Combating Terrorism

Combating Terrorism
Strategies and Approaches

William C. Banks
Syracuse University

Renée de Nevers
Syracuse University

Mitchel B. Wallerstein
Syracuse University

CQ PRESS

A Division of Congressional Quarterly Inc.
Washington, D.C.

CQ Press
1255 22nd Street, NW, Suite 400
Washington, DC 20037

Phone: 202-729-1900; toll-free, 1-866-4CQ-PRESS (1-866-427-7737)

Web: www.cqpress.com

Photo Credits: AP Images, 285

Cover design: El Jefe Design

∞ The paper used in this publication exceeds the requirements of the American National
Standard for Information Sciences—Permanence of Paper for Printed Library Materials,
ANSI Z39.48-1992.

Printed and bound in the United States of America

11 10 09 08 07   1 2 3 4 5

Library of Congress Cataloging-in-Publication Data

Banks, William C.
  Combating terrorism : strategies and approaches / William C. Banks, Renée de Nevers,
Mitchel B. Wallerstein.
      p. cm.
  Includes bibliographical references and index.
  ISBN 978-0-87289-299-6 (alk. paper)
  1. Terrorism—United States. 2. Terrorism—United States—Prevention. 3. Terrorism—
Government policy—United States. 4. Terrorists—United States. 5. Civil defense—United
States. I. De Nevers, Renée. II. Wallerstein, Mitchel B. III. Title.

  HV6432.B355 2008
  363.325'1560973—dc22

                                    2007035734

To our students

About the Authors

William C. Banks is professor of law and public administration, as well as director of the Institute for National Security and Counterterrorism, at Syracuse University. He is recognized internationally as an expert on constitutional and national security law and counterterrorism. He has written extensively on national security, domestic and international terrorism, and emergency preparedness and response. He coauthored the definitive text in the field, *National Security Law,* Fourth Edition, and in 2007, Banks and coauthors Stephen Dycus and Peter Raven-Hansen published *Counterterrorism Law* to help define this emerging field. He has also served as special counsel to the United States Senate Judiciary Committee and worked with the committee on the confirmation hearings for Supreme Court nominee Stephen G. Breyer.

Renée de Nevers is assistant professor of public administration at the Maxwell School of Citizenship and Public Affairs at Syracuse University, teaching courses in international and national security. She has taught at the University of Oklahoma and was a research fellow at the Kennedy School's Belfer Center for Science and International Affairs; the Center for International Security and Cooperation and the Hoover Institution, both at Stanford University; and the International Institute for Strategic Studies. Her research interests include U.S. cooperation with multilateral institutions in combating terrorism, regulation of the private security industry, and the linkages between international norms and the use of force. She has written numerous articles on international security and is the author of *Comrades No More: The Seeds of Change in Eastern Europe* (2003).

Mitchel B. Wallerstein is dean of the Maxwell School of Citizenship and Public Affairs and professor of political science and public administration at Syracuse University. He has written numerous books, articles and studies on national security matters. Wallerstein previously was vice president of the John D. and Catherine T. MacArthur Foundation, where he directed the Program on Global Security and Sustainability. From 1993 to 1997, he served as deputy assistant secretary of defense for counterproliferation policy and as senior representative for trade security policy. During his tenure at the Department of Defense, he helped found and subsequently cochaired the Senior Defense Group on Proliferation at NATO. He has taught at M.I.T., George Washington University, Georgetown University, and the Johns Hopkins University School of Advanced International Studies. He is a member of the Council on Foreign Relations and the International Institute for Strategic Studies and recently was elected president of the Association of Professional Schools of International Affairs.

Brief Contents

Contents

Boxes, Tables, Figures, and Maps

Boxes

Tables

Figures

Maps

Preface

Six years after the September 11, 2001, terrorist attacks, terrorism and what to do about it remain in the vortex of policy, political, and legal debates and analyses in the United States. And it is not likely that there will be a significant downturn in the importance attached to combating terrorism anytime soon. Ironically, since the swift and effective U.S. campaign to remove the Taliban and al Qaeda from Afghanistan, al Qaeda has reportedly regrouped along the Pakistan-Afghanistan border, terrorist cells have developed a lethal and effective franchise in Iraq, and the world has witnessed the emergence of "homegrown" terrorism in London and Madrid. Meanwhile, the U.S. government continues to maintain that additional terrorist strikes on one or more domestic targets are likely, and it has argued successfully that the prospect of more terrorism targeting Americans justifies intrusive new measures to conduct surveillance, without a court order, of the electronic communications of those suspected of ties to terrorism.

Combating Terrorism: Strategies and Approaches seeks to lay out in straightforward terms the challenges confronting U.S. decision makers today and for the foreseeable future as they attempt to anticipate and respond to terrorist threats. The aim of this book is to bring into focus the dominant set of policy problems posed by terrorism in the twenty-first century. Students will find the book particularly useful in helping them to understand what is admittedly a disturbing and complicated subject and in reaching their own conclusions about which responses are likely to be effective. The book concentrates primarily on terrorist activity aimed at the United States, whatever its source.

Combating Terrorism has been written for undergraduate and graduate students studying terrorism and national or international security. It seeks to provoke thought and to generate understanding about some of this era's most vexing problems. Although this book assumes basic knowledge of U.S. government institutions and processes, any upper-division student should be able to work effectively with the text. The book also should be readily understandable to the layperson who is seeking an approachable explanation and enhanced understanding of issues that appear virtually every day in the newspapers and on television.

The Approach and Organization of This Book

Before the mid-1990s, terrorism occupied little space in the curricula of higher education or even in the popular literature. Even though terrorism has been a facet of international relations and internal strife within nations throughout human history, any attention to incidences of terrorism was typically treated within a survey of international relations, a history or political science course focusing on ethnic or religious groups within a region or nation-state, a seminar on foreign relations, or a criminal law course. After the first attack on the World Trade Center in 1993 and the Oklahoma City bombing in 1995, terrorism gained some additional attention as an academic subject. After the attacks of September 11, 2001, and the launching of the "global war on terrorism" by the George W. Bush administration, the subject of terrorism became an overnight sensation; it has subsequently generated significant academic attention, both within traditional fields of study and as a new area. The newly emerging academic interest in terrorism is not likely to be short-lived. The growing disparity between the haves and have-nots, along with the demonstrated impact of asymmetric warfare waged by terrorists, signals that, like it or not, systematic and longer-term understanding of terrorism and the response to it will have to be part of higher education for many years to come.

This book is our contribution to this understanding of terrorism. A central strength of the book is its interdisciplinary approach. The problems posed by terrorism are multidimensional, and, to be successful, strategies developed as a response must draw on a variety of disciplines and perspectives. Thus uniquely, *Combating Terrorism* pays considerable attention to legal issues, including civil liberties problems, interdictions and extradition, money laundering, and international organized crime. The book's ten chapters systematically describe and assess the range of strategies, policy options, and approaches that the United States employs—or could employ—for responding to terrorism. The introductory chapter defines the subject and provides its historical perspective, then assesses the strategies and approaches generally available to counter terrorism. Chapter 2 identifies and assesses the modern terrorist threat. The remaining eight chapters explore the approaches in depth, from looking at why terrorists might strike and what might be done to lessen the root causes of terrorism to using military force to combat terrorism. In between, law enforcement and investigation, planning for homeland security, responses to terrorist incidents, international cooperation, and the use of the media and public affairs function are considered.

Each chapter introduces the approach or strategy featured, suggests the issues and questions addressed in the chapter, and then presents case studies that explicate the themes. These case studies are designed to give students a quick study and analysis of a particular terrorist incident and provide further insight into the complexities of combating terrorism. The case studies bring the materials to life and provide excellent material for teachers to use in generating discussion, projects, or opportunities for writing papers or engaging in further research. Boxed features offer interesting asides and conclude with provocative questions to aid in student learning. Each chapter also summarizes what has been presented and concludes with a list of readings for additional information.

We, the authors, are closely affiliated with the Institute for National Security and Counterterrorism (INSCT), an academic center jointly sponsored by the Maxwell School of Citizenship and Public Affairs and the College of Law at Syracuse University. In keeping with the mission of INSCT, we bring political science, public affairs, law, and government service backgrounds to our abiding interest and deep commitment to the problems posed by terrorism. Also, as we do in our academic endeavors at Syracuse, we believe that the issues presented by terrorism are best understood and analyzed through the prism of varying disciplinary perspectives, a sentiment that motivated the writing of this book. The pages of this book reflect the influences of our different backgrounds. We hope that readers will agree with us that our differences strengthen the final product.

Acknowledgments

We have enjoyed working with the excellent staff at CQ Press. At each step of the process, CQ Press provided us with enthusiasm, support, and direction. Chief acquisitions editor Charisse Kiino encouraged us to develop this book, and Kristine Enderle nurtured the manuscript as its development editor. Freelance copy editor Sabra Bissette Ledent was superb, and the production editors, including Anna Socrates, did first-rate work while keeping us on schedule. We also appreciate the thoughtful contributions of our reviewers for CQ Press: Kimberly Fox, Shippensburg University; James Lutz, Indiana University–Fort Wayne; Harold Molineu, Ohio University; Stephen Sloan, University of Central Florida; and Barry Steiner, California State University–Long Beach. We would also like to acknowledge the excellent research assistance provided by Lacey I. Rubin and Jesse Blinick, and the support of Syracuse students affiliated with the Student Association on Terrorism and Security Analysis (SATSA), whose enthusiasm and dedication helped to develop and sustain INSCT and our work on this book.

Chapter 1 **Combating Terrorism: An Introduction**

A t lunchtime on February 26, 1993, a twelve-hundred-pound bomb enclosed in a rented van exploded in the parking garage underneath the World Trade Center complex in downtown Manhattan. The blast killed six persons, injured over a thousand, and immeasurably harmed America's notions of security from terrorism.

The men charged with engineering the bombing had entered the United States using fake passports or fake visas, or they had claimed political asylum. Their base, the Al-Salam Mosque in Jersey City, had been since 1990 a center for the teachings of Sheikh Omar Abdel Rahman, a blind Egyptian cleric who had adopted the most violent strands of Islamic thought. Sheik al-Rahman, along with eventual co-conspirator Ramzi Yousef, a highly trained terrorist from Pakistan and veteran of the Afghan jihad, were on a State Department list of persons suspected to have been involved in politically motivated violence, and thus they were by law excludable from the United States. Rahman had entered the country using a visitor's visa from Sudan. By the time officials realized their mistake, he had claimed political asylum. After being taken into custody, Rahman was released, in part because of the overcrowded detention centers, and he was told to appear for a hearing on his asylum application within eighteen months. Yousef, who had entered the country using a fake Iraqi passport, had sought asylum on the basis that he would face persecution by Iraq if ordered to return. He also was released because of lack of detention space.

Once released, the perpetrators made preparations for the bombing. On November 30, 1992, Mohammed Salameh, a Palestinian from the West Bank who had entered the United States on a Jordanian passport and who was Yousef's roommate, rented a storage locker in Jersey City under an alias. Federal Bureau of Investigation (FBI) agents would later testify that this locker contained chemicals and bomb-making devices. On February 23, 1993, Salameh and Nidal Ayyad, a chemical engineer who was born in Kuwait, but was a naturalized U.S. citizen educated at Rutgers University, rented a van from a rental agency in Jersey City. On February 25, Mohammad Salameh visited the rented locker.

Post-bombing activities further implicated these men. Less than two hours after the explosion on February 26, Mohammad Salameh appeared at the rental agency, claiming that his van had been stolen. Salameh then returned

1

repeatedly over the next few days in an attempt to reclaim his deposit. Meanwhile, FBI agents recovered the vehicle identification number from a piece of the van that carried the explosives, which allowed them to trace the van to the rental office in Jersey City. Federal agents waited for Salameh's return to the rental agency, watched him complete paperwork on the missing van, and then arrested him when he left the agency. When they searched Salameh's rented locker, FBI agents found chemicals (including sulfuric acid and shotgun powder), beakers, tubing, and a fuse.

The other actors fled the country. Yousef, thought to have planned the bombing, fled to Pakistan on the day of the bombing, and continued to engage in terrorist activities. Eyad Ismoil, a childhood friend of Yousef and the driver of the bomb-carrying van, fled to Jordan the same day. After a two-year pursuit, Yousef was apprehended in Pakistan, and Ismoil was arrested in Jordan. In the interim, two related trials were held. On March 4, 1994, Mohammad Salameh, Nidal Ayyad, Mahmud Abouhalima, and Ahmad Ajaj were convicted of various offenses connected with the bombing of the World Trade Center.[1] On October 1, 1995, ten defendants, including Sheikh Rahman and Yousef, were found guilty of charges related to a thwarted plan to blow up the United Nations headquarters and other New York City buildings, bridges, and tunnels. Evidence at this trial included statements in Yousef's computer about a coordinated plan to bomb twelve U.S. jetliners within a forty-eight-hour period.

Throughout its investigation of terrorist groups before and after the World Trade Center bombing, the FBI employed wiretaps and an informant, Emad A. Salem, a former Egyptian intelligence officer. FBI infiltration of the group planning to bomb the New York City landmarks resulted in the failure of the plot and led to the 1995 convictions. Although Salem did not penetrate the cell made up of those who were convicted of the World Trade Center bombing, his testimony was critical in the 1995 trial.

The culminating trial of Yousef and Ismoil was held in 1997 in New York. At the end of the three-month trial, a jury convicted Yousef of directing and helping to carry out the World Trade Center bombing and Ismoil of driving the van that carried the bomb into the underground garage of the World Trade Center. Both received life sentences for offenses involving the use of explosives to kill.

Although the government developed much of its case against Yousef in the earlier trials, new testimony was admitted from a Secret Service agent who accompanied Yousef on his flight to the United States from Pakistan in 1995. According to his testimony, Yousef not only admitted to and explained in detail his role in the plot, but he expressed regrets that it had not resulted in more death and destruction. The Secret Service agent further recounted that Yousef said the explosion was intended to topple one of the towers into the other, killing up to 250,000 people. Yousef also reportedly told the agent that he had recruited the conspirators, picked the target, directed the construction and delivery of the bomb, and set its fuse, all to avenge the Palestinian people and to retaliate against the United States for its support of Israel. Moreover, Yousef apparently confessed to plans for a suicide attack on the Virginia headquarters of the Central Intelligence Agency and an attempt to assassinate President Bill Clinton with phosgene gas. Ismoil admitted to authorities that he had driven the van that carried the bomb, although he claimed that he thought he was delivering cartons of shampoo.

With the benefit of hindsight, one might now wonder how America's defenses could have been so easily penetrated, and why intelligence and law enforcement officials were unaware of the plot to bring down the towers. More broadly, this incident raises the question of how the U.S. government should have responded to the revelation that the nation was vulnerable to more and potentially far worse acts of terrorism.

What Does It Mean to "Combat Terrorism"?

As the opening vignette illustrates, even relatively ineffective terrorist attacks can do grave harm. The damage can be measured in lives lost or injuries, in property damage and other material costs, or in something less easily quantifiable—the fear that another attack is coming. As this text will reveal, mounting effective counters to terrorism is an especially difficult task. Because of the stealth and surprise that accompanies terrorism, the anonymity of the attackers, and the frequent willingness of terrorists to die for their cause, tackling terrorism is daunting at best. Yet for as long as terrorists have struck, governments have devised ways to counter the threat that terrorism poses. The list of possible counterterrorism strategies is long and growing, in part because of the evolving dynamics of the terrorism threat.

Combating terrorism requires a multifaceted set of strategies and tactics. Although negotiation and diplomacy have not proven especially effective in most terrorism situations, it would be foolish to discount these approaches in combating terrorism. Similarly, intelligence investigations may succeed in uncovering and then thwarting terrorism before it occurs, and yet the terrorist attacks against the United States on September 11, 2001, provide a stark reminder of what may happen when intelligence operations come up short. Still, it would be irresponsible for a government not to invest heavily in intelligence to combat terrorism.

Traditional deterrence theory suggests that a detailed and comprehensive set of criminal prohibitions against terrorist activities might diminish terrorism, even though many terrorists are not, in fact, deterred by criminal sanctions (think of suicide bombers). Another measure might be the installation of security screening operations—at mass transit nodes or at the entrances of public buildings, malls, or sporting events. Yet such screening operations intrude on privacy, and they can be overcome by determined terrorists. Or officials may decide to "harden" targets by building barriers, installing video surveillance, and adopting new design techniques and technologies. But, yet again, terrorists have found ways around every innovation to date. Finally, a government might choose to go after terrorists with military force; after all, the United States and some other Western nations have far more military might than any terrorist organization. But experience has shown that even though military force is sometimes effective against terrorists, at other times its bluntness as a policy instrument imposes costs in lost lives, injuries, and damaged property beyond those terrorist organizations targeted. The use of military force to counter terrorists may have the unintended effect of engendering more terrorism if the military response causes extensive civilian casualties.

In short, combating terrorism is a work in progress. Governments are fighting terrorism using a multiple set of strategies and tactics, and none of them operates to the exclusion of another. Similarly, none of them has been singularly effective. But no matter what combination of strategies and approaches are followed, there will be trade-offs between competing priorities or the values at stake in countering terrorism. The most prominent trade-off might be thought of as a set of choices: how much liberty are people willing to sacrifice in return for greater security?

Many of the approaches examined in the remainder of this book offer some greater protection from the threat of terrorism, but at a cost, such as more intrusive forms of surveillance of citizens or more inspections and searches of the personal items of those riding mass transit or entering a shopping mall or sporting event. Making informed policy choices about trade-offs like these in countering terrorism is especially difficult because decision makers cannot say how great the risk of terrorism is, or how much security will be gained by adopting the surveillance and inspection measures.

Difficult trade-offs also lurk below this strategic level. If the United States invests heavily, for example, in biometric screening or sophisticated imagery equipment that can see inside homes or offices, what opportunities to direct the invested capital (dollars and human resources) toward the advancement of medical research or better education will be forgone? Then there is the elephant in the room in any discussion about terrorism—fear. It is not known to what extent the policy choices in combating terrorism are driven by the fear of a terrorist threat rather than by terrorism itself. Should Americans make significant commitments of resources, sacrifice liberties, and incur massive opportunity costs out of fear of an unknowable threat of terrorism? The answer to that question depends on finding ways to quantify or otherwise make more concrete the variables involved in deciding how and at what costs Americans should invest in combating terrorism. And it depends on whether these choices can be made wisely when the "game" of terrorism and countering terrorism are front and center on a daily basis.

Learning about terrorism and its countermeasures is challenging for various reasons. For starters, this field of study crosses traditional disciplinary lines, incorporating elements of history, government and political science, psychology, law, mass communications, international relations, and philosophy. Adding to the challenge, this field of study is interdisciplinary as well—that is, the learning and knowledge required to become an accomplished student of combating terrorism lies at the intersections of these disciplines and in the new and emerging insights gained by bringing together the perspectives of more than one discipline in addressing policy problems. Although the field of counterterrorism is a difficult one, it can be intellectually exciting and rewarding. Few fields of study today rival counterterrorism in its immediate application to real-world events and people's daily lives.

This chapter constitutes a primer for the balance of the book. First, it examines the perennial problem of definition—what is terrorism? Apart from canvassing a range of perspectives on what counts as terrorism, the aim is to arrive at some attributes that are widely agreed to be at the core of terrorism. The chapter then presents a brief history of terrorism simply to provide background for further study. That history is followed by synopses of the problems presented by state-sponsored terrorism, the "new terrorism," and the terrorism pursued by Islamic extremists. These categories capture the most vexing contemporary terrorism dilemmas, and they present the most difficult challenges in combating terrorism. Finally, this chapter provides an overview of the remainder of the book by presenting a survey of the strategies and approaches used by the United States to combat terrorism.

What Is Terrorism?

Understanding the dynamics of combating terrorism depends on developing a clear picture of what terrorism is. What associations does terrorism bring to mind? What distinguishes a terrorist organization from a guerrilla group? From insurgents? From a criminal gang? From a seemingly insane, lone assassin? Does the violence itself count as terrorism, independent of who did it and for what reasons?

Scholars have identified dozens of definitions of terrorism, and a like number may be found by perusing the laws of the United States and other Western nations. One explanation for the large number of definitions is linguistic sloppiness—the label "terrorism" sometimes is affixed to something that policy makers simply wish to condemn. Another explanation is international politics. Governments and international organizations struggle with the political reality that, to some degree, what counts as terrorism is driven by whose side one is on.

From the perspective of the target, an attack may be terrorism, while from the attacker's vantage point, or a supporter's, the attack is justified and so is not terrorism. As Palestinian Liberation Organization (PLO) chairman Yasser Arafat said while addressing the UN General Assembly in 1974, "The difference between the revolutionary and the terrorist lies in the reason for which each fights. For whoever stands by a just cause and fights for the freedom and liberation of his land from the invaders, the settlers and the colonialists, cannot possibly be called terrorist." [2]

One example of such a situation can be found in South Asia. In Jammu and Kashmir, local Muslims have been fighting against Indian control of their region for a long time. The Muslims view themselves as insurgents, waging a guerrilla campaign against Indian military forces. But attacks against civilians in the region occur regularly, including bombings of local movie houses and attacks against candidates for parliament. Should these attacks be viewed as terrorism? Or are they part of a freedom movement by insurgents fighting an organized military force?

Taking this perspective into account, groups widely considered to be terrorist may embrace monikers such as the National Liberation Army, the Popular Front for Liberation, Shining Path, Basque Fatherland and Liberty, or Afrikaner Resistance Movement. Groups that have succeeded even for a time in challenging what they view as an oppressive government call themselves anything but terrorists, incident to their efforts to attain legitimacy in the eyes of the people.

Box 1.1 **Defining Terrorism at the United Nations**

In the summer of 2005, after ten years of negotiations, it appeared that the United Nations might reach agreement on key principles, including a definition of terrorism, that would lead to adoption of a Comprehensive Convention on International Terrorism. A draft version of the convention contained this statement: "The targeting and deliberate killing of civilians and non-combatants cannot be justified or legitimized by any cause or grievance." [a] The U.S. ambassador urged that the words "by terrorists" be inserted between "killing" and "of." [b] Some governments sought to exclude from the definition of terrorism actions that are taken in "resistance to occupation" and to add language that would include collateral damage caused by military action. When government leaders gathered in September 2005, they approved an agenda-setting document in anticipation of the sixtieth session of the General Assembly that avoided these controversies by simply deleting all of the definitional language.

- Why would the U.S. ambassador seek to amend the proposed definition?

- Why would some nations wish to exclude resistance to occupation by another country and include collateral damage caused by military action?

- What does this episode suggest about the difficulties encountered in defining terrorism?

---

[a] See the "Advanced Unedited Version," August 5, 2005, at www.un.org/ga/59/hlpm_rev.2.pdf.
[b] See letter from John R. Bolton (no date) at www.un.int/usa/reform-un-jrb-ltr-terror-8-05.pdf.

Although this book focuses primarily on U.S. responses to terrorism, the United States struggles to define terrorism in the larger international context, and some common understanding of what terrorism means may be integral to the success of countermeasures. Most policy makers share at least some common views about the elements or attributes that define terrorism. One definition that captures a set of widely accepted criteria has been adopted by the U.S. Department of State for the purpose of collecting data about international terrorism. According to this definition, terrorism is "premeditated, politically motivated violence against noncombatant targets by subnational groups or clandestine agents, usually intended to influence an audience."

An alternative definition can be found in the International Convention on the Suppression of the Financing of Terrorism, an international treaty adopted by the UN General Assembly in 1999 and ratified by over 130 countries. It says that terrorism is "any . . . act intended to cause death or serious bodily injury to a civilian, or to any other person not taking an active part in hostilities in a situation of armed conflict when the purpose of such act, by its nature or context, is to intimidate a population, or to compel a government or an international organization to do or to abstain from doing an act."

And then the U.S. Department of Defense defines terrorism this way: "The unlawful use, or threatened use, of force or violence against individuals or property to coerce and intimidate governments or societies, often to achieve political, religious, or ideological objectives."

These definitions contain more similarities than differences. From them, it is possible to isolate the most obvious common ingredients of terrorism:

- Violent, premeditated—either actual violence or intended and threatened violence that is not impulsive but is the result of some planning
- Motivated not by personal gain, but by a political, religious, or ideological objective, such as religious freedom or social change
- Intended to have psychological and social impacts beyond the immediate violence
- Targeted toward unarmed, noncombatant persons or those otherwise unable to defend themselves (with indiscriminateness to achieve significant psychological and social disruption)
- Carried out by subnational groups or clandestine agents.

Terrorism involves *violent, premeditated actions*—that is, the violence is planned and always purposeful. An impulsive, deranged shooter is not a terrorist. Because of the fear of terrorism and the dread it evokes among those targeted, terrorism may consist of either actual or threatened violence. For example, the September 11 use of airliners-as-weapons caused a massive downturn in passenger air travel for months after the attacks.

Terrorism is distinguishable from violent crime, often based on the difference in *motivation*. The violent criminal acts in order to achieve personal objectives, such as to gain revenge or to steal money. For the terrorist, the violence is a means of communicating a political, religious, or other ideological message. To be sure, the political nature of terrorism means that what is considered to be terrorism remains subject to varying interpretations. The adage that "one man's terrorist is another man's freedom fighter" only begins to portray the analytic, political, cultural, and legal difficulties in defining terrorism.

As just noted, terrorists use violent acts to make political, religious, or other ideological statements. In doing so, they are seeking *an audience*. And they want that audience to be captive in two different ways. First, the terrorists hope that through media coverage their "issue," whatever it is, will be firmly implanted in the public consciousness. Second, and related to the first, the terrorists want people to fear such violent acts and to expect more violence, so that in their fear and dread they will either pressure their government to accede to the terrorists' political agenda or increasingly distrust their own government's capacity to protect them from terrorist violence. If the latter distrust grows to a sufficient level, the government may lose the capacity to govern, and the terrorists will have achieved a victory. Beyond the immediate audience, terrorists seek to reach potential recruits and those who may support their actions in more passive ways.

Armed forces of a state wear uniforms, insignias, and follow a chain of command. Terrorists share none of these characteristics. Their targets typically are not the combatants of an opposing army; rather, their targets are the *noncombatants*. National militaries follow rules and norms, even during wartime. These rules, many codified in the Geneva and Hague Conventions and others that have grown out of custom developed by state practice over time, include protecting civilians, ensuring humane treatment of detainees, and protecting neutral territory and its people. Military forces may mistakenly kill civilians, such as in 1988 when the United States shot down Iran Air Flight 655 in the Persian Gulf after a U.S. warship mistook the airliner for an attacking jet. But the mistaken strike was not terrorism. When Libyan agents conspired to place a bomb that brought down Pan Am Flight 103 the same year, it was a clear act of terrorism—the Libyans deliberately targeted hundreds of civilian travelers.

Violent attacks in a military campaign are decidedly not terrorism, even attacks that are covert. As such, those carrying out a terrorist attack are also not members of a uniformed military force and are instead members of a *subnational or clandestine group*, organized or not, large or small. Or a single actor may be the attacker, whether a member of a group or a "lone wolf." The terrorist organization may be highly structured. Or the group might be structured as a cell, made up of a small number of persons who communicate with each other, but do not report to a central authority, at least not for operational instructions.

In thinking about definitions, it is important to pay careful attention to one salient point: terrorism is a method or means of doing something. Terrorism itself is not an enemy—that is, terrorism is not the "who" that is of concern, or the "what" that the perpetrators of violence are seeking to achieve. Indeed, calling the U.S. response to the attacks of September 11 the "war on terrorism" or the "global war on terrorism" is at best confusing and at worst misleading. Such labels obscure the nature of the enemy and make it more difficult to distinguish among different kinds of terrorist threats and to weigh the capabilities of, and strategies to counter, different terrorist organizations.

As demonstrated by the capacity of policy makers to shape counterterrorism policies, even those who are aware that the United States itself defines terrorism in different ways for different purposes are not reticent to deliberate and decide policies to counter terrorism. Those responsible for a segment of terrorism policy identify the terrorism they see and make policy accordingly. For the student of countering terrorism, understanding the range of considerations that must be taken into account in deciding what is inside and outside the terrorism box is important. However, except for lawyers who must match a definition of terrorism to someone's behavior in law enforcement or intelligence-gathering settings, or in targeting a military response, precision may not be required.

Origins of Terrorism

Terrorism has ancient origins, first documented in the Old Testament stories of politically inspired murder. The operations of organized terrorist groups were also described early in recorded human history. Among them was the extremist Jewish group, the Sicari, who attacked Romans and other Jews during the Roman occupation of Palestine. Their principal weapon was the *sica*, a short dagger, but they also burned houses, palaces, and government archives. The Order of the Assassins, another early group, was an eleventh-century Muslim sect that sought to transform Islam by killing Sunnis and Christians in Persia, Syria, and Palestine. The Assassins accomplished little, but they apparently originated the notion of the suicide attacker, disguised as an innocent worshiper. Although violence and religious wars were commonplace in much of the world during the Middle Ages and thereafter, little of what is considered terrorism today occurred during those times.

Ironically, the term *terrorism* was first used widely during the French Revolution—the *regime de la terreur*—and it was applied in positive terms to describe the system used by the new government to establish order after the anarchy that prevailed after the Revolution. Although French revolutionary leader Maximilien Robespierre declared that the harsh tactics of the regime of terror were merely a tool needed to induce and protect democracy, the revolutionary rhetoric and its leaders soon collapsed under the weight of their own tactics. Thereafter, *terrorism* became a term used to describe abuses of power, whether by the state or by others attacking the state.

Traditionally, terrorist groups attacked the state in some way. The groups that carried out terrorist attacks were clearly organized, usually in a hierarchical structure. More recently, what some call "new terrorism" is distinguished by a tendency to target noncombatants for vaguely articulated political or religious objectives and by the indiscriminateness of attacks, which are designed to achieve significant psychological and social disruption. These new groups, which may be organized less traditionally or organized only in small cells, are also feared because of their potential for striking with weapons of mass destruction (WMD), usually defined to include nuclear, biological, and chemical weapons, and sometimes construed to include radiological weapons.

Traditional Terrorism

For most of the twentieth century, analysts focused on states as the sources of terrorism, typically through the subjugation of groups by terrorist means (for example, the Kurds in Iraq, groups inside the Soviet Union by Joseph Stalin, indigenous people by the Guatemalan government). But since the last decades of the twentieth century, the threats posed by non-state actors have become dominant. (See Table 1.1 for some examples of nineteenth- and twentieth-century terrorist groups.)

Terrorism by Subnational Groups

What today is considered traditional terrorism grew out of nationalism and its tensions with the Industrial Revolution, including the Industrial Revolution's boon to capitalism and its social and economic winners and losers and the rise of communism or Marxism. These nineteenth-century economic and social dislocations proved to be the roots of the antistate and revolutionary justifications for terrorism that came to fruition in Europe and later spread to Latin America and elsewhere.

Narodnaya Volya (People's Will), which came together as a socialist movement inside Russia in the 1870s, was organized to combat the country's tsarist government. Moderates inside Narodnaya Volya believed that, spurred by a nonviolent propaganda campaign, workers would rise up against the tsar's failure to meet the basic needs of the working class in Russia. A more radical group advocated violence to overthrow the government. The radicals looked for justification to the theory of "propaganda by deed," credited to the Italian republican Carlo Pisacane. According to Pisacane, "ideas result from deeds, not the latter from the former." Thus, based on this view, violence was needed to inform and to rally the people behind the revolution. Simple persuasion and propaganda by words could not achieve the desired ends.

When the tsar began to arrest and to detain moderate members of Narodnaya Volya, the radicals won control of the organization, and it began to carry out random assassinations of police and minor government officials, and of members of the tsar's family. Although the leaders of Narodnaya Volya recognized that their campaign of selective assassination would not bring down the tsarist government, they reasoned that the growing preoccupation of the

Table 1.1 Some Nineteenth- and Twentieth-Century Terrorist Organizations

Group	Period	Tactics	Objective
Narodnaya Volya (People's Will, Russia)	1870s	Targeted assassinations, widespread dynamite attacks, crudely fashioned bombs; avoided harm to innocents	Combat and overthrow the tsarist government
Armenian National Movement (Eastern Turkey)	1880s–1890s	Targeting Ottoman rulers	Reestablish an Armenian state
Inner Macedonian Revolutionary Organization (Greece, Bulgaria, Serbia)	1890s–1920s	Armed guerrilla struggle with Ottomans, political assassinations	Establish autonomy of Macedonia
Mlada Bosna (Young Bosnia, Bosnia)	Early twentieth century	Fighting Habsburg dominance in Bosnia, assassinating Habsburg archduke Franz Ferdinand and others	Achieve unification of Serbia and other southern Slavic lands
Ku Klux Klan (United States)	1865–??	Terrorizing black citizens and Reconstruction governments, burning crosses, lynching, bombing	Establish white supremacy in the United States
Provisional Irish Republican Army (Ireland, England)	1969–2005	Riots targeting British Army and economic assets, judges, politicians and British government officials; bombings	Overthrow Northern Ireland and found a United Ireland
Hamas	From 1987	Suicide attacks of civilian and military targets	Destroy Israel and create a Palestinian state
Al Qaeda	From 1998	Coordinated attacks on infrastructure targets, seeking mass casualties	End Western influence in the Middle East, destroy Israel

government with its own security would weaken its responses to Russian society's general disaffection with the government. In other words, the terrorists practiced a kind of patience. If the government became obsessed with countering the terrorists, it would neglect its duties and eventually fall.

Narodnaya Volya made at least eight attempts on the life of Tsar Alexander II. Once Narodnaya Volya began the widespread use of dynamite and crudely fashioned bombs—the first terrorist group to do so—it eventually succeeded. In 1881 an assassin blew up both the tsar and himself by detonating dynamite as he approached the tsar's carriage. But this success of Narodnaya

Volya was also its downfall. The government reacted to the killing of the tsar by tracking down and arresting the leadership of the group, robbing Narodnaya Volya of its initiative.

Groups such as Narodnaya Volya, along with other Russian terrorist groups and those inspired by their ideology, are distinct in important ways from contemporary terrorists. These groups claimed that they used terrorism only because the governments they fought were hopelessly corrupt and unresponsive to the needs of the people. In theory, Narodnaya Volya sought civil liberties like those embodied in the U.S. Constitution. They planned their attacks assiduously to avoid harm to innocent victims, and they picked their targets after determining that the victim had committed brutal or corrupt actions against the people of Russia. Narodnaya Volya maintained that, once its goal of overthrowing the tsarist government succeeded, it would fully participate in a replacement government that permitted the people an active role.

Anarchism (the rejection of any central governing authority) and the political assassination tactics of some individual anarchists and anarchist groups gained adherents in Europe and elsewhere after Narodnaya Volya and its exploits. (See Table 1.1.) The Armenian National Movement attacked Ottoman rulers in Eastern Turkey in the 1880s and 1890s, and the Inner Macedonian Revolutionary Organization adopted a similar campaign in Greece, Bulgaria, and Serbia just before the start of World War I. The Armenians were the victims of genocide during that war, and the Macedonians' organization collapsed when efforts to create an independent Macedonia failed.

An individual anarchist succeeded in assassinating U.S. president William McKinley in 1901, and over the surrounding decades other anarchists assassinated President Sadi Carnot of France (1894), Empress Elizabeth of Austria (1898), King Humbert I of Italy (1900), and King George I of Greece (1913). A group of nationalist Serb students and intellectuals known as Mlada Bosna (Young Bosnia) fought the Habsburg dominance in Bosnia, and arguably through their actions sparked World War I when a Young Bosnia member assassinated the Habsburg archduke Franz Ferdinand in Sarajevo in 1914. Young Bosnia was aligned with at least one other Bosnian nationalist group at the time—Black Hand—and some historians maintain that Serbian government officials were supporters of the terrorist groups, at least insofar as supporting efforts that forced the events leading to war. Despite the assassinations, throughout the period from the heyday of the Narodnaya Volya until World War I, the anarchists' limited numbers had little impact on the governments or the policies they challenged. Still, the anarchists succeeded in instilling fear in many places, and their techniques of bomb making and suicide attacks serve as models for contemporary terrorists.

Parallel developments in the nineteenth century included the birth of an American version of the secret societies that were practicing terrorism. Born out of the Civil War, the Ku Klux Klan, or KKK, was organized to terrorize black citizens and the Reconstruction governments in the South. The Klan operated as a secret society, led by a Grand Wizard and state and local leaders, known as Grand Dragons, Grand Titans, and Grand Cyclopses. KKK terrorists wore intimidating symbols—white robes and hoods—and they burned crosses while they terrorized their targets. The Klan later expanded its targets to include religious minorities, organized labor, and foreigners, although the primary targets of bombings and other KKK violence remained black citizens and civil rights groups.

After World War II, violent nationalist revolutions were brought against colonial governments throughout Africa and the Middle East, most notably in Algeria, Kenya, and Cyprus. When violence was prosecuted against these colonial powers, or more generally by nationalist groups inside these Third World countries against the West, it became popular to label them "freedom fighters," not "terrorists." Over time, the use of terrorist methods to further revolutionary aims by nationalist and ethnic separatist groups took root in the Middle East (the Palestine Liberation Organization), Canada (the Québécois separatist group Front de libération du Québec, or FLQ), and Spain (the Basque separatist group Basque Fatherland and Liberty, or ETA). The separatists employed terrorism directly in the futile pursuit of their separatist objectives, but also in order to draw international attention to their causes. Thus, whether the groups were freedom fighters or terrorists, they sometimes employed terrorism to attain their objectives.

State-Sponsored Terrorism

Sovereign states can sponsor terrorism in a variety of ways. Typically, states provide financial or in-kind material support to terrorist organizations. For example, states may compensate the families of suicide bombers. Or states may provide some form of sanctuary for terrorists from other states seeking to apprehend the terrorists.

State sponsorship of terrorism has a horrific history. The 1930s brutalization of Jews and other disfavored groups and citizens by the German Nazis, Italian Fascists, and Russian Stalinists are easily the most vivid and storied examples. State-sponsored terrorism was also practiced by Greece in the 1970s, and by several Latin American governments from the 1970s onward—Argentina, Chile, Colombia, El Salvador, Guatemala, and Peru.

Contemporary state-sponsored terrorism may take the form of governments using terrorism as a way of waging war through employed surrogate terrorists. For example, since 2003 the government of Sudan has employed Janjaweed militia, primarily members of nomadic Arab tribes, who, on behalf of the government in Khartoum, raid towns and villages inhabited by darker-skinned African tribes. The Sudanese government pays the Janjaweed a monthly salary in return for their acts of terrorism against the villages, from which non-Arab liberation movements have taken up arms against the central government. Some reports suggest that Janjaweed attacks are preceded by bombing raids by the Sudanese air force, and that Janjaweed militia wear combat fatigues identical to those worn by the Sudanese army. Refugees from the Darfur region allege that Janjaweed leaders encourage their militiamen with racist slurs, and urge the men to rape the villagers while looting and burning down their homes during their raids.

The Sudan example illustrates that, for the terrorist group that carries out state-sponsored terrorism, the benefits of sponsorship can be considerable. The state's intelligence, military, and diplomatic resources can provide logistical and intelligence support, as well as training and revenue for otherwise ill-equipped groups of amateurs.

At other times, the state-sponsored terrorist may be a fully capable, independent operator and the person or group may or may not be ideologically driven by the state's political cause. For example, the Abu Nidal Organization (ANO), led by Palestinian terrorist Sabri al-Banna, furthered the terrorist aims of Iraq, Libya, and Syria, while amassing considerable wealth. The Japanese Red Army (JRA) serviced the Popular Front for the Liberation of Palestine (PFLP) and attacked the Lod Airport in Israel in 1972 and the French embassy in The Hague and a Paris discotheque in 1974. In 1986 Libyan terrorists attacked a Berlin nightclub and killed two U.S. servicemen and wounded over two hundred U.S. soldiers and others. After the United States responded by bombing targets in Libya, the JRA agreed to mount attacks on behalf of Libya under the alias Anti-Imperialist International Brigades (AIIB). For about two years, the JRA attacked U.S. and European targets, using car bombs and rockets. At least one AIIB/JRA attack was foiled, however, when police stopped JRA terrorist Yu Kikumura on a New Jersey highway. The police found hollowed-out fire extinguishers packed with explosives and roofing nails that Kikumura apparently planned to place outside a U.S. Navy recruiting station in Manhattan. The bombs were timed to explode during the crowded lunchtime traffic near Wall Street.

In the 1980s and 1990s, state-sponsored terrorism was practiced against civilian populations, forcing them to abandon their homes and lands. For example, South Africa engaged in state-sponsored terrorist attacks from the 1960s to 1980s, principally through operations targeting neighboring states. South African agents allegedly were involved in a 1961 airplane crash in Zambia that killed UN Secretary General Dag Hammarskjüld, and in a 1986 crash that killed Mozambican president Samora Machel. South Africa also supported the insurgent groups UNITA and RENAMO, which employed terrorist tactics in Angola. Likewise, Pakistan was accused of involvement in terrorist activities in Jammu and Kashmir against the Indian government. Meanwhile, the United Kingdom supported Loyalist groups inside the UK and Ireland that arguably engaged in terrorist activities, while the United States supported an anti-Soviet Afghan mujahideen during the 1980s, and helped dissident groups fighting the government of Iraq after the 1991 Gulf War. The religious and ethnic conflicts at the center of most of these incidents sometimes stemmed from ancient rivalries, but often from restructured relationships in the post–Cold War world. These mass terror campaigns, which have included the policy of ethnic cleansing or genocide, have played out from the Caucasus and Balkans to central Africa and South Asia.

For many years, the U.S. State Department listed seven countries as sponsors of terrorism: Cuba, Iran, Iraq, Libya, North Korea, Sudan, and Syria. Sudan, the newest member of this list, was added in 1993. Some countries on the list—Cuba, North Korea, Sudan, and Syria—were placed there not so much as current active sponsors of international terrorism, but because of their role in providing passive forms of support such as training facilities and sanctuary for terrorists. Until recently, the Muammar al-Qaddafi regime in Libya attacked the United States and Britain (through support of the Irish Republican Army) repeatedly.

Likewise, Iran supports extremist Palestinian groups such as Hamas and the Palestinian Islamic Jihad (PIJ), and it has supported terrorist attacks throughout the Middle East. Saddam Hussein's Iraq brutalized its citizens, terrorized the Kurds living inside Iraq, and attacked the United States wherever it could, including the failed plot in 1992 to assassinate former president George H. W. Bush in Kuwait.

As of 2007, only three of those states continued to covertly sponsor international terrorism: Iran, Sudan, and Syria. North Korea remains on the State Department list of state sponsors, but its intentions in this area are unknown, and Iraq was removed as a state sponsor after its government fell after the U.S.-led invasion in 2003. Libya was removed from the list in 2006 after the Libyan government agreed to a series of international initiatives, including forsaking terrorism and allowing inspections of its weapons facilities. Cuba remains on the list only as a symbol of U.S. distaste for the Castro regime. All in all, the remaining state-sponsored terrorism represents a small part of international terrorism.

State sponsorship of terrorism is not necessarily an all-or-nothing proposition. Even though states may be passive supporters, their culpability can be nearly as great as that of active sponsors, or at least sufficient to merit attention in shaping a state's policies to counter state involvement. Because active state sponsorship of terrorism has declined in recent years, terrorist groups have benefited from less overt means of support such as tolerance of terrorist fund raising, open or underenforced borders, and acquiescence in a terrorist organization's recruiting and operations.

A surprisingly large number of nations may be culpable in this passive way. For example, al Qaeda carried out much of the recruiting and fund raising for the September 11 attacks in Germany and Saudi Arabia, two of the closest allies of the United States in fighting al Qaeda. Moreover, the September 11

Box 1.2 **The United States: A Leading Sponsor of Terrorism?**

Some opponents of the United States—most notably Cuba, North Korea, and
Venezuela—claim that its record of supporting terrorist strikes abroad and its
record on human rights, before and during the war on terrorism, make it a leading sponsor of terrorism. In the 1980s, the International Court of Justice (ICJ,
or World Court) ruled that the United States had engaged in the unlawful use
of force in its support of the contras, a rebel group alleged to use terrorist tactics in fighting the elected government of Nicaragua. On several occasions,
the CIA sought through terrorist means to overthrow or assassinate Cuban
leader Fidel Castro, most famously in the Bay of Pigs invasion in 1962. In the
1970s, congressional investigators found evidence that the CIA supported the
assassination of heads of state in Congo, Guatemala, and Iran.

- Based on the characteristics of terrorism reviewed earlier in this chapter,
  do these examples appear to support the contention that the United
  States has been a state sponsor of terrorism?

- Do any of the events mentioned constitute terrorism? If so, how would
  you characterize the U.S. role in them?

operations were planned in part inside Malaysia, and operatives in the attacks
traveled to and lived openly inside the United States. Before and since September 11, Pakistan has had murky but certain links to al Qaeda, and it has
provided sanctuary to the Taliban leadership since their overthrow in
Afghanistan. Elsewhere, the Greek government long tolerated the violent
Revolutionary Organization 17 November, while the United States allowed
significant domestic fund raising for the Provisional Irish Republican Army
(PIRA) and its terrorism directed at Britain.

The reasons a nation provides passive support for terrorism are similarly
diverse. Sometimes, the tolerance or acquiescence stems from the widespread
support for the terrorist organization inside the state (Pakistan and al Qaeda,
for example). At other times, the state may not itself be threatened by the terrorist organization and thus determines that it will incur little direct cost in
tolerating the group's activities (France and Basque separatists, for example).
Although some passive state supporters of terrorism might simply lack an
effective counterterrorism capability, most of them, such as Saudi Arabia, simply choose not to invest in countering a threat their governments perceive as
not directed at them. In other situations, such as Pakistan's murky relationship with al Qaeda, the state may confront uncomfortable dilemmas: challenging al Qaeda too vigorously may alienate many citizens and even threaten
the government's stability, while turning a blind eye to al Qaeda will cost Pakistan vital financial support from the United States.

The "New Terrorism"

Beginning in the late 1960s, hostage taking for political purposes, often accompanied by aircraft hijackings, ushered in a new era of terrorism. This section describes some of the developments characterizing the changing nature of terrorism during this period.

First, terrorists began to routinely cross international borders to carry out their actions. For example, in July 1968 the Popular Front for the Liberation of Palestine hijacked an El Al flight from Rome to Tel Aviv, and forced Israel to negotiate directly with it for prisoner releases in return for the release of hostages. In 1970 the PFLP hijacked three airliners during a six-day period that Palestinians later called Black September. The hijackers landed the planes in Jordan, and, enjoying worldwide media attention, demanded an exchange of Palestinian political prisoners from various Western European jails in return for hostages. As the hijackers later explained, the unrealistic prisoner exchange demands were of only secondary interest to the PFLP. What they really wanted they got—attention on the world stage. Scenes of the 276 hostages and their PFLP captors were broadcast to millions over the six-day saga. After negotiations broke down, the PFLP was attacked by the Jordanian army, the hostages were freed, civil war erupted in Jordan, and the PFLP was expelled from the country.

Second, the "new terrorists" learned to target important political symbols of a state. In the 1980s in Northern Ireland, the Provisional Irish Republican Army (PIRA) sought British withdrawal of military support for the Protestant majority. The strategy adopted by the PIRA emphasized indiscriminate bombing attacks against the British military, the Royal Ulster Constabulary, and members of the British government in Ireland and England. In 1984 PIRA placed a hundred-pound bomb in a Brighton hotel where British prime minister Margaret Thatcher and her cabinet were staying. In the explosion, four government officials were killed and forty were injured. This attack and other bombings attracted considerable media attention for the PIRA, as did their prison hunger strikes and interviews and documentaries.

Finally and perhaps most notably, terrorists learned to exploit the media attention to a terrorist event to their advantage. During the 1972 Munich Summer Olympic Games, a group of Palestinian terrorists from the Black September group took eleven Israeli athletes hostage. While a worldwide viewing audience of hundreds of millions watched, the terrorists demanded the release of Arab prisoners held in Israeli jails. After negotiations failed, the terrorists engaged German police at the Munich Airport, where all eleven Israelis, five of the terrorists, and one police officer were killed. Despite the operational failure, the propaganda value of the stunning attacks was of immeasurable value for the Palestinian cause, which clamored for the creation of a Palestinian state and recognition of the Palestinian people.

Although the number of incidents of international terrorism declined during the 1990s, the number of fatalities attributed to terrorist attacks grew dramatically during the 1990s and into the 2000s. (See Table 1.2.) The new generation of terrorists appears to have little if any regard for massive and indiscriminate targeting of civilians. Those same terrorists perceive that only large-scale devastation will capture their opponents' attention and compel their opponents to give in to their demands. (See Chapter 9.) In addition, the improved security adopted by many traditional terrorist targets has sent the groups in pursuit of "softer" targets such as public buildings, shopping malls, or transit systems, frequented by large numbers of people. On the technical front, improved bomb-making equipment and supplies and widely available "how to" manuals are enabling terrorists to build more lethal explosives. As the Japanese religious cult Aum Shinrikyo demonstrated in the 1990s, terrorists possessing religious fanaticism, money, and scientific and technical capabilities can develop WMD.

In the United States, extremist right-wing terrorism became a serious issue in the 1990s with the white supremacist movement linked to the Christian Identity Movement. In addition to the Ku Klux Klan and neo-Nazi skinhead groups, these terrorists bombed abortion clinics and targeted doctors. Other extremists were arrested in 1996 for conspiring to bomb the Los Angeles federal building, an IRS office in Utah, and a synagogue in Phoenix. The eye-opening attack for many Americans, however, was the bombing by Timothy McVeigh and Terry Nichols—both linked to the white supremacist movement—of the Alfred P. Murrah Federal Building in Oklahoma City in April 1995; 168 died.

Islamic Extremist Terrorism

Only after the devastating attacks of September 11 did analysts and counter-terrorism officials begin to develop a fuller understanding of the nature of the threat posed by al Qaeda and Islamic fundamentalist terrorism. Al Qaeda is not sponsored by any state, nor is it affiliated with a particular government or set of governments. Thus there is no way to negotiate or to pursue diplomatic or even military solutions against a known enemy. In 1996 Osama bin Laden issued a "Declaration of War against America," followed in 1998 by a similarly blistering fatwa (religious edict). He called on every Muslim to kill Americans, as a religious duty, and to include civilians at every opportunity. Although the fatwa and other al Qaeda statements are veiled in religious rhetoric, their objectives are political—to force the United States to withdraw from Saudi Arabia and the Persian Gulf region. Al Qaeda also seeks the end of secular regimes in Muslim nations such as Egypt, Pakistan, and Saudi Arabia, and it aspires to an Islamic-ruled region, governing according to what it views as "true" Islam.

Table 1.2 Major Terrorist Incidents in the 1990s

Year	Location	Incident	Terrorist organization/individuals	Fatalities and injuries
1991	India	Assassination of former Indian prime minister Rajiv Gandhi	Liberation Tigers of Tamil Eelam (LTTE)	16 killed
1992	Argentina	Bombing of Israeli embassy	Hezbollah	29 killed, 242 wounded
1993	United States	World Trade Center bombing	Islamic terrorists	6 killed, 1,000 injured
1994	West Bank	Hebron massacre	Jewish extremist	29 killed, 150 injured
1995	Japan	Tokyo subway station attack	Aum Shinrikyo	12 killed, 5,700 injured
	United States	Oklahoma City bombing	Timothy McVeigh and Terry Nichols	168 killed, hundreds injured
	Israel	Bus bombing	Hamas	6 killed, over 100 injured
	Pakistan	Egyptian embassy attack	Three Islamic groups claim responsibility.	16 killed, 60 injured
1996	Sri Lanka	Central bank bombing	LTTE	90 killed, 1,400 injured
	Israel	Bus bombing	Hamas	26 killed, 90 injured
	Israel	Dizengoff shopping center bombing	Hamas and Palestinian Islamic Jihad both claim responsibility.	20 killed, 75 injured
	Saudi Arabia	Khobar Towers	Many claim responsibility.	19 killed, 515 injured
1997	Egypt	Tourist killings	Al-Gama'at al-Islamiyya	62 killed, 26 wounded
1998	Kenya/Tanzania	Embassy bombings	Osama bin Laden/al Qaeda	301 killed, over 5,000 injured

After al Qaeda took responsibility for the September 11 attacks, there was no longer any doubt that this nontraditional network of terrorists could strike with great lethality, killing indiscriminately, and that they might strike at any place and time, possibly with WMD. Captured documents and records indicate that al Qaeda has actively sought to acquire such weapons, and, if it has them, there is little doubt that they will be used.

Perhaps al Qaeda owes much of its success to its organization. Instead of hierarchical arrangements, the structure of al Qaeda is loose and network-based. Although Osama bin Laden and his key associates are the leaders of al Qaeda, the operational structure is flat, and the loosely networked cells can and do act with considerable autonomy. Groups such as al Qaeda do not depend on sponsorship from states. Rather, their worldwide sympathizers provide funds and the means to carry out attacks.[3]

Strategies and Approaches Employed by the United States to Counter Terrorism

Historically, terrorism has always been a concern in the United States. Threats of political assassination and anarchic acts against the government have sporadically emerged since the early years of the nation, including during the Civil War with the assassination of President Abraham Lincoln and the Reconstruction era attacks by groups such as the Ku Klux Klan. These acts gravely threatened the survival of the Union. Though less dire, activities by anarchists at Haymarket Square in Chicago and the assassination of President McKinley around the turn of the twentieth century reminded the nation that terrorists could strike at any time.

Based on the experience drawn from the terrorist attacks carried out in the early to mid-1990s on New York's World Trade Center, in Oklahoma City, and on the Tokyo subway, U.S. government officials began to emphasize preparedness to counter terrorism threats through homeland security. Policy makers noted with alarm the possibility that terrorism could become significantly more lethal than before, entailing mass slaughter and indiscriminate attacks. These concerns were driven in part by reports of lax security in the former Soviet Union within chemical and biological weapons programs and at nuclear weapons facilities. The scale of the Soviet chemical and biological weapons programs were described by defectors as large, producing sufficient quantities of lethal biological agents to cause massive human casualties—that is, on the scale of a nuclear weapon. These programs were also beset by accidents and security problems, including the ongoing uncertainty that the makers of these agents may have undertaken similar work in new places, such as Iraq, taking their lethal agents with them.

There is no question but that countering terrorism has become one of the most devilish set of policy problems facing the United States in contemporary times. It has tried to deal with terrorism through enhanced investigative tools, in the hope of interdicting terrorism before it strikes; as a law enforcement issue; as a matter for international cooperation and diplomacy; and as a species of war best fought by the military. These approaches are not mutually exclusive. Nor are they exhaustive. Nor have they been all that successful. Meanwhile, policy experts and government officials are trying to determine why terrorists strike and what might be done to lessen the root causes of terrorism, and they are studying the dynamics of homeland security planning and recovery, as well as the role of the media and the government's public affairs function.

That said, one of the lessons gained from trying to define terrorism bears repeating: terrorism is a method, a way that some people and groups seek to attain their objectives. As such, there is no common enemy in fighting terrorism. Nor is there a common cause for the terrorists. Combating terrorism, then, requires challenging, some might say "civilizing," the ways in which states, groups, and individuals carry out their political or religious agendas.

Root Causes of Terrorism

For a phenomenon as disruptive, destructive, and prevalent as terrorism, it is inevitable that governments and experts from a range of disciplines are devoting considerable energy to trying to identify its underlying causes. Many experts believe that only efforts to address the root causes of terrorism will lead to its significant decline. The causes—poverty, political repression, lack of education, and discrimination, among others—remain in place, and out of the caldron of seemingly intractable root causes are recruited the new generations of terrorists.

The United States has done little, however, to counter the root causes of terrorism. Using investment and direct aid to improve the education systems in those parts of the world where terrorists are most commonly recruited may be an attractive, albeit expensive, option. So are direct cash payments—that is, cash assistance in return for disbanding a terrorist group—although no such successes have been reported. Encouraging political reforms and greater opportunities for participation by all people in a nation's government is another option. The United States may use diplomatic means for this end, or a combination of financial or trade-based incentives. Other incentives toward economic development in target areas also may be effective, such as micro-credit schemes, loans and grants, or job training programs.

Policy makers have not paid attention to the root causes of terrorism in part because the relationships between the conditions giving rise to terrorism and the actual terrorist acts are complex and little understood. It has always been difficult to show a cause-and-effect relationship with terrorism, because, if shown, the links between carnage from a terrorist attack and the root causes of the attack are of questionable reliability. For example, suicide bombers are often secular, belonging to a religion other than Islam. Although the bombers' martyrdom is often glorified with reference to religious ideals, the real cause of their terrorist act is more likely political.

Some of the other factors compounding the difficulties in trying to understand the root causes of terrorism include the following:

- In recent years, terrorism has occurred more frequently in open and free societies than in closed societies.
- Successful peace processes may inflame a minority interest group.
- Poverty in a nation or area does not always produce terrorism. For example, in Africa Niger has no terrorism and very low economic standards, whereas Kenya has significant terrorism with relatively higher economic standards.
- Groups that develop cohesion as terrorists may be sustained by group affiliations, independent of any policy changes outside the group.

In addition, those who make and carry out counterterrorism policy are not the same people or even the same offices that consider root causes and how to alleviate them. For the most part, the study of root causes is an academic enterprise, complemented in some places by government offices that are only distantly connected to the policy-making apparatus. When a terrorist attack occurs and countermeasures are imminently needed, talk about why the terrorists struck is shoved to one side.

Interdiction and Investigation

The best way to combat terrorism is to stop an attack before it occurs, or interdiction, which is obviously easier said than done. Still, the United States has tried very hard to learn about terrorist activities in their nascent planning or talking stages, and then take steps to break up or arrest the terrorists or otherwise defuse the plot. Investigation refers to the various methods employed to learn about terrorist plots before they become operational.

Interdiction can be accomplished on its own, without intelligence or any advance warning about a terrorist plot. For example, sensors might detect a bomb or a biological agent in a mass transit facility or at some other checkpoint. Likewise, biometric screening of those who seek entrance to a major sporting or entertainment event might identify someone on a terrorism watch list and prevent a terrorist attack. But these methods are technologically challenging and expensive. They also are imperfect—the technologies may produce false positives, thereby subjecting an innocent person to scrutiny because of imperfections in the system.

Gathering intelligence to counter terrorism has great potential, and the United States invests heavily in this strategy. Intelligence investigations differ from the traditional law enforcement investigations. Instead of looking for evidence that a crime that has been committed or, if investigators are lucky, is about to be committed, intelligence investigations generally pursue information about terrorist plans and intentions where no crime may have occurred and there is no probable cause that a crime is about to be committed. Because of the privacy and free expression protections in the U.S. Constitution, law enforcement investigators generally are required to obtain a warrant from a judge before placing a wiretap on a telephone or looking at e-mail or conducting a search.

If investigators are seeking intelligence about a potential international terrorism incident, more relaxed rules apply, designed to ensure the secrecy of the investigation. Intelligence investigators also must take great care not to trample on the rights of innocent individuals, or to stereotype terrorism suspects based on their ethnicity or race, religion, age, or gender, which can lead to profiling—conducting secret and potentially intrusive investigations based on one or more of those personal characteristics rather than on any demonstrated affiliation with terrorism. Further complicating matters is the current trend in the United States to criminalize terrorism, with the result that law enforcement and intelligence investigations of the same targeted persons may be running on parallel tracks, with shared information. If the intelligence investigators uncover a crime while conducting their secret investigation, can the police use their material as evidence at trial? These and other issues are explored in Chapter 5.

One problem in studying interdiction and investigation is that often the successes are not revealed; such information is classified, so that adversaries do not know how their plots were thwarted—that is, what the intelligence community refers to as its "sources and methods." Instead, those studying interdiction and investigation must examine some instances in which the investigation failed or was flawed to learn about how to structure interdiction and investigative activities.

Planning for Homeland Security

Securing the U.S. homeland has always been a central mission of the U.S. government, but after the Civil War nearly brought the nation to an end, no serious threat to the country's borders was encountered until al Qaeda struck on September 11, 2001. Even so, after the World Trade Center bombing in 1993 and the bombing at the Oklahoma City federal building in 1995, government officials began to give more attention to homeland defense. When the Japanese cult group Aum Shinrikyo used sarin nerve gas to attack the Tokyo subway system in 1995, some officials, including President Clinton, began to consider the possibility that terrorists might strike with nuclear, biological, chemical, or radiological devices that could inflict mass casualties inside the United States.

In 2002 Congress enacted the Homeland Security Act and created the Department of Homeland Security (DHS) in a mammoth government reorganization that effectively relocated twenty-two agencies and 170,000 employees to the new department. Faced with the daunting task of using its huge new bureaucracy to provide a secure homeland, DHS struggles with problems of organization, personnel management, and mission.

Through a series of presidential directives and DHS planning documents, a National Response Plan (NRP) and National Incident Management System (NIMS) were put into place in 2004 and 2005, respectively. They were designed to provide a template for responding to a terrorist attack on the homeland. Growing awareness of terrorist capabilities and U.S. vulnerabilities has spurred the private sector to work at security as well in order to protect critical infrastructure assets, such as telecommunications, energy, and banking. Protecting the borders and international shipping and air points of entry has received considerable attention. Meanwhile, state and local governments, with varying degrees of investment and intensity, have also launched planning initiatives, but some are lagging for lack of resources, and others are provoking critics to wonder out loud whether policy priorities call for significant investment in homeland security for some of the more remote states such as Montana.

A concern in any homeland security initiatives is civil liberties. For example, should citizens be subject to video surveillance in shopping malls or mass transit facilities, or undergo searches before boarding a bus or commuter train? It is not clear how much additional security such measures are likely to provide. It also is not clear whether the investments in airline security since September 11 are worth the cost, or whether they are simply an example of "fighting the last war," in which policy makers plug a security gap that has already been exploited while the terrorists make preparations to find a different vulnerability. In short, are the trade-offs in liberty for security worth the price?

Incident Management and Recovery

Many experts believe it is inevitable that the best efforts at intelligence, interdiction, and planning will fail to prevent a major terrorist attack. In the event of another such incident, the actions that government and the people take during the crisis will go a long way toward determining just how grave and how costly the incident will be. Indeed, determining just what part of government and what level of government will manage the response to a terrorism incident is perhaps the central issue in incident management. Incident management and recovery consists of a structure for managing a wide range of tasks, the processes for managing them, and the leadership and cooperation needed to get them done.

Beyond fashioning a command structure of some sort and assigning the principal management and recovery tasks, incident managers must decide how communications and other essential services will be provided in the event of a major terrorist attack, and how people will be advised of what steps or precautions they should take. Often, incident management requires paying considerable attention to the public health dimensions of a crisis. After the crisis stage of an incident, recovery may present as challenging a set of tasks, with similar questions, as management during the crisis.

If a small cell of terrorists or even a lone terrorist managed to release a contagious biological agent in an urban setting—smallpox, for example—events could quickly spiral out of control. Because smallpox can be released in an aerosol form and would be difficult to detect, those infected, perhaps a few dozen or a few hundred, would not know about their infection and would go about their lives, including interacting with others and traveling, for the ten to fourteen days before symptoms appear. Once the outbreak is evident, public health, emergency management, and other personnel critical to infrastructure would be severely stressed. Meanwhile, who would be in charge in such an outbreak? The city officials where the outbreak first occurs? The governor of the affected states? The president?

Other decisions would have to be made about how to distribute the smallpox vaccine to local health providers, how those who are potentially infected would be isolated, and where those who are already sick would receive treatment. Travel restrictions would likely be imposed, and businesses and schools would be closed. Thus some part of government would have to provide essential services. If panic sets in and looting or other unrest breaks out, the military may have to play a role in enforcing the laws.

Law Enforcement and Its Methods

The effective enforcement of criminal law has always been an important instrument in assuring security in organized societies. In theory, terrorism could be treated like other crimes. Criminalize the terrorist actions, round up the violators, and try, convict, and imprison them. Over time, the sanctions will deter others from terrorism. But it is not so simple. First, determining what exactly should be forbidden by the criminal law and then defining the crime and its elements in clear language are challenging tasks. Drafters of such laws must avoid encroaching on civil liberties and ensure that the forbidden actions are understood by the average person. Second, the investigations raise many of the problems just identified in connection with investigating terrorism generally. Third, problems of classified or other secret information may compromise the defendant's right to a fair trial, and the questionable extraterritorial application of U.S. laws may prevent reaching some of those most culpable. Finally, there is little evidence that stiff criminal penalties, including in some cases the death penalty, will deter others from carrying out terrorist attacks, especially if they are motivated by messianic religious beliefs.

Since the mid-1990s, the United States has amplified its criminal laws against terrorist activities in a wide-ranging array of new offenses. Among the most pervasive are a set of measures forbidding "material support" of terrorism. In the new laws, providing material support could include financial contributions, logistical support, weapons or other instruments of terrorism, and the use of one's self as personnel for the terrorists. Because material support could be and is defined in so many ways, prosecutors have used these provisions to charge hundreds of persons in recent years. In many of these prosecutions, the accused has defended himself or herself by claiming that the activities charged—raising funds for a charity, for example—are protected expressive activities and thus may not form the basis for a conviction. But the government has argued, with considerable success, that fund raising for a charity is not protected if the charity, in turn, supports terrorist activities.

In its most extreme law enforcement strategy, the Bush administration decided late in 2001 by a military order to create a status of detainees in the war on terrorism—"enemy combatants"—and to hold them indefinitely in military detention. Then, if it chooses, it can bring them to trial before military commissions. The commissions are not unprecedented—military commissions have been employed in other U.S. wars—but, unlike their predecessors, these were not (until late 2006, that is) authorized by Congress, and they exist outside the traditional system for military justice. In a still ongoing series of controversial rulings, the administration has moved forward with plans to try accused terrorists by military commission. Meanwhile, the federal courts are weighing the extent to which the law demands more fairness than the military order (and new statute) provide. Some issues that have been raised are whether military commissions should provide the kinds of procedural protections afforded the accused in criminal cases in the United States, or perhaps those given to service personnel accused of violating the Uniform Code of Military Justice.

International Cooperation

Just as terrorism transcends international boundaries, so, too, must any effective response strategy. One tool that is as old as international relations is diplomacy—that is, the process of engaging foreign governments, communicating policy to them, persuading them of its desirability, and then reaching informal or formal agreements on the policy. In part, diplomacy can address the root causes of terrorism by explaining the message the United States wishes to send to those who might be susceptible to terrorist recruiting. More directly, diplomacy can aim to persuade states that sponsor terrorism to desist, and to dissuade the states that harbor terrorist groups from doing so. Often diplomacy may be needed simply to provide support or protection in the foreign state for U.S. interests.

In the United States, the Department of State plays the leading role in shaping international cooperation, although intelligence and law enforcement agencies, as well as the Departments of Defense, Treasury, and Homeland Security, often join in international initiatives and programs. Since the 1970s, international treaties and agreements have been a central front in combating terrorism. For example, the European Convention on the Suppression of Terrorism, adopted in 1977, provides for cooperative measures for countering terrorism by European nations. In 1997 the UN General Assembly adopted the International Convention for the Suppression of Terrorist Bombings, and as of 2007 the convention has been ratified by over 120 nations. This convention also includes instruments for international cooperation. Whether bilateral or multilateral, treaties and agreements can provide for the rendition of suspected terrorists or other mutual law enforcement assistance; resolve to adopt common laws and policies against terrorism, or to condemn a terrorist group or state supporter; and adopt conventions against specific terrorist actions, such as hostage taking or maritime navigation, and thus provide an agreed set of standards to ease implementation and enforcement across borders.

Weapons proliferation, a product of the Cold War, historically revolved around a state's acquisition of nuclear weapons. Today, even with the end of the cold war, nuclear weapons issues remain a problem in the form of managing the existing stockpiles in the former Soviet Union and closely following the activities of the other governments that possess nuclear weapons and exhibit worrisome tendencies (most notably, Pakistan, North Korea, and potentially, Iran). The specter of WMD and the growing ease with which countries can acquire chemical, radiological, and biological weapons also have led to ramped-up efforts to reach enforceable international agreements to control the proliferation of these weapons.

And yet a host of problems confound these initiatives. The nuclear weapons of the former Soviet Union are not fully secured in a reliable, systematic way. While the current Russian weapons stockpiles are generally secure, there are substantial supplies of fissile material that are not. In addition, the scientists who worked for the Soviet nuclear and biological weapons programs (the Soviet Union had the world's largest and most sophisticated biological weapons program) are not all accounted for, which means that they may have taken their talents to other nations or to work for terrorist organizations. Another problem is that some forms of WMD, such as chemical weapons, can be acquired or made relatively cheaply, rendering control all the more difficult. If non-state terrorists can develop a biological agent and then weaponize it, for example, only excellent intelligence and luck would allow the states that are potential targets to know about a possible attack and perhaps prevent it.

In the end, of course, international cooperation and diplomacy may be of limited effectiveness in combating non-state terrorists. States that are victimized by terrorists do not make it their policy to negotiate with terrorists.

The Media and Public Affairs

Until the coming of age of the mass and electronic media and the 24/7 worldwide news cycle, news reporting about terrorism was not a significant part of the dynamics of terrorism. Now, however, the media are omnipresent, pervasive, and influential. Combating terrorism requires understanding a complex set of relationships between terrorists, governments and their citizens, and the media.

In 1975 terrorism expert Brian Jenkins observed that terrorists do not want a lot of people dead; rather, they want a lot of people watching and listening.[4] Although Jenkins's statement may, after the horrific attacks of September 11 and other more recent ones, be only half-right, his point remains powerful. Terrorism is often designed first and foremost to call attention to the terrorists' cause. The Palestinian attack on the Israeli athletes at the 1972 Summer Olympic Games in Munich is an instance against which others may be judged. Over the span of two days, millions of television viewers watched the drama unfold and end in a tragic bungled raid by German police in which all the Israelis, all but three of the terrorists, and one German policeman died. However, the Palestinians accomplished their objective: to broadcast to the world their demand for a Palestinian state.

But reporting about a subject as dynamic and potentially sensationalistic as terrorism is tricky. The media must decide how much attention should be paid to the terrorists and their message, whether implicit or explicit, and to what extent they should cover graphic violence and the attendant carnage. Meanwhile, the media must ask themselves whether they are playing into the hands of the terrorists by merely following the story.

In the United States, as in other nations where terrorist attacks have occurred, the government plays a central role in conducting public affairs—that is, putting out the official government message, whether it be a policy about terrorism, a response to terrorists' demands, or instructions to citizens on how to respond to a terrorist threat or incident. Many Americans learned soon after the events of September 11, when letters tainted with anthrax began to arrive, that a mixed or inconsistent (and occasionally inaccurate) public affairs voice and message can exacerbate the tendency toward fear and panic that is a central element of the terrorism agenda.

The Internet has also served as a powerful tool for terrorist organizations, independent of the media and their reporting. Terrorist groups use the Internet to promote themselves and to spread propaganda about their goals and causes either to known adherents and more widely to e-mail distribution lists they obtain from charities or perhaps nonprofit groups. The Internet thus also serves as a means of recruiting new sympathizers for the terrorist organization, no matter where they might live. Once a curious individual expresses an interest in an organization's Web sites or electronic mailings, a single return e-mail to the Web site may lead to other forms of contact by the terrorist organization.

Military Responses to Terrorism

The use of military force to counter terrorism has historical roots as deep as those of terrorism. Although nations have always strived to defend themselves and their citizens, a range of problems render the use of military force in combating terrorism the option of last resort in most instances. For one thing, if military force is contemplated to combat an ongoing attack such as a hostage taking or a series of bomb attacks, the force used as a counter may cause more casualties among the innocents than the use of other options. For example, the German attempt to rescue Israeli athletes from Palestinian terrorists during the 1972 Olympic Games resulted in fatalities on both sides. Although the U.S. and other Western nations worked thereafter to develop specially trained commando units for hostage situations, few such terrorist attacks have occurred since, and the operational risks associated with the use of force remain large. U.S. special operations forces have developed impressive capabilities, but their use in hostage situations remains fraught with pitfalls.

Military force is more likely to be considered in response to a terrorist attack. Striking back may be thought of as retaliation—an eye for an eye—or as a kind of anticipatory self-defense, hitting the terrorists before their plans to strike, or strike again, can be carried out. Retaliation is not lawful—imagine an endless cycle of strikes and counterstrikes escalating without end. However, in the modern era of terrorism in which secret attacks by non-state actors are capable of inflicting massive casualties, the line between forbidden retaliation or reprisal and self-defense is shifting to permit greater discretion to use the military option as a means of preventing and deterring future attacks.

Another problem that confronts decision makers when the use of military force is considered is its effectiveness. Does a military strike succeed in preventing or deterring the next or subsequent terrorist attacks? This question is important in part because the imprecision of the military option may produce civilian casualties and thus inflict harm beyond that intended. Significant strides have been made in making the military option more precise—guidance systems for missiles and the use of high-technology drones to identify targets in close detail, for example. In fact, several strikes have been launched against al Qaeda and Osama bin Laden, taking advantage of the new technologies and systems, but, aside from their symbolic value, they do not appear to have undercut al Qaeda's capabilities or deterred future attacks. The strikes launched in 1998 in Sudan and Afghanistan after terrorists bombed U.S. embassies in Kenya and Tanzania arguably only emboldened al Qaeda to hit the United States again and again, with greater lethality, while U.S. missiles killed innocents on the ground. However, after the September 11, 2001, attacks, the U.S. military operation in Afghanistan to capture or kill al Qaeda and its Taliban hosts was widely viewed as successful. In a few months, most of the military operation had been completed, a new government was in place, albeit tentatively, and al Qaeda and its capabilities were damaged considerably, at least temporarily.

Finally, the 2003 U.S.-led invasion of Iraq revealed that the use of military force abroad can itself incite terrorism. Faulty intelligence was at least partly responsible for the invasion, predicated on the view that Saddam Hussein was poised to strike at the United States and the West with his WMD. Instead, the invasion and removal of Saddam inspired jihadists from outside Iraq to infiltrate an Iraqi insurgency and attack the United States and other Western interests inside Iraq.

Conclusion

Of the strategies used by the United States in responding to terrorist threats, and described in coming chapters, no one approach should be selected or even preferred over the others. Some would say that the United States has followed the "kitchen sink" approach—throwing anything available at the problem in the hope that something might work. But, in fact, combating terrorism is, in this respect, not all that different from many policy problems—resolution or even adequate management of the problem requires a multifaceted response. The problems associated with tobacco, smoking, and health costs offer one example. Once the health effects of smoking and second-hand smoke were widely understood, the government at first tried to discourage smoking by providing health information about smoking and by inserting health warning labels on tobacco products. After the government threatened to ban advertising of tobacco products on television, the tobacco industry and broadcasters agreed to a set of voluntary controls. When levels of tobacco use failed to decline significantly, regulators sought to control the access of potential teenage smokers to tobacco products. When this approach was invalidated by the courts, Congress considered restrictions in the form of legislation.

The study of combating terrorism is so important for many of the same reasons that it is so difficult. The stakes are extremely high when WMD and potential mass-casualty events are assessed, along with the attendant disruptions in U.S. society and in the international sphere. In the years since the September 11 attacks, the demand for education about terrorism, combating terrorism, and homeland security has placed a high premium on students who are prepared for new careers and challenges in this rapidly expanding field. Every assignment and every class devoted to the issues described in this book will invoke the events and controversies described daily in newspapers, in televised newscasts, and on Web sites. There is simply no timelier subject than combating terrorism, nor one that presents Americans with more challenges in gaining greater understanding of how to shape policy in this area so fraught with drama and uncertainty.

FOR FURTHER READING

Heymann, Philip. *Terrorism, Freedom, and Security: Winning without War.* Cambridge: MIT Press, 2003.

Pillar, Paul R. *Terrorism and U.S. Foreign Policy.* Washington, D.C.: Brookings, 2001.

Richardson, Louise. *What Terrorists Want.* New York: Random House, 2006.

Stern, Jessica, *The Ultimate Terrorists.* Cambridge: Harvard University Press, 2001.

Chapter 2 Identifying and Assessing the Modern Terrorist Threat

Before the attacks of September 11, 2001, how would the average American have described a "typical" terrorist? In all likelihood, the description would have been something like this: a poor, angry young man with little or no formal education, whose deeply held extremist views are the result of a life of deprivation and poverty or extensive political or religious indoctrination. The typical terrorist also may or may not have been characterized as being "Arab" or "Muslim," because many Americans were aware that terrorists were active in places as geographically distinct (and non-Muslim) as Peru or Colombia in Latin America or India and Sri Lanka in Asia. Since September 11, however, with the country fixated on the threat of *Islamic* terrorism, the image of a terrorist has become generalized as virtually any person of the Islamic faith. In reality, however, neither of these images is accurate.

The modern terrorist threat is complex and nuanced, and it is virtually impossible to typecast the person who typically turns to terrorist violence or to neatly categorize his or her motivations. Thus to assess and analyze the full scope of the terrorist threat in the twenty-first century, this chapter will explore the following questions: What and who are terrorists? What are their motivations? What are their tactics? How do they organize? And where do they recruit, train, and operate?

What and Who Are Terrorists?

As just noted, the term *terrorist* covers a lot of ground, and there is often disagreement about whether certain groups should be considered terrorist organizations or legitimate political or social movements. It is not surprising, then, that it is equally difficult to describe the profile of a person who joins a terrorist organization and engages in violent acts.

Many people assume that individuals who resort to acts of mass violence against innocent civilians necessarily must be either "true believers" in the thrall of a particular extreme ideology, religion, or cult; desperately poor or downtrodden individuals who feel that they have little or nothing to lose; hardened criminals; or psychopaths. Although it is true that each of these "types"—and perhaps more than one—could be applied to those who engage in violent acts, there is simply no common profile, whether psychological, political, or social, of the modern terrorist. Indeed, people appear to turn to terrorist activities, whether on an individual or collective basis, for a variety of reasons. For some, it may be the inevitable culmination of years of ineffectual (but peaceful) political activism. For others, it may be the result of a recent religious conversion or personal epiphany. For still others, it may be a convenient cover for other criminal activities—for example, the narco-terrorists who operate in certain lawless areas of some countries. Or it may be the culmination of a long slide into serious mental illness.

As for the demographics of those who decide to resort to terrorism and especially suicide terrorism, are they young or old, male or female? Are they single "loner" types or people with families? Are they a member of a particular ethnic group or religious group that disproportionately produces terrorists? Are they poor and illiterate or possessing a high school or even college education and regular income? The answer may be surprising: terrorists encompass *all* of these characteristics and more—so much so that they simply defy easy classification. As Bruce Schneier has pointed out, "Those who say that terrorists are likely to be Arab males have it wrong. Richard Reid, the shoe bomber, was British. Jose Padilla, arrested in Chicago in 2002 as a 'dirty bomb' suspect, was a Hispanic-American. . . . Terrorists can be male or female, European, Asian, African or Middle Eastern." [1]

It is even difficult to develop an accurate profile of those who are prepared to take their own lives for a cause—that is, those who engage in the most dangerous and insidious type of terrorist activity, suicide bombing. Indeed, even though the terrorists involved in the attacks of September 11, 2001, apparently were prepared to commit suicide to complete their mission (and though it has been suggested that not all the hijackers may have known that the objective was to crash the planes into buildings), it has now been fairly well documented that none of these individuals fit the profile typical of a suicidal personality—that is, they were not suffering from mental illness, nor had their life circumstances left them with little or nothing to lose by sacrificing their lives. At the same time, they were not uneducated, desperately poor, or simple-minded, meaning that they were not duped into unwittingly carrying out a suicide mission.[2] Apparently, the only thing that appears to have bound them together was their total commitment to the Islamic jihadist cause.

Marc Sageman, in a recent path-breaking book, undertook an analysis of terrorist networks, and particularly the al Qaeda cells operating in Hamburg, Germany, and Montreal, Canada, that were connected to the September 11 attacks on New York City and Washington, D.C.[3] Based on intensive study of 172 individual biographies, he further refutes the notion that the members of these networks were motivated to turn to terrorism based on poverty, trauma, mental illness, or lack of education. Instead, he suggests that they appear to have been motivated by social bonds (for example, lifelong friendships, family relationships, or community connections) that predated their ideological commitment, and that it was these social networks that inspired the young men (and they were all men) to join the radical jihadist elements and become willing to seek martyrdom through suicide attacks.

Even if the analysis here were confined just to what is known about the main leaders of al Qaeda, the socioeconomic and educational differences among them are striking. Osama bin Laden is the scion of an extremely wealthy Saudi family involved in large construction projects throughout the Middle East. He had every possible advantage growing up, including extensive education, wealth, and connections at high levels within Saudi society. Bin Laden's second in command, Ayman al-Zawahiri, is an Egyptian medical doctor, who has a middle-class background. By contrast, Abu Musab al-Zarqawi, the self-identified head of al Qaeda in Iraq who was killed by U.S. forces on June 7, 2006, was a poor, uneducated Jordanian, who had already served time in prison. Clearly, then, at some point each of these men, though from distinctly different backgrounds, became radicalized and committed to financing, planning, and carrying out violent terrorist acts in support of a common, radical jihadist vision.

Terrorism in the twenty-first century reflects a trend toward a level of resources, ingenuity, and training that far exceeds the capabilities of the typical terrorist organization of the 1970s and 1980s. In those early days, a jet-liner could be hijacked (for the purposes of blowing it up on the ground) or hostages could be captured (such as the Israeli hostages at the 1972 Munich Summer Olympic Games) by a small but committed group that had at least some rudimentary weapons training and were prepared to be killed or captured during the act. By contrast, today the operations of al Qaeda, which is a network and not a terrorist group per se, are global and highly complex. They involve the use of advanced technology (such as computers, encrypted software, untraceable telecommunications, and, perhaps in the future, biological or nuclear weapons), and they require substantial capital and a great many trained operatives. Thus, although the uneducated "true believer" may still have a role as the terrorist foot soldier, the backgrounds of the September 11 hijackers suggest the emergence of a new breed of better-educated and more sophisticated terrorist operative.

Yet another trend in evidence during the past decade is the shift away from terrorism as the nearly exclusive domain of men. Although a few women were involved in some of the terrorist groups of the 1970s and 1980s (for example, the Baader-Meinhof Gang in Germany was co-led by a woman), up through the end of the 1990s violent terrorism was overwhelmingly undertaken by males. Since then, however, this situation has begun to change. Multiple successful female suicide bombings have been carried out in Iraq, Israel, and elsewhere in the Middle East. And many of these female suicide bombers were later revealed to be well educated—some even holding Ph.D.s and other advanced degrees—and virtually all were solidly middle class. Women have also been members of the IRA and certain terrorist groups operating in Latin America.

Finally, just to reiterate a point made in Chapter 1, although today the world is focusing intently on individuals and groups associated with radical, Islamic jihadist terrorism, many other active terrorists are of other ethnic and religious backgrounds and are pursuing causes, to the extent that they can be identified, that appear to be unrelated to the radical Salafist form of Islam. Examples include the Tamil Tiger separatist movement in Sri Lanka, the narco-terrorists who operate in some Latin American countries, and the Basque separatist movement in Spain.

What Are Their Motivations?

Now that it has become clearer that terrorists are not easily stereotyped and that they may come from many different socioeconomic, religious, and ethnic backgrounds, it is useful to explore their motivations for engaging in violent terrorist activities, including those that may involve suicide attacks. It has been observed that individuals and groups often resort to terrorism when they conclude that their needs or their political or ideological agendas are being ignored, if not actively opposed, by the established order. Terrorism is, in this respect, a way of demanding attention and gaining legitimacy for a set of political, social, economic, religious, or other demands. The many historical examples include the struggle by the Irgun, a group of Israeli fighters active in the 1940s, which resorted to terrorist tactics to demand that the British recognize the existence of the state of Israel. A current example is the struggle by Palestinian groups that have been using similar tactics to seek control over the same land. Other terrorist acts, however, are more difficult to connect to a particular issue agenda or demand for legitimacy. For some, the motivation may result from an obscure, and often highly personalized, ideology or worldview; for others, the motivation may be pure anarchism, with no broader objective than to attack and bring down the existing order.

Table 2.1 provides a typology of the major (known) motivations or rationales for terrorist violence. Because individuals or groups decide to commit a terrorist act, or help others do so, for dozens of reasons, only those that are most common and seem to explain the majority of known terrorist attacks are presented here.

Motivations for State-Sponsored Terrorism

State-sponsored terrorism is a potentially risky game in which a duly constituted government provides financial, logistical, and other kinds of support, including arms and explosives (and the training to use them), to terrorist organizations under its control or influence. This is risky primarily because where evidence directly connects the state sponsor with the actions of a terrorist group, the security—and possibly the continued existence—of a state may be placed in jeopardy. Perhaps the most well-known example of this danger is the 1986 U.S. bombing of the family compound of Muammar al-Qaddafi in Libya in retaliation for the terrorist attack on a discotheque in Germany that was frequented by U.S. soldiers, or the political and economic embargo put in place

Table 2.1 Typology of Terrorist Motivations

Nature of terrorist group or individual	Motivation	Definition
1. State-sponsored	Political	A group that is funded, trained, and supplied directly by the state to carry out its policy agenda
	Religious	A group that acts on the religious principles of a theocratic government
	Ideological	A group that shares, or is organized to support, the philosophical principles of a government
	Failed-state anarchism	A group that takes advantage of the failure of a government or its inability to govern effectively (especially in remote areas)
2. Non-state-sponsored	Political	A group with a policy agenda, often involving the overthrow of the existing regime
	Religious	A group motivated by religious principles, either of an existing religion or one created by its founders
	Ideological	A group motivated by philosophical principles that may be either broad (such as communism) or narrow (that is, unique to the group)
	Personality-driven	A group, usually in the form of a cult, that is driven by the vision and charisma of its leader
	Organized crime	A group that either derives its operating resources from illegal sources (such as narcotics) or is protected or financed by organized crime syndicates
	Single-issue	A group that focuses on an individual cause, such as the environment or animal rights, or is extremist in relation to issues such as race or religion
3. Individual	Ideological	An individual motivated by a particular philosophy or belief, often of his or her own creation
	Religious	An individual of deep faith motivated by the teachings of an organized religion
	Anarchist	An individual who does not accept the authority of governments and who struggles actively to resist such authority and control
	Single-issue	An individual who focuses exclusively on a single "cause" such as the environment or abortion

against Libya in response to its other major support for terrorism—its role in sponsoring the 1988 destruction of Pan Am Flight 103 over Lockerbie, Scotland. (See Chapter 8.)

Recent examples of state-sponsored terrorism include the Libyan government (until its radical change in behavior and then removal from the terrorist state watch list)—both its indirect support (arms and financing) of terrorist groups such as the IRA and others in Europe and the Middle East and its direct terrorist activities in Europe, including the destruction of Pan Am Flight 103; the North Korean government, which has conducted terrorist-style attacks in South Korea, Thailand, and elsewhere in Asia over the years; the Iranian government (since it became an Islamic theocracy in the late 1970s), which has financed and armed Hezbollah in its fight against Israel and may be implicated in the present-day insurgency in Iraq; and the Syrian government, which has long hosted Hezbollah in Lebanon (which it controlled until recently) and in Damascus.

Many people would argue that failed states—that is, those in which the central government can no longer effectively govern much of its territory, such as Afghanistan (under the Taliban) or Somalia—or even partially failed states, such as Sudan, also should be considered state sponsors of terrorism. After all, major atrocities of a terrorist nature, such as the attacks by the Janjaweed in the Darfur region of Sudan, have been—and continue to be—committed in these places. Yet because the governments of truly failed states (such as Somalia) are, by definition, unable to govern, they cannot be considered a direct sponsor of terrorism. At the same time, the situation in Sudan is more nuanced, because the government in Khartoum continues to be in control and yet denies involvement with the Janjaweed, despite the press reports alleging that it is supporting the attacks.

Governments sponsor terrorism—and individuals carry out such acts on their behalf—for a variety of reasons. Based on the historical evidence, the principal motivations for state-sponsored terrorism are generally political and religious (and often a mixture of the two) or, in some cases, ideological. Until its recent shift in policy, for example, Muammar al-Qaddafi's government allegedly provided financial support for various terrorist groups largely on the basis of Qaddafi's publicly stated ideological "solidarity" with their stated aims and objectives. Elsewhere in the Middle East, the Iranian state, together with Syria, continues to provide financial, military, and other support to terrorist groups opposing the existence of the state of Israel, based on both religious and political motivations.

Motivations for Non-State-Sponsored Terrorism

The number of terrorist groups not sponsored or supported in some fashion by governments is enormous, and, as indicated in Table 2.1, their motivations vary widely. This category includes the dozens of radical single-issue groups, some of which continue to exist even in the United States. These groups range from those that espouse racial purity and separation of the races, to those that believe violence is justified in connection with social issues such as abortion, to those that feel they must take radical action in order to protect the environment. This category also includes larger and more broadly focused organizations and networks such as al Qaeda that are motivated by religious, political, or ideological beliefs or by a combination of economic and political motivations—such as those behind organized crime and narco-terrorists.

Because there are so many different non-state-sponsored terrorist groups, each with its own mission and philosophical rationale, they are divided here into four broad categories: (1) political/ideological, (2) religious, (3) organized crime, and (4) issue-specific. A look at some examples of terrorist groups in each of these categories will reveal their motivations, and the case studies in this chapter will provide greater detail on some of these groups and especially on their motivations and objectives.

Political/Ideological Terrorist Groups

Certainly, the largest and most diverse category of non-state-sponsored terrorist groups is those whose motivations are political or ideological in nature. Such groups cover the waterfront of ideas and political orientations from extreme left to extreme right to no political orientation at all (that is, those that adhere to a purely anarchist ideology that challenges all forms of political and organizational authority). Some groups focus exclusively on changing the political relationships within the specific country in which they operate—or, at least, on gaining political influence and legitimacy for themselves. Others espouse a much broader (and often vaguer) global agenda. Some of these terrorist organizations are, in reality, composed of a small band of deeply committed individuals; in some cases, the group itself may take the form of a cult, revolving around the personal philosophy and ideology of a charismatic leader.

Many people would argue that the network of terrorist organizations known as al Qaeda (which, loosely translated, means "the foundation" or "the base") is as much a political/ideological terrorist group as anything else. However, because of its fundamental connection to the radical Salafist form of Islam, al Qaeda is addressed in the following section on religious groups. Examples of terrorist groups that have in the past or currently are espousing a broad range of political and ideological motivations in justification of their violent acts include, on the left, the Red Brigades, a militant group in Italy in the 1970s that kidnapped and later murdered the former Italian prime minister Aldo Moro; the Red Army Faction (also known as the Baader-Meinhof Gang), which operated in West Germany in the 1970s; and the Symbionese Liberation Army (SLA), which was an American terrorist group that considered itself the vanguard of an African American, urban guerrilla movement. (See Case Study 2.1.)

CASE STUDY 2.1

The Symbionese Liberation Army: An Early Example of U.S. "Homegrown" Terrorism

Active during the 1970s, the Symbionese Liberation Army was a tiny American terrorist group that considered itself to be a vanguard army. The SLA, which adopted its rhetoric from Maoism and South American revolutionaries, engaged in selected violent acts such as murder, kidnapping, and robbery in order to attract media attention and, its members hoped, popular support. The media-hungry group distributed photographs and press releases and taped interviews that explained their activities.

The SLA emerged out of a Vacaville, California, prison visitation program that linked student ideologists at the University of California, Berkeley, with prisoners affiliated with a radical left-wing group called the Black Cultural Organization. In 1971 some of these students, all middle or upper class and white, founded an organization to fight oppression and poverty. In 1973 this group connected with Donald DeFreeze, an escaped convict from the Vacaville prison, and other student radicals. DeFreeze became the leader—and the only African American member—of the SLA. The group adopted the slogan "death to the fascist insect that preys upon the life of the people" and a seven-headed cobra as its symbol. Members rejected their given names and took on new revolutionary names.

On November 6, 1973, the SLA murdered Oakland, California's first black school superintendent, Dr. Marcus Foster, using hollow-point bullets dipped in cyanide. Although the group claimed the attack was to protest Foster's plan to introduce identification cards into the public school system, in reality Foster had opposed the use of ID cards. In addition, he was well respected and popular in the black community and among left wing political groups. His violent murder thus appalled people across ideologies and alienated the group from its radical roots. Members of the SLA went into hiding after Foster's murder.

On February 4, 1974, the SLA made its next move by kidnapping publishing heiress Patricia (Patty) Hearst, then a college student at Berkeley. The group chose Hearst to garner media attention, and they succeeded. The first television media frenzy took place outside of the Hearst family mansion after the kidnapping. Thereafter, the SLA communicated to police and the Hearsts only through the radio and newspapers, and it insisted they do the same. The original plan was to negotiate a prisoner swap, but the group switched gears and demanded instead that food be distributed to the poor.

Meanwhile, the FBI's search for Hearst was proving ineffective; negotiations were becoming more heated; and Patty Hearst's public communications with her family were becoming more strained. On April 1, she renounced her name and adopted the SLA identity of "Tania." Her parents claimed she had been brainwashed. Some experts suggested that she suffered from Stockholm syndrome (a psychological response to abduction in which the hostage can show signs of loyalty to the abductor, regardless of the risk to the hostage). Other observers believed Hearst had adopted radical terrorism to rebel against her upbringing. Two weeks later, Hearst was caught on a security camera participating with the SLA in a bank robbery in San Francisco. Afterward, she fled with the SLA to Los Angeles.

When found by the Los Angeles Police Department the next day, the SLA engaged police in one of the biggest shootouts in the city's history. DeFreeze and five other members (the majority of the SLA) died in a fire during the shootout. Hearst and two other SLA members watched the event on television from their hotel, and then they fled to Berkeley to regroup. The group resurfaced the following September, when Hearst and three other SLA members were arrested for the robbery. When booked, Hearst listed her occupation as "urban guerrilla."

After a very public trial in March 1976, Patty Hearst (who had reclaimed her old identity soon after her arrest) was found guilty of armed bank robbery and sentenced to seven years in prison. She served twenty-one months before President Jimmy Carter commuted her sentence. President Bill Clinton granted her a full pardon in January 2001. The other SLA members were not so lucky; most of the remaining members were given major prison sentences.

This case study describes only one of a number of terrorist groups that have been spawned in the United States over the last forty years. (Another example is the so-called Weather Underground group that grew out of the anti-Vietnam war movement.) The particular motivations and objectives of each group have varied and usually have been related to the ideological views and personal proclivities of its members. This case study also illustrates how terrorist groups seek to use the media and publicity to advance their agendas and make their demands known. The SLA case attracted major national publicity, particularly after the group kidnapped newspaper heiress Patty Hearst and she allegedly became a part of the group (though she later claimed she had been brainwashed). ■

Examples of terrorist groups or individuals operating from a political or ideological orientation on the right include the Aryan Nations, a white, antigovernment, virulently anti-Semitic, ultranationalist group founded in the 1970s, along with a parallel network of imprisoned gang members known as the Aryan Brotherhood, and the Neo-Nazi Skinheads, a movement that began in the UK in the 1970s advocating the completion of the racial and religious cleansing begun by Adolf Hitler and a world run only by and for white people.

One subcategory of political/ideological terrorist groups is those engaged in long-standing political struggles within a particular country. Often known as *separatist movements* because of their desire to win the independence of a region or people or those of a particular religious or ethnic persuasion, they are of relevance here because they frequently resort to terrorist tactics. These tactics have included bombings of public places (in order to maximize casualties), targeted assassinations of government officials, and various violent acts intended to intimidate local businessmen and others into cooperating and helping to finance their activities. Among the many examples of separatist groups that have recently resorted to terrorism as a political tactic are the Basque separatist group ETA, which in the Basque language means "Fatherland and Liberty" and which has long been fighting for a separate political state for the Basque people, independent of Spain and France, in the physical land area adjacent to the Spanish-French border. Although ETA has been responsible for more than nine hundred killings and other acts of violence over the years, it declared a unilateral ceasefire in March 2006 and stated that henceforth it would work through the political process for the rights of the Basque people. Unfortunately, a spate of bombings during 2006 left the ceasefire more or less defunct.

The Liberation Tigers of Tamil Eelam (LTTE), also known as the Tamil Tigers, are seeking the independence of the Tamil people on the island of Sri Lanka. The Tamil Tigers have employed particularly violent guerrilla or terrorist tactics, including suicide attacks, against the non-Tamil people in their quest for independence from the government of Sri Lanka. Each member of the group, which is highly centralized and disciplined, reportedly carries a cyanide capsule around the neck to be used in the event of capture.

The Irish Republican Army, another separatist group, was formed in 1969 as the clandestine military wing of the political party Sinn Fein in Northern Ireland. Its purpose was to apply pressure on the British government to remove its forces from Northern Ireland and to allow its reunification with the Republic of Ireland to the south, which had been granted independence from Britain in 1920. Before the July 1997 ceasefire, the IRA was responsible for hundreds of bombings, kidnappings, assassinations, and extensive criminal activities (such as drug running) to support its activities. After the 1997 ceasefire, a fragile, bipartisan political process was established in Northern Ireland that eventually allowed the IRA to "decommission" its hidden weapons (but without public documentation or confirmation), and in July 2005 the organization publicly called on its members to disarm and to work henceforth through the political process.

Another type of political/ideological terrorist group is the *cult,* or *sect,* most of which are formed around the (often semi-irrational) thinking—and preaching—of a charismatic leader who demands absolute loyalty and discipline based on his or her personal ideology and beliefs. The cult leader typically preaches a messianic or apocalyptic vision that prophesizes, in one way or another, the coming end of the world and the possibility of salvation. Although history is littered with examples of cults, including many in the United States, most have been relatively peaceful and law abiding. Indeed, most simply wanted to be left alone to practice their beliefs. In the 1980s and 1990s, however, two cults turned to violence and terrorist tactics in obedience to their leader's instructions: the Rajneeshi cult in Oregon and the Aum Shinrikyo cult in Japan.

The Rajneeshi cult is of interest here because, like the second example, the cult members turned to terrorism as a way of achieving their instrumental political objectives—in this case, the attempted political takeover of a rural town in Oregon. The Rajneeshi cult, which was founded in India in the early 1970s by Bhagwan Shree Rajneesh, attracted a considerable following in the United States and in Europe. After being forced out of its base in India, the cult purchased agricultural land in Oregon, but soon ran into strong political opposition from the local and county governments over its plans to build an entirely autonomous town of about ten thousand people. In response, cult leaders plotted to use salmonella bacteria, which they managed to produce, to sicken large numbers of local residents, thereby preventing them from voting in a local election. If successful, the plot would have enabled the cult to take control of the government of The Dalles, Oregon. After cult members surreptitiously inserted the salmonella into the salad bars of ten local restaurants, over four hundred people became ill, and nearly fifty of those required hospitalization. Members of the cult also attempted, unsuccessfully, to poison the town's water supply. Ultimately, however, the attack failed to influence the outcome of the election, and the cult later abandoned its efforts to use biological agents—although it did not abandon terrorism. Instead, it began targeting a list of "enemies," using conventional weapons. One such "enemy" was Oregon's U.S. attorney, Charles H. Turner. But these plots were discovered; the cult ringleaders were arrested, tried, and convicted; and Bhagwan Shree Rajneesh was deported from the United States, which led to the demise of the cult in Oregon.[4]

The use of chemical and biological weapons by the Aum Shinrikyo cult in Tokyo is perhaps one of the best documented of the pre–al Qaeda terrorist events. (For more detail, see Case Study 2.2.) Aum Shinrikyo was a Japanese apocalyptic cult led by Shoko Asahara, a charismatic individual whose stated objective was to politically dominate Japan, and eventually the world. When the cult failed to achieve even its first objective by legitimate means, in March 1995 Asahara ordered his followers to carry out a large-scale chemical weapons attack using deadly sarin gas (the cult had been experimenting with sarin for years) in the Tokyo subway system.

CASE STUDY 2.2

Aum Shinrikyo: Mass-Casualty Terrorism Perpetrated by
a Religious Cult

Aum Shinrikyo, a Japanese apocalyptic cult led by Shoko Asahara, a partially blind former yoga instructor who claimed to have messianic powers, was the first non-state terrorist group to successfully launch a large-scale chemical weapon attack against civilians. Asahara established Aum in 1984 as a yoga school and publishing house. After a series of visions, he changed the group's name in 1987 to Aum Shinrikyo, Sanskrit for "supreme truth." Aum's teachings drew from pseudoscience, Nostradamus, Buddhism, millenarian Christianity, and Eastern mysticism, and included apocalyptic revelations about Aum saving or re-creating the world through magic and science. Asahara believed that Japanese society was corrupt and that its destruction was imminent.

Aum proceeded to launch an aggressive recruitment campaign, emphasizing its spiritual teachings and focusing its efforts on attracting intellectuals, including scientists and university students. The cult also established its own political party, but all twenty-five of its candidates lost in Japan's 1990 parliamentary elections. About this time, the group apparently shifted its goal from taking control of Japan to precipitating a nuclear attack by the United States on Japan. Between 1989 and 1995, the cult expanded to six countries (including the United States and Russia), and its membership increased from a hundred to more than fifty thousand, and its net worth from some $4.3 million to $1 billion. The cult raised funds through donations, the sale of religious paraphernalia, and seminars and training courses. But it also was linked to insurance fraud schemes and the manufacture of illegal drugs, for which it had a marketing agreement with the Japanese mafia (the Yakuza).

Aum's huge membership provided the intellectual and physical labor it needed to support its attempted development of biological, chemical, and nuclear weapons. The goal was to traumatize Japanese society, disrupting it so that Asahara could intervene and lead his followers to a takeover of the government. Aum went about this in numerous ways. In 1993 Asahara led a group of sixteen cult doctors and nurses to Central Africa purportedly on a medical mission, but the real purpose of the mission was to learn how to collect samples of the deadly Ebola virus (a virtually impossible task, because the virus is so deadly that it would have killed most of those coming in contact with it). The cult purchased chemical processing equipment and chemicals in Japan, and it attempted to obtain additional supplies through the U.S. subsidiary, Aum USA; but it failed to obtain the special export license needed to do so. After establishing its own nuclear weapons program proved too complex, Aum attempted to acquire a fully functional nuclear weapon either from sources in the former Soviet Union or another willing seller. When this foray failed as well, the cult planned to spread in downtown Tokyo unprocessed uranium mined from its Australian sheep ranch, but the attack was never carried out.

Aum's efforts to produce and obtain mass-casualty weapons never came to the attention of any intelligence agency in Japan or elsewhere. Indeed, even if the Japanese authorities had suspected Aum's activities, they would not have been able to act because there was no provision in national legislation at the time addressing the attempted acquisition of WMD by a domestic group.

During the early 1990s, Aum tried to acquire, manufacture, or use at least seventeen toxic chemical agents, such as the deadly nerve agent sarin, and biological agents, such as anthrax and botulism. But most of these attempts failed or were extremely limited in effect because of the technical issues Aum encountered in creating and dispersing agents. One such attack was carried out in the city of Matsumoto on June 27, 1994. Members of Aum used refrigerated delivery trucks equipped with spraying mechanisms to disseminate sarin into the domicile of three judges set to hear a case against the cult. However, the wind blew the sarin into the surrounding neighborhoods, where it sickened fifty-four people (including the judges) and killed seven. The attack was not attributed to Aum at the time, but many experts now see it as the precursor to its later, much larger attack on the Tokyo subway.

On March 20, 1995, five members of Aum released sarin in a coordinated attack on Tokyo's subway system. Packages resembling shopping bags, but containing a chemical mixture of sarin, were placed on the floors of five different trains bound for Kasumageseki, an area of central Tokyo where most government ministries are located. When cult members punctured the bags with sharpened umbrella tips, the chemical material spilled onto the floors of the subway cars, evaporating and spreading throughout the cars. By the end of the day, fifteen subway stations had been affected, twelve people had died, five thousand had become ill, and over a thousand had required hospitalization.

In the six months following the attack, Japanese authorities responded by arresting almost four hundred cult members and charging them with offenses ranging from murder to conspiracy to kidnapping, assault, obstruction of justice, and theft. However, the attacks by Aum continued, possibly to distract authorities from forming a case against Asahara. On May 5 and July 4, 1995, Aum left crude chemical explosives in the public restrooms of five Tokyo subway stations, but all of them either failed to detonate or were discovered before they could. Police arrested Asahara on May 16, 1995, and in October of that year the Japanese government revoked its recognition of Aum as a religious organization. As for the cult leader, after a trial lasting many years Asahara was sentenced to death, and he has now exhausted all of his appeals. It is still not clear, however, when the sentence will be carried out.

The case of the Aum Shinrikyo cult remains one of the most important examples of non-state-sponsored terrorism. It demonstrates how a group can form around the extremist views of a charismatic individual and, with the necessary access to technical expertise and substantial amounts of money, can develop or obtain mass-casualty (chemical or biological) weapons. It also demonstrates how a national government can fail to understand the danger presented by such a cult (unless it successfully infiltrates the group), and how the constitutional and legal protections of organized religion can be used to shield a cult from police surveillance. Finally, Shoko Asahara, the cult's paranoid leader, is an example of the power that charismatic figures espousing extremist views cloaked as religious dogma (and there have been many others) can have over those who are often innocent but naive and who are simply searching for something in which they can believe. ∎

Religion-Based Terrorist Groups

Because of the events of September 11, 2001, and their aftermath, al Qaeda is undoubtedly the best known of the religiously motivated terrorist groups, perhaps in all of history. As noted earlier, al Qaeda is actually not a single group at all, but rather a loosely coordinated network of individuals and groups all sharing the same (or similar) radical jihadist beliefs. The group's origin can be traced to the period following the 1979 invasion of Afghanistan by the Soviet Union, when foreign Muslim fighters came to the aid of the Afghan mujahideen who were resisting the Soviets. Eventually, the collective forces succeeded in forcing the Soviets to withdraw. In the aftermath of the Afghan conflict, and particularly after the United States and coalition states inserted forces into the Arabian Peninsula in 1991 to repel Saddam Hussein's invasion of Kuwait, al Qaeda and its leaders, Osama bin Laden and Ayman al-Zawahiri, turned their focus from Russia to secular Arab states and then to the West.

After the Soviets left Afghanistan, al Qaeda provided training, logistics, and financial support for the jihad against the secular governments of the "near enemy" in Egypt, Saudi Arabia, and Yemen. The shift toward the "far enemy" in the West was marked by bin Laden's 1996 declaration of "War Against the Americans Occupying the Land of the Two Holy Places (Expel the Infidels from the Arab Peninsula)."

In February 1998, bin Laden issued a binding religious edict, or fatwa, entitled "World Islamic Front Against the Jews and Crusaders." The fatwa declared that it was the duty of Muslims everywhere to kill Jews and Americans in all parts of the world in order to liberate the Al-Aqsa Mosque in Jerusalem and to force all "crusaders"—read: American and other foreign forces—to leave the Arabian Peninsula and the greater Middle East. (It remains unclear whether Osama bin Laden had sufficient religious training or any legal authority to issue an official fatwa in the first place, although this point now seems largely moot in view of the tragic events of the last six years.)

In all likelihood, the planning for the September 11 attacks on New York City and Washington, D.C., began during this same time period. In some respects, al Qaeda's stated goals and objectives are as much political as they are religious. Yet it is clear that the continuing series of terrorist violence that has taken place both before and since September 11 has been motivated and justi-fied on the basis of the religious fatwa that bin Laden issued in 1998. Among the major terrorist acts attributed to al Qaeda, in addition to the 2001 attacks on the World Trade Center in New York City and the Pentagon in Washing-ton, are the near-simultaneous bomb attacks on the U.S. embassies in Nairobi, Kenya, and Dar es Salaam, Tanzania, in August 1998 that left 258 people dead and more than 5,000 injured; the suicide attack on the U.S. Navy destroyer USS *Cole* in a Yemeni port in October 2000 that killed seventeen U.S. sailors; and the bombing of two nightclubs on the resort island of Bali, Indonesia, in Octo-ber 2002 that killed 202 people and injured another 209. (Details on many of these pre–September 11 attacks by al Qaeda are presented in Case Study 2.3.)

CASE STUDY 2.3

Pre–September 11 al Qaeda Terrorist Acts

Khobar Towers

On June 25, 1996, shortly before 10:00 p.m., three roof guards at the Khobar Towers military housing complex in Dhahran, Saudi Arabia, saw two men park a fuel truck in a parking lot eighty feet from the complex and then get into a car and drive away. Four minutes later, a twenty-thousand-pound bomb exploded, killing nineteen members of the U.S. Air Force and injuring hundreds of other Americans and Saudis. The attack on Khobar Towers revealed to the world the vulnerability of U.S. military and other installations abroad.

After the bombing, President Bill Clinton declared that the bombers would be brought to "justice." Teams of FBI agents and forensic and technical personnel were deployed to Saudi Arabia to conduct a thor-ough criminal investigation. The government of Saudi Arabia, which arrested six of the bombers soon after the attacks, was very cooperative and supportive of the FBI investigation. Some five years later, in June 2001, the U.S. Justice Department charged fourteen members of the Saudi Hezbollah, a Shiite Muslim extremist group, with the Khobar bombing. Federal officials said the accused had received support and inspiration from individuals within the Iranian government, but no Iran-ian officials were named in the indictment. In 2004 the commission appointed by President George W. Bush to investigate the September

11, 2001, attacks determined that the Sunni Muslim extremist group al Qaeda may have played some kind of role in the attack as well. Osama bin Laden called the attack a "praiseworthy act of terrorism," and it is possible that he lent logistical and material support to the operation, temporarily overcoming the long-standing Shiite-Sunni rivalry against a perceived common enemy.

East African Embassies

On August 7, 1998, two car bombs exploded nearly simultaneously outside of the U.S. embassies in Nairobi, Kenya, and Dar es Salaam, Tanzania, killing more than 250 people (most of them African civilians) and wounding over 5,000. In Nairobi, which experienced the brunt of the violence, the local infrastructure proved insufficient to cope with a disaster of this magnitude. Al Qaeda faxed messages to media outlets in the United Arab Emirates and France announcing its responsibility for the attacks, thereby bringing the terrorist network and its leader, Osama bin Laden, into the international spotlight for the first time since the first World Trade Center bombing in 1993. During a January 1999 interview with the Arabic news channel al Jazeera, bin Laden noted that the U.S. embassy in Nairobi was targeted "because it was the major U.S. intelligence center in East Africa." The embassy bombings took place eight years to the day after the United States established a military presence on Saudi soil as part of a UN coalition to contain Iraqi leader Saddam Hussein during the Persian Gulf War.

The U.S. embassy bombings in East Africa provoked international concern and speculation about al Qaeda's choice of targets. The U.S. interests in Kenya and Tanzania were vulnerable for several reasons. Although relatively stable nations, Kenya and Tanzania suffer from public corruption, porous borders, and endemic poverty. They also struggle to counterbalance political instability elsewhere in the region, in nations such as Uganda and Somalia. These conditions, then, were favorable for international criminal and terrorist organizations.

In stark contrast to its response to the Khobar Towers bombing three years earlier, the U.S. government was very proactive in its response to the embassy bombings, employing military, economic, and legal means. On August 20, 1998, President Clinton put the multipronged U.S. response into action. As FBI investigators worked with local law enforcement in Tanzania and Kenya to gather evidence and make arrests, Clinton signed an executive order freezing the assets of bin Laden and al Qaeda and prohibiting U.S. citizens and firms from doing business with them. He also ordered the commencement of Operation Infinite Reach, a series of cruise missile strikes on two terrorist targets: a terrorist training camp in Khost, Afghanistan, and a pharmaceutical facility in Khartoum, Sudan, suspected of involvement in chemical weapons production and affiliation with al Qaeda.

After the attacks, the U.S. government faced international and domestic scrutiny for its security policies. Its embassies were located in the centers of Nairobi and Dar es Salaam, not on the outskirts with most of the other foreign embassies. As a result of these attacks, security measures at U.S. diplomatic missions overseas were tightened, bolstered by a dramatic increase in the budget and resources of the Diplomatic Security Service. Meanwhile, the Clinton administration was being widely criticized for its decision to employ a military response, for the secrecy of its decision-making process, and for its choice of targets.

Fingers were also being pointed at the Kenyan, Tanzanian, and U.S. law enforcement agencies, which had overlooked the signs of an impending al Qaeda attack in East Africa. For example, in 1997 the FBI, CIA, and Kenyan officials had raided the home of Wadih el Hage, a known secretary for al Qaeda. In a confiscated computer, Kenyan officials discovered a letter discussing a clandestine cell in Nairobi, operating under instruction from bin Laden. Other documents were not translated because U.S. intelligence lacked Arabic translators, and el Hage moved to the United States soon afterward. In another overlooked sign, in the fall of 1997 Egyptian Mustafa Mahmoud Said Ahmed had walked into the Nairobi embassy and informed CIA officers that a group planned to detonate a truck bomb in the embassy's parking garage. The CIA vetted and discredited the information. Ahmed, who was arrested in Tanzania after the bombing, was believed to be a key figure in the Dar es Salaam attack, but the charges were dropped in 2000. In yet another sign, in early 1998 bin Laden had issued a fatwa calling for attacks on the United States and Israel.

USS Cole

On October 12, 2000, the U.S. Navy destroyer USS *Cole* was attacked by suicide bombers, who drove a small, explosives-filled boat into the side of the ship during a routine refueling stop in the harbor of Aden, Yemen. The destroyer's rules of engagement prevented its guards from firing on the small boat without first obtaining permission from the *Cole*'s captain or another officer. The attack killed seventeen members of the ship's crew, wounded thirty-nine others, and seriously damaged the ship. The CIA later concluded that the attack could have killed three hundred and sunk the ship if it had been executed slightly more skillfully. Although al Qaeda never claimed responsibility for the attack, the tactic resembled the truck bombs it had used to attack the U.S. Marine Corps barracks in Beirut in 1983 and Khobar Towers in 1996.

After the attack, President Clinton declared, "If, as it now appears, this was an act of terrorism, it was a despicable and cowardly act. We will find out who was responsible and hold them accountable." However, an attack against a military target does not meet the legal definition of terrorism under U.S. law. Unlike the Saudi, Kenyan, and Tanzanian governments, Yemeni security services were reluctant to cooperate with U.S. investigations of the bombing. The criminal investigation, led by the FBI, was complicated by political pressures to maintain strong U.S.-Yemeni relations and to bolster the floundering Arab-Israeli peace process. Both the Clinton and George W. Bush administrations were criticized for failing to respond adequately to the *Cole* attack.

In November 2002, the CIA fired an AGM-114 Hellfire missile from a Predator unmanned aerial vehicle (UAV) at a car carrying Abu Ali al-Harithi, a suspected planner of the *Cole* bombing, and Ahmed Hijazi, a U.S. citizen. The operation, which was carried out on Yemeni territory, killed both men. In 2004 a Yemeni judge sentenced two men to death and four more to prison terms of five to ten years for their roles in the *Cole* bombing. The indictment charged that the conspirators, all al Qaeda operatives, engineered a plot in mid-1999 to conduct an attack on U.S. Navy ships in the port at Aden. According to the indictment, one of the men facilitated the attack and planned to film it. Another was a key al Qaeda operative recruited by members of Osama bin Laden's inner circle. He helped to procure safe houses in Aden for the terrorists, as well as the boat and truck used to tow the boat to the harbor. The plot is thought to have included sixty people, including a carpenter, a welder, and a corrupt Yemeni policeman.

The 1996 Khobar Towers bombing in Saudi Arabia, the simultaneous bombing of the U.S. embassies in Kenya and Tanzania in 1998, and the 2000 attack on the USS *Cole* in Yemen were three major terrorist attacks by al Qaeda that preceded the September 11, 2001, attacks in New York City and Washington. The three attacks had a significant impact on U.S. security and foreign policy in the 1990s. They also acquainted the world with Osama bin Laden's al Qaeda terrorist network and demonstrated al Qaeda's reach (well beyond the Middle East itself) and its intent to continue its terrorist attacks against the United States until it withdrew from Saudi Arabia and the remainder of the Islamic world. ■

Two other groups—Hamas and Hezbollah—have frequently relied on terrorist tactics and are, in fact, identified officially as terrorist groups by the U.S. government and most governments belonging to the European Union, but it is difficult to know precisely how to characterize them. Although both groups invoke strong religious justifications for their actions—and their claims on the territory of the state of Israel—both also have become ever more deeply involved in the political life and culture of the Palestinian Authority and the country of Lebanon. Hamas, or Harakat al-Muqawama al-Islamiyya (Islamic Resistance Movement), is a Sunni-based organization that wrested control of the legislature of the Palestinian Authority from Fatah in January 2006. In June 2007, Hamas moved militarily against Fatah and succeeded in gaining unilateral control of the Gaza Strip. It has so far refused to renounce explicitly the use of force against Israel or its official position that Israel has no right to exist and must be eliminated. Its central belief is that the land of Israel is an inalienable Islamic bequest, and that the struggle to regain control of Israeli territory is the duty of every observant Muslim. Hamas has engaged in acts of terrorist violence since 1989, and it began the use of suicide bombings in 1993. With Israel's withdrawal from the Gaza Strip in September 2005, Hamas began using homemade Qassam missiles to randomly shell Israeli towns located near the border.

Hezbollah (The Party of God), a Shia-based Islamic organization, is at the same time a religious movement, a Lebanese political party, a social movement and charitable organization, and a tenacious military organization that employs terrorist tactics. Formed originally to force Lebanon to become a single-party Islamic state, it later abandoned this goal in favor of focusing on elimination of the state of Israel. Hezbollah, which is closely aligned with Iran and Syria, has been engaged in terrorist actions against Israel since 1982, when Israel first invaded southern Lebanon to form a "security zone" beyond its northern border. It also is alleged to have been responsible for the devastating bomb attacks against the U.S. embassy and U.S. Marine barracks in 1983 in Beirut, Lebanon, and for a series of well-publicized hostage-taking episodes. In June 2006, Hezbollah provoked a war with Israel by staging a cross-border raid and kidnapping two Israeli soldiers. The ensuing hostilities, much of which involved aerial bombardment by both sides, resulted in enormous devastation and loss of life, especially in southern Lebanon. The conflict marked the first time that a state actor (Israel) was forced to engage a non-state actor (Hezbollah). The result was that Hezbollah successfully resisted the overwhelming military advantage of the Israel Defense Force by hiding its weapons and fighters among the civilian populations in the Lebanese villages.

Organized Crime and Terrorism

Beginning in the 1980s, there was evidence of a growing convergence between the interests of "narco-traffickers," who processed large volumes of cocaine and heroin in poor developing countries and distributed the drugs for sale in wealthy industrialized countries, and the interests of the separatist guerrilla groups, who were using terrorist tactics to attempt to destabilize and eventually overthrow existing national governments. The term *narco-terrorist* was actually coined as early as 1983 by the president of Peru, Fernando Belaúnde Terry, when describing attacks on the Peruvian narcotics police. Over the last twenty years, narco-traffickers in countries as diverse as Mexico, Colombia, Myanmar, and Afghanistan have at times employed terrorist tactics to intimidate and otherwise threaten the governments of the countries in which they were operating. At the same time, some terrorist groups, including FARC (Revolutionary Armed Forces of Colombia), Hezbollah in Lebanon, and al Qaeda in Afghanistan, have themselves resorted to narco-trafficking as a means of quickly raising large amounts of capital to finance their violent attacks. Thus in some respects, the problem has now become global as more and more terrorist organizations see narco-trafficking as a way to support the high costs of their operations.

Another potentially worrisome trend is the involvement of other organized crime groups in aiding and abetting terrorist groups. For example, there appears to be active collaboration between the Russian mafia and Chechen separatists, who continue to fight against the political control of the Russian government. In addition, according to some reports, smugglers in possession of small quantities of nuclear material have been intercepted on the borders of Georgia, Turkey, and Armenia. These smugglers allegedly were hired by Russian organized crime, and the worry is that the intended buyers may well have been terrorist groups seeking to acquire sufficient quantities of highly enriched fissile material to build a nuclear device or a dirty bomb (the latter does not actually require highly enriched material and does not produce a nuclear chain reaction).[5]

In Russia and some other states of the former Soviet Union, corruption is massive and widespread; indeed, it is, in effect, part of the normal way of doing business. Because organized crime has extensively penetrated the construction and transport sectors in Russia—and parts of the police force—it is relatively easy for crime syndicates to move such contraband through and out of the country. Thus if nuclear or other potentially dangerous materials (such as biological agents) are either stolen or purchased on the black market, crime syndicates can readily move the items into the hands of willing buyers, who almost certainly would include terrorist organizations.[6]

Single-Issue Terrorism

A final set of non-state actors that have, at various times, resorted to terrorist tactics in pursuit of their goals is the single-issue group. This highly eclectic mix of organizations—some of them formally declared and others existing only as secretive underground networks—have found it necessary or expedient to resort to violence as a means to either call attention to their issue or position or to exact revenge on the individuals or organizations whose actions they oppose. Among the most well-known single-issue groups that have employed physical violence are: Earth First, a radical underground environmental group that has been accused of "spiking" old-growth trees with metal rods that would injure loggers attempting to cut down the trees; extreme antiabortion groups that have undertaken bombing attacks on medical clinics where legal abortions are performed; and animal rights groups that have broken into and destroyed laboratories where animal testing is being conducted.

The phenomenon of single-issue groups resorting to violent tactics is not confined to the United States. In Europe, animal rights activists are reportedly undertaking similar initiatives in opposition to animal testing in Britain (in 2005 they succeeded in securing a ban on foxhunting). In the oil-rich delta of Nigeria, local tribal groups demanding a fair share of that country's enormous oil profits have taken over, and at times damaged, oil pumping and storage facilities. They also have taken foreign workers and oil company executives hostage. Finally, in a variety of incidents in Europe, South Asia, and elsewhere, antiglobalization activists have attacked the facilities and retail outlets of major transnational corporations.

Motivations of Individual Terrorists

It is difficult to characterize comprehensively all of the motivations of individuals who commit violent acts in the name of a particular cause. Clearly, some of these people are mentally disturbed, and so may turn to violence as a way of acting out, based on delusional thinking. Others, however, may hold personal grudges against society or particular organizations in society, or they may have aberrant ideological beliefs that motivate them to use violence to seek revenge or to attack individuals or organizations that they perceive have wronged them personally or are opposed to their beliefs. Sometimes, these individuals demonstrate behavior that could be characterized as that of a social misfit, shunning organized groups and, in some cases, society in general. The motivations of individuals who commit acts of terrorism may be ideological, religious, ecological ("ecoterrorism"), or perhaps issue-specific such as extreme opposition to abortion. The descriptions of the three individual terrorists that follow demonstrate the range of behavior and motivation of individuals who have perpetrated terrorist violence based on their personal beliefs.

Timothy McVeigh

Perhaps the best known—and most infamous—example of an act of terrorism by an individual was the bombing of the Alfred P. Murrah Federal Building in Oklahoma City on April 19, 1995, by Timothy McVeigh, with the active support and assistance of an accomplice, Terry Nichols. The attack resulted in the death of 168 people; 850 were seriously injured. McVeigh, with help from Nichols, packed a rental truck with over five thousand pounds of ammonium nitrate, a common agricultural fertilizer, and nitro methane, a highly explosive motor fuel used in race cars. He then parked the truck in front of the Murrah office building (which included a daycare center for the children of the federal workers) just after it opened for the day and detonated the bomb via a time-delay fuse. The incident remains the most deadly act of domestic terrorism ever perpetrated by a U.S. citizen.

Although McVeigh never revealed the precise motive for the attack, written material found by the FBI provided evidence of his libertarian, neofascist, and antigovernment views. McVeigh's defense lawyers, acting on his instructions, attempted to justify the attack as a response to what the accused apparently considered were crimes committed by the federal government in ending the 1993 siege of the Branch Davidian cult compound in Waco, Texas. Timothy McVeigh was executed for his crimes on June 11, 2001. (Also see Chapter 9.)

Theodore Kaczynski

Theodore (Ted) Kaczynski, also known as the "Unabomber" (it was his FBI code name, which stood for "university and airline bomber"), sent bombs through the U.S. mail to several airlines and universities from the late 1970s through the early 1990s, killing three people and wounding twenty-nine. Kaczynski was a brilliant, but highly eccentric, mathematician, who was trained at Harvard University and the University of California, Berkeley. At the time of his capture, he was discovered living a hermitic, survivalist existence in rural Montana. Apparently, his motivation for the bombings was a felt need to call public attention to the dangers of modern technology, which he believed would eventually subjugate the entire human race. There also was some evidence that Kaczynski believed that corporate interests were attempting to develop technology that would lead to "mind control." Ultimately, however, he never revealed why he targeted airlines and universities, although some of the bombs sent to universities appeared to target faculty members involved in computer science. After an insanity defense was rejected by the courts, Kaczynski agreed to plead guilty, accepting a sentence of life in prison without the possibility of parole. In return, the U.S. government dropped its demand for the death penalty. (Also see Chapter 9.)

Eric Rudolph

A third example of terrorist activity by an individual was the series of bomb attacks carried out by Eric Rudolph in the 1990s. The attacks killed three people and injured 150. Rudolph's most famous terrorist act was the bombing in Central Olympic Park in Atlanta, Georgia, on July 27, 1996, in the midst of the Atlanta Summer Olympic Games. In 1997–1998, Rudolph perpetrated bombings of two abortion clinics and a gay nightclub. Although Rudolph's motivations for the bombings of the abortion clinics and the gay nightclub were never fully explained, various media reports attributed them to his extreme Christian beliefs that considered abortion to be a capital crime and homosexuality a cardinal sin. His motivation—or, at least, justification—for the Olympic bombing is better understood. According to a statement he made after his arrest, he undertook the bombing in an attempt to stop the Games because of his opposition to "global socialism" and to satisfy his desire to embarrass the U.S. government because it sanctioned legal abortion.

Rudolph, a trained survivalist, went underground after the last bombing in 1998, and he successfully evaded capture for five years by living in the

Appalachian wilderness, most likely with local help. He was captured almost accidentally in March 2003. Like Ted Kaczynski, he eventually accepted a plea agreement in order to avoid the death sentence; in his case it was three consecutive life terms. As part of the plea agreement, Rudolph agreed to lead federal authorities to a cache of 250 pounds of dynamite that he had hidden in rural North Carolina.

What Are Their Tactics?

The tactics used by terrorist groups, both state and non-state sponsored, have been in near-constant evolution since the emergence of terrorism as a global phenomenon during the Cold War. Indeed, state-sponsored terrorism was more prominent during the Cold War, as both the United States and the Soviet Union often subsidized proxy groups to attempt the overthrow of governments that one side or the other opposed on ideological grounds. Both sides invested heavily, and in some cases over a long period of time, but each was always careful not to threaten the other directly out of fear that things could quickly spiral out of control and lead to a nuclear confrontation, as they nearly did in Cuba in the early 1960s.

During the 1970s, the world witnessed the rise of non-state-sponsored terrorism, particularly in the Middle East. Such terrorist groups were interested primarily in placing the international spotlight on their causes, using the media as their vehicle. As such, they were not interested in causing mass casualties; rather, they wanted to gain—and retain—positive media attention that would help to increase public sympathy and support for their causes. Accordingly, groups such as the Palestine Liberation Organization engaged in various "made for media" terrorist acts, including hijacking jet airliners, many of which were blown up after the passengers had been freed. In the 1980s, terrorist tactics began to change, however, as groups searched for ever larger (that is, more outrageous) "media spectaculars." As a result, the self-imposed limitations on the size and scope of attacks and the partial avoidance of attacks against civilian populations were rejected, at least by some groups.

The 1990s saw continued escalation in the scope and lethality of terrorist tactics perpetrated against both military and civilian targets, including the use of suicide bombing on a large scale. Although hardly a new tactic (for example, Japan resorted to the infamous Kamikaze suicide air attacks against Allied naval vessels during World War II), Islamic jihadist violence, including the Beirut bombings, has frequently involved the use of suicide attackers. Moreover, the Second Palestinian Intifada—or "Uprising"—which began in 2000, has been marked by an upsurge in the use of pedestrian suicide bombers, who infiltrate Israel and detonate themselves on buses, in markets, and in other public places with substantial loss of life among innocent civilians. The desirability of the suicide bombing tactic stems from the fact that it is virtually unstoppable once the bomber has passed beyond security checkpoints; it allows the terrorist to "deliver" the weapon with great precision and flexibility; and it evokes maximum terror impact because of its random nature and its ability to target vulnerable, undefended places.

The advent of large-scale suicide bombing tactics and the gradual elimination of restraints on mass-casualty events and the taking of innocent civilian lives served as a prelude to the tactics adopted by al Qaeda and its nationally based affiliates in the 1990s and 2000s. Indeed, the attacks on the World Trade Center in New York City and the Pentagon in Washington, D.C., which killed about three thousand people, represented, in retrospect, a tactical watershed, not only because of the diabolically clever (and largely unforeseen) use of jet airliners as flying fuel bombs, but also because the attacks demonstrated clearly that the radical Islamic jihadist approach to terrorism now seeks to *maximize* civilian casualties and destruction by whatever means possible. Any pretense about distinguishing between innocent civilians and combatants has been dropped. All those people who live in countries targeted by the radical jihadists, as well as the nationals of those countries who live abroad, are now considered legitimate targets.

The crossing of this casualty threshold is leading, in turn, to the final—and ultimately, most worrisome—tactical evolution: the potential terrorist use of nuclear, biological, or chemical weapons, or what has been termed "catastrophic terrorism." The details on how terrorists might acquire or develop such weapons and how they might intend to use them have received extensive coverage, especially since the September 11 attacks.[7] The following scenarios are of greatest concern:

- *Terrorist acquisition and use of an intact nuclear weapon.* This scenario could occur only if a group succeeded in buying or stealing a weapon from Russia, one of the other successor states of the Soviet Union, or another nuclear-capable state such as Pakistan. Such a weapon might be "delivered" via intermodal shipping container, delivery truck, or intercoastal freighter.
- *Terrorist acquisition of fissile (that is, highly enriched, radioactive) material to construct and detonate a crude improvised nuclear device.* Again, this material would most likely be obtained from one of the same sources as above and delivered in much the same way as a nuclear weapon.
- *Terrorist acquisition or development and use of bacteriological or viral agents as a biological weapon.* Terrorists find biological weapons attractive because they are relatively easy to conceal during manufacture and transport and potentially can be used anonymously, thereby making it extremely difficult for national authorities to identify the perpetrator.
- *Terrorist acquisition or manufacture and use of chemical weapons.* Although they would not create the kinds of mass casualties that would result from a nuclear or biological attack, chemical weapons are appealing because they are low-tech, low-cost, and relatively easy to manufacture.

They would lend themselves particularly to use in large, indoor public spaces such as sports arenas and public transportation terminals.

It is indeed fortunate that the world has yet to witness a catastrophic terrorist attack (other than the idiosyncratic use of jetliners in the September 11 attacks). Documents captured after the Taliban and al Qaeda were driven out of Kabul, Afghanistan, have revealed, however, that the leadership of these groups has placed a high priority on the acquisition or development of nuclear and biological weapons. Moreover, there is little doubt that any terrorist group succeeding in these efforts would be highly likely to actually use the weapons, because once such a capability was discovered, governments of potentially threatened states would make an all-out effort to find and neutralize it, thereby instilling in terrorist groups a "use it or lose it" mentality.

How Do They Organize?

The structure of terrorist organizations has evolved significantly over the years. Because terrorists engage in violent, and frequently criminal, activities, they typically strive to be as secretive as possible about how they are organized and about which individuals hold positions of leadership. After all, the Israeli government, among others, has had substantial success in undertaking programs of "targeted killings," designed to eliminate the key leaders of both Hamas and Hezbollah. What is known about the organization of most terrorist groups is that, in order to survive the increased scrutiny and pressure from intelligence services, the police, and the military, they have moved away from the traditional hierarchical leadership structure, with its single paramount leader, a few top lieutenants, operational commanders, and a larger number of field agents. Instead, they are increasingly utilizing a flat organizational structure made up of many semi-independent cells capable of mounting attacks with little or no direction from or approval required by a central leadership. This new "metastasized" cellular structure has been facilitated greatly by the enormous expansion in the use of the Internet.

Since the Taliban and al Qaeda were driven out of Afghanistan and Osama bin Laden and his deputy, Ayman al-Zawahiri, were forced into hiding—presumably in the rugged western provinces of Pakistan—al Qaeda has evolved considerably. Today, indigenous al Qaeda cells are operating in dozens of countries, often with little or no direct contact with or operational control by the organization's leadership, other than through the video messages that bin Laden and al-Zawahiri release periodically. In addition to making it much harder for intelligence and police authorities to identify and track the movements of the cells and take them down, this decentralized organizational structure encourages the rise of local leaders, the identification of local sources of financing, and the general "indigenization" of the radical Islamic jihadist movement in various parts of the world.

This indigenization process has, in turn, raised concerns in many countries about the possible existence of homegrown terrorist cells—that is, clandestine groups that either were put in place ahead of time to hide in the target country awaiting orders to act (what are commonly known as "sleeper cells") or local groups of terrorist sympathizers who have become radicalized and are prepared to undertake terrorist violence within their own countries and against their fellow citizens. For example, some of the suicide terrorists who took part in the September 11 attacks were inserted into the United States more than a year ahead of time while plans were being finalized for commandeering airliners to attack the World Trade Center and the Pentagon. By contrast, based on the evidence collected so far, the group that perpetrated the bombing of trains in Madrid in 2004 was composed largely of naturalized Spanish citizens who had emigrated from North Africa. (See Case Study 2.4.) Likewise, the British nationals who planned and carried out the suicide bombings of the London transport system (buses and subways) in July 2005 apparently were a completely indigenous terrorist cell, because all of the known members were born in the UK.

CASE STUDY 2.4

The Madrid Train Bombings:
A Terrorist Attack Perpetrated by an Indigenous al Qaeda Cell

During morning rush hour on March 11, 2004, ten explosives-filled backpacks detonated almost simultaneously on four commuter trains in three stations in Madrid, Spain. One hundred and ninety-one people died and almost eighteen hundred were injured in the second-worst terrorist attack in Europe. On their way to the city center, all four trains had passed through the Alcalá de Henares station, where bombers had placed in the cars the explosives that were then detonated by cell phone as the trains neared Madrid's central station. The attacks, called by some the "Madrid Massacre," took place three days before Spain's general election. On March 14, Spain's Socialist Party won a surprise victory after voters appeared to turn against the ruling government in response to the Madrid attacks.

After the bombings, Spain's ruling party publicly blamed the militant Basque separatist group ETA for the attacks. Although ETA had historically used terrorism to disrupt elections, evidence found at the scenes quickly implicated Islamic militants. Also, the attacks bore many similarities to other al Qaeda operations, such as the element of surprise, the use of cell phones to detonate the explosives, and the targeting of heavily trafficked areas to inflict as much human and infrastructural damage as possible.

A stolen van containing seven detonators and an Arabic-language tape was discovered near a Madrid station; in addition, three backpack bombs that had failed to explode were discovered. The backpacks contained cell phones that were traced to three Moroccans, including Jamal Zougam, who had been monitored previously by Spanish authorities for his alleged ties to the suspected leader of an al Qaeda cell in Spain. It is speculated that the unexploded bombs were intended to be detonated once the trains had entered the crowded central station of Madrid, which would have resulted in the deaths of thousands of additional people.

On April 2, 2004, an unexploded bomb was discovered on a high-speed train track between Madrid and Seville. Tests indicated that the explosives matched the size and type used in the March 11 attacks, thereby sending a message of defiance to the Spanish public and authorities. On April 3, following a warrant issued the previous week, police arrived at an apartment building in the Madrid suburb of Leganes, where five suspects, including the alleged ringleader of the Madrid plot, were thought to be located. However, the suspects in the second-floor apartment shot at the approaching police while chanting in Arabic. As police prepared to enter the building, the suspects detonated a large explosive, blowing out the walls and windows of the apartment, killing a police officer, and wounding eleven others. Later, it was found that the seven suspects actually in the apartment possessed more explosives prepared for use. Two more suspects may have escaped the scene.

In the months after the attacks, police arrested dozens of suspects in six countries. Over one hundred suspects were arrested throughout the investigation. In April 2005, twenty-nine persons were indicted for involvement in the bombings. Five of them, including Zougam, were charged with all 191 deaths in the bombings and 1,755 attempted murders, and twenty-four others were charged as accomplices who collaborated to help the other five gain access to bomb-making materials, including explosives stolen from a mine that were later used in the attacks. At their trial, which began in Madrid in 2007, the defendants denied involvement in the bombing and refused to answer questions in court.

Investigators believe the Madrid attacks were orchestrated by an indigenous network composed mainly of Moroccan Islamic militants who were seeking to disrupt Spain's upcoming general elections and to draw attention to Spain's controversial support for the U.S.-led invasion of Iraq. Although no direct links with al Qaeda have been established, the indictment alleges that the bombers were inspired by al Qaeda as their role model. According to the indictment, the suspects studied a report posted on the Web site of the Global Islamic Media Front in which a committee of al Qaeda experts suggested an attack in Spain before the general elections of March 14 in retaliation for Spain's sending thirteen hundred troops to Iraq as part of the U.S.-led forces.

Other nations, including the United States, have been deeply affected by the Madrid bombings. Although less is known about the July 7, 2005, attacks on the London transit system, the Madrid bombings are often seen as their precursor. In addition, the pursuit of justice in Spain has involved many other nations in Europe and North Africa. A trial began in Italy in 2006 for Rabei Osman Sayed Ahmed, the suspected mastermind of the Madrid bombings, who later sought to recruit more terrorists in Milan. The Moroccan government also sent its own team of investigators to examine a connection between the Madrid bombings and a suicide bombing in Casablanca in 2004 that killed forty-five persons.

Spain, like many Western European nations, has a large and growing population of Muslims, mainly immigrants from North Africa. In the next fifteen years, Muslims will make up an estimated 20 percent of Europe's population, and yet they have traditionally been disenfranchised and are therefore not fully integrated into Spanish (or other European) societies. The bomb attacks in Madrid and London may therefore be only a precursor to additional terrorist violence elsewhere in Europe in the years to come.

For residents of the European Union, both the Madrid and the London bombings have clearly driven home the point that they are not immune from the kind of attacks that occurred in the United States on September 11, 2001. Indeed, those attacks revealed that the longtime ethnic schisms and religious discrimination found in Europe could well be the reason European states have been targeted.   ■

Many terrorist organizations remain local or "regional" in their focus. Hamas and Hezbollah, for example, are dedicated exclusively to opposing Israel, just as the Tamil Tigers are concerned solely with their struggle against the government of Sri Lanka. But even such terrorist organizations have had to adapt their structures to make themselves less vulnerable to penetration by intelligence services and to the targeted assassination of their leaders.

As noted earlier in this chapter, there is evidence that some terrorist organizations are joining forces with organized crime groups—or are themselves turning to organized crime as a means of financing their operations. The "unholy alliance" of terrorists and organized crime syndicates offers advantages to both sides. In Colombia, for example, where the terrorist group FARC controls large portions of the country's rural areas both politically and militarily, there appears to be an alliance of convenience between FARC and the drug cartels. FARC provides security for the narco-traffickers, who, in turn, devote a share of their profits to financing FARC's operations. In other parts of the world, organized crime groups also act as go-betweens to help give terrorist groups access to weapons and other controlled equipment and technology, including nuclear material. Some also use their economic influence over corrupt politicians and government bureaucrats to give terrorist groups the protection they need to operate in certain areas of a country with relative impunity.

Where Do They Recruit, Train, and Operate?

With the passage of time, there is an accumulating body of information about the recruitment techniques, training arrangements, and operational tactics of various terror organizations. Although many groups organize and operate in a highly idiosyncratic fashion, it is possible to discern patterns or trends even from such individualized behavior.

Recruitment

Most analysts agree that for many years before the attacks of September 11, 2001, terrorist groups, especially in the Middle East, were most successful in adding new foot soldiers to their ranks by recruiting among the refugee camps and poverty-stricken urban neighborhoods where unemployment ran high and where anger and frustration—especially among young men—was large and growing. Today, middle-class men and women are also joining terror networks in increasing numbers. This development may stem in part from the highly effective use of the Internet by al Qaeda and other indigenous groups to communicate Islamic jihadist propaganda. (See Chapter 9 for more discussion of this phenomenon.)

It has become increasingly clear that the war in Iraq and the insurgency it fostered has enormously aided terrorist recruiting efforts. Scenes of death and destruction in Iraq (and in Afghanistan) have permeated the global media since the outset of war in Iraq in 2003. This situation has been exacerbated by the unfolding evidence of prisoner abuse at U.S. military facilities such as Abu Ghraib prison in Iraq and the detainee detention center at Guantánamo Bay, Cuba. In effect, Iraq has become a "terrorist magnet," drawing foreign jihadists to fight against what Osama bin Laden refers to as "the Crusaders" (U.S. and coalition forces). Some terrorist attacks in other countries such as Britain and Spain also appear to have been motivated specifically by events in Iraq, and they were intended as retaliation. Many of the foreigners who came to fight in Iraq will—or already have—return to their home countries, well trained, battle-hardened, and ready to recruit still more terrorist fighters. And there is every indication that these foreign fighters are finding an enthusiastic reception, both because they themselves are viewed as heroes and because the youthful demographics in many Islamic countries provides many young targets for easy recruitment.

Training

To the extent that it is known, terrorist training is believed to include both physical and psychological preparation. On the physical side, recruits are put through rigorous conditioning and drilled extensively in paramilitary tactics, including weapons handling, the construction and use of improvised explosive devices (IEDs), and specialized urban guerrilla training such as ambushes and booby traps. On the psychological side, terrorist recruits are trained in how to make themselves fit in and look inconspicuous (especially on missions outside of their home territories or countries), how to avoid detection by the intelligence and police authorities that may be searching for them, and how to cope with any feelings of doubt or remorse in situations of mass-casualty violence. Clearly, for Islamic jihadist terrorist groups this kind of training takes on a strongly religious orientation. Terrorist recruits being prepared for possible suicide bombing missions require extensive additional psychological and religious counseling as well.

As noted earlier, the insurgency in Iraq has provided an extraordinary training ground for both foreign fighters loyal to al Qaeda and indigenous fighters (mostly Sunnis) who oppose the new Iraqi government. In many respects, this "real world" experience is far more effective than any terrorist training camp. Indeed, there is a certain irony in the fact that the violent insurgency in Iraq has become the principal training ground for new terrorists, because, earlier, Osama bin Laden and his al Qaeda organization were forced to leave Sudan in response to diplomatic pressure by the United States and other governments, and later they had to flee Afghanistan after the Taliban government was overthrown by the United States and coalition forces. During Operation Enduring Freedom in Afghanistan, U.S. forces (both air and ground) completely destroyed what was left of the al Qaeda training camps.

Although there is evidence that the al Qaeda leadership has reconstituted itself in the western provinces of Pakistan and may even have resumed training activities on a limited scale, it is also becoming apparent that the new generation of global terrorists does not need to attend central terrorist training schools. For one thing, it is now possible for terrorists to obtain most of the information they need from the how-to manuals on bomb making and other tactics posted on the many jihadist Web sites or made available to them covertly on CD-ROMs. (See Chapter 9.) For another, because the basic organizational structure of al Qaeda has apparently now evolved into a disaggregated "cellular" structure, much of the physical and psychological training can be undertaken locally. And, of course, some terrorist groups, such as Hamas and Hezbollah in the Middle East and the Tamil Tigers in South Asia, have always operated their own homegrown programs and training operations, including the indoctrination and training of those prepared to carry out suicide attacks.

Operations

To achieve their mission objectives, terrorists must be either located near or have access to their intended targets. In some cases, they can gain access at the time of their intended attack—for example, the suicide terrorists who manage to penetrate Israeli border security and successfully blow themselves up, usually in the midst of civilian population centers in Tel Aviv and elsewhere. In others, terrorist attacks may require substantial advance planning and complicated logistics, including the positioning of sleeper cells. There is strong evidence that this was the modus operandi of at least some of the nineteen hijackers who participated in the hijacking of the U.S. jet airliners on September 11, 2001. Interestingly, many of the September 11 perpetrators were hiding in plain sight in the United States for many months. And, as is now well known, while in the United States some even enrolled in programs offering limited flight training, which obviously was an essential requirement of their plan.

It is also true, however, that terrorist organizations require a hospitable "home" environment in which to develop their plots, identify and train the foot soldiers who will carry them out, and attend to such matters as financing, logistics, and propaganda. During the period in which most terrorism was connected to a state sponsor, the home was provided by the sponsoring government, though typically this link was never admitted publicly. It is thus no coincidence that both Hezbollah and Hamas have offices in Damascus, Syria, through which they obtain financial resources, weapons, and military advisers, many of whom find their way into southern Lebanon, for Hezbollah, and the Gaza Strip and West Bank, for Hamas.

Terrorist organizations have also often sought other safe havens. In the early 1990s, Osama bin Laden established his initial base for al Qaeda in Sudan, and he remained there until political pressure on the Sudanese government became too intense and he was asked to leave. Bin Laden and his organization then moved to Afghanistan, where they were the guests of the extremist Taliban government that had recently won the long civil war that had ensued after the withdrawal of Soviet forces from the country. Afghanistan under the Taliban provided the perfect operating base for al Qaeda: the country was weak and still politically divided, and the government needed the financial support that bin Laden was able to provide. In return for this support, the Taliban permitted the terrorist organization to establish training camps that ultimately were attended by thousands of foreign jihadist recruits until shortly before U.S. and coalition forces overthrew the Taliban government after the September 11 attacks.

Ironically, earlier the United States almost had an opportunity to capture bin Laden, courtesy of Taliban cooperation. The brash, aggressive manner of bin Laden and al Qaeda did not mesh comfortably with the austere Taliban world. During 1997 and 1998, the United States held negotiations with the Taliban regime that ultimately led to a tentative deal that would have handed bin Laden over to the United States in return for U.S. concessions to Taliban needs in Afghanistan. The deal came undone, however, when the U.S. embassies in Kenya and Tanzania were attacked by al Qaeda, which prompted the United States to respond by sending cruise missiles to Sudan and Afghanistan.

With the loss of its operating base in Afghanistan, al Qaeda and the indigenous terrorist organizations that it encouraged had to search for new operating and training bases. Some groups have had the freedom to operate, and even undertake training, in the countries in which they are located (for example, Indonesia and the Philippines). At the same time, the leadership of al Qaeda has managed to continue to produce a steady stream of propaganda messages while in hiding (as noted earlier, most likely in the rugged and isolated westernmost provinces of Pakistan). These messages are released either through friendly broadcast networks or via the Internet. Even though it is unclear to what extent the al Qaeda leadership still has the freedom to conduct operational planning, to communicate freely and openly, or to recruit and train new terrorists, there is growing concern that al Qaeda may be reconstituting itself in Waziristan without any active opposition or interference from the government of Pakistan.

Conclusion

This chapter has looked comprehensively at terrorist activity on a historical and a worldwide basis. This examination has revealed some important characteristics of terrorists that readers should keep in mind while proceeding through the rest of this volume. First, those who engage in terrorism today do not fit the stereotype often portrayed by the media—that is, they are not necessarily poor and uneducated, criminal, or psychotic; indeed, they are most often quite the opposite: coolly rational, middle class, and well educated. Moreover, Islamic jihadist groups are but one of many types of terrorist organizations active in the world today. Second, while state-sponsored terrorism continues on a limited basis, the overwhelming majority of terrorist activity is of the non-state-sponsored variety. Yet within this broad category there is enormous variation in underlying motivations, agendas pursued, and operating methods employed. Third, particularly for those groups that engage in terrorist violence based on religious agendas, the constraints that previously discouraged the large-scale murder of innocent civilians apparently no longer exist. This situation has, in turn, raised the specter of catastrophic terrorism, based on the use of mass-casualty weapons, including nuclear devices. Finally, the various means by which terrorist groups recruit and train their members and organize themselves, often in a highly flexible, nonhierarchical fashion, renders these organizations difficult to identify and destroy.

FOR FURTHER READING

Allison, Graham. *Nuclear Terrorism: The Ultimate Preventable Catastrophe.* New York: Henry Holt, 2004.

Hoffman, Bruce. *Inside Terrorism.* New York: Columbia University Press, 2006.

Pape, Robert. *Dying to Win: The Strategic Logic of Suicide Terrorism.* New York: Random House, 2005.

Sageman, Marc. *Understanding Terror Networks.* Philadelphia: University of Pennsylvania Press, 2004.

Chapter 3   The Causes of and Responses to Terrorism

In the wake of the terrorist attacks on the World Trade Center in New York City and the Pentagon in Washington, D.C., on September 11, 2001, Americans tried to come to grips with the greatest human-caused act of violence (other than war) ever to befall the United States. Perhaps the most frequently asked question was "Why do they hate us?" The subject was endlessly discussed, written about in newspapers and magazines, and debated on both television and radio. Inevitably, experts and nonexperts alike pointed out that, to try to answer the "Why do they hate us?" question, it was necessary to understand—and ultimately to address—the root causes of terrorism. These root causes include the variety of circumstances and factors that motivate individuals and organizations to turn to unprovoked physical violence as the only means available to pursue their interests and grievances.

This chapter begins by examining the numerous hypotheses that attempt to explain why and how individuals become sufficiently alienated, desperate, or otherwise motivated to adopt terrorist violence as their primary recourse. Although these explanations do not hold universally and are not necessarily consistent across all national or sociocultural and political contexts, they do at least offer a way to begin to understand the equivalency in the terrorists' minds between the conditions or circumstances that have affected them personally, or their family, ethnic group, or society (either within their lifetime or historically), and the violence that they now seek to perpetrate on others. Quite naturally, when policy makers and other experts have thought about how the global community might ultimately "solve" the problem of terrorism, they have found a compelling logic in the idea that, if the root causes of terrorism can be understood and addressed in some fashion, the threat of such violence would cease—or at least be reduced significantly.

As already established in Chapter 2, the many different terrorist groups in the world today have many and varied motivations and agendas. As a result, the responses that governments and international organizations have developed sometimes seek to address the root causes of terrorism, but more frequently they are characterized by more expedient, shorter-term measures. Thus the second objective of this chapter is to examine the range of responses to terrorism and terrorist organizations. Ultimately, it seeks to answer the question of whether the responses developed to date actually address the conditions that motivate terrorism in the first place.

Identifying the Causes of Terrorism

Why might a person become sufficiently angry or radicalized to resort to, or to at least support, the planning and execution of terrorist attacks? Could it have something to do with a person's social and economic circumstances? In other words, do conditions of poverty, illiteracy, and poor health serve as the roots of terrorism? Are people more likely to become engaged in terrorism in situations in which there are huge disparities in wealth and political power, or in which there is extensive political persecution or corruption? What roles do external influences and actors play—such as introducing through the media alien ideas or practices that appear to threaten the values of the dominant religious ideology?

These are just some of the questions that must be asked—and answered—to understand the causes of terrorism. But, because these causes are linked closely to the macroeconomic and social disparities with which the world continues to struggle, a framework must be imposed on the analysis in order to make it comprehensible and not over-encompassing. Accordingly, this chapter first considers the *internal* sources of terrorism—that is, those that arise within a country or in an area in which the terrorism occurs or the terrorist group is based. Attention then turns to the *external* sources of terrorism—that is, the impact of the behavior of other state and non-state actors and conditions, both current and historical, that may motivate the creation of or support for terrorist organizations. Finally, the chapter examines whether U.S. foreign and defense policies and U.S. international corporate activities warrant treatment as a special case because of the unprecedented military, economic, political, and cultural reach and influence of the United States in today's world. This typology is summarized in Table 3.1.

Internal Sources of Terrorism

The root causes of many incidents of terrorism from recent history have been associated with specific social, political, and cultural disparities and injustices within a particular country. However, with the advent of al Qaeda, which purports to be a *global* network of anti-Western terrorist groups, the focus is now changing. This section, however, examines the internal sources of terrorist violence.

Socioeconomic Factors

As just noted, one hypothesis about the causes of terrorism is that the particular circumstances within a country can create a context in which individuals become radicalized and willing to engage in activities that support the interests of organizations that engage in terrorism, even if they themselves do not commit terrorist crimes. Indeed, evidence suggests that the conditions of

Table 3.1 Sources of Terrorism

Level	Type	Examples
Internal	Socioeconomic	Sendero Luminoso (Shining Path, Peru), FARC (Colombia), refugee camps (world)
	Political/colonial	Zapatista Army of National Liberation (Mexico), Irgun (Israel), Mau Mau uprising (Kenya), Sandinistas (Nicaragua), Chechen conflict (Russia), ETA (Spain), Abu Sayyaf Group or al-Harakat al-Islamiyya (Philippines)
	Cultural/ethnic/religious	Madrassas (Islamic religious schools), Taliban (Afghanistan), IRA and Ulster Volunteer Force (Ireland), Jewish Defense League (Israel/U.S.), Kurdistan Workers Party (Turkey)
External	Colonial/neocolonial	Iranian revolution
	Regional/historical	Israel versus Syria and Iran, Pakistan versus India
	Failed states/lawless areas	Afghanistan, Waziristan (Pakistan), Somalia, Sierra Leone, Sudan, tri-border region of Brazil, Argentina, and Paraguay
	Penetration of foreign cultures	Al Qaeda, other jihadist groups
	"Clash of civilizations"	Al Qaeda

people living in poverty may, under certain circumstances, create a fertile breeding ground for terrorist ideologies. In the urban slums and squatter settlements and remote rural areas of the developing world, where people often do not enjoy even the limited benefits of economic development such as access to health care, education, potable water, or electricity, it is easy to develop a sense of despair and hopelessness that one's quality of life will ever improve under the current political system—especially if that system is demonstrably corrupt and often authoritarian.

At times, this despair can lead to anger and to a willingness to use—or at least condone the use of—violence to achieve political, economic, and social change. Indeed, sometimes even those in the middle class have been driven to support political violence in the face of evidence of massive government corruption and authoritarian rule. Some scholars have observed, however, that desperately poor and hungry people are typically too busy trying to stay alive to be politically active, much less to engage in terrorism.[1] And yet when radical indigenous groups have been able to promise better living conditions and less poverty, people whose social and economic future seems otherwise hopeless have shown a willingness to listen and respond to their message. Two specific examples, both drawn from Latin America, illustrate how indigenous political groups have sought to recruit poor rural peasants to their cause:

Sendero Luminoso, or Shining Path, in Peru and the Revolutionary Armed Forces of Colombia, or FARC.

Shining Path is a Maoist guerilla organization that was created as an off-shoot of the Communist Party in Peru. Throughout the 1980s, Shining Path gained support from poor peasants in rural areas by filling the political void left by the central government—that is, it provided "popular justice" by exe-cuting cattle rustlers, managers of the state-controlled farming collectives, and well-to-do merchants, who were perceived to be exploiting poor farm labor. As a result of these actions, the peasantry of many Peruvian villages, especially in the impoverished, neglected, and remote regions away from the national capital, Lima, expressed sympathy with Shining Path's ideology.

But Shining Path did not confine itself to the countryside. It also mounted attacks against the infrastructure in Lima, sabotaging electrical transmission towers (in multiple instances), thereby producing urban blackouts; setting fires to an industrial plant and several shopping malls; and bombing the offices of the governing party, Popular Action. Shining Path also engaged in selec-tive assassinations, targeting specific individuals—notably leaders of other left-ist groups, local political parties, and even peasant organizations that opposed it. By 1991 Shining Path had gained control of much of the center and south of Peru and had a large presence on the outskirts of Lima.

Shining Path's brand of Maoism was never broadly popular, especially with urban dwellers of Lima. Ultimately, even the rural peasants stopped supporting the group because of its brutality and its practice of killing peas-ants and popular leaders for even minor offenses. Some peasants went so far as to form anti–Shining Path groups. They also disliked Shining Path's pol-icy of closing small, rural markets in order to end small-scale capitalism and to try to starve Lima of food. Thus the attempts by an indigenous, radical political organization to radicalize and recruit poor peasants from the Peru-vian countryside ended in failure. Eventually, the government captured the organization's leadership, though remnants of Shining Path continue to exist today.

A second example of an indigenous group that has attempted to radicalize and recruit largely from among the poor rural population is FARC in Colom-bia. Also a communist offshoot organization, FARC claims to represent the rural poor in their struggle against Colombia's wealthy classes. It also opposes the U.S. influence in Colombia in the form of U.S. multinational corporations and the fight by the U.S. Bureau of Alcohol, Tobacco, and Firearms (ATF) against the cocaine trade. FARC's stated objective is to seize power in Colom-bia through an armed revolution, which it funds principally through extor-tion, kidnapping, and participation in the illegal drug trade. FARC also frequently recruits children as soldiers and informants, usually by force, although some join voluntarily as a means of escaping rural poverty and unem-ployment. FARC's involvement in narco-trafficking has included coca plant harvesting, protection of coca crops, and protection of cocaine manufacturing sites. At times, FARC has overrun and massacred small communities in order to silence and intimidate those who do not support its activities, but also to enlist new (and often underage) recruits by force, to distribute propaganda, and to rob local banks.

By some estimates, FARC has under its control between fifteen and eighteen thousand soldiers. Colombian president Álvaro Uribe has tried various tactics to convince FARC to end its insurgency, including direct negotiations and the declaration of a temporary truce. The results, however, have been mixed, and FARC remains active and politically viable in rural areas of the country. Unlike the situation in Peru, however, the close continuing relationship between FARC and Colombian narco-traffickers has produced large quantities of cash to finance terrorist operations and to encourage the loyalty and cooperation of poor rural peasants.

The refugee camps in the Middle East and elsewhere also may be a fertile breeding ground for terrorists and terrorist ideologies, and some evidence lends credence to this concern. A typical camp contains thousands—and in some cases, tens of thousands—of extremely poor refugees, most of whom have been forcibly removed from their lands and their homes as a result of armed conflict. Since the end of the 1948 Arab-Israeli War, the United Nations Relief and Works Agency (UNRWA) has operated refugee camps in the Gaza Strip, the West Bank, Jordan, Lebanon, and Syria for over four million Palestinian refugees. In many of these places, there is now a second (or, in some cases, a third) generation of young people who have never lived outside of the camps. Understandably, they harbor deep feelings of despair and anger over their homeless, stateless condition and over the lack of economic opportunity they face. Gaza, in particular, and to a lesser extent the West Bank are the base of operations for the terrorist group Hamas, which recruits actively in the refugee camps and uses them as places to store weapons and to hide from Israeli forces. During the two intifadas,[2] news reports indicated that the suicide bombers who managed to cross into Israel and detonate their explosives among civilian populations began their fateful journeys in the refugee camps of the Gaza Strip and the West Bank.

Political Factors

Poverty, illiteracy, and ill health do not, of course, occur in a vacuum. They typically are the result of systematic neglect and underinvestment in social programs, mismanagement of the national economy, and often the diversion of resources by corrupt politicians who are uninterested in addressing the needs of the poor. Although these conditions exist widely today in many developing countries, in most of these countries there is no evidence of terrorism or the formation of terrorist organizations. As noted earlier, because of the immediate exigencies of their daily lives, the poor typically lack the time or the motivation to engage in organized violence.

When control of a country is in the hands of a privileged elite who are known to be exploiting the economy for their own financial gain at the expense of the poor, or when those running the government are corrupt and are diverting resources for their own profit (often sending large sums of money out of the country), the situation may be different. Also, if the socioeconomic gap between rich and poor is actually *widening*—a reality observed in almost any major Third World city today—even the most destitute eventually begin to question the reasons for their poverty. Those seeking to recruit new members of terrorist networks or to organize new terrorist groups can point to these socioeconomic disparities and convince the poor that radical violence is the only viable means of bringing about change.

An example of a revolt against wealth disparity and poverty, and one that interestingly did *not* result in terrorist violence, was the Zapatista Army of National Liberation in Mexico. The Zapatistas, who took their name from the famous Mexican revolutionary Emiliano Zapata, were organized to call the world's attention to the large disparities in the distribution of wealth in the Mexican state of Chiapas and to the fact that the rights of the indigenous Mayan population had been systematically ignored for many decades by the federal government in Mexico City. The Zapatistas also protested the signing of the North American Free Trade Agreement (NAFTA), which they believed would only intensify the gap between the rich and the poor in Chiapas. The group did not demand independence from Mexico; rather, it wanted greater autonomy and greater control over the profits from the natural resources being extracted from Chiapas. Although the "Zapatista revolution" was briefly violent, it soon became long-term, nonviolent political negotiations intended to improve economic and social conditions and to meet other demands of the indigenous populations. Even today, those negotiations continue, on and off. (See Chapter 9.)

National governments have frequently reacted to the growing demands for social and economic justice or greater political rights, or even full political autonomy, with repressive measures designed to neutralize the power and influence of those calling for such changes. Organizers are threatened, and later arrested, and protests are broken up, often violently. Such repression may continue for extended periods of time, becoming more severe and lawless as it continues, especially if there is organized resistance. Under these circumstances, resistance groups may view the resort to violence, including terrorist tactics, as the only viable response, especially in situations in which peaceful political protest has become too dangerous or ineffective. There are many examples of groups that, organizing in response to political, economic, and social repression, often as a result of colonial rule (in the late nineteenth and early twentieth centuries), have resorted to terrorist tactics. Examples include the Irgun in Israel (1931–1948); the Muslim Brotherhood in Egypt (1935–present); the Mau Mau uprising in Kenya (1952–1960); and, more recently, the Chechens in Russia (1990–2004). The Chechen uprising, which has consisted of a protracted struggle between the Russian military and Chechen rebels, has produced some major terrorist incidents both in Moscow and elsewhere. (See Case Study 3.1.)

Another source of political violence that at times has assumed terrorist characteristics is derived from national policies that marginalize, alienate, and de facto exclude certain ethnic groups or nationalities from the economic, political, and social benefits of mainstream society. These types of policy initiatives, whether or not sanctioned by national law, have become more widespread as a result of rising global (and often illegal) immigration, especially in Western Europe and, to a lesser extent, in certain parts of Asia. Government refusal to recognize ethnic groups or minority nationalities has a long history in many countries and is undertaken as a matter of national policy.

One example is the Basque people of northeastern Spain (and part of France), who have struggled for separate recognition by the Spanish government since at least the nineteenth century—first with the Spanish monarchy and more recently with elected Spanish governments. In 1959 they established Basque Fatherland and Liberty, or ETA, demanding sovereignty and self-determination for the Basque people. As a result of the continuing efforts by the Spanish government to suppress and destroy the ETA, particularly during the rule of Spanish dictator Francisco Franco, the organization turned to terrorism. To date, the ETA has taken responsibility for over nine hundred killings, mostly of Spanish government officials, in the name of Basque independence. The organization supposedly declared a "permanent ceasefire" in 2006 in the expectation that the Spanish government would negotiate some sort of partial autonomy for the Basque region, but the bombings resumed in 2007, and the ETA has now declared the ceasefire to be at an end. It therefore remains unclear whether a political solution can be found.

In some respects, a more pernicious source of terrorist motivations may be the isolation and discrimination based on language, race, or ethnicity experienced by immigrants, especially when they are recent arrivals who may well have no more than guest worker status (if they are legally in the country to begin with). Many governments seeking to assimilate immigrant communities ban discriminatory practices. But often extensive de facto discrimination may take the form of lack of access to such things as housing, jobs, and education. Some immigrants have even been forced to adhere to local practices that may violate their own religious or cultural traditions. For example, the government of France has banned Muslim girls from wearing the hijab, or head covering, at school (it actually has banned all other religious accoutrements such as yarmulkes and crosses as well). However, for most Muslim girls and women the wearing of the hijab is an important religious and cultural practice, and so they feel violated and discriminated against when forced to go out in public without it.

France is certainly not the only country in Europe struggling with how to socially, politically, and economically assimilate people who are from outside the traditional mainstream culture. But the problem in France has been brought into sharp focus by the ongoing violence and riots by Muslim minorities on the outskirts of Paris, and especially by the youth, most of whom are from Algeria and other countries in North Africa (a French colonial possession) and are living in economic and social isolation from mainstream French society. There is evidence that some of the most alienated among this youthful population also may be engaged in the formation of local terrorist cells that are loosely connected to al Qaeda.

Concern has been expressed that the same alienation motivating the rioters could drive them to adopt more extreme forms of Islam as a rejection of the West. Although religious radicalism is thought to be minimal among France's Muslims, Salafism, an extreme form of Islam that has supported the struggle of jihad in some forms, has gained ground in some communities. In addition, the intelligence community has traced multiple cases of terrorism back to Western Europe. Examples include the 2001 World Trade Center attacks, which were facilitated by an al Qaeda cell based in Hamburg, Germany; "Shoe Bomber" Richard Reid, who was recruited in a British jail; and Zacharias Moussaoui, the so-called twentieth hijacker from the attacks of September 11, who found his calling in a London mosque. Some analysts have argued that such radicalization took place in Europe because of European national identities rooted in their ethnicities, in contrast to the United States, which, although it still struggles with integration, conceives of itself as a nation of immigrants and thus far has had limited experience with homegrown radicalism.

At the opposite extreme, governments have at times actively encouraged the persecution and "removal" of those elements of society that threaten their legitimacy or control. This persecution is typically carried out by so-called militias—or, in some extreme cases, death squads—that are not formally affiliated with the government and thus can claim to operate outside of its direction or control (although the truth may be significantly different). Some examples of countries in which these paramilitary groups operate, or have operated in the past, and in which violent, "terrorist-like" tactics, including targeted assassinations and bombings, have been used to scare certain elements of society into submission or exile are Argentina, Chile, Colombia, and Guatemala. In Argentina and Chile, the conservative regimes adopted lawless, terroristic behavior in a "Dirty War" against leftists and communists in the mid-1970s and early 1980s. Thousands of people "disappeared" (were murdered) with no record of their arrest, much less their execution.

Finally, like the separatist group ETA, which has used terrorism to pursue its demands for some form of autonomous region for a Basque homeland, some groups are motivated to turn to terrorism in support of true separatist objectives. Chapter 2 described the Tamil Tigers in Sri Lanka, a group that seeks a separate, independent Tamil state on that island nation. In the southern Philippines, the Abu Sayyaf Group (ASG), also known as al-Harakat al-Islamiyya, or "Father of the Sword," has been fighting since the early 1990s for a separate

Islamic state in the western part of the Philippine island of Mindanao and the Sulu Archipelago. More broadly, the ASG envisions breaking away from the Philippines, a predominantly Roman Catholic country, and forming a pan-Islamic state across much of Southeast Asia.[3] The ASG has engaged in bombings, assassinations, kidnappings, and extortion in its fight for independence. The Philippine military has responded in force to the ASG separatist challenge, supported technically by special forces of the U.S. military, and apparently has succeeded in suppressing, and almost entirely eliminating, the group.

Cultural Factors

The years since September 11, 2001, have revealed that, unfortunately, certain cultural institutions and practices have also acted as significant sources or conduits of terrorist thinking and recruitment. For example, in the aftermath of the al Qaeda attacks the media devoted significant attention to the role played by madrassas, or traditional Islamic religious schools, in providing students with a narrow, doctrinaire, ideologically slanted view of the world, and of the Western world in particular. Although there is now some disagreement among experts about the extent to which the madrassas have actually contributed to the growth of al Qaeda and other terrorist groups, there is concern that the atmosphere in the madrassas may have rendered their graduates, including those who might be willing to martyr themselves as suicide bombers, particularly vulnerable to the messages of terrorist recruiters. Likewise, during the period the Taliban were in control of the government of Afghanistan, the cultural institutions of the country were subjected to a broad-based effort to impose extreme, orthodox Islamic values on the entire citizenry. These efforts included permitting male children to receive only Islamic education in madrassas and effectively closing all secular institutions of higher education; prohibiting women's education altogether; banning all forms of music and sports and the watching of television; and destroying (with explosives) the ancient, world-famous "Buddhas of Bamiyan" because they represented a "craven image" considered offensive to Islam. And, of course, until it was overthrown by U.S.-led coalition forces after the September 11 attacks, the Taliban provided safe haven for the leadership of al Qaeda.

The role of religion as a radicalizing force and fertile recruiting ground for those holding extremist views—and who are prepared to use violence in support of those views—is by no means confined to Islam. The long, religious-based conflict in Northern Ireland between the Roman Catholic and Protestant communities, each with its own radical groups—the Catholics' IRA versus the Protestants' Ulster Volunteer Force, both of which frequently resorted to terrorist tactics, especially bombings and political murders—provides demonstrable evidence that similar circumstances prevail in the Christian world as well. And Judaism, too, has had radical groups that resorted to terrorist tactics. Those groups include the Irgun, a militant Zionist group that struggled against

British rule in Palestine from 1931 until Israel's independence in 1948, and, more recently, the Jewish Defense League, a right-wing group founded in the United States but which has operated in both the United States and Israel and has used violence as a tactic in responding to anti-Semitic attacks.

There are many examples from history, and from the present time as well, of government efforts to suppress the culture, language, and political rights of ethnic minorities. Earlier in this chapter, the French government's effort to ban the hijab from French schools was noted. In some countries, these efforts at suppression have continued over long periods of time, creating deep resentments and even hatreds within the persecuted populations, who see their culture being threatened, if not systematically destroyed. An important, present-day example of this suppression, which has led directly to terrorism, is the suppression of the large Kurdish minority in Turkey. That country's Kurdish population numbers some fifteen million people, or about 20 percent of the total population. Perhaps because it is such a large ethnic minority with its own language and traditions, the unwillingness of the Kurds to assimilate into mainstream Turkish society led the Turkish government, beginning in the 1920s, to impose increasingly restrictive measures, which included bans on speaking the Kurdish language in public, teaching Kurdish in the schools (even as a second language), and forming political parties based on ethnic issues or concerns.

In 1973 this suppression of Kurdish culture and rights led to the establishment of the Kurdistan Workers Party (PKK), which actively supports the separation of the Kurdish area, Kurdistan, from Turkey. To that end, the PKK has engaged in a long-running series of terrorist attacks against Turkish government officials, as well as government and corporate facilities. The Turkish government has responded in force. Although most of its top leaders are now in prison, the PKK remains active as a separatist organization, and it continues to employ terrorist tactics in pursuit of its demands. Resolution of the problem is complicated by the fact that Kurdish populations reside not just in Turkey but also in neighboring Iran, Iraq, and Syria.

CASE STUDY 3.1

Repression of an Indigenous Terrorist Group: Chechnya and Russia

Chechnya, a republic of Russia, is located in the Northern Caucasus mountains, bordering the Republic of Georgia. The nation of 1.5 million people has almost always been part of Russia since it was conquered in the late nineteenth century, and it continues to fight what has been an often brutal Soviet (and later Russian) suppression of Chechen autonomy that began in the final years before the breakup of the Soviet Union in 1991. Once that breakup occurred, Chechen separatists intensified efforts to pursue their goals of sovereignty and independence. After the outbreak of hostilities in 1994, Chechen fighters began to choose civilian targets in Russia, including public transportation, theaters, hospitals, and schools. On the heels of the September 2001 terrorist attacks on the United States, Russian authorities, up to and including President Vladimir Putin, began to stress the involvement in Chechnya of international terrorists and associates of Osama bin Laden, in part to generate Western sympathy for Russia's ongoing (and often brutal) military campaign against the Chechen rebels.

The conquest of the entire Northern Caucasus was a fundamental strategic objective during the early expansion of Bolshevism and the establishment of the Union of Soviet Socialist Republics. After the breakup of the Soviet Union, the preservation of Chechnya as part of Russia became an issue of national interest and pride. The fear in Moscow is that if Chechnya becomes independent, more ethnic groups will seek to break away from Russia, leading to its disintegration. In addition, Chechen territory enhances Russian power; it provides access to the oil of the Caspian Sea (via Azerbaijan) and extends Russia's circle (or threat) of influence to key allies in the Middle East and Central Asia.

The Chechen-Ingush Autonomous Soviet Socialist Republic, as it was officially known, was imposed on Chechnya by the Bolsheviks (communists) in 1922. The Chechens rose up against Soviet rule during World War II, resulting in the deportation of one million Chechens (three-quarters of the population) to Kazakhstan and Siberia in 1944. Soviet dictator Joseph Stalin argued that the deportation was necessary to prevent the Chechens from assisting Nazi Germany. One-third of those deported died in the process. The Chechens were allowed to return to their homeland after 1956, during the Nikita Khrushchev's de-Stalinization program. In February 2004, the European Parliament recognized the 1944 deportation as an act of genocide. This incident remains a major source of Chechen anger and resentment toward Russia.

After the dissolution of the Soviet Union in 1991, Chechnya declared independence from Russia. However, Russian president Boris Yeltsin rejected Chechnya's independence and sent a small force to its airport. Chechnya's newly elected president, former Soviet air force general Jokhar Dudayev, declared martial law and mobilized the Chechen national guard. Yeltsin's outnumbered forces ultimately returned to Moscow. When Yeltsin attempted to send a more substantial force, the move was blocked initially by the Russian Supreme Court. In December 1994, Yeltsin declared a state of emergency in the Chechen region and sent forty thousand troops to recapture the capital, Grozny. Russian forces then leveled Grozny, but even with vastly superior technology and manpower, they were unable to overcome the Chechens' guerrilla tactics to establish control over the mountainous areas.

Analysts described the Chechen separatists as a loose network of cells consisting of clan-based fighters led by semi-independent commanders.

The Chechen separatist movement used a wide range of tactics, including social activism, strategic crime, and terrorism, to complement guerrilla warfare. By most accounts, rebel leader Shamil Basayev was instrumental in introducing terrorism to the movement. Basayev planned and carried out the 1991 hijacking of a Russian airliner, forcing it to land in Ankara, Turkey, and then holding a press conference to draw attention to Chechnya's plight.

After the 1994 invasion, Chechen terrorism grew more violent. In 1995 Basayev led a group of rebels in taking seventeen hundred civilians hostage in a hospital in the town of Budennovsk in southern Russia. They demanded the withdrawal of Russian troops from Chechnya, and they called for their own state outside of Russian sovereignty—demands that would be echoed in future attacks by Chechen rebels. One hundred hostages were killed, some during the three bungled rescue missions, before Basayev negotiated the hostages' release and safe passage for him and his accomplices. The hostage taking was broadcast live on Russian television, and it greatly contributed to the Russian public's disillusionment with Yeltsin's war in Chechnya.

In August 1996, the demoralization of Russian forces and public disapproval of the war in Chechnya prompted Yeltsin to agree to a ceasefire, which supposedly led to a negotiated settlement. However, after a series of Moscow apartment buildings were bombed, allegedly by Chechen rebels in September 1999, killing three hundred people, Putin, who was then Russia's prime minister, initiated a second and much larger military campaign into Chechnya in late September. When Putin was elected president of Russia in March 2000, he was bolstered by a high public approval rating for his hard-line stance on Chechnya. In May 2000, Russia gained control of Grozny, and Putin declared direct rule of Chechnya, although guerilla warfare continued in the mountains. It is estimated that between 70,000 and 250,000 civilians were killed in both military campaigns and that about 400,000 were displaced. Russian military casualties were estimated at about 11,000. Meanwhile, the Russian government faced international criticism and scrutiny for attacking civilian targets, and human rights groups reported cases of murder, rape, and hostage taking against civilians, although these incidents occurred substantially after the September 11, 2001, attacks in the United States.

Chechnya's brief taste of quasi-independence from 1995 to 1999 was characterized by lawlessness and the rise of Islamic extremism. Warlords fought each other, and kidnappings were frequent and highly publicized, often undertaken for ransom. In this environment, Islamic fundamentalism gained a greater following, although its size is widely disputed. In 1999 Islamic law was established in Chechnya. This final change was evident in Basayev. He began his career as a nationalist and an admirer of Cuban revolutionary Che Guevara, but by the time he was killed in an explosion of questionable origin in 2006 he was adhering to fundamentalist Islam. Some analysts claim that his shift to Islam was mainly to attract funding from the movement in the Middle East, but few believe he ever had contact with Osama bin Laden. In addition, it is likely that a small contingent of Arab fighters, possibly linked to other Islamic extremist groups, were fighting with the rebels in Chechnya.

Today, Russia continues intermittently to suffer brutal suicide bombings and hostage takings carried out by Chechen rebels. Until his death, Basayev was instrumental in their coordination. In October 2002, Chechen suicide bombers took about eight hundred people hostage in a Moscow theater. After a three-day standoff, Russian special forces pumped nerve gas into the theater and then stormed the building. One hundred and twenty-nine hostages died from exposure to the gas. All forty-one hostage takers were killed as well. In August 2004, female suicide bombers blew up two Russian airliners on the same day, killing eighty-nine people. Two weeks later, over three hundred people, mostly children, were killed when thirty Chechen rebels took twelve hundred people hostage in a school in Beslan in southern Russia. The school attack outraged the international community, and it is widely thought to have undermined any remaining sympathy for the Chechen cause. It also lent credibility to Russian authorities' argument that Chechen terrorists are the world's foes in the war on terrorism, although there was substantial evidence of ineptitude on the part of the Russian special forces who attempted to take back the school and free the hostages.

Presently, nearly three-quarters of Chechnya's population of more than one million people are without jobs, electricity, and telephone services, and a substantial portion of this population is displaced in refugee camps because of the widespread destruction. Hundreds have disappeared in kidnappings blamed on all sides. Chechen rebels are also in extremely close proximity to insufficiently secured Russian nuclear facilities, prompting some analysts to worry about the possibility of catastrophic terror in Russia.

The Chechen case is significant not only because of what it demonstrates about the effect of weak central control (especially just after the breakup of the Soviet Union) in dealing with separatist groups prepared to use terrorist tactics, but also because of what it reveals about how historical injustices—in this case including genocide—can be carried forward even after the nature of the regime in power has changed profoundly. Terrorism by some Chechen insurgents also was, and continues to be, driven by a deep ethnic alienation from Russian culture and political control. Thus, despite the Russian government's apparent success in suppressing the separatist movement, it remains unclear whether the insurgents have permanently abandoned the use of terrorism to achieve their political objectives. ■

External Sources of Terrorism

Conditions of inequality, discrimination, and cultural threat, whatever their cause within a given country, are also the result of external actors, forces, and social conditions, both historical and present-day, that threaten the existing "order" or bring about changes that are considered by many to be inimical to the national interest and that must be resisted with violence if necessary. This section addresses these external sources of terrorism.

Colonialism and Neocolonialism

The legacy of colonialist occupation and neocolonialist (that is, economic) domination is still felt strongly in many parts of Africa, Asia, and Latin America. Because colonialism and neocolonialism are, with the exception of Japan, associated almost exclusively with the historically dominant nation-states of Western Europe and the United States, many scholars and policy makers hold the West (including Japan) responsible for much of the underdevelopment and inequitable ownership of land and other resources that characterize so much of the developing world. Even though the era of political colonialism has been over since the middle of the twentieth century, foreign economic ownership of national assets and resources has continued—and, in some cases, has actually increased. Unfortunately, there are also too many examples of governments intervening, often covertly, in the affairs of other countries (usually developing ones) on behalf of the economic interests of their citizens and corporations. Memories of these interventions tend to be long, and they can provide a common rallying point for those seeking retribution.

One example of the volatile legacy of neocolonial interventionism, driven in large measure by dependence on oil exports and geopolitical self-interest, is Iran. The 1979 Iranian revolution deposed Shah Mohammad Reza Pahlavi, despite the active support of the United States, and brought to power Ayatollah Ruhollah Mussaui Khomeini, who founded the Islamic Republic, targeting the United States as its implacable foe. Among the many reasons that conditions were favorable for the overthrow of the Pahlavi throne was the Shah's strong pro-Western policy and close identification with the United States—after all, he came to power in 1953 with the substantial assistance of the U.S. Central Intelligence Agency. As a result, many Iranians considered the Shah to be little more than a puppet of the United States and the West. After the rise of the Khomeini government, the United States was and continues to be characterized by Iranian propaganda as "the Great Satan," amidst allegations of U.S. political intervention and control and economic exploitation. In view of the many serious issues that now complicate U.S.-Iranian relations, including Iran's suspected efforts to develop a nuclear weapon and its alleged support for the insurgency in Iraq and the arming of Hezbollah in southern Lebanon, the earlier history of neocolonialism and political intervention has proved to be a powerful and enduring obstacle to better relations.

Regional Conflicts and Historical Enmities

In some instances, the roots of terrorism can be traced to a history of antagonistic, and often bellicose, relations between neighboring countries, or countries occupying the same region and competing for power and influence. For example, Israel has long claimed that the terrorist groups Hamas, Hezbollah, and Palestinian Islamic Jihad are armed and financed by many of the same regional neighbors (Syria, Iran, and perhaps Saudi Arabia) with whom it has fought a series of wars during the last forty years. The Israelis argue, with some credibility, that these countries appear to be using the three non-state actors as proxies to continue the armed struggle for control of what they believe is, or should be, Palestinian territory.

Pakistan, which is Muslim, and India, which is predominantly Hindu, have had tense relations—and occasional military conflicts—since their partition in 1947. The struggle has focused primarily on control of the contested state of Jammu and Kashmir and the demarcation of a permanent border between the two countries, but it also has concerned the treatment of the large Muslim community that has continued to reside in India. Although these disputes have been taken up most recently through diplomatic channels established as part of a joint peace process, this effort has failed to prevent a continuing series of terrorist attacks in India—almost all of which were blamed on Pakistan and, more specifically, on the Pakistani military's Inter-Services Intelligence agency (ISI). The obvious question, of course, is why the ISI would be instigating or assisting in the planning of major terrorist activities in India while the two governments are at the same time talking about resolving their differences peacefully. (See Case Study 3.2.)

Failed/Failing States and Lawless Areas

The term *failed state* (or *failing state*) refers to a nation whose system of governance has collapsed or is extremely weak and ineffective because of political paralysis, factional violence, rampant corruption, terrorism, or other causes. Indeed, often many of these factors are working in combination. Each of the failed or failing states that has emerged since the end of the stable bipolar order of the cold war period has had its own particular circumstances and difficulties in reestablishing a workable, functioning government. In the partial vacuum created when a government is unable to govern, terrorist organizations, whether indigenous or foreign, are presented with a situation in which there are few, if any, restrictions on their operations and there is little fear of political pressure, much less police scrutiny. Al Qaeda and other groups have taken advantage of such lawlessness to set up training camps and other kinds of support operations in places such as Afghanistan and Somalia.

Perhaps the best-known example of a failed state playing host to terrorism is Afghanistan after the collapse of the government in 1992 and the takeover by the Taliban. During this time, the leadership of al Qaeda, which had been forced to leave Sudan, was able to reestablish itself in the territory of Afghanistan. It did so, in part, by providing substantial sums of money to help the Taliban maintain control of the country. Until it was dislodged once again and forced to flee when U.S. and coalition forces invaded Afghanistan after the September 11 terrorist attacks, al Qaeda was able to operate openly. It established camps that reportedly trained thousands, if not tens of thousands, of terrorist fighters, who later dispersed to other countries.

As noted in earlier chapters, after its defeat at Tora Bora the al Qaeda leadership likely relocated in the westernmost part of Pakistan in the province of Waziristan. Waziristan, a "Federally Administrated Tribal Area" of Pakistan that has been semi-independent since the late nineteenth century, has always been a lawless place dominated by sometimes feuding local tribes and religious leaders. These tribes are overtly hostile not only to the efforts of the Pakistani government to rein them in, but also to the idea of permitting a military or police presence by foreign powers—especially non-Islamic states such as the United States. Waziristan is then, in many ways, an ideal place for Osama bin Laden and Ayman al-Zawahiri, both of whom are now wanted international fugitives, to hide and to continue to run their al Qaeda organization. At the same time, apparently the remnants of the Taliban also have been given sanctuary in Pakistan, where they can rest, train, and rearm in preparation for slipping back into Afghanistan to conduct additional terrorist acts.

Similar lawless areas can be found in other parts of the world as well. One such example is the tri-border region where Brazil, Argentina, and Paraguay meet, and where an effective police presence is lacking. In the failed or failing states of Lebanon, Sierra Leone, Somalia, and Sudan, lawlessness and lack of effective governance have created opportunities for terrorist organizations to establish safe havens for wanted terrorist criminals, bases of operation for training, and logistical support platforms for foreign attacks. For example, in the wake of the sudden and unexpected overthrow of the rump Islamic government of Somalia by Ethiopian forces in early 2007, the United States refocused its attention on al Qaeda cells operating in the southern part of the country. These cells, which are suspected of having perpetrated the bombing of the U.S. embassies in Kenya and Tanzania, had managed to establish a foothold because of the chaotic, lawless situation in Somalia.

Penetration of Foreign Cultures and Lifestyles

Clearly, one of the central factors motivating the struggle by al Qaeda and other Islamic jihadist organizations is their resentment of the unwanted penetration of Western values, lifestyles, and culture into traditional, conservative Islamic societies.[4] Cultural penetration happens in many ways and through many different modalities. Some of it is purposeful—such as advertising and religious proselytizing—and some of it is the unintended result of the offer-

ings of the mass media, movies, videos, and music, as well as global communications, including the Internet. Whatever its source, cultural penetration is
a largely unstoppable phenomenon, unless a country wishes to cut itself off
entirely from the outside world, such as North Korea or Myanmar. It is also
beyond the control of governments, because much of it happens in real time
and through multiple private channels.

The resentment of cultural penetration in some Islamic countries stems
from the prevailing strict religious orthodoxy, which, among other things, for-
bids women from showing themselves in public (or on film), from driving cars,
or, in extreme cases, from receiving an education. Both sexes may be forbidden to consume alcohol or pork products; to listen to certain types of music—
or perhaps music of any kind; or to read works of fiction containing themes
that are considered blasphemous or improper. If, as a result of media penetration, advertising, or direct personal contact, people living in such conservative settings are exposed to information, ideas, or messages that are deemed
culturally insensitive and possibly threatening, those who view themselves as
the guardians of the culture have demonstrated a willingness to take steps to
prevent these practices and, at times, to use violence against the organizations
and countries producing such content, which usually are in the West.

"Clash of Civilizations"

Since the attacks of September 11, 2001, in New York City and Washington,
many people have speculated about the "real" motivations or demands of al
Qaeda. To put it somewhat differently, many people have asked themselves
what exactly are the goals of radical Islamic terrorists, and what would it take
to convince them to renounce violence and seek change peacefully through
the political process. Unfortunately, the leaders of al Qaeda have, presumably
for strategic reasons, never been very specific about their real demands,
thereby making it difficult, if not impossible, to undertake any direct negotiations or explore possible compromises with them.

What is known, however, is that those who adhere to Salafism not only
reject and actively oppose the penetration of Western culture and values,[5] but
also demand, in various combinations, (1) the total withdrawal of Western
military forces from the Arabian peninsula (it is considered sacred to the
Islamic religion); (2) the elimination of Western political influence and domination from the entire Islamic world; (3) the reestablishment of the caliphate[6]
that, according to some radical jihadist statements, would seek to unite all the
Islamic peoples of the world under a single Islamic governance that would
even include some lands now part of the Western world;[7] and (4) elimination
of the state of Israel. Because these demands are being expressed through
unprovoked acts of violence directed against the United States and other
Western countries, the prospects for political negotiation and accommodation
seem almost nonexistent. Indeed, Samuel Huntington[8] points to the increas-

ing likelihood of "fault line wars," which in this case would be hostilities based explicitly on the divisions between the countries of the Islamic world and Western countries that adhere to a Judeo-Christian heritage.[9] To be clear, however, Huntington also suggested several "fault line war" scenarios, many of them not involving Islamic states.

The growing civilizational divide also has a psychological dimension: the sense of humiliation and rage that many Muslims feel about their individual and collective treatment, both historically and in the current era. Although it may well be that Osama bin Laden and his adherents would have chosen in any event to pursue a strategy based on the use of violence and terrorism, the anger and frustration felt by many in the Islamic world, especially in Arab countries, have actually spurred the widespread dissemination of al Qaeda's message and attracted many new adherents. The resonance of the radical jihadist message with the "Muslim street"—that is, with the typical person, who is likely to be a young, and possibly unemployed, male—is the result, in part, of a substantial historical legacy of colonialist subjugation and underdevelopment and authoritarian rule by local elites and clans. However, it also is the result of a deep and abiding sense of frustration and hopelessness produced by the current lack of economic opportunity and, in many countries, the perception that the gap in living standards and access to the benefits of modern society is actually widening, although this gap may well be the result of internal resource inequalities. Rather than looking at the factors within their societies that may be causing such inequities, adherents often find it easier to simply blame external actors and circumstances.

CASE STUDY 3.2

Regional Conflicts and Historical Enmities: India, Pakistan, and Jammu and Kashmir

When the British dismantled their South Asian colonial empire in 1947, they partitioned the Indian subcontinent into two nations: India, which is secular and Hindu-dominated, and the Muslim nation of Pakistan. The two nations have been adversaries ever since, beginning with a violent partitioning process that led to the displacement of two million people and half a million deaths. Indeed, India and Pakistan have fought three wars, two over India's disputed Himalayan state of Jammu and Kashmir.

Over the last ten years, between thirty and sixty thousand people have died in the Kashmir conflict. Although most of the state is controlled by India, Pakistan also lays claim to it, because it is majority Muslim. Both nations maintain troops along the so-called Line of Control, which is the ceasefire line through Kashmir from the first Indo-Pakistani war. Because both nations now have nuclear capabilities, this rivalry has wide implications for the South Asian region and the international community.

In 1989 armed Kashmiri resistance to Indian rule broke out. The insurgency was indigenous at first, consisting of multiple separatist groups, some advocating independence for Jammu and Kashmir and others advocating union with Pakistan. However, in the 1990s Islamic jihadist fighters who had fought in Afghanistan against the Soviet Union in the 1980s traveled to fight alongside the Kashmiri separatists. This development fueled an ideological shift from that of self-determination to that of holy war, which coincided with an escalation of violence in Kashmir and terrorist attacks in India.

India has been a frequent target of terrorist attacks by militant groups. The attacks have been concentrated in Indian-controlled Jammu and Kashmir and other northeastern states, in areas of Hindu worship nationwide, and in national, financial, or social interests in the major cities of Mumbai (formerly Bombay) and New Delhi. These tragic events have repeatedly soured diplomatic relations between India and Pakistan and raised tensions between Indian Muslims and Hindus, sometimes leading to retaliatory violence.

One of the worst attacks occurred on March 12, 1993, when a series of fifteen bombs exploded over a two-hour period at key civilian centers throughout Mumbai, killing 257 people and wounding 713. Although 123 defendants were tried and convicted in 2006, Indian authorities were unable to capture the alleged mastermind behind the attacks, Dawood Ibrahim. Ibrahim, the leader of an international organized crime syndicate, allegedly orchestrated the attacks from Dubai, one of the United Arab Emirates, and then fled to Karachi, Pakistan. Some analysts allege that Ibrahim coordinated the attacks on behalf of the Pakistani military's Inter-Services Intelligence agency (ISI). Whatever the truth, U.S. and Indian intelligence agencies report that, once in Pakistan, Ibrahim developed close ties with al Qaeda when he allowed it to use his smuggling routes. The Pakistani government denied Dawood's presence in the country for a long time, and it still refuses to extradite him.

Historically, Indian authorities have been quick to blame Pakistan for providing a safe haven to militant groups, supporting their activities, and permitting them to cross the border into India to smuggle arms and commit acts of violence and terrorism. (Pakistan is equally quick to point out that Hindu extremist attacks have been carried out on Muslims in India as well.) Pakistan claims to lend only "moral" support to the Kashmiri insurgency, and cites India's massive human rights violations in Jammu and Kashmir as the cause of the ongoing strife. India has repeatedly accused Pakistan of providing training and arms to the insurgency and of supporting "cross-border terrorism." There is widespread speculation that Pakistan's strategy is to use militant groups as an added line of defense against a militarily superior India should another war break out. In 1999 the two nations almost went to war a fourth time when

Pakistani forces infiltrated Indian-controlled Jammu and Kashmir. Pakistan considers that area fundamental to its identity, and the insurgency is a legitimizing force for Pakistan's president, Gen. Pervez Musharraf, whose predecessor backed down in the 1999 face-off.

September 11, 2001, marked a shift in Pakistan's policy toward militant groups. In order to support the war on terrorism and the U.S. invasion of neighboring Afghanistan, the Pakistani military had to turn its focus away from Jammu and Kashmir and to its borders with Afghanistan. President Musharraf also cracked down on militant groups operating in Pakistan by banning them, but this move was widely unpopular with Pakistanis, and the extent to which this crackdown has been sustained remains unclear.

On December 13, 2001, five men disguised as military commanders entered and attacked the Indian parliamentary complex in New Delhi. In the ensuing shootout, the attackers and nine other people died (none of them politicians), and twenty-two were wounded. The government of Pakistan and separatist groups based in Indian-controlled Jammu and Kashmir condemned the attacks, and no one came forward to claim responsibility. Through their investigation, Indian officials identified the five assailants as Pakistani nationals and alleged that they were members of two Pakistan-based militant Islamic groups, Lashkar-e-Taiba and an al Qaeda affiliate, Jaish-e-Mohammed. Pakistan's ISI and kingpin Dawood Ibrahim were implicated in the planning; Pakistani officials denied all accusations and demanded evidence.

The attack on India's parliament brought India and Pakistan close to war yet again. During the ensuing ten-month period, there was a buildup of one million troops along both sides of the Indo-Pakistani border. With pressure from the United States, both nations eventually withdrew, and in January 2002 President Musharraf gave a keynote speech pledging that Pakistan would not allow terrorists to operate from Pakistani soil. Soon afterward, it was reported that President Musharraf cut off all support to several militant groups, including those linked to the parliament attacks, and shut down the ISI wing allegedly responsible for funding Islamic militant groups. In 2004 Pakistan started reducing its activity along the Line of Control in Kashmir. After an earthquake in Jammu and Kashmir killed nearly eighty thousand people in 2005, military activity on both sides came to a near halt, but tensions across the Line of Control continue.

The India-Pakistan rift is important both because the two nations have nuclear weapons capabilities, which make the stakes enormous should a terrorist attack spiral out of control, and because it is so clearly driven by ethnic, religious, and political differences. It also demonstrates, however, that national governments, if they are willing to exercise control over non-state actors operating on their behalf, can at times contain and even prevent terrorist attacks.   ■

The United States as an Immediate Cause of Terrorism

Since the Iranian hostage crisis in 1979, when sixty-three U.S. diplomats and three other U.S. citizens were held captive for 444 days in the U.S. embassy in Tehran by radical Muslim students, the government of Iran has frequently referred to the United States as "the Great Satan." Based on world events since that time and similar rhetoric emanating from other countries in the Middle East, Iran is not alone in this view (although it is by no means clear that this view is held by the average Iranian citizen, or necessarily by citizens of other Middle Eastern countries). What has caused the United States to receive this unique and unenviable moniker and condemnation? And is the United States, as a result, being viewed as a special target or threat by Islamic terrorist organizations?

As noted earlier in this chapter, the United States has a long and not altogether meritorious history in the Middle East region. It has taken sides in various internal political struggles; the CIA has been involved in the overthrow of governments; the U.S. government is widely viewed by the Islamic populations of the region as siding openly with Israel in its struggle with the Palestinians; and there is a deep suspicion that most U.S. actions there are conditioned, first and foremost, by the need to assure reliable access to Middle Eastern oil. Radical Islamists take particular offense that U.S. forces are stationed in Saudi Arabia, not too far distant from the holy city of Mecca, and, of course, in Iraq and Afghanistan. Ultimately, because of its size, military power, and global economic and political reach, the United States, as the sole remaining superpower, is frequently viewed as a threat simply because of its *presence* in the region.

The reality, however, is far more nuanced. The United States also has been a force for peace at many points in contemporary Middle Eastern history. It has contributed billions of dollars in foreign aid to the region, and it liberated Kuwait after it was invaded by Iraqi dictator Saddam Hussein on April 2, 1990. Although Osama bin Laden and al Qaeda have labeled the United States as the "infidel" and U.S. soldiers as "crusaders"[10] whose objective is to destroy Islam, they conveniently overlook the fact that it was the United States that led the effort to build a military coalition to protect Muslims living in Croatia, Bosnia, and other parts of the former Yugoslavia when it broke up in the early 1990s. Nevertheless, the fact remains that the large physical presence of the U.S. military and political and intelligence operatives in the Middle East and Southwest Asia, combined with the perception that the U.S. government has consistently sided with conservative and repressive (and often corrupt) regimes that oppose the ideological agenda of the radical jihadists, has produced a situation in which the United States is viewed "as public enemy number one," which must be driven out if the caliphate is to be reestablished.

A Cause and Effect Explanation for Terrorism?

So far this chapter has explored a wide variety of factors, both internal and external, that explain why individuals and organizations turn to terrorism to achieve their goals and objectives. It may well be asked, however, whether any of these explanations really proves a direct cause and effect relationship between specific socioeconomic, political, and cultural circumstances and the violent acts that terrorists perpetrate, most often against innocent civilians. Indeed, is there ultimately a difference between the factors that contribute to terrorism and those that contribute to other types of political and social change, including some that result in or utilize violence to achieve a desired outcome (such as the violent overthrow of a despotic government)?

The answer is that conditions of inequality and disenfranchisement undoubtedly can and do motivate much-needed political change under certain circumstances—one example is the struggle of the African National Congress to end the "whites only" domination of the apartheid government in South Africa. Such conditions also can be used by political leaders as a rationale for pursuing their own personal agendas, whether it be the acquisition of great personal wealth or the pursuit of extreme ideological beliefs, and for attacking a legitimately elected government. Examples are the rebels under Charles Taylor in Liberia and the FARC's collusion with and protection of the narco-traffickers in Colombia. In this regard, it is always important to bear in mind that terrorism is a means to a political objective, whether good or bad; it is *not* an end in itself.

At the same time, the emergence of radical Islam, and particularly the Salafist principles followed by the leadership of al Qaeda, has added a new dimension to the explanation of terrorism. Although al Qaeda's rationale for terrorism, to the extent that it has ever articulated one, certainly refers to the historic and current inequalities and alleged mistreatment of the people of the Islamic world, it appears to go much further. It seeks to justify terrorism and violent attacks on innocent civilians, both non-Muslims and Muslims alike, using the words of the Qur'an, the sacred writings of the prophet Muhammad. The argument is based on a view of world history and current political realities that is fundamentally at odds with that held by most of the international community. When combined with a zealous belief in the principle of personal martyrdom in support of jihad, radical Islam presents extremely difficult and dangerous challenges to world order that have no easy answer or resolution.

The Range of Responses to Terrorism

Over the years, governments—and sometimes nongovernmental organizations (NGOs)—have developed a range of policies and initiatives for responding to threats of terrorism. Some responses are internal, and some are external. At various times, these responses have been employed both singly and in com-

Table 3.2 Responses to Terrorism

Level	Type	Examples
Internal	Promotion of social and economic integration	United States
	Explicit secularization of public life	Turkey, France
	Establishment of truth and reconciliation commissions	Argentina, Rwanda, South Africa
	Restrictions on communication and access to information	China, United States
	Increased domestic surveillance initiatives	UK
	Restrictions on internal movement in a country	Israel in the Palestinian territories; UK in Northern Ireland; U.S. and coalition forces in Afghanistan and Iraq
	Border controls and immigration restrictions	United States, Canada, Australia, Japan
	Suppression through intelligence and police action	Colombia versus FARC; Saudi Arabia versus al Qaeda; Afghanistan versus Taliban
	Direct engagement	IRA, ETA, LTTE
External	Cultural and educational exchanges	U.S. Fulbright Scholars, NGOs, Israeli-Palestinian symphony
	Public diplomacy	United States
	Targeted bilateral foreign assistance	Most advanced wealthy countries
	Investment in infrastructure and economic development	UN, World Bank
	Investment in police, military, and intelligence training	United States, Japan
	Anti–money laundering efforts	United States, UN
	Economic and political sanctions	UN versus Libya
	Military action (covert and overt)	U.S. global "war on terrorism"

bination. As the severity and frequency of terrorist attacks have increased, governments often have found it necessary to resort to harsher and more repressive measures, which are included in the typology shown in Table 3.2.

Internal Responses to Terrorism

National governments have employed a variety of strategies and tactics to contain, neutralize, and attempt to eliminate terrorist threats within their borders.

The responses described here are listed in ascending order of their severity and restrictiveness.

Promotion of assimilation and economic and social integration. In an ideal world, many of the socioeconomic, ethnic, and cultural problems and differences that radicalize people and motivate them to commit or support acts of terrorism can be mitigated by policies that actively seek to integrate, and ultimately assimilate, immigrant or minority communities into the mainstream of society. This approach is, of course, the implicit logic behind the "melting pot" theory that has been pursued in the United States ever since its founding. Particularly in the post–September 11 context, there is evidence that the U.S. policy of assimilation has paid enormous dividends. With a few isolated exceptions, the United States does not have the marginalized populations of young, unemployed, and disaffected Islamic youth who have rioted as in some European cities. To the contrary, Islamic religious and community leaders have played a major role since the terrorist attacks in calming their communities and keeping them engaged in the political process. As a result, so far there has been little evidence of homegrown terrorist cells, such as those uncovered in the UK, France, Germany, and the Netherlands.

Explicit secularization of public life. Many scholars would argue that the United States, because of the circumstances associated with its settlement in the seventeenth and eighteenth centuries, is unique, and that elsewhere it is therefore unreasonable to expect terrorism to be mitigated anytime soon through policies that simply encourage assimilation. Some countries have adopted instead an approach that calls for the explicit secularization of society, attempting to remove religious symbolism and religion itself as something that separates or isolates people, or that ultimately becomes a recruiting tool for terrorist organizations. Perhaps the two most well-known adherents to this policy are France and Turkey. As noted earlier in this chapter, the government of France has banned the wearing in public of *any* religious symbols, including headscarves by Islamic women, yarmulkes by Jewish men, or Christian crosses. Turkey has legally banned religious symbolism and the wearing of head cover since the founding of the modern Turkish state in 1923 by Mustafa Kamal Atatürk.

Establishment of truth and reconciliation commissions. In some countries, the sources of terrorism may be found in the atrocities recently committed (even rising to the level of genocide) but never officially acknowledged, much less redressed, by governments. Some successor governments have established truth and reconciliation commissions to investigate and make public what actually happened—and, it is hoped, bring the perpetrators to justice. The idea is to remove the events as a source of grievance for the wronged parties. Two well-known examples of countries that have used truth and reconciliation commissions successfully are Argentina—to investigate the "dirty war" carried out from 1976 to 1983; and Rwanda—to investigate and bring to justice the perpetrators of the 1994 genocide against the Tutsis.

Restrictions on communication and access to information from public sources. One of the principal ways in which terrorist groups communicate with each other and plan their attacks, especially since they discovered their use of land-based telephone lines and cell phones was being monitored, is the Internet and e-mail. Apparently, terrorist groups have mastered sophisticated techniques to encrypt e-mail communications to "embed" secret communications in publicly available Web sites, and to use information widely available via the Internet to select the targets for their attacks and to plan the logistics. The United States and some other countries have now begun to monitor Web sites aggressively and to take measures to deny—or at least degrade—access to those people engaged in facilitating terrorism. This is a difficult task, however, because Web sites discovered and shut down can be replaced almost instantaneously. Since September 11, 2001, the United States also has taken steps to remove from government Web sites any information that might be useful to terrorists either in designing weapons or in planning attacks on specific targets. But many Web sites that contain information are not under the purview of the government.

Increased domestic surveillance. In countries such as the United Kingdom, where terrorist threats and attacks have been a way of life for decades, the government has resorted increasingly to video surveillance,[11] along with aggressive internal intelligence, to monitor the whereabouts and movements of known or suspected terrorists and to provide investigators with rapid and reliable evidence in the wake of a terrorist attack. Such video footage was used to good effect, for example, in the case of the terrorist bombing of the London Transport system in 2005, and again in 2007 in the failed car bombings in London and Glasgow, Scotland. One school of thought maintains that, except in situations in which terrorists are determined to commit suicide in executing their attack, the perpetrators of terrorist attacks generally want to escape capture for their act in order to live to fight another day. Thus the knowledge that most high-value targets are monitored by video cameras is thought to serve at least as a partial deterrent. That said, there is obviously no substitute for intelligence gathering, which normally involves following suspected perpetrators or staking out suspected targets. But this approach works only if the perpetrator or the target is known, which frequently is not the case when it comes to terrorist organizations.

Restrictions on internal movements within a country. Some of the countries that have been the frequent targets of terrorist attacks, especially those involving suicide bombings, have established mobile internal checkpoints within their borders that can be and are moved without notice. The logic of this approach is that the more screenings a would-be terrorist must endure, especially if the screens are established outside or away from high-value targets and urban areas, the greater the likelihood that the perpetrator will be discovered and neutralized before reaching the intended target. Since the onset of the Second Intifada in 2000, Israel has had great success to the use of moveable internal checkpoints. This tactic also was used by the British in Northern Ireland to deal with IRA terrorism, and more recently by the U.S. and coalition forces in Iraq and Afghanistan with more mixed results.

Border controls and restrictions on visas and immigration. For countries adjoining large oceans—the United States, Canada, Australia, and Japan are examples—border controls may be at least partially effective in preventing would-be terrorists from entering their territory. Controls on entry typically include visa requirements, forgery-resistant passports, and, increasingly, the use of biometric indicators such as fingerprinting and iris scans. As discussed further in Chapter 8, controls also are being imposed on cargo—especially shipping containers—destined for the United States (and some other countries) in an attempt to prevent a nuclear device or other mass-casualty weapon from being shipped covertly into the country. In the many countries that have common land borders, including the member states of the European Union, it is far easier for dangerous cargo and people to move without detection.

Complete suppression through aggressive intelligence and police action. Many states have responded to terrorism carried out within their borders by domestic elements by attempting to suppress, and if possible destroy, the perpetrators and their organizations. These efforts have achieved varying degrees of success. It has depended largely on the effectiveness of the central government and the extent to which it can mount successful domestic intelligence and police or military action and control its borders so that terrorists cannot escape or operate from an adjoining country. The government of Colombia, for example, has tried for many years to capture or otherwise destroy the leadership of FARC, but so far it has failed to do so, perhaps because the central government often has been politically weak and unable to project its police or military power into the remote rural areas where FARC operates. By contrast, the government of Saudi Arabia has achieved notable success in identifying and destroying al Qaeda cells operating within the kingdom, in part by arresting clerics that give sanctuary to the terrorists. At the present time, the weak central government of Afghanistan is struggling, even with the help of North Atlantic Treaty Organization (NATO) forces, to prevent the resurgence of the Taliban, which is able to operate with impunity from sanctuaries in the remote western provinces of neighboring Pakistan.

Direct engagement with terrorist organizations. Most often, the preferred approach for any government facing terrorist threats or attacks is to engage the terrorist organization in direct talks with the hope of eventually drawing them into the mainstream political process. Unfortunately, direct negotiation has been established and implemented successfully in only a few instances. Perhaps the most well-known success is the long effort to convince the Irish Republican Army and its political arm, Sinn Fein, to fully "decommission" its weapons and permanently abandon the use of terrorist tactics. This effort is now well advanced; the IRA announced in July 2005 that it was formally renouncing violence and would henceforth work through the political process. Other attempts at direct negotiation—for example, between the Spanish government and the Basque separatist group ETA and between the government of Sri Lanka and the Tamil Tigers—have been episodic and ultimately unsuccessful. (See Case Study 3.3.)

External Responses to Terrorism

Beyond the responses that individual governments have fashioned within their own borders, a variety of measures have been pursued by governments, both bilaterally and multilaterally, through the United Nations and other international nongovernmental organizations. Some of the more significant examples are described in this section.

Cultural and educational exchanges. Many people believe that terrorism, and the hatred that motivates it, is largely the result of negative cultural and political stereotyping and the enormous amount of hate-filled propaganda that is propagated through the Internet and other media channels. One way to overcome such profound misunderstandings is by increasing the public's exposure to the culture and people of the adversary. This strategy has been tried many times, with varying degrees of success, by both governments and NGOs. The Fulbright Scholars program, which is partially financed by the U.S. government, is an example of a long-standing effort to place U.S. students and faculties in foreign countries and bring foreign scholars to the United States. One example of a privately financed cultural exchange designed, in part, to reduce some of the misunderstanding and hatred between the Israeli and Palestinian peoples is the symphony orchestra directed by the internationally acclaimed conductor Daniel Barenboim and made up of young Palestinian and Israeli musicians.

Public diplomacy. The term *public diplomacy* refers to the effort to organize and disseminate information and positive messages in support of diplomatic objectives. In the view of many critics, the failure of the United States to counter the negative publicity associated with the invasion of Iraq (including the abuses at Abu Ghraib prison) and other actions taken since the September attacks—again, much of it disseminated as hate-filled propaganda through the Internet—has greatly exacerbated the terrorist threat to the United States. The problem was considered sufficiently important that the U.S. Department of State decided to establish a senior position of under secretary of state for public diplomacy and public affairs. And yet many analysts believe that the U.S. government is still doing a poor job of winning the hearts and minds of those in the Middle East and other regions where terrorist organizations operate and recruit new members.

Targeted bilateral foreign assistance. Another way to win hearts and minds, especially in the Islamic countries of the developing world, especially where al Qaeda and other terrorist groups are recruiting members, is carefully targeted programs of foreign assistance that contribute significantly toward improved living conditions and reducing poverty. Foreign aid is a controversial and often politicized instrument—at both the sending and receiving ends. But if it can be used, for example, to address the HIV/AIDS crisis or to bring potable drinking water or new roads to underdeveloped areas, it will demonstrate that the United States or other developed countries are not the "devils" they are portrayed to be in terrorist propaganda, thereby helping to counteract the steady drumbeat of attacks that drive people to support terrorist ideology.

Investment in infrastructure and economic development. A similar logic pertains to multilateral assistance provided through various UN agencies and to the low-interest or no-interest loans offered through the World Bank. Increasingly, large donors to multilateral development institutions, such as the United States, are pressing for these investments to be targeted wherever possible in ways that will address—and possibly ameliorate—some of the basic socioeconomic factors addressed earlier in this chapter that may prompt people to sympathize with those supporting terrorism.

Investment in the training of police, military, and intelligence personnel. One consistent pattern not only in the fight against Islamic terrorism but also in other, long-standing terrorist struggles is the ineffectiveness of police, intelligence, and military personnel in many countries, whether because of lack of training, lack of the right equipment and weapons, or lack of funding. Accordingly, the United States, Japan, and some western European governments have been offering special assistance to governments that have shown they lack the capacity to monitor terrorist activity within their borders or to suppress and destroy terrorist organizations or terrorist cells once identified. (Also see Chapter 8.) Pakistan is one example of a country in which there is substantial terrorist activity—including the harboring of foreign terrorist fighters (allegedly including Osama bin Laden and Ayman al-Zawahiri)—but the government appears either unwilling or unable to address the problem. The Pakistani case is complicated, however, by the ethnic and religious makeup of the country and by the remoteness and lack of law and order in its western provinces near the border with Afghanistan.

Disruption of terrorist financing and the movement of money and high-value goods. Since September 11, both individual countries and the United Nations have made ongoing efforts to restrict the ability of terrorist organizations to gain access to and move large amounts of cash to finance their attacks. This topic is discussed extensively in Chapter 8.

Economic and political sanctions against nations that support terrorism. When a state sponsor of terrorism can be identified, ample precedent exists for imposing bilateral and/or multilateral sanctions involving both restrictions on imports and exports and political penalties of various kinds. The objective of sanctions, which to be effective must be as fully multilateral as possible, is to create conditions in which the costs of directly sponsoring or otherwise supporting terrorism outweigh the benefits to be derived by not doing so. The sanctions imposed on the Libyan government of

Box 3.1   **Public Diplomacy as a Response to Terrorism**

The United States has a serious image problem. Attitude polls and media surveys of the world's diverse Arab and Muslim nations indicate that their publics think the United States is anti-Islam, that it conspires to keep Arabs and Muslims disunited and weak, and that it supports any injustice if it furthers American political and economic interests (especially oil). In fact, public opinion of the United States has fallen in almost every nation since 2001.

Traditional diplomacy consists of government-to-government relations and interactions, such as trade negotiations. It generally has a minimal impact on public opinion, and it often takes place behind closed doors. By contrast, public diplomacy is the process of a government engaging the public of another country. This kind of diplomacy takes a long-term perspective and encompasses a wide range of activities, including educational and cultural exchanges, sports, targeted radio programs in multiple languages, and information campaigns abroad in the hope of building an intercultural understanding. In this way, governments can gauge foreign culture and attitudes, learn what shapes them, and use this information to inform and influence foreign publics to support policies favorable to the nation engaging them. Ideally, public diplomacy helps traditional diplomacy formulate and articulate policies that will garner the support of—or, at least, less criticism from—foreign publics. Although enhanced intercultural understanding can serve multiple policies, in the field of counterterrorism it is a crucial way of limiting the influence of terrorist groups.

Public diplomacy gained credibility and acceptance as a foreign policy tool during World War II. When the Nazis and Soviets began to broadcast their radio programs in other languages to attract international support, the United States and Britain funded their own counterpropaganda efforts for this purpose. Radio Free Europe, which was established later (during the Cold War) by the United States, provided information to people living under Soviet censorship. Many analysts believed it was the key to extending Western influence and contributing to the fall of the Soviet Union. During the Cold War, the Soviet Union and the United States honed deep understandings of the language and culture of each other in order to develop a rapport with each other's public. During this period, the United States established the U.S. Information Agency (USIA), which created and implemented a long-term public diplomacy strategy.

Public diplomacy can facilitate counterterrorism efforts in two interrelated ways: first, it can build support for the United States, and second, it can reduce the attractiveness of terrorism to potential supporters and terrorists. After the Cold War ended, U.S. public diplomacy efforts did not keep pace with the country's technological, economic, political, cultural, and military growth. Indeed, public diplomacy has always struggled to find a permanent home in the U.S. government. In 1999 USIA was merged with the State Department, where it lost influence and resources. Meanwhile, its radio outreach programs continued to operate independently. By September 11, 2001, the world had

continues . . .

changed, but American public diplomacy capabilities and priorities remained outdated and diminished. With the onset of the information age, more people around the world had access to a variety of news and other resources, and therefore were more aware of international affairs and how to exchange information. As post–9/11 U.S. foreign policy took shape, the government realized it lacked the long-term structures necessary to launch a diplomatic effort to address terrorism issues.

In 2002 the Bush administration made permanent the Office of Global Communications, a once-temporary unit used to troubleshoot foreign public opinion issues during wartime. Analysts and policy makers began to refer increasingly to the need to win the war of ideas against al Qaeda and to win over the hearts and minds of the foreign public. The State Department's Office of Public Diplomacy also was expanded, and briefly attracted a public relations executive, Charlotte Beers, as its under secretary. (She left after seventeen months, and her successor left a mere six months later.) The same year, Congress allocated funds for a radio station, later called Radio Sawa, to broadcast throughout the Middle East and Central Asia, and in 2004 a television station, Alhurra, was also established. The potential radio audience alone was estimated at as many as 99 million listeners ages fifteen to thirty-four, and the combination of Western and Middle Eastern music and pro-American news attracted an audience—albeit a skeptical one. By contrast, Television Alhurra faces stiff competition in a saturated market—including from al Jazeera, which had already captured a large share of the news market in the region from CNN and the BBC by presenting information with a pro-Arab, pro-Islamic slant—and its prospects are therefore dim. Both stations have been criticized for not being able to measure or demonstrate whether they have achieved their mission of countering biases that the United States perceives in the Arab world's news media.

The State Department thus has struggled to regain its footing in the public diplomacy world. Experts agree that it was ill-prepared to handle the increased demands of a global fight against terrorism, lacking in resources and expertise. In 2002 the department produced videos, pamphlets, booklets, and other materials, including an advertising campaign intended for broadcast in Muslim countries depicting religious tolerance and thriving Muslims in the United States—but it showed a shorts-clad woman jogging. Several Arab nations refused to run the TV ads, and they were discontinued after they failed to resonate with Jordanian focus groups. Some of the pamphlets also received negative media attention, such as one that used a photograph of lead September 11 hijacker Mohammed Atta, accompanied by descriptions of Zacharias Moussaoui, the "twentieth hijacker." The Office of Public Diplomacy was forced to divert its resources to damage control, and critics allege that the United States has yet to recover the credibility lost from these blunders. In 2005 President Bush tapped his longtime aide and former White House counselor Karen Hughes to be the new under secretary for public diplomacy at the State Department. The greater influence and funding at its disposal offered a new

continues . . .

lease on life to an area of U.S. foreign policy that, by most accounts, cannot afford to fail.

The Department of Defense has not been without its critics as well. In 2002 the Pentagon was assailed for a series of fliers it dropped over Afghanistan, depicting dead people in turbans (presumably supporters of the Taliban) and an altered photograph of Osama bin Laden in a Western suit with the caption "Osama bin Laden, the murderer and coward, has abandoned you." Experts pointed out that this tactic was both ineffective and offensive, because the altering of a photograph and the use of graphic imagery could elicit mistrust among flier recipients. Even the Department of Defense itself has faced a massive public diplomacy challenge. According to observers, stories such as the prisoner abuse scandal at Abu Ghraib, the treatment of detainees at Bagram and Guantánamo Bay, and the abuse of the Qur'an at Guantánamo have all served to undermine foreign public support of the United States. The department did create the Iraqi Media Network to broadcast messages from the Coalition Provisional Authority to the Iraqi public after the United States invaded Iraq, but it mainly reported news and held press conferences; it did little to manage scandals.

For many Americans, the knee-jerk reaction to news stories about the low esteem in which the United States is held in the Islamic world and elsewhere was once "Who cares? We're far more powerful." But the consensus is growing among policy makers and analysts and thoughtful people among the general public that foreign attitudes and understanding are a significant strategic concern, because they can have a major impact on the success or failure of U.S. initiatives overseas. This consensus is especially relevant to U.S. counterterrorism strategies, which have thus far been unable to defeat terrorism militarily.

- Does it matter what people in the Islamic world and elsewhere think of the United States, or does U.S. military and economic power make this concern irrelevant?

- How can it be that the country that invented public relations and commercial product advertising is unable to create a consistent, positive message to convey to the rest of the world?

- Because al Qaeda is known to be using the Internet to disseminate hate-filled propaganda and to recruit new members, should the United States be making a concerted effort to issue counterpropaganda (much as it did during World War II) also via the Internet?

Muammar al-Qaddafi as a result of the 1988 bombing of Pan Am Flight 103 over Lockerbie, Scotland, that killed 270 people are described in detail in Chapter 8.

Covert and overt military action against terrorist organizations. After the attacks of September 11, 2001, President George W. Bush announced the launch of a global war on terrorism, and authorized a U.S. military invasion that succeeded in driving the Taliban and al Qaeda out of Afghanistan. It failed, however, to result in the capture of Osama bin Laden or his top lieutenants. Later, in 2003, the United States invaded Iraq. A variety of justifications were offered for the invasion, ultimately including the prevention of further terrorism. Direct military action against global terrorism well predated the Bush administration, however, and it has taken a variety of forms, including standoff attacks using cruise missiles and other air assets; full-scale frontal military assaults using large numbers of ground forces, tanks, and artillery; and surgical attacks and low-intensity operations, often carried out covertly by special forces or intelligence operatives. These actions historically have achieved uneven success, although the remarkable accomplishments of the relatively small numbers of U.S. special forces in Afghanistan are certainly worthy of note. Further details on military responses to terrorism can be found in Chapter 10 of this volume.

CASE STUDY 3.3

Negotiating Directly with a Terrorist Organization:
The Government of Sri Lanka and the Tamil Tigers

For more than two decades, Sri Lanka, a nation of roughly twenty million on an island slightly larger than West Virginia, has been fighting a civil war with the terrorist group Liberation Tigers of Tamil Eelam (LTTE). Best known for inventing the tactic of suicide bombing, LTTE uses both conventional warfare and terrorism to pursue its goals of self-rule and government for Sri Lanka's Tamil minority. Over sixty thousand people died and more than a million were displaced in the conflict during the 1980s and 1990s, and the violence continues, despite a negotiated ceasefire in 2002.

In the early twentieth century, British colonial rule of Sri Lanka exacerbated long-standing ethnic tensions between the Tamils, who practice Hinduism, and the Buddhist Sinhalese majority. The Tamils are the largest ethnic group in northern and southern Sri Lanka, but after independence in 1948 they faced institutional discrimination and political disenfranchisement. Initially, the Tamils formed political parties to advocate for the creation of an autonomous Tamil state, but when Buddhism was declared Sri Lanka's national religion in 1972, a younger generation of more radical Tamils emerged and formed the radical Tamil New Tigers Party. In 1975 the group initiated a campaign of relatively low-intensity violence against policemen and politicians; the next year it gave up its party affiliations and became the LTTE. In 1983 the LTTE ambushed a military patrol, killing thirteen soldiers in the north of Sri Lanka in what came to be known as the first battle of Sri Lanka's civil war. Anti-Tamil riots broke out, leading to the deaths of several hundred Tamils and more fighting between the Sri Lankan military and the LTTE in the north. In July 1985, the LTTE gunned down 146 Sinhalese at a holy Buddhist site, signaling that its targets had expanded to include innocent civilians.

Although numerous Tamil liberation organizations were in existence in the early 1980s, LTTE's extreme indoctrination practices and the political leverage it gained from suicide bombings allowed it to eliminate competing liberation groups and gain the de facto support of the Tamil population. The LTTE benefited from a steady stream of volunteers from this population, who faced persecution and retribution from the Sri Lankan government and Sinhalese mobs.

LTTE members are known for their discipline and devotion to the organization's cause, and they are famous for the cyanide capsules they reportedly wear around their necks to avoid being captured alive. LTTE's force is estimated at ten thousand men and women, who are trained in the use of artillery, surface-to-air missiles, and rocket launchers. The LTTE also recruits underage children to fight. The organization's elite wing of suicide terrorists is called the Black Tigers; in 1984 it established a naval wing called the Sea Tigers.

The LTTE's international wing is responsible for raising funds from the Tamil diaspora in Europe, Asia, and North America. The LTTE also has used extortion, fraud, and money laundering to generate economic resources. In its spending, the LTTE has been linked to the purchase of sophisticated weaponry from countries in the former Soviet Union and the capture of large quantities of weapons from Sri Lankan security forces. Until 1987 the LTTE received material support from the Indian state of Tamil Nadu, and some analysts claim that India's national intelligence agency also has provided training and arms. In recent years, however, many nations have classified the group as a terrorist organization, which will likely restrict its fund-raising abilities.

The LTTE has proved itself to be a formidable adversary for the Sri Lankan military, whom it engages in military battles in northern and eastern Sri Lanka. Although boundaries often shift, the LTTE-controlled territory in the Jaffna district of Sri Lanka has become the de facto Tamil state. The group is blamed for the ethnic cleansing of Jaffna, including the expulsion of its entire Muslim population in 1990. After the LTTE assassinated former Indian prime minister Rajiv Gandhi by suicide bomb in 1991, India became the first nation to ban the LTTE as a terrorist organization. Throughout the 1990s, the LTTE carried out a series of devastating suicide bombings in the nation's capital, Colombo, killing civilians and politicians and putting pressure on Sri Lanka's democratic processes.

Repeated attempts have been made to negotiate a peaceful solution to this conflict, including rounds of peace talks in 1985, 1989–1990, and

1994. In 2000 the International Red Cross in Sri Lanka was able to secure an agreement to enable the movement of civilians in the northern war zone. Two years later, with Norway acting as a mediator, the government and the LTTE negotiated an open-ended ceasefire agreement, but stalling on both sides and political turmoil in the Sri Lankan government have all but officially ended the initiative. Many observers believed the December 2004 tsunami disaster would be a unifying force for Sri Lanka, but the LTTE alleged that the government withheld the distribution of international aid to Tamil areas. In spite of a 2006 reconfirmation of the ceasefire, escalating violence between the two sides resulted in the deaths of hundreds of people, indicating that the agreement has allowed both sides the opportunity to regain their strength and resume hostilities.

The LTTE's struggle against the government of Sri Lanka is noteworthy for three reasons. First, as noted earlier, the separatist group is generally credited with inventing the tactic of suicide bombing—a phenomenon that U.S. soldiers have become all too familiar with in Iraq and Afghanistan. Second, this conflict is unusual in that, apparently with substantial success, terrorist tactics and strategy have been combined with the more traditional military approaches, which have even included naval engagements. Finally, the LTTE case provides demonstrable evidence of how difficult it is to negotiate an end to a long-standing struggle involving the use of terrorism.   ■

Conclusion

This chapter has examined a wide range of the causes or sources of terrorism—that is, the conditions or circumstances that drive people to engage in or support the use of violence to achieve political, socioeconomic, or cultural change. It also has considered a range of policies that governments, intergovernmental organizations, and NGOs have adopted in response to terrorism. The question, however, is whether the responses to terrorism—both those already implemented and those proposed—actually address the root causes that have been identified here. For example, do they address the sense of rage and humiliation expressed today by many young people in the Islamic world, especially in the countries of the Middle East? Do they ameliorate peoples' perceived sense of violation when Western cultures penetrate traditional, conservative, non-Western societies? Are they perceived as addressing in any meaningful way the underlying poverty, lack of economic development, political corruption, and authoritarian rule that characterizes so much of the world in which terrorism breeds and terrorist groups organize and train? And, ultimately, to what degree are the more punitive responses to terrorism (including military action) actually likely to prevent or significantly reduce the likelihood of additional attacks in the future—or do they sometimes have the *opposite* effect by radicalizing even more people in the affected country or region and driving them to support, or at least condone, further terrorist violence? These are among the questions that the informed reader should be asking.

FOR FURTHER READING

Anonymous (Michael Schauer). *Imperial Hubris: Why the West Is Losing the War on Terror*. Washington, D.C.: Brassey's, 2004.

Benjamin, Daniel, and Steven Simon. *The Next Attack: The Failure of the War on Terror and a Strategy for Getting It Right*. New York: Times Books, Henry Holt, 2005.

Huntington, Samuel P. *The Clash of Civilizations and the Remaking of World Order*. New York: Simon and Schuster, 1996.

Chapter 4 Preventing Terrorism: Interdiction and Investigation

Early on September 11, 2001, Mohammed Atta and Abdul Aziz al Omari headed for the Portland, Maine, airport to catch their 6 a.m. flight to Boston and then a connecting flight to Los Angeles. When he checked in for his flight, Atta was selected by the Computer Assisted Passenger Prescreening System (CAPPS) for special security measures. As a result, his checked bags were held until he was aboard the flight. Once in Boston, Atta and al Omari and the eight others who joined them there checked in for their two different flights to Los Angeles. All ten passed through security checkpoints, where they were screened by metal detectors calibrated to detect items with at least the metal content of a .22-caliber handgun. Apparently, at least a few of the men carried box cutters or pocket utility knives, which in those days were permitted on flights.

At about the same time, five colleagues of the Boston travelers checked in at Dulles Airport in Washington for still another flight bound for Los Angeles. CAPPS selected two of the four, brothers, for additional screening. One had no photo identification and spoke no English, and the other struck the airline customer service representative as suspicious. As in Portland, their bags were held until they boarded the flight. Because several of the Dulles travelers set off the metal detectors, they were hand-wanded by security personnel before being passed through security. Four other men checked in for another flight bound to Los Angeles from Newark Airport at about the same time, and they had similar check-in and security experiences.

These nineteen men together boarded four transcontinental flights. They planned to commandeer the planes and turn them into missiles, each loaded with as much as 11,400 gallons of jet fuel. By 8 a.m. on September 11, these hijackers had overcome all the security measures that U.S. civil aviation had in place to prevent a hijacking.

The missed opportunities to learn about the September 11 hijackers and analyze their activities before they could carry out their plot have been examined at length in efforts to improve the ways in which the United States protects itself against terrorism. But the task is daunting. How can this or any other nation anticipate terrorism? Protecting against terrorism involves the use of programs and methods to interdict terrorists and their means of attack, as well as an array of investigative tools used to collect information about terrorists and their plans before those plans become operational. This chapter describes and assesses interdiction and intelligence as techniques for preventing terrorism. The sections on these topics illustrate the challenges that terrorists' efforts at evasion and their tendencies to operate in difficult-to-detect cellular structures pose to those trying to mount successful programs. The third and fourth sections of this chapter examine how government should organize itself to prevent terrorism, and how information collected in combating terrorism is shared with other agencies and governments. A brief final section reviews the problems of interdiction and intelligence collection abroad and how other nations manage these same tasks.

Interdiction

Apart from eliminating its root causes, the best way to combat terrorism is to prevent it before it occurs. In the United States and in most other organized societies, criminal laws and their enforcement provide a logical preventive. The punishment and incarceration of those who commit crimes are intended, in part, to deter others, discourage repeat offenders, and reduce the number of people in the community who are likely to commit crimes. (See Chapter 5 for an exploration of law enforcement in combating terrorism.)

Deterrence in Theory and Practice

Deterrence theory often breaks down in combating terrorism, however, because those most likely to carry out terrorist attacks are not likely to be deterred by the conventional social pressure to conform or fear of criminal punishment. Despite these shortcomings, one U.S. counterterrorism strategy has been to develop legislation and law enforcement programs dedicated to catching and punishing would-be terrorists before they strike, on the theory that interdiction of these early-stage crimes may, over time, deter future terrorism. (See Chapter 5.)

At the other extreme, deterrence could be enhanced by adopting policies of retaliation—that is, punishing terrorists after they strike by supporting their domestic opponents, for example, or by targeting their families for abduction or even lethal force. Experience has shown, however, that such policies may backfire. For example, when the Palestinian group Hamas began suicide attacks against Israelis soon after the Oslo peace accords were signed in 1993, Israel countered with an aggressive response. Within a few months, Israeli commandos had successfully killed the Palestinian leaders who were believed to be directly responsible for planning suicide operations. But, instead of generalized deterrence, the Israeli response to Palestinian terrorism created martyrs and generated new recruits for suicide bombings directed at Israeli targets. Hamas bombers struck five times in two weeks and killed fifty-nine Israelis. Their success not only affected the national elections in Israel in 1996, but also effectively sidelined the peace process that had been begun by Israeli prime minister Yitzhak Rabin, who was assassinated in 1995.

Deterrence is also complicated by the difficulties in attributing terrorist attacks to an identifiable group or state. After an attack takes place against the United States, attribution is normally possible through conducting good police work and collecting evidence. But sometimes even good police work does not lead to the perpetrators of terrorism. One vivid example is the six-year-old investigation of the 2001 anthrax letter attacks on government leaders in Washington that killed five people, injured several others, and closed down four public buildings for extended periods. Those simple letters caused widespread fear and panic and imposed decontamination costs in the neighborhood of more than $1 billion. In 2006 the investigation went cold, and since then no credible leads have emerged. The early arrest of Dr. Steven J. Hatfill, a bioweapons expert, proved to be a false start. Hatfill is now pursuing a lawsuit against the United States and several journalists who revealed his name as a suspect in the investigations.

With threats of terrorism, even highly credible threats, it is not always so easy to identify the perpetrators in order to activate deterrence measures. And in situations in which the threat is believed to be state-sponsored, deterrence is complicated by the calculus of determining whether taking hostile action against that state will produce unacceptable responses, or whether the United States is willing to act against a state with which it is otherwise friendly.

Another reason the United States does not rely on law enforcement methods and processes alone to stop terrorism is that, even if the threat of criminal punishment were to deter some would-be terrorists, the harm caused by even a single terrorist incident could be so grave that society would not accept an approach that simply seeks to arrest, prosecute, and incarcerate those responsible for violent terrorist attacks. Effective prevention must, then, be broadened to include other ways to stop terrorism before it happens. Broad strategic prevention policies must be shaped, and implementation of those policies must be managed, by those parts of government capable of paying careful attention to the tactical details of staying on top of the terrorist threat.

Stopping Terrorists before They Strike

In its purest form, interdiction permits isolating a known terrorist from a potential target, thwarting the operational plans for an attack, finding all the operatives and their supporters, and arresting and prosecuting the suspects. Successes have included the following:

- The group responsible for the 1993 World Trade Center bombing was prevented from implementing its plan to destroy other New York City landmarks, as well as its plan to assassinate Egyptian president Hosni Mubarak.
- Working with foreign counterparts, U.S. investigators disrupted a bomb plot in 1995 that, if carried out, would have resulted in the destruction of a dozen U.S. commercial jumbo jets flying Asian-Pacific routes.

- U.S. law enforcement officials arrested in 1999 a suspect who attempted to enter the United States from Canada with powerful explosives and timing devices, from which he intended to manufacture a bomb that would have been detonated at Los Angeles International Airport.

Additional successful interdiction efforts are described in a fact sheet distributed by the White House in October 2005 and reproduced in Box 4.1.

Box 4.1 **Fact Sheet: Plots, Casings, and Infiltrations Referenced in President Bush's Remarks on the War on Terror**

Overall, the United States and our partners have disrupted at least ten serious al-Qaida terrorist plots since September 11—including three al-Qaida plots to attack inside the United States. We have stopped at least five more al-Qaida efforts to case targets in the United States or infiltrate operatives into our country.

10 Plots

1. The West Coast Airliner Plot: In mid-2002 the U.S. disrupted a plot to attack targets on the West Coast of the United States using hijacked airplanes. The plotters included at least one major operational planner involved in planning the events of 9/11.

2. The East Coast Airliner Plot: In mid-2003 the U.S. and a partner disrupted a plot to attack targets on the East Coast of the United States using hijacked commercial airplanes.

3. The Jose Padilla Plot: In May 2002 the U.S. disrupted a plot that involved blowing up apartment buildings in the United States. One of the plotters, Jose Padilla, also discussed the possibility of using a "dirty bomb" in the U.S.

4. The 2004 UK Urban Targets Plot: In mid-2004 the U.S. and partners disrupted a plot that involved urban targets in the United Kingdom. These plots involved using explosives against a variety of sites.

5. The 2003 Karachi Plot: In the Spring of 2003 the U.S. and a partner disrupted a plot to attack Westerners at several targets in Karachi, Pakistan.

6. The Heathrow Airport Plot: In 2003 the U.S. and several partners disrupted a plot to attack Heathrow Airport using hijacked commercial airliners. The planning for this attack was undertaken by a major 9/11 operational figure.

7. The 2004 UK Plot: In the Spring of 2004 the U.S. and partners, using a combination of law enforcement and intelligence resources, disrupted a plot to conduct large-scale bombings in the UK.

8. The 2002 Arabian Gulf Shipping Plot: In late 2002 and 2003 the U.S. and a partner nation disrupted a plot by al-Qa'ida operatives to attack ships in the Arabian Gulf.

continues . . .

9. The 2002 Straits of Hormuz Plot: In 2002 the U.S. and partners disrupted a plot to attack ships transiting the Straits of Hormuz.

10. The 2003 Tourist Site Plot: In 2003 the U.S. and a partner nation disrupted a plot to attack a tourist site outside the United States.

5 Casings and Infiltrations

1. The U.S. Government & Tourist Sites Tasking: In 2003 and 2004, an individual was tasked by al-Qa'ida to case important U.S. Government and tourist targets within the United States.

2. The Gas Station Tasking: In approximately 2003, an individual was tasked to collect targeting information on U.S. gas stations and their support mechanisms on behalf of a senior al-Qa'ida planner.

3. Lyman Faris & the Brooklyn Bridge: In 2003, and in conjunction with a partner nation, the U.S. government arrested and prosecuted Lyman Faris, who was exploring the destruction of the Brooklyn Bridge in New York. Faris ultimately pleaded guilty to providing material support to al-Qa'ida and is now in a federal correctional institution.

4. 2001 Tasking: In 2001, al-Qa'ida sent an individual to facilitate post-September 11 attacks in the U.S. U.S. law enforcement authorities arrested the individual.

5. 2003 Tasking: In 2003, an individual was tasked by an al-Qa'ida leader to conduct reconnaissance on populated areas in the U.S.[a]

Other successes in preventing terrorist attacks necessarily remain secret because of ongoing investigations or to protect the identity of the sources or methods used in exposing the plots.

- What problems are posed by the widespread use of terrorist interdiction techniques?

- Should Americans sacrifice some portion of their liberties for the security promised by these efforts?

---

[a] Entire text taken from White House, "Fact Sheet: Plots, Casings, and Infiltrations Referenced in President Bush's Remarks on the War on Terror," www.whitehouse.gov/news/releases/2005/10/20051006-7.html.

There have not been many more successes beyond the ones described here, at least in part because information about terrorist attack plans is rarely concrete and specific enough to disable discrete attacks. One exception, albeit one that did not deter any intended terrorist act, occurred in 2002 when U.S. intelligence agencies received word that a North Korean ship, the *So San,* was transporting missiles from North Korea to an undetermined destination. After monitoring the movement of the *So San* for some days, the U.S. Navy asked a Spanish warship in the area to intercept the *So San* and then deploy personnel to board the vessel while on the high seas some six hundred miles off the coast of Yemen. The Spanish naval commander agreed to cooperate with the United States, and, after the North Korean ship tried to evade capture, two Spanish ships in the area fired warning shots across its bow. When the *So San* continued to flee, the frigate *Navarra* deployed by helicopter a boarding team of Spanish marines, who later were joined by U.S. Navy personnel. Together, they placed the crew under guard and searched the *So San,* where they discovered fifteen North Korea–made unassembled Scud missiles and their components, hidden beneath the declared cargo of the vessel. After a request from the government of Yemen, the purchaser of the missiles, the ship and its cargo were eventually released. The United States acquiesced in the Yemeni government's transaction because, in an agreement, Yemen pledged to the United States that it would use the missiles only for defensive purposes, and that it would not acquire the components of weapons of mass destruction. In addition, there was no evidence that the Yemenis intended to use the missiles for WMD delivery or for any other illicit purpose. The fact is, however, that the transaction was consummated before the new agreement, and the United States did not want to dissuade the Yemenis from future cooperation in combating international terrorism. Even though the transaction was completed, the interdiction demonstrated that intelligence assets could detect, locate, and follow shipments of possible delivery vehicles for mass-casualty weapons at sea, over long distances. Detecting the mass-casualty weapons themselves presents additional challenges. (See Case Study 4.1.)

Interdiction through "Pre-Crime" Arrests?

The more likely interdiction scenario occurs where intelligence indicates that U.S. embassies or interests in a certain region are likely to be hit. Or Internet chatter may suggest that a traveling diplomat will be kidnapped, but there is no indication of which traveler, where, or when. Intelligence in these instances at the strategic level might be good—that is, information about the general level and sources of the threat—but specific information, or tactical intelligence, has usually not been available.

More terrorist attacks could be prevented if officials were able to arrest or detain those persons who are the subjects of even an uncorroborated tip or nonspecific threat information. Although officials would surely make many mistakes—arresting or detaining those who have done nothing wrong—this kind of "pre-crime" prevention strategy would surely prevent some terrorist activities.

In the film version of Philip K. Dick's short story "The Minority Report," government officials believe that they have found the ultimate form of preventive law enforcement. Relying on the visions of a trio of seemingly unerring psychics, police are able, without fail, to detect crime before it occurs. Sometimes, officials can even detect the crime and detain the perpetrator even before he begins to contemplate the actions that would lead to the criminal conduct. What author Dick calls "pre-crime" is thus the perfect realization of a law enforcement dream—all criminal harms (even terrorism) are avoided, and no persons are wrongly accused. As actor Tom Cruise dramatically demonstrates in the film version, however, the psychics are fallible, their predictions can be wrong, and the risk of falsely accusing those who are innocent of criminal wrongdoing cannot be so easily avoided.

In the United States and in many other nations, traditional civil liberties protections written into law limit the potential effectiveness of this form of interdiction, because the law requires that there be "probable cause" or some other measurable degree of targeted suspicion that the suspect has committed or will soon commit a crime before an arrest can be made. And, if arrested, the suspect cannot be detained beyond the time needed for trial. In the United States, immigration law authorities have been used, particularly since September 11, to detain or remove or deny entry at U.S. borders to those suspected of involvement in terrorist activities. More generally, intelligence efforts have been enhanced to gather information about potential terrorist attacks, thereby enabling greater prevention.

Interdiction through Profiling?

Another vexing problem in setting and implementing policies to interdict terrorism occurs when officials select for screening or some other special scrutiny persons of certain racial or ethnic groups because they fit a profile of terrorist suspects. Aside from the inevitable false positives problem (singling out those who are innocent) that arises in any program that engages in profiling, the persons so targeted may reasonably believe that the government has engaged in unlawful discrimination against them because officials have made an assumption about their proclivities toward terrorist acts based simply on their race or ethnicity, not on individualized grounds for suspicion. With that in mind, the U.S. Department of Justice offered this guidance to federal law enforcement agencies:

> In making routine or spontaneous law enforcement decisions, such as ordinary traffic stops, Federal law enforcement officers may not use race or ethnicity to any degree, except that officers may rely on race and ethnicity in a specific suspect description. . . .
>
> In conducting activities in connection with a specific investigation, Federal law enforcement officers may consider race and ethnicity only to the extent that there is trustworthy information, relevant to the locality or time frame, that links persons of a particular race or ethnicity to an identified criminal incident, scheme, or organization. . . .
>
> In investigating or preventing threats to national security or other catastrophic events (including the performance of duties related to air trans-

portation security), or in enforcing laws protecting the integrity of the Nation's borders, Federal law enforcement officers may not consider race or ethnicity except to the extent permitted by the Constitution and laws of the United States.[1]

How might this guidance be applied to a concrete example? Suppose the FBI learns that persons affiliated with a foreign ethnic terrorist group plan to use suicide bombers to assassinate their country's president during a visit to the United States. Should federal law enforcement or intelligence personnel focus their attention on members of that ethnic group in the United States? If so, what scrutiny would be permissible? Consider these opposing views:

- "Young Muslim men bombed the London tube and attacked New York with planes in 2001. From everything we know about the terrorists who may be taking aim at our transportation system, they are most likely to be young Muslim men. Unfortunately, this demographic group won't be profiled. Instead, the authorities will be stopping Girl Scouts and grannies in a procedure that has more to do with demonstrating tolerance than with protecting citizens from terrorism. . . . [Profiling is] based on statistics. Insurance companies profile policyholders based on probability of risk. That's smart business. Likewise, profiling passengers based on proven security risk is just smart law enforcement." [2]
- "Look at the 9/11 hijackers. They came here. They shaved. They went to topless bars. They wanted to blend in. They wanted to look like they were part of the American dream. . . . Could a terrorist dress up as a Hasidic Jew and walk into the subway, and not be profiled? Yes. I think that profiling is just nuts." [3]

Chapter 1 introduced the moral and legal barriers to profiling for investigation, which are based on the premise that singling out suspects on racial or ethnic grounds conflicts with the norm that all persons should be treated with equal respect and concern. In addition, the experience gained from investigating terrorism has shown that racial profiling focuses on an "unstable" trait, one that can easily be switched. For example, in the 2005 London transit bombings the planners of the attack apparently recruited East Africans to carry the bombs because of local scrutiny of Arab and Pakistani men. Similarly, suicide bombers in Israel tended to be young, militant Muslim men, but now they include secular Palestinians, women, and teenage girls.

On the subject of profiling, New York City police commissioner Raymond Kelly has asked: "Whom do you profile? Forty percent of New Yorkers are born outside the US. Who am I supposed to profile?" [4] In fact, the use of profiling raises many questions: Is the use of race, color, nationality, or ethnic identity impermissible discrimination where there is solid evidence of disparate offending between racial or ethnic groups? Is there a difference between "statistical discrimination" and racial bigotry? Is there a significant difference from a policy point of view between schemes that use race or ethnic origin as part of a multipart profile and those that use race or ethnicity as the exclusive basis for the profile?

Technology-Based Interdiction

A variety of strategies are available for detecting terrorist activity before it occurs, including technology-based methods for gathering information. However, even though satellite images may reveal training camps or safe houses, they do not reveal what kind of training is under way in the camp or what objectives those receiving the training will pursue. In other words, the technology may provide useful information, but additional intelligence must be collected before an operation to combat the threat can be mounted. Even surreptitious electronic surveillance has limited utility, because terrorists are adept at evading these means of detection by using satellite phones or fax machines, or perhaps simply passing paper notes to one another. For example, Osama bin Laden reportedly stopped using cell phones and fax machines in late 2003 after al Qaeda operatives learned that technical intelligence collection devices were monitoring their communications. Techniques for gathering intelligence on terrorist activity are explored later in this chapter.

Interdiction by Designation

One preventive strategy practiced by the United States since statutory authority for the strategy was enacted in 1996 allows the secretary of state to designate an entity as a foreign terrorist organization (FTO). Once a group is so designated, any assets belonging to it inside the United States are frozen.[5] In addition, according to the statutory authority, members of the FTO are barred from entering the United States,[6] and all persons within the reach of U.S. law enforcement are forbidden from "knowingly providing material support or resources" to the FTO.[7] Violators are subject to lengthy prison terms. The secretary of state can designate an organization as an FTO if it engages in "terrorist activity" that "threatens the security of United States nationals or the national security of the United States."[8] Dozens of groups have been designated as FTOs over the last ten years. (See Table 4.1.) And although this deterrent by itself is hardly sufficient, the dire effects of designation may affect the behavior of some groups.

Regulating the Means of Attack

When interdiction cannot be accomplished directly by identifying terrorist suspects for arrest or detention, prevention efforts may require longer-term, ongoing efforts. One set of preventive measures is aimed at regulating or even

Table 4.1 U.S.-Designated Foreign Terrorist Organizations, as of October 2005

Name and base of operations	Description	Goals and targets	Estimated strength	Year founded	Alleged activities
Abu Nidal Organization (ANO), aka Fatah—Iraq	Transnational organization composed of functional committees	Targets U.S., UK, France, Israel, moderate Palestinians, the PLO, Arab countries	A few hundred	1974	Attacks in 20 countries, killing or injuring 900; leader Abu Nidal died in 2002.
Abu Sayyaf Group (ASG)—Philippines, Malaysia	Separatist group composed of several semiautonomous factions	Aims to create Islamic state in Philippines; profit-driven terrorism	200–500	1991	Kidnappings, bombings, assassinations, extortion
Al-Aqsa Martyrs Brigade—West Bank, Gaza Strip, Israel	Small cells of Fatah-affiliated activists	Aims to drive out Israelis and to establish a Palestinian state	Unknown	2000	Shootings, suicide operations (first Palestinian female suicide bombing)
Ansar al-Islam (AI)—Iraq	Iraqi Kurds and Arabs	Aims to create an Islamic state in Iraq; allied with al Qaeda	500–1,000	2001	Ambushes, attacks
Armed Islamic Group (GIA)—Algeria	Islamic extremists	Aims to replace Algerian regime with an Islamic state	Fewer than 100	1992	Massacred thousands of civilians; targeted foreigners
Asbat al-Ansar—Lebanon	Sunni extremist group associated with Osama bin Laden	Aims to create Islamic state; opposes peace with Israel	300	1990s	Assassinations, bombings of Western targets, failed coup
Aum Shinrikyo (Aum)—Japan, Russia	Cult established by Shoko Asahara	Claims U.S. will start World War III with Japan, beginning Armageddon	1,950	1987	Chemical attacks on Tokyo subways; no recent activity
Basque Fatherland and Liberty (ETA)— Spain, France	Group established to create an independent Basque homeland	Targets Spanish and French government interests, tourists	Unknown	1959	Since 1960, attacks in which more than 850 killed, hundreds injured

Table 4.1 U.S.-Designated Foreign Terrorist Organizations, as of October 2005 (continued)

Name and base of operations	Description	Goals and targets	Estimated strength	Year founded	Alleged activities
Communist Party of the Philippines/New People's Army (CPP/NPA)—Philippines	CPP's military wing, formed to overthrow the government through guerrilla warfare	Targets Philippine security forces, politicians, judges, government informers, NPA rebels	Fewer than 9,000	1969	Assassinations, murders, attacks on U.S. personnel and interests
Continuity Irish Republican Army (CIRA)—Northern Ireland, Irish Republic	Splinter group of IRA; also called Continuity Army Council and Republican Sinn Fein	Targets British military, Northern Ireland security forces, loyalist paramilitary groups	Fewer than 50	1990s	Bombings, assassinations, kidnappings, hijackings, extortion, robberies
Gama'a al-Islamiyya (Islamic Group, IG)—Egypt	Egypt's largest militant group now split into two factions, one calling for a cease-fire	Aims to replace Egypt's government with an Islamic state	Unknown	1973	1993 World Trade Center bombings, attacks on tourists
Hamas (Islamic Resistance Movement)—West Bank, Gaza Strip, Israel	Outgrowth of the Palestinian branch of the Muslim Brotherhood	Aims to replace Israel with Palestinian Islamic state using political and violent means	Unknown	1987	Large-scale suicide bombings and attacks against Israelis
Harakat ul-Mujahedin (HUM)—Pakistan	Islamic militant group aligned with the radical Jamiat Ulema-e-Islam-Fazlur (JUI-F) faction	Targets Indian troops, Kashmiri civilians, Western interests	Several hundred	1985	Linked to al Qaeda; hijacked Indian airliner in 1999
Hezbollah (Party of God)—Lebanon, worldwide cells	A radical Shiite group seeking to create an Iranian-style Islamic republic	Aims to eliminate Israel; is also anti-U.S.	A few hundred	1982	Suicide bombings, hijacked TWA Flight 847 in 1985; rocket attacks against Israel in 2006
Islamic Jihad Group (IJG)	Islamic militants active in Central Asia	Targets Americans and U.S. interests	A few hundred	2004	Bombing attacks

Name	Description	Aims	Strength	Year	Activities
Islamic Movement of Uzbekistan (IMU)—South Asia, Tajikistan, Iran	Islamic militants opposed to Uzbekistani president Islom Karimov's secular regime	Aims to remove Karimov, establish an Islamic state, fight anti-Islamic opponents	Fewer than 500	1991	Car bombs, taking foreign hostages; most active in Kyrgyzstan and Tajikistan
Jaish-e-Mohammed (JEM, Army of Mohammed)— Pakistan	Islamic extremist group formed after Masood Azhar's release from prison	Aims to unite Kashmir with Pakistan; targets Indian government and political leaders	Several hundred	2000	Murder of U.S. journalist, Indian Parliament bombing, anti-Christian attacks
Jemaah Islamiya Organization (JI)	Southeast Asia cells of militant Islamists	Aims to create an idealized Islamic state	Unknown	1990s	Bombings in Indonesia and Philippines; plots against tourist spots, foreign diplomatic buildings
Al-Jihad (AJ)—Cairo, Egypt, Yemen, Afghanistan, Pakistan, Lebanon, UK	Egyptian Islamic extremists, merged with al Qaeda in 2001	Aims to replace the Egyptian government with Islamic state, attack U.S. and Israeli interests	Several hundred	1970s	Attacks on Egyptian government personnel; assassinated Anwar Sadat
Kahane Chai (Kach)—Israel, West Bank	Jewish extremist group	Aims to restore the biblical state of Israel; organizes protests against the Israeli government	Unknown	1994	Threats against Arabs, Palestinians, Israeli officials
Kongra-Gel (KGK), aka Kurdistan Workers Party (PKK)—Turkey, Middle East	Marxist-Leninist insurgent group	Aims to create a democratic Kurdish state; targets Turkish security forces, officials, and villagers who oppose organization	4,000–5,000	1974	Attacks on diplomatic and commercial facilities, bombings of tourist sites
Lashkar-e-Tayyiba (LT, Army of the Righteous)—Pakistan	Armed wing of a Pakistan-based Sunni anti-U.S. missionary group	Targets Indian troops and civilians in Kashmir	Several thousand	1989	Attacks on border security forces and Indian Parliament
Lashkar i Jhangvi (LJ)—Pakistan, Afghanistan	Sunni sectarian radical group banned in Pakistan in 2001; anti-Shiite	Aims to create a Muslim state in Pakistan	Fewer than 100	1996	Armed attacks, bombings, attempted assassinations

Table 4.1 U.S.-Designated Foreign Terrorist Organizations, as of October 2005 (continued)

Name and base of operations	Description	Goals and targets	Estimated strength	Year founded	Alleged activities
Liberation Tigers of Tamil Eelam (LTTE)—Sri Lanka	Most powerful Tamil nationalist group in Sri Lanka	Aims to create a Tamil state in Sri Lanka; targets key personnel, senior political and military leaders	8,000–10,000	1976	Assassinations, suicide bombers: "The Black Tigers"
Libyan Islamic Fighting Group (LIFG)—Libya, UK, other countries	Libyans who had fought against Soviet forces in Afghanistan and the Qaddafi regime in Libya	Pledges to overthrow un-Islamic government of Libyan president Muammar al-Qaddafi	Several hundred	1990s	Suicide bombings, assassination attempt against Qaddafi
Moroccan Islamic Combatant Group (GICM)—Morocco	Formed in the 1990s by veteran mujahadeen of the war against the Soviets in Afghanistan	Aims to create an Islamic state in Morocco	Unknown	1990s	2003 terrorist attack on Casablanca; 2004 Madrid bombing
Mujahedin-e Khalq Organization (MEK)—Iraq	Marxist-Islamic group expelled from Iran and receiving Iraqi support; largest armed Iranian opposition group	Advocates a secular Iranian regime	Over 3,000	1960s	Assassinations, terrorist bombings, foreign military-aided assaults
National Liberation Army (ELN)—Colombia, Venezuela	Marxist insurgent group inspired by Fidel Castro and Che Guevara	Targets foreign employees from large corporations	3,000	1965	Kidnappings, hijackings, bombings, extortion
Palestinian Islamic Jihad (PIJ)—Israel, West Bank, Gaza Strip	Militant Palestinians committed to destroying Israel through holy war	Targets Israeli military and civilians; opposes secularism	Unknown	1970s	Suicide bombings, attacks on Israeli interests
Palestine Liberation Front (PLF)—Iraq	Broke away from PFLP-GC and split into pro-PLO, pro-Syria, and pro-Libya factions	Targets Israel; known for its aerial attacks	Unknown	1970s	Attacked Italian ship Achille Lauro; murdered a U.S. citizen

Organization—Location	Description	Strength	Year	Targets	Activities
Popular Front for the Liberation of Palestine (PFLP)—Syria, Lebanon, Israel, West Bank, Gaza Strip	Marxist-Leninist group that broke away from the Arab Nationalist Movement	Unknown	1967	Targets Israel's "illegal occupation" of Palestine and opposes negotiations with Israel	International terrorist acts in the 1970s, attacks against Israel and moderate Arab targets since 1978
Popular Front for the Liberation of Palestine—General Command (PFLP-GC)—Syria	Group that split from the PFLP to focus on fighting; opposes PLO	Several hundred	1968	Targets Israel, West Bank, Gaza Strip	Unusual attacks in Europe and the Middle East: hot air balloons, hang gliders, Lebanese guerrilla operations
Al Qaeda— Afghanistan until 2001, Southeast Asia, Middle East, worldwide cells	Osama bin Laden's network of Arabs who fought against the Soviet Union	Several thousand	1980s	Aims to establish a worldwide pan-Islamic caliphate; targets non-Islamic regimes and U.S. citizens	Bombings of embassies and USS Cole; September 11, 2001, attacks on U.S.
Real IRA (RIRA)—Northern Ireland, UK, Irish Republic	Armed wing of the 32 County Sovereignty Movement (32CSM) to unify Ireland	Fewer than 100	1998	Targets civilians, military, police, Protestant communities	Bombings, assassinations, robberies
Revolutionary Armed Forces of Colombia (FARC)—Colombia	Oldest and most capable Marxist insurgency with ties to drug trafficking	9,000–12,000	1964	Targets Colombian political, military, economic interests; also foreign citizens	Bombings, mortar attacks, kidnappings, extortion, guerrilla warfare, drug trafficking
Revolutionary Nuclei (formerly ELA)—Athens, Greece	Group that emerged from antiestablishment and anti-U.S./NATO/European Union (EU) leftist groups	Believed small	1995	Targets U.S. and European interests and government buildings in Greece	Arson attacks, low-level bombings, usually striking in early-morning hours

Table 4.1 U.S.-Designated Foreign Terrorist Organizations, as of October 2005 (continued)

Name and base of operations	Description	Goals and targets	Estimated strength	Year founded	Alleged activities
Revolutionary Organization 17 November—Athens, Greece	Radical leftist group named for student uprising in 1973	Seeks removal of U.S. bases and Turkish military and severing of NATO and EU ties	Believed small	1975	Assassinations, bombings, improvised rocket attacks; supported by bank robberies
Revolutionary People's Liberation Party/Front (DHKP/C)—Turkey	Marxist-Leninist group: "Party" refers to its political activities, "Front" to its militant operations	Targets U.S., NATO, Turkish establishment	Unknown	1978	Attacks on U.S. interests, suicide bombings
Salafist Group for Preaching and Combat (GSPC)—Algeria	Outgrowth of GIA and the most effective armed group in Algeria	Targets military and government targets; pledges to avoid civilians	Several hundred	1992	Attacks on military, police, government convoys
Shining Path (Sendero Luminoso, SL)—Peru	Group based on Maoist teachings	Aims to build communist regime and destroy Peruvian institutions; targets political enemies	300	1960s	Attacks leaving 30,000 dead, assassinations, bombings, village raids
Tanzim Qa'idat al-Jihad fi Bilad al-Rafidayn (QJBR), aka al-Zarqawi Network and al Qaeda in Iraq—Iraq	Group established soon after start of Operation Iraqi Freedom to bring together jihadists and other insurgents; merged with al Qaeda	Aims to expel Coalition forces and establish Islamic state in Iraq, then move to Syria, Lebanon, Israel, Jordan	Unknown	2003	Many bombings, killing hundreds; assassination of key Iraqi political figures; beheadings of Americans
United Self-Defense Forces of Colombia (AUC)—Colombia	Umbrella organization that consolidates paramilitary groups	Targets "insurgents" from FARC and ELN	8,000–11,000	1997	Assassinations, guerrilla warfare, drug trafficking

SOURCE: U.S. Department of State, Office of Counterterrorism.

prohibiting the sale of the materials needed to carry out terrorist attacks, such as explosives. In the September 11 attacks, the terrorists found a way to direct their weapons—fully fueled jetliners—into the World Trade Center and Pentagon. Beyond that, they needed only rudimentary flight and navigation skills, simple weapons, and enough hijackers to take control of the airliners. Anticipating a similar attack, since September 11 the U.S. government has made it harder to gain access to the cockpits of airliners, enhanced preboarding screening for anything that could be used as a weapon, and authorized shooting down planes that may be threatening to target a domestic target.

Similar reasoning leads to policies that deny access to the fissile materials needed to build a nuclear weapon. Because no legitimate reason exists for anyone to possess fissile materials, aside from those few who are authorized to do research on or to handle such materials for the U.S. and a few other governments, policy makers are quick to agree to strict prohibitions on access to such materials. The difficult challenge is how to also deny such access to those who would trade in nuclear technology or fissile materials, or who would steal or pay a bribe to obtain such materials. Once groups seeking to develop a nuclear weapon or trade nuclear technology are identified, close monitoring of the group's activities through the use of informants or other means is possible.

When prevention cannot be directed at a known possessor of nuclear materials, or even a group known to be pursuing them, the preventive actions are more diffuse. The critical component in nuclear terrorism is, of course, obtaining the fissile materials or operational nuclear devices. (Most experts agree that any terrorist group that acquires fissile materials may have or can find the expertise to produce a crude nuclear weapon or device.) The most prominent sources of fissile, weapons-grade materials are the states of the former Soviet Union, where some materials are still poorly guarded. Corruption and black markets are adding to an already unstable protection scheme inside Russia, and confirmed instances of efforts to acquire Russian fissile materials continue to mount (although many attempts many have later proven to be hoaxes). The United States and other nations are helping to provide security for the Russian fissile materials, but it is believed that some fissile materials, or at least non–weapons grade materials, have already been taken from the former Soviet sites.

Elsewhere, a Pakistani nuclear scientist is now known to have produced and sold nuclear materials and technology, including uranium-enriching centrifuges and plans for the actual design of nuclear weapons. Abdul Qadeer (A. Q.) Khan was a principal force behind Pakistan's successful program to build a nuclear bomb. After decades of failure, Khan stole Western designs for the production of enriched uranium and adapted them for Pakistan's use in the 1980s. Even before the September 11, 2001, terrorist attacks, it was suspected that Khan and others in Pakistan's nuclear program might be seeking ways to spread nuclear technology to other Islamic countries. The United States learned later in 2001 that a few weeks before the September 11 attacks a campfire meeting was held in Afghanistan, attended by Osama bin Laden, his peer

Ayman al-Zawahiri, and two Pakistani delegates from Pakistan's atomic energy commission. Their discussion could not be overheard.

Agents have been collecting extensive intelligence on A. Q. Khan for some time. After the interdiction in October 2003 of a ship bound for Libya revealed the presence of centrifuges traced to Khan's organization, the intelligence community was able to work backward and identify a worldwide business in nuclear technology and determine that Khan's suppliers included firms in Europe and the Middle East. By the late 1990s, the Khan network of companies and suppliers could count Libya, Iraq, Iran, and North Korea among its customers. In fact, Khan and the Pakistanis were so brash that they advertised Khan's services and took an ad in an English-language newspaper. By 2000 the United States had evidence that Khan was selling specialized centrifuge technology that would permit the buyer to enrich uranium, the necessary predicate for building a nuclear weapon. By late 2001, the centrifuge equipment was being transported to the governments of Libya, Iran, and North Korea.

After the September 11 attacks, ever greater intelligence efforts were directed at monitoring Khan's network. In 2002 and early 2003, pressure was placed on the government of Pakistan to stop Khan's activities, but these efforts only meandered along. Meanwhile, the United States learned from CIA investigators that the German ship *BBC China* had left Dubai en route to Libya carrying centrifuge equipment. At the request of the United States, the ship diverted to an Italian port, where an inspection revealed the nuclear equipment, manufactured at Khan's production facility in Malaysia. Khan was then arrested in Pakistan, and Khan's customers realized that the United States had known of their nuclear purchases and trades. And yet with so much technology and even fissile materials already on the black market, interdiction efforts were severely limited.

The 2003 seizure of the *BBC China* gave the United States an opportunity to express public surprise and outrage at what it had known for a long time. At the same time, the openness of the seizure gave Pakistani president Pervez Musharraf the political cover he needed to put a stop to A. Q. Khan's activities. Although there is substantial reason to believe that elements of the Pakistani government were complicit in Khan's efforts (or at least looked the other way when technology and other items were being exported), President Musharraf was never pressed to investigate or reveal the degree to which members of his government were involved because the United States needed Pakistan's cooperation in the global war on terrorism.

Different but equally challenging problems are faced by counterterrorism officials trying to interdict terrorism associated with biological agents, which could cause catastrophic harm. Biological agents can be spread by human contact, through an explosion, or with an aerosol device. States may threaten to use such agents, or states may sell biological agents to non-state terrorists. Although considerable technical expertise is required to isolate most pathogens, a terrorist group might acquire pathogens from those who have legitimate (research) reasons to have them, and then replicate or preserve the germs.

The possession and use of biological weapons, which are already forbidden by international treaty, are a criminal offense in the United States and in some other nations. Beyond traditional forms of deterrence, detection is complicated by the fact that the facilities in which germs may be made are typically small and unobtrusive. In addition, much of the activity in such facilities may be legitimate, such as producing medicines or fertilizers. Thus one interdiction technique used for biological agents is to regulate their ingredients by requiring licenses for the sale and purchase of quantities of such materials, tracking the shipment of such agents through manifests or other monitoring systems, and adding taggants or other markers that would trace the origins of the substance.

Apart from readily identifiable targets, interdiction by controlling access to targets is mostly guesswork and heavily limited by the availability of resources and the difficulties of imagining how terrorists will strike next. A crude nuclear device, for example, could be delivered in a small van or pickup truck. The bomb itself also could be stored in the vehicle and transported without much risk of disclosure and the need to meet only moderate safety requirements. The fissile materials would be no harder to smuggle into the United States than drugs.

Screening for Security

Similar but perhaps less dramatic challenges are confronted in interdicting terrorists in public places. Local, state, and federal officials face many questions: To what extent should they impose security controls before admitting access to public buildings? To airports and subway stations? To shopping malls and large arenas? If restrictions on access are imposed, what should constitute sufficient proof that the applicant does not pose a terrorist threat? Should physical searches of the person and the applicant's possessions be required? Some sort of background check?

In response to the high incidence of airplane hijackings in the 1960s, the United States and many other nations began to impose searches of air travelers. At first, passengers were frisked if they fit a subjective hijacker profile and activated a metal detector. After 1973 a new program in the United States subjected all passengers to metal detector screening, required that they submit to a search if requested, and subjected all carry-on bags to an X-ray scan. After the attacks of September 11, 2001, even more stringent controls were implemented. A Terrorist Screening Database is continually being generated and maintained by contributing government agencies, based on intelligence collection, and names are forwarded to airline officials to enable additional passenger screening. Air travelers must now also show government-issued identification as part of the screening process.

Two of the September 11 hijackers, after being identified earlier in 2001 by the CIA as potential terrorists, had been added to the State Department watch list called TIPOFF. The TIPOFF list was designed to prevent terrorists from getting visas to travel to the United States. But, for whatever reason, the TIPOFF list was not shared with the Federal Aviation Administration (FAA). The FAA kept its own "no-fly" list, which included persons banned for air travel because of the threat they were thought to pose. The FAA also kept a "selective list," which included persons who would be subjected to further screening before being allowed to fly. None of the September 11 hijackers were on either FAA list. Repairing such bureaucratic failures requires adopting other security measures that would be effective in screening traveling, such as a national identity card. But any such policies have to take into account the problem of "false positives"—such as when an innocent person is erroneously included on a watch list.

Screening could be applied to other transit targets as well. In 2005 the New York City subway system adopted a random "container inspection program" to address the threat of an explosive device being taken into the subway in a carry-on container or backpack. New York City officials acted after the Madrid commuter train bombings on March 11, 2004, that killed more than two hundred persons, another train bombing in 2004 in Moscow that killed forty, and the London subway bombings in July 2005 that killed fifty-two. The New York City program permits inspectors to stop passengers randomly to inspect containers. An individual may refuse to permit the inspection at the cost of being denied entrance to the subway with the uninspected item, but a refusal does not subject the individual to arrest. Officials concede that the inspection program does not completely secure the subway system, but they maintain that it will deter some terrorists.

Following the Money

A different interdiction technique seeks to track and then seize or control the funds used to further terrorist aims. By 2002 the United States had launched programs, based on international banking agreements, that permitted the government to track such funds as they moved through accounts all over the world. Even nations not friendly to the United States had an interest in cooperating in this process to avoid being designated as supporters of terrorism. If the link with terrorists was established, the questionable assets could be frozen under the terms of the international agreements. More important, the ability to follow the money trail was a fairly effective way to keep tabs on the actors and their activities, and, in the longer term, perhaps curtail terrorists' access to cash and thus force them to cut back on operations. These international efforts are explored further in Chapter 8.

Complicating Factors

Interdicting terrorism is complicated by some of the common traits of terrorists and their organizations. First, some terrorists, such as Oklahoma City federal building bomber Timothy McVeigh or Unabomber Ted Kaczynski are "loners," who do not affiliate with extremist groups or otherwise provide any noticeable advance warning that they will carry out terrorist acts. Second, terrorist organizations themselves can be very hard to penetrate. Access is carefully controlled, as is information, and the cellular structure of many terrorist organizations limits considerably the information obtainable from any one member or group of members. Communications themselves are typically difficult to intercept, because terrorist groups have learned to evade detection by using multiple technologies or by eschewing technological means of communicating in favor of passing notes or face-to-face meetings. Third, terrorist organizations are primarily international or multinational, and their aims and means cross national borders. Interdiction thus requires the cooperation of foreign governments, the provision of security for U.S. persons and interests abroad, and new legal arrangements that permit U.S. officials to operate in other nations.

CASE STUDY 4.1

Interdiction at the Border: The Millennium Plot

In 1994 Algerian Ahmed Ressam used a falsified French passport to immigrate to Canada. After admitting to Canadian immigration officials that he used a fake passport under a false name, Ressam claimed political asylum on the basis of a fabricated story about political persecution in Algeria. After he failed to attend his political asylum hearing in 1995, asylum was denied and Ressam was arrested. Later, however, he was released, he again failed to show for his hearing, and then he was arrested four times over the next few years for petty theft crimes. He was neither jailed nor deported.

Eventually, Ressam fraudulently obtained a genuine Canadian passport under the name Benni Antoine Noris. In 1998 Ressam traveled to Afghanistan, where he received explosives training at an al Qaeda training camp. There, he planned with other Algerians to attack U.S. targets, and he left Afghanistan in 1999 equipped with materials for chemical weapons hidden in toiletry bottles, instructions on assembling bombs, and plenty of cash.

Back in Canada, Ressam acquired more bomb-making materials and false documents, and he decided by late summer of 1999 to attack the Los Angeles International Airport, where, he believed, he could move about most easily without recognition and do the most damage. In December 1999, Ressam spent a week in Vancouver, preparing the explosive mixture, renting a car, and packing more than one hundred pounds of explosives in the car's spare tire well in the trunk.

On December 14, Ressam approached the car ferry at Victoria, B.C., where he would cross to Port Angeles, Washington. U.S. immigration officials at Victoria were mildly suspicious of Ressam. They ran his genuine but fraudulently obtained Canadian passport through a range of databases. Because the passport was not in Ressam's name, the U.S. officials did not pick up the outstanding Canadian arrest warrants. Officials also cursorily searched the trunk of Ressam's car, but they found nothing and permitted him to board the ferry.

At Port Angeles, U.S. Customs agent Diana Dean noticed that Ressam appeared nervous and that he gave tentative answers to her questions. While she asked Ressam for identification, other agents began to search his car. When the agent began to pat down Ressam, he panicked, ran, and was caught and arrested. Inspectors searching the car trunk found the explosives concealed in the spare tire well, although they at first believed that the white powder-like substance they discovered was drugs until one inspector identified a timing device hidden inside a box.

Officials did not learn of the Los Angeles Airport plan until they found and seized evidence in Montreal later in 2000. Ressam began cooperating with investigators in 2001, and he revealed the existence of al Qaeda cells within the United States. After pleading guilty on July 27, 2005, Ressam was sentenced to twenty-two years in prison.

Is this case about the fortuity of Diana Dean's keen awareness of Ressam's nervousness, or does the interdiction of the "Millennium Plot" have more portable lessons? The importance of using well-trained personnel as investigators and screeners in combating terrorism is undeniable. The human side of interdiction is sometimes overlooked in an era in which technologies offer so many sophisticated ways to conduct surveillance. In addition, the Ressam case illustrates the importance of international cooperation in stopping terrorism before it occurs. The cooperation between the United States, France, and Canada led investigators to discover the full extent of Ressam's plans and to his eventual decision to cooperate with investigators. (See Chapter 8 for additional aspects of the Ressam investigation.)   ■

Gathering Intelligence to Prevent Terrorism

Intelligence, simply put, is the gathering and processing of information, as well as the label that is affixed to what is found. In the counterterrorism setting, intelligence officials often refer to intelligence as *chatter*, a term that implies, correctly, that what is gathered is often not the kind of precise or specific tactical intelligence that is the stuff of classic espionage stories. Instead, chatter refers to a modicum of the communications of suspected terrorists and their movements and is normally expressed in terms of a pattern—more chatter, less chatter, lots of chatter. In other words, the use of "chatter" to describe the intelligence used to combat terrorism reflects the imprecision and uncertainty inherent in the field.

Whatever the descriptor, terrorism-related intelligence is collected by field agents who must travel to the sources of information about terrorist activities and possibly infiltrate terrorist circles and by home-based agents who review publicly available ("open source") materials and monitor technical means of surveillance, such as satellite photography and electronic surveillance. The raw data are then interpreted by analysts, whose reports are given to policy officials.

Efforts to collect intelligence may target the leaders of terrorist groups to study their behavior for signs of planned action. Likewise, efforts may target the supporters of terrorism, states or private actors, especially those who provide financial support. Intelligence gatherers can target known or likely infrastructure for terrorist activities—safe houses and movement of supplies, transportation nodes, logistical support, or storage facilities. Similarly, agents may be able to penetrate and observe terrorists' command and control schemes and communications and intelligence capabilities. Finally, much may be learned about potential terrorist attacks by following the recruitment of operatives or supporters and their indoctrination in training camps.

As discussed earlier, deterrence efforts are imperfect at best. Assuming for the foreseeable future that terrorists will attack the United States, perhaps the single most important tool in the government's counterterrorism arsenal is intelligence. For those terrorist plots whose details are sufficiently clear, the attack itself may be disrupted. In those cases and some others, the persons responsible may be arrested and prosecuted for conspiracy or inchoate crimes. Failing sufficient evidence for prosecution, officials may still be able to detain those suspected of planning the terrorist attack, detain and possibly deport those who are aliens, or take steps to freeze the financial assets of those thought to be responsible for supporting the suspected attack.

As revealed in previous chapters, modern terrorism has evolved in ways that complicate identifying the likely acts and actors in advance. Thus it has become extraordinarily difficult to learn about upcoming terrorist activities. For one thing, operational secrecy and the element of surprise have become a top priority in modern terrorism. Therefore terrorists work hard to thwart counterterrorism intelligence gathering. For another, the perpetrators of terrorism are no longer typically identified with sovereign states. Instead, the groups are diffuse, loosely organized (if they are organized at all), capable of blending in local environments, and difficult to penetrate. Another problem is that at least some terrorists have proven willing and able to inflict significant violent harm, either through suicide attacks or through the use of highly lethal explosives. Finally, modern communications technologies, including the Internet, have greatly expanded the ways in which terrorists can communicate with each other and with potential recruits and thus facilitated evasion.

As U.S. officials grew increasingly concerned about the international terrorism in the 1980s and 1990s and the possibility that the United States might be attacked at home or abroad, intelligence efforts to combat terrorism were expanded. Among other things, government agencies created watch lists of suspected terrorists and their supporters, so that these databases could be shared with intelligence and other agencies. Even though intelligence agencies were encouraged to share their information—collected, for example, by means of high-powered satellite and video camera technologies—little sharing, in fact, occurred.

Changes in technology and in the ways of the world have greatly enhanced intelligence agencies' capacities to gather information through technical means, and the explosion of information sources has made information easier to come by but less trustworthy. As collection has become more complex, the need to protect intelligence processes from penetration has become a major activity within the intelligence community.

The end of the Cold War and the emergence of asymmetric attacks on the United States are presenting unprecedented challenges for U.S. intelligence agencies. Instead of a single-minded focus on the Soviet Union, intelligence agencies now must confront a wide range of targets across the globe, including states and lethal non-state actors intent on doing harm to the United States. As technology ushered in the information era, the intelligence challenge of digging for secrets was replaced by the need to sift through masses of data in pursuit of a reliable understanding of an intelligence target. That terrorists would infiltrate U.S. cities and then succeed in inflicting catastrophic harm on September 11 underscored Americans' vulnerability, while causing significant rethinking about how the U.S. intelligence structure is organized and how its assets are deployed.

Intelligence operations and objectives are currently experiencing a remarkable change. Covert operations are now seeking to disrupt terrorist groups and ward off their planned attacks, to foil narcotics shipments, and to thwart the financial transactions of black market weapons traders. Computer technology is being used increasingly to disrupt the financial activities of hostile governments and to mine masses of data in pursuit of suspicious persons and groups. Activities such as influencing elections abroad or spreading democratic ideas and programs, once covert, are carried out in the open, either by governments or privately.

At the same time, counterterrorism investigations are seeking to anticipate terrorism rather than find the perpetrator of a crime already enacted. In the latter setting, investigators work from a crime scene, taking advantage of forensic clues, whereas countering terrorism through investigation is something like constructing a mosaic. Bits and pieces of information, from disparate sources, gathered over time may provide the information that could allow officials to prevent a terrorist strike. The information may be gathered by people or machines, but it must be analyzed and disseminated to be of practical value.

In the ideal counterterrorism investigation, suspects are identified, probably from the intelligence collected on their previous activities, such as forensic evidence from prior events or statements from those who inform on the suspects. Terrorists can make identification of those initial suspects difficult, however, by, for example, minimizing the knowledge that any one participant has of the operational plans. As those suspects and their contacts are monitored, the intelligence expands. These additional contacts are developed through physical surveillance, telephone or e-mail records, and perhaps Internet usage or even records from commercial activity, such as credit card usage, bank accounts, and educational or employment records. Informants may be recruited, and agents may seek to infiltrate the terrorist group. The surveillance, probably some combination of physical observation and electronic surveillance, will maintain constant contact with the suspects. As a planned attack moves toward its implementation, intelligence gathering continues and arrests are made and detention follows. Combating terrorism by gathering intelligence is thus now predominantly programmatic in nature, not episodic or after the fact.

Organizing Intelligence to Combat Terrorism

Until the post–World War II reform of the defense and intelligence agencies in 1947, there was no permanent legal structure for conducting intelligence activities in the United States. In the National Security Act of 1947, Congress created the Central Intelligence Agency and the National Security Council (NSC). Although the CIA was given a broad charter to collect foreign intelligence and to perform "other functions" as directed by the president or the NSC, Congress prohibited the CIA from having "law enforcement or internal security functions." The CIA was created to be the eyes and ears of the United States in the area of foreign intelligence gathering—in those days principally concerning the Soviet Union and Cold War issues.

Table 4.2 U.S. Intelligence Community, 2007

Central Intelligence Agency	
Department of Defense agencies	Other intelligence units
• Air Force Intelligence • Army Intelligence • Navy Intelligence • Marine Corps Intelligence • Defense Intelligence Agency • National Geospatial Intelligence Agency • National Reconnaissance Office • National Security Agency	• Coast Guard Intelligence • Department of Energy • Department of Homeland Security • Department of State • Department of the Treasury • Drug Enforcement Administration • Federal Bureau of Investigation

SOURCE: United States Intelligence Community, www.intelligence.gov/1-members.shtml.

Particularly after the country's experiences in fighting Nazi Germany in World War II, there was no enthusiasm in U.S. policy circles for creating a domestic security service as part of the U.S. intelligence bureaucracy. Instead, any intelligence collection on domestic targets was thought to be a job for the FBI—the federal police. The prohibition on the CIA performing "internal security functions" did not, however, bar the agency from operating inside the United States. In other words, pursuit of foreign intelligence was and remains the domain of the CIA wherever that search might lead. The CIA has the authority to monitor the movements of a suspected foreign terrorist inside the United States, but it may not conduct surveillance on domestic suspects, such as Oklahoma City federal building bomber Timothy McVeigh or Unabomber Ted Kaczynski.

The techniques for learning about the plans of a terrorist group are more or less the same whether the purpose of collecting the intelligence is prevention or prosecution. Operational concerns in the two types of investigations differ to the extent that greater care is taken to protect the sources and methods of counterterrorism intelligence, so that they can continue to be employed. Sometimes, valuable insiders can be persuaded to "turn" and work for investigators by the offer of financial inducements or, if conditions permit, a willingness to bargain for a plea to a lesser criminal charge.

Human Intelligence

In the United States, humans have been collecting intelligence directly since the administration of President George Washington, who retained spies to gather intelligence on foreign powers. Either as direct observers and listeners or as infiltrators or informants who gain admission to and the confidences of the group being targeted, human intelligence has always played an important role in protecting national security.

Human intelligence (HUMINT) runs the gamut, from classic cloak-and-dagger espionage to the overt collection of open source information such as Web browsing, reading government and media reports, and simple physical observation. HUMINT is performed primarily by the CIA, operating abroad, although Defense Department agencies and the Departments of Justice, State, and Treasury also employ human intelligence. HUMINT may include U.S. personnel deployed to embassies overseas or "assets" that are "handled" by U.S. officials—that is, foreigners who provide the intelligence.

Electronic Surveillance

At its most effective, electronic surveillance—also known as ELSUR—captures conversations and movements about plans to commit a terrorist act and thus allows the government to step in before the crime occurs. However, electronic surveillance may impose a heavy cost. An array of personal privacy and expressive freedoms are threatened by electronic surveillance, especially surveillance that is undertaken on a long-term, full-time basis. Those who know or suspect that their conversations are being monitored censor themselves. Individual interests in anonymity are compromised, as are choices about self-determination and freedom of association. As the U.S. Supreme Court has noted, electronic surveillance for national security purposes may implicate a "convergence of First and Fourth Amendment values not present in cases of 'ordinary' crime" when it targets peoples whose activities are politically motivated.[9] Government interests may be stronger in these areas, but there is also a greater risk of jeopardizing protected expression, including the freedoms of speech and association.

Special Rules for Collecting Foreign Intelligence in the United States

In the United States, the use of traditional law enforcement techniques is accompanied by the traditional Fourth Amendment requirements, including, under the Omnibus Crime Control and Safe Streets Act, the need to establish that a crime has been committed or is imminent before a warrant to conduct electronic surveillance is issued by a judge. Because of the gravity of the threat of terrorism and the consequences of those acts, the government has sought the authority to undertake surveillance with something less than the criminal law standard. Rather than permit warrantless surveillance by the executive branch for foreign intelligence information inside the United States, Congress enacted the Foreign Intelligence Surveillance Act of 1978 (FISA) to prescribe rules for the conduct of such surveillance. Following FISA procedures, federal investigators, normally the FBI, may obtain orders from a secret court—the Foreign Intelligence Surveillance Court (FISC)—to engage in electronic surveillance or a physical search for foreign intelligence information inside the United States. The more permissive FISA regime is arguably justified on the grounds that the danger of international terrorism is grave and that the privacy intrusions are limited to the collection of information for foreign intelligence purposes.

In addition, something like FISA procedures may be justified because terrorists in a loosely defined cellular structure are hard to identify in general, and they are typically trained not to engage in criminal conduct that would justify the criminal variant of electronic surveillance. The electronic surveillance undertaken in conjunction with ordinary crimes requires that the application for a warrant contain detailed information about the alleged criminal offense, the facilities and communication to be intercepted, the identity of the target (if known), the period of time of the surveillance, and an explanation of whether other investigative methods could achieve the same objective.

Because of the need for secrecy and the often more open-ended need to monitor a target for foreign intelligence, ordinary crimes warrant procedures are ill-suited for foreign intelligence gathering. Clearly, something less than a completed act of international terrorism should be required before launching electronic surveillance in pursuit of foreign intelligence. However, deciding just how much evidence of a connection between a potential target and a terrorist group or terrorist activities should be required is a nettlesome problem. Without sufficient controls, electronic surveillance is an especially ominous form of investigation because, in a digital world, it records and may store and retrieve forever not just the information that investigators seek but everything that the target communicates, no matter how unrelated to the purpose of the surveillance.

Signals Intelligence

One set of intelligence-gathering disciplines is heavily dependent on technology. Signals intelligence (SIGINT) gathers communications through electronic, digital, and light signals. At times, even unmanned aerial vehicles (UAVs) equipped with surveillance technologies and missiles have been used to permit the real-time identification and then targeting with lethal forces of a known terrorist. The National Security Agency (NSA) is the predominant provider of SIGINT and its close relation imagery intelligence (IMINT), which is information gathered by photography or other image collection means. Satellites and aircraft are used to collect IMINT. Both SIGINT and IMINT can become even more useful by employing measurement and signature analysis (MASINT). Technical means of collection were developed by and large for the purpose of keeping tabs on the Soviet Union and other nations during the Cold War. Most of the collection targets were large and fairly static over time.

Terrorism presents entirely different challenges for collecting technical intelligence, whether the medium is telephone, e-mail and the Internet, or data from government or private sector databases such as credit reports or banking records. Although these technical means of collection play an important role in countering terrorism, typically the role is in support of other intelligence sources because it is harder to track terrorists' smaller footprints and dynamic movements with technical means. Technical collection is also limited because terrorists are knowledgeable about the monitoring capabilities of Western governments. As a result, electronic communications methods are often not used by terrorists for salient operational messages, and those communications that are made electronically may be encrypted or otherwise disguised using sophisticated evasive techniques.

The methods for collecting technical intelligence are further complicated in combating terrorism by the wide range of foreign languages encountered in collection and the relatively poor state of the foreign language capabilities of the U.S. intelligence agencies.

Finally, because terrorism does not respect geographic boundaries, the collection of technical intelligence on terrorist activities must be undertaken inside the United States, not just abroad. When a technical intelligence target is inside the United States, the legal restrictions on NSA and CIA activities in the United States may forbid such activities. If so, the FBI might carry out the domestic operation, but legal rules also require that it obtain permission from the FISA court before most forms of electronic surveillance can be conducted.

Covert Operations

Covert operations—intelligence operations that go beyond just collecting information—also may be conducted to counter terrorism. Covert operations may be undertaken in support of a military coup or an insurgent campaign against an unfriendly government. However, they can also be conducted to support investigations through infiltrating foreign groups or governments in order to spread propaganda or false information—and to learn about intelligence activities at the same time—or to foil an anticipated hostile operation by various means.

Inevitably, any U.S. involvement with foreign intelligence assets in seeking to learn more about terrorist activities leads to difficult judgments about affiliating with unsavory characters in return for gaining what might be valuable intelligence. So-called dirty assets have plagued U.S. intelligence operations at various times. When it is reported in the media, for example, that a paid CIA operative is known to be engaged in the narcotics trade or in human trafficking or in torture, U.S. intelligence agencies reconsider how to vet an asset before he or she is engaged, and whether an asset's record of unlawful conduct should deter a future relationship. (See Case Study 4.2.)

CASE STUDY 4.2

Dirty Assets

One risk in employing private intelligence operatives is the difficulty encountered in controlling the operative's or asset's behavior. The prototype of the intelligence asset is a foreign national who is sought out by U.S. intelligence officials because they believe the asset can deliver useful intelligence in one form or another.

Ali Hassan Salameh

In the early 1970s, the CIA succeeded in penetrating the Palestine Liberation Organization (then the most feared terrorist organization), which had targeted the United States and its citizens in the Middle East. After concluding a secret deal with the PLO's chief of intelligence, Ali Hassan Salameh, the CIA obtained detailed and extensive information about a range of terrorist activities and terrorist groups. Salameh even intervened personally to stop some planned attacks. Apparently, Salameh believed that his work in support of the CIA could help the PLO to achieve its political goals in the Middle East. But Salameh was a known terrorist. He was a member of Yasser Arafat's "Black September" organization, and he was chief of operations in planning the murders of Israeli athletes at the Munich Summer Olympic Games in 1972. The CIA reportedly targeted Salameh for assassination at the same time the agency was working with him, until Israeli intelligence operatives killed him in 1979.

The Deutch Rules

In 1995 Director of Central Intelligence John M. Deutch promulgated guidelines for the CIA, and, through them, ordered a review of all intelligence assets in the employ of the agency. Deutch acted after widespread media attention and litigation focused on allegations that CIA assets in Guatemala had been involved in the torture, disappearance, and death of U.S. citizens in that country since 1984. Deutch was also prompted to act after President Bill Clinton directed the Intelligence Oversight Board (IOB) to review these and related allegations. The IOB found that maintaining a CIA influence in Guatemala required that the CIA deal with some unsavory characters, but that the human rights records of Guatemala security services were widely known to be "reprehensible." The IOB found that the CIA had given insufficient attention to human rights abuses by agency assets and that the agency had failed to inform members of Congress about the issues, thereby preventing Congress from providing effective oversight.

The Deutch rules required central approval of the recruitment and employment of dirty assets in the future. However, a June 2000 report of the National Commission on Terrorism criticized the Deutch rules as deterring and delaying efforts to recruit valuable assets and making intelligence personnel who might recruit assets "risk averse." After the September 11 attacks, the criticisms of weak and failed efforts at collecting human intelligence were renewed. Soon thereafter, the Deutch rules were ignored by the agency and then were formally rescinded in 2002.

Intelligence officials face ethical and operational challenges if they learn that an asset is "dirty"—that is, the asset behaves unlawfully or uses extreme tactics and methods not condoned by the asset's employer. Recent experiences suggest that it remains unclear whether the United States should screen such dirty assets before they are retained. On the one hand, the United States might prefer to assume the risk that some "bad apples" will taint the otherwise good reputation of its intelligence agencies. On the other, unlawful and extreme tactics embraced by even one asset could set an example inside the agency that could be repeated by others. ◼

Analyzing Intelligence

Analyzing intelligence to counter terrorism is just as complicated a task as collecting intelligence. The terrorism environment is dynamic; the threats change and evolve, sometimes suddenly. Thus decisions have to be made about how best to prioritize analytic resources. Should the lion's share be devoted to Osama bin Laden and al Qaeda? What about the cells of jihadists who appear otherwise unaffiliated, and those whose threats are nascent but credible? To what extent should analysis be focused on threats posed by states or groups that are state-sponsored? Taking into account the vast amounts of data that can be collected through technical means, the mass of information that may be relevant to investigations of terrorism is truly overwhelming. Realistically, there is no way to process, evaluate, and disseminate assessments of all the terrorism-related intelligence produced by U.S. collectors. As a result, the U.S. government, along with those of some other Western states, has begun to conduct some of the analytic work through automated means.

The NSA employs data-mining techniques as an adjunct to its surveillance activities. (See Box 4.2.) Data mining involves using data analysis tools to discover previously unknown patterns and relationships in data sets. Data mining may use association techniques (one event is connected to another), a sequence or path analysis (one event leads to another), clustering (documenting groupings such as geographic location), and forecasting (patterns that permit reasonable predictions about future activities). In countering terrorism, data mining can be used to identify questionable money transfers, communications among terrorist suspects, or travel by suspects.

Box 4.2   **The NSA and Data Mining: The Terrorist Surveillance Program (TSP) and the Call Data Program**

On December 16, 2005, the *New York Times* reported that, according to government officials, President George W. Bush had secretly authorized the National Security Agency to eavesdrop on Americans and others inside the United States to search for evidence of terrorist activity without the court-approved warrants normally required for domestic surveillance. Pursuant to a secret executive order signed by the president in 2002, the NSA has monitored the telephone and e-mail communications of thousands of persons inside the United States where one end of the communication was outside the United States, without warrants, to learn more about possible terrorist plots. President Bush defended the program as "crucial to our national security," and he ordered an investigation into the leak of the existence of the program to the media.

Later dubbed the Terrorist Surveillance Program (TSP), this controversial surveillance program has generated immense media attention, congressional

continues . . .

hearings, and dozens of lawsuits. According to the Bush administration, the NSA intercepts communications into and out of the United States of people linked to al Qaeda or an affiliated terrorist organization. The purpose of the program is to establish an early warning system to detect and prevent another terrorist attack on U.S. soil. Using powerful NSA computers connected to telephone switching stations inside the United States, the NSA can quickly employ its voice recognition programs to reach an identified suspect's network of callers and then subject the individuals inside that network to similar scrutiny. By repeating the pattern, the NSA can increase geometrically the numbers subject to surveillance.

In May 2006, *USA Today* reported that the NSA also had been secretly collecting telephone call data (the numbers dialed and the dates and times of the calls, not the contents of the calls) on tens of millions of Americans in order to create a database of every call made within the nation's borders. The collected data may be used to identify calling patterns that could indicate an activity of interest to intelligence investigators. Once calling numbers of interest are identified, the same computer power associated with the TSP could be used to generate the social network of the caller, and so on.

Both the TSP and the call data program have been challenged in court as violations of the civil liberties of Americans. In January 2007, President Bush announced that the TSP would end, because the Justice Department had arranged to obtain orders for necessary surveillance from the Foreign Intelligence Surveillance Court (FISC). As noted, that special court requires that orders approving electronic surveillance for collecting foreign intelligence be based on a showing by the Justice Department that there is probable cause to believe that the surveillance target is engaged in activities related to international terrorism. Because the TSP had been less discriminating than the FISC guidelines in its targeting decisions, it remains unclear (because the court orders and accompanying applications are classified) just what foreign intelligence surveillance collection activities are under way.

- What arguments might be made for and against the lawfulness of these programs?

- Should Congress be the one to decide whether to permit these programs to operate? Or should their development and implementation be left to the executive branch?

- What are the benefits and drawbacks of data mining in combating terrorism?

Intelligence Failure?

The September 11, 2001, attacks on the World Trade Center and the Pentagon prompted widespread finger pointing at what some critics regarded as massive failures of intelligence. The two congressional intelligence committees and the Bush-appointed National Commission on Terrorist Attacks upon the United States (9-11 Commission) found that inadequate organization and management of the intelligence community prevented the director of central intelligence (DCI) from ensuring that information about the hijackers' plans was shared with agency analysts, who could have "connected the dots" and perhaps even uncovered the plot in advance.[10] The 9-11 Commission also noted that limited legal authority forced the DCI to "direct agencies without controlling them." The commission pointed out that, especially for intelligence elements within the Department of Defense, the DCI "does not receive an appropriation for their activities, and therefore does not control their purse strings." [11] Similarly, the congressional joint inquiry found that even after DCI George Tenet ordered the intelligence community to give the Osama bin Laden network its highest priority, his words had little effect beyond the CIA.

Later, the Bush administration case for the 2003 Iraq War relied heavily on intelligence-based assertions that the Saddam Hussein regime had stockpiles of WMD that would imminently be used against the United States and its allies. After President Bush declared an end to major combat operations in Iraq in 2003 and investigators cleared the battlefield rubble, no WMD were found. In March 2005, a presidentially appointed commission found "that the Intelligence Community was dead wrong in almost all of its prewar judgments about Iraq's weapons of mass destruction." The commission found an "inability to collect good information," "serious errors in analyzing" the information collected, and a failure to distinguish assumptions from evidence in its analysis. (See Case Study 4.3.)

The intelligence failures of September 11 and Iraq appeared to many observers to be symptomatic of a larger struggle by the nation's intelligence agencies to confront the post–Cold War environment that includes dozens of high-priority targets. Today and for the foreseeable future, the intelligence environment is composed not only of a growing number of states, but also of highly diffuse transnational terrorism, crime, and proliferation networks. As noted earlier in this chapter, advances in technology and potential dual uses of goods have also made detection of weapons and facilities harder and made their concealment easier.

In its July 2004 report, the 9-11 Commission recommended several changes in the structure of the intelligence community:

- unify strategic intelligence and operational planning against Islamist terrorists across the foreign–domestic divide with a National Counterterrorism Center.
- unify the intelligence community with a National Intelligence Director.
- unify the many participants in the counterterrorism effort and their knowledge in a network-based information-sharing system that transcends traditional governmental boundaries.

- unify and strengthen congressional oversight to improve quality and accountability.
- strengthen the FBI and homeland defenders.[12]

Although the Bush administration supported the recommendations of the 9-11 Commission, the president declared that he could meet the new challenges through executive branch rules changes and appointments. When congressional interest in legislative responses to the 9-11 Commission recommendations developed significant momentum in 2004, after President Bush had implemented some reforms inside the executive branch, the president eventually supported new legislation.

An Intelligence Czar?

In December 2004, Congress approved the most extensive reorganization of U.S. intelligence in more than half a century. The Intelligence Reform and Terrorism Prevention Act of 2004 responded, at least in part, to those who sought the creation of a cabinet-level intelligence czar. It created the position of director of national intelligence (DNI), appointed by the president and confirmed by the Senate, and subject to the "authority, direction, and control of the President." (See Figure 4.1 for an organization chart of the Office of the Director of National Intelligence.) The DNI cannot serve simultaneously as director of the CIA or as head of any other component of the intelligence community.

The DNI serves as head of the intelligence community and as principal adviser to the president, National Security Council, and Homeland Security Council "for intelligence matters related to the national security." The director also oversees and directs implementation of the National Intelligence Program. The DNI is responsible for establishing "objectives, priorities, and guidance" for elements of the intelligence community and for managing intelligence collection, analysis, production, and dissemination by entities of the intelligence community.

In addition to developing and determining the annual consolidated National Intelligence Program budget, the DNI directs the allocation of appropriations through the heads of departments containing agencies or organizations within the intelligence community and through the director of the CIA. Although the director of national intelligence was given considerable new budgetary authority with which to manage the intelligence community, he or she has no direct prescriptive authority over intelligence support to military operations through the Department of Defense.

The DNI has direct authority over a Senate-confirmed principal deputy and up to four personally appointed additional deputy directors, a National Counterterrorism Center, a National Counterproliferation Center, a general counsel, a director of science and technology, and a National Intelligence Council.

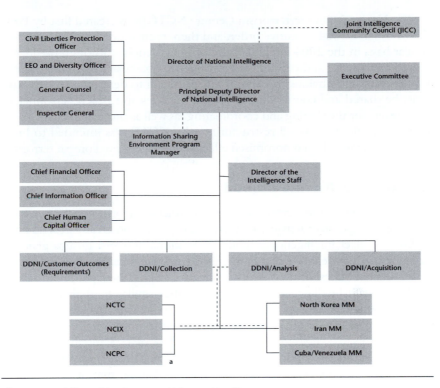

Figure 4.1 Office of the Director of National Intelligence

SOURCE: Office of the Director of National Intelligence, http://www.dni.gov/aboutODNI/organization.htm.
°Acronyms used herein: National Counterterrorism Center (NCTC); National Counter Intelligence Executive
(NCIX); National Counter Proliferation Center (NCPC); Mission Manager (MM)

The DCI post was eliminated, and the job of running the CIA was given to a director of the CIA.

Implementation of the reforms has been piecemeal. Former U.S. ambassador to the United Nations John Negroponte was confirmed as the first DNI in 2005, and most of the subordinate positions were filled later that year. Meanwhile, on March 31, 2005, the Silberman-Robb Commission (see Case Study 4.3) recommended that the president create a new national security service within the FBI that would include the Counterterrorism and Counterintelligence Divisions and the Directorate of Intelligence, all subject to the budget and coordination authorities of the DNI. The Silberman-Robb Commission also recommended that the principal national security elements of the Department of Justice be placed under a new assistant attorney general for national security. President Bush accepted these recommendations, ordered the attorney general to implement them, and asked Congress to create the new assistant attorney general position. The Congress did so in 2006.

The National Counterterrorism Center (NCTC) was created first by President Bush in a 2004 executive order, and then its creation was confirmed on a similar basis in the 2004 intelligence reform legislation. Although the idea of shared intelligence and coordinated intelligence operations to counter terrorism has wide and obvious appeal, it is more difficult to determine exactly what must be shared and coordinated and what agencies and which personnel are responsible for the sharing and coordinating, as well as the leadership in a joint operation. Like the overall restructuring, the NCTC was intended to break down old barriers that compromised effective intelligence to combat terrorism.

Collecting Intelligence Abroad

The capabilities of the United States to interdict a terrorist attack or even to monitor the aggregate activities of a terrorist organization greatly depend on its ability to collect intelligence abroad. International terrorist groups generally organize, train, raise funds, recruit members, and plan their attacks from outside of the United States, or they almost always do. If U.S. intelligence officials are unable to gain intelligence abroad in quantities similar to their intelligence "take" during domestic operations, their ability to prevent attacks will diminish.

Intelligence can be obtained from abroad either through the cooperation of those states in which terrorist groups operate or by U.S. intelligence agents abroad collecting the intelligence themselves. Unfortunately, many times host states may not cooperate. Some states such as Yemen may simply lack the capacity to be helpful except in the most rudimentary ways. Other states—such as Saudi Arabia, Sudan, and Syria—may argue that such cooperation constitutes too direct a threat to their own sovereignty, or that they do not want the local population to observe that the government is collaborating with a nation that is trying to apprehend local persons whose organization might actually be viewed favorably by many people. In addition, the very prospect of U.S. cooperation with the intelligence services of some nations—again Syria, for example, a nation known to systematically violate human rights in intelligence interrogations—might suggest to some observers that the U.S. commitment to human rights and the rule of law is for sale.

When a major investigation of terrorist activities abroad is under way, typically after a significant attack or credible threat, a joint task force is created to satisfy the needs for an extensive U.S. presence and for international cooperation. The State Department would likely coordinate such an effort, as it did with the investigation of the bombing of Pan Am Flight 103 over Lockerbie, Scotland, in December 1988. In that investigation, the State Department managed a complex interagency and transnational operation that eventually succeeded in identifying the bombers and their Libyan sponsors.

U.S. intelligence operations carried out abroad to combat terrorism resemble domestic operations in that the intelligence collected often arrives in bits and pieces that are understandable only as part of a larger mosaic. Collecting those bits and pieces abroad can be particularly challenging because the U.S. personnel doing so are obviously not part of the local culture. Sometimes a "walk-in" to a U.S. facility or agency official will provide helpful information because he expects to be paid, or because he has some other reason to expose the activities of the eventual target. Although walk-ins are notoriously unreliable, and U.S. officials must exercise extreme care in evaluating their information, sometimes the relationship pays dividends. In 1993 Mir Aimal Kansi stood brazenly outside the CIA's headquarters in Virginia and killed two CIA employees with an AK-47 assault rifle. He then managed to flee undetected, first to Afghanistan and then to Pakistan. The United States offered a $2 million reward for information leading to Kansi's arrest, and ensured that the reward was widely publicized. Four years later, informants hoping to collect the reward approached U.S. officials in Pakistan and succeeded in arranging for Kansi to appear at a designated time and place. He was then arrested by a disguised FBI team that flew with him back to the United States to stand trial. The informants claimed the reward.

Postscript: A Note on Counterterrorism Investigations in Other Nations

Some nations, such as Israel and the United Kingdom, have relaxed detention rules so that they permit a suspected terrorist to be held even though he or she has not been convicted of a crime. These nations also permit coercive interrogation for the purpose of obtaining information about terrorist activities. In Israel, after the suicide bombings of buses in Jerusalem and Tel Aviv in 1995, the intelligence agency Shin Bet was allowed to use "moderate physical force" in its interrogations of those detained on suspicion of terrorist activities.

In response to terrorism in Northern Ireland, the British and Irish security, police, and military personnel have been allowed to conduct warrantless searches. Such searches follow a determination, eventually reviewable by the courts, that there is a "reasonable suspicion" that the target of the search is engaged in terrorist activities. In Germany, the government, in the face of ongoing concerns about violent domestic terrorist groups and the growing evidence of a jihadist terrorist presence, is advancing the use of computer-driven intelligence collection and advanced data mining techniques to combat terrorism. Collection activities are more loosely tethered in Germany, where the intelligence agency may target any "efforts" that threaten "the free democratic constitutional order" in Germany.

CASE STUDY 4.3

Curveball: The Value of Vetting

Before the United States launched the Iraq War in 2003, the principal justification for the invasion of Iraq was the need to rid Iraq of the WMD presumably poised to attack the United States and its allies. On the eve

of the war, Secretary of State Colin Powell made a powerful, albeit ultimately unsuccessful, appeal for UN Security Council support for the
invasion based on a detailed presentation of alleged Iraqi biological
weapons sites. After U.S. and coalition forces failed to find the WMD,
President George W. Bush appointed the Commission on the Intelligence Capabilities of the United States Regarding Weapons of Mass
Destruction (also known as the Silberman-Robb Commission because it
was cochaired by Judge Laurence Silberman and former senator Charles
Robb) to investigate how the prewar certainties about Iraq's WMD
could have been off the mark. In March 2005, the commission reported
that "the Intelligence Community was dead wrong in almost all of its
pre-war judgments about Iraq's weapons of mass destruction. Its principal causes [included] the Intelligence Community's inability to collect
good information about Iraq's WMD programs."

In particular, the commission reported the story of a "pivotal source"
code-named "Curveball," whose claims about Iraqi biological weapons
were asserted to be true by Secretary of State Powell in his address to the
UN Security Council on the eve of war. The information on Iraqi WMD
supplied by Curveball, who claimed to be an Iraqi chemical engineer,
was routed through his refugee home in Germany. Curveball had begun
working with the German Federal Intelligence Service in 2000 in
exchange for an immigration card, and the U.S. Defense Intelligence
Agency (DIA), which handled Iraqi refugees in Germany, forwarded the
German intelligence reports to the CIA. Curveball soon began providing technical drawings and other detailed reports that Saddam Hussein
had secretly constructed lethal germ factories on trains and trucks.

Except for a brief meeting between Curveball and a DIA medical staff
technician in 2000, the Germans refused to let U.S. officials interview
Curveball until 2004, well after the war began. Neither the DIA nor the
CIA checked his background, although the DIA medical technician
questioned his reliability, as did other foreign intelligence service contacts. When German intelligence officials realized that he was "out of
control" and a mentally unstable alcoholic, they did not wish to express
their doubts in public. Instead, at a private lunch with the CIA chief of
the European Division, a German intelligence officer reported that
Curveball "is a fabricator and he's crazy."

In short, Curveball was not a terrorist or a drug dealer; he was a liar.
The CIA chief of the European Division reported his concerns up the
chain of command at CIA headquarters, but word of Curveball's fabrications apparently never made it to the top. Some senior officials who
later retired from the CIA claimed that the CIA chain of command knew
about the lack of credibility of the reports, but allowed them to be used
by the Bush administration in furtherance of its war plans. Others said
that they had no idea that Curveball had lied. And some assumed that

his reports were only part of the prewar picture of Iraqi WMD being painted by the administration, but, in fact, Curveball's fabrications were the sole source. After concluding that his story was "all-too-familiar," the commission recommended that the CIA systematize and standardize the asset validation procedures inside the agency to ensure that the information provided to them is truthful and accurate.

Unlike the dirty assets situation, where vetting may or may not be practical or even desirable in some situations, the Curveball debacle underscores the importance of careful evaluation of intelligence sources. Where foreign policy considerations prevent vetting the source, intelligence officials should clearly state the uncorroborated nature of any information coming from the source. ■

Conclusion

After more than five years of waging a war on terrorism, the United States remains unclear about whether interdiction and intelligence have made the country more secure. Bush administration officials claim that three-quarters of al Qaeda's senior leadership have been either killed or are in custody, and yet terrorists claiming affiliation with al Qaeda continue to carry out attacks around the world. Over time, it appears likely that al Qaeda and allied radical jihadist terrorists will be even more loosely aligned than in the past, so that practically free-standing cells will receive general direction and support but plan and carry out operations independently. To the extent this diffusion is occurring, the interdiction and intelligence challenges are greater than before. At the same time, the fact that the United States has not been attacked on its own soil since September 11 could reflect the terrorists' lack of capacity to do so, the hardening of U.S. targets, and improved detection hand in hand with successful deterrents—or simply that the next attack has yet to arrive.

FOR FURTHER READING

Keefe, Patrick Radden. *Chatter: Dispatches from the Secret World of Global Eavesdropping.* New York: Random House, 2005.

Lowenthal, Mark M. *Intelligence: From Secrets to Policy.* 3d ed. Washington, D.C.: CQ Press, 2006.

Odom, William E. *Fixing Intelligence: For a More Secure America.* 2d ed. New Haven: Yale University Press, 2003.

Ranelagh, John. *The Agency: The Rise and Decline of the CIA.* New York: Simon and Schuster, 1987.

Chapter 5 Law Enforcement and Its Methods

José Padilla, a former gang member and U.S. citizen, was arrested in Chicago in May 2002 when he disembarked from his international flight at O'Hare Airport. He was then transported by the FBI to New York City, where he was held as a material witness in the ongoing investigation of the September 11, 2001, terrorist attacks. Two days before a hearing in which Padilla was expected to challenge his continued detention, the president signed an order classifying Padilla as an enemy combatant and ordered that he be transferred from the civilian facility to military confinement. The media reported that Padilla was suspected of organizing for al Qaeda a dirty bomb attack inside the United States.

For three and a half years, Padilla remained in military detention, the first American citizen arrested in his own country to be classified as an enemy combatant. In 2004 the Justice Department reported that Padilla had not, after all, been planning to attack with a dirty bomb. Instead, he planned to blow up apartment buildings using conventional explosives to detonate the natural gas lines feeding into the buildings. Then, in December 2005, the government changed course again and sought permission to have Padilla released from military custody and tried in civilian court.

For as long as the U.S. government has viewed terrorism as a significant national security concern, it has struggled with the dilemma of how to deal with the threat posed by terrorists. Are they enemy belligerents in a time of war who commit war crimes and are thus amenable to military detention and trial by military commission, even when operating and captured inside the United States? Or are they criminals who should be tracked down, arrested, detained, charged, and convicted through the traditional civilian law enforcement process? If terrorism possesses attributes of both models, which one should prevail, or should some altogether new framework for adjudicating alleged terrorists be created?

To an extent, the answer to the dilemma has been "all of the above." After September 11, the United States developed a controversial new framework for military detention and adjudication of alleged terrorists outside the decades-old military justice system. At the same time, since the 1980s Congress and the executive branch have developed a still-growing and now extensive set of laws that criminalize terrorism and related activities. As a result, some important convictions of terrorists for heinous crimes have been achieved. However, experience has shown that mounting successful criminal prosecutions presents many challenges and imposes considerable costs, and some critics continue to question the wisdom of devoting significant resources to fighting terrorism with law enforcement tools. From a very different perspective, others are alarmed that the broader net being cast by prosecuting inchoate schemes and by charging those who may only inadvertently provide support to terrorism through their contributions or expressive activities threatens to chill the exercise of protected constitutional freedoms.

This chapter explores these themes. It begins by examining the pluses and minuses of using criminal law enforcement as a strategy for combating terrorism. The reasons to favor prosecution are evenly matched by the drawbacks and difficulties in successfully prosecuting terrorism crimes. It then traces the development of the criminal laws that proscribe terrorism-related activities, and, along the way, it follows the expansion of U.S. laws to reach prospective criminal defendants virtually anywhere in the world. The chapter discusses as well rendition—the practice of bringing suspected terrorists back to the United States or, in recent and extreme instances, sending them to a third country for indefinite detention and interrogation through a controversial practice known as "extraordinary rendition." This discussion is followed by an examination in greater detail of the principal mechanisms now used by the United States to criminalize terrorism, including those laws that permit reaching financiers and others less directly involved in the acts of violence, and the laws that forbid inchoate plans for terrorist activities. The final section considers the prospects for international tribunals to adjudicate alleged terrorists, including the recently constituted International Criminal Court.

The currency of the law enforcement strategy for fighting terrorism was brought into stark relief soon after September 11. Within weeks of the terrorist attacks, Attorney General John Ashcroft announced that the Department of Justice would shift its primary focus "from investigating and prosecuting past crimes to identifying threats of future terrorist acts, preventing them from happening, and punishing would-be perpetrators for their plans of terror." The new "paradigm of prevention" marked a dramatic change in the way in which the U.S. government responded to threats of terrorism, and it generated new interest in the potential uses of law enforcement as a counterterrorism tool. But if the strategy is to prevent first and prosecute second, how will the criminal laws fit the new paradigm?

The Benefits and Costs of Relying on Law Enforcement to Combat Terrorism

The list of reasons to commend the use of the criminal laws to combat terrorism is in some ways like any set of benefits in using law enforcement to reduce deviant behavior. As reviewed in Chapter 4, a classic justification for criminal laws and the punishment that violators face is to deter any future violations of the law. Deterrence certainly is among the reasons that law enforcement methods are used to combat terrorism, but its effectiveness is difficult to measure. Would-be terrorists who are motivated by the righteousness of their cause may not be deterred by the prosecution of others before them, and deterrence has no effect on those who would be suicide bombers.

Sometimes the successful prosecution of a single terrorist has direct and indirect benefits. For example, the capable and nefarious Ramzi Yousef, mastermind of the first World Trade Center bombing in 1993 and planner of many other plots, was sentenced for his crimes to life imprisonment without parole plus 240 years in a U.S. maximum security prison. (See Case Study 5.1.) Thus the direct benefit of his prosecution was that Yousef would not strike again.

As for the indirect benefits, Yousef's capture in Pakistan and rendition to the United States with the assistance of the government of Pakistan revealed several important symbolic gains. First, it showed that the United States would adjudicate alleged terrorists under the rule of law. Although this reputation has since been compromised by the controversial interrogation, detention, rendition, and adjudication practices put in place by the Bush administration since the September 11 attacks, an important revelation is that a state victimized by terrorist attacks is capable of trying those accused of the violence by the same methods and standards of fairness applied to everyday crimes.

Second, the capture and conviction of Yousef demonstrated that prosecution can be an effective weapon in the arsenal to combat terrorism. Considerable effort and expense were devoted to finding Yousef, capturing him alive, and protecting his legal rights once he was detained. In the end, the investment may have paid off.

Finally, the fate delivered to Yousef may deter others who might follow in his footsteps. Just as successful prosecutions of high-profile gang or organized crime kingpins may, at least in some instances, deter those criminal activities, prosecuting terrorists may pay dividends in combating terrorism.

Related to the symbolic gains of a high-profile conviction is the advantage that it confers on the investigators and police who track the activities and movements of accused terrorists. Suspects who have evaded capture are made aware by successful prosecutions that the United States and cooperating nations are able to track down fugitive terrorists virtually anywhere in the world. Similarly, the successful cooperative venture between the governments of the United States and Pakistan could encourage other nations to stiffen their efforts to combat terrorism and to assist in the efforts to detain and bring to justice those accused of terrorist crimes.

The downside in favoring criminal prosecution as a strategy to combat terrorism is formidable. First, as mentioned earlier, the deterrent effects of prosecution are uncertain, and, at least for religious zealots and suicide terrorists, they do not register at all. In addition, the prosecution of terrorists and their imprisonment will likely induce retaliation in the form of new terrorist attacks, including hostage taking to secure the release of imprisoned terrorist colleagues. For example, after the conviction and sentencing of blind cleric Sheikh Omar Abdel Rahman (discussed later in this chapter), U.S. officials suspected that his followers in Egypt would be inspired to strike out against the United States. Likewise, the arrest and conviction of Mir Aimal Kansi for killing CIA personnel at CIA headquarters apparently inspired the 1997 killing of four U.S. businessmen and their driver in Karachi, Pakistan. (See Case Study 5.1.)

Second, the public trials of prominent terrorist suspects may serve to draw further attention to the cause the terrorists represent. As Chapter 9 reveals, a basic objective of terrorism is to gain publicity. Media coverage of terrorist prosecutions may provide more benefits for the terrorist organization than the cost to the group of losing a leader.

Third, criminal prosecution is typically successful only in charging the operatives who carry out terrorist attacks, not the leaders or masterminds. Finding the evidence needed to prosecute leaders successfully is a daunting challenge. In this respect, the conviction of Yousef was exceptional. More often, the foot soldiers who are caught have left a trail that criminal investigators can follow, whereas the leaders and organizers are removed, inaccessible even to the operatives in many cases. Thus the successful prosecution of the underlings may do little to thwart the terrorism directed by the leaders. For example, after the 1998 bombings of the U.S. embassies in Kenya and Tanzania, effective police work and cooperation from Kenyan and Tanzanian authorities enabled the prosecution and conviction of some low-level operatives involved in those attacks, but mastermind Osama bin Laden could only be indicted as a co-conspirator who remained a fugitive.

Likewise, the 1988 bombing of Pan Am Flight 103 over Lockerbie, Scotland, eventually resulted in the government of Libya handing over two operatives to stand trial, but those responsible for ordering and planning the attack were never punished. Although the trials and convictions in the Pan Am Flight 103 and African embassy bombings cases may have provided some measure of justice and closure in those instances, in other respects neither justice nor closure was achieved. The masterminds and leaders remained free, and the victims could never be fully compensated for their losses.

These problems with use of the prosecution approach to combating terrorism are confounded by the difficulties of the prosecution cases themselves. At the outset, once an alleged terrorist is arrested and the commitment to prosecute becomes known, anything less than conviction and significant prison time will be viewed as a counterterrorism failure. Because criminal conviction requires proof of guilt beyond a reasonable doubt, the proof in a case alleging terrorist activities must go well beyond the evidence that might suffice to associate a person with terrorist activities for the purpose of targeting that person for investigation. Finding evidence of direct involvement by those who did not actually take part in the terrorist attack may be difficult or impossible, and, depending on the crime or crimes alleged, prosecutors and other government officials may determine that a difficult-to-prove case is too risky.

The building of the case itself is also complicated by some factors unique to terrorism-related crimes. First, the sources and methods for gathering the intelligence that led to the arrest and detention of the accused would in the normal course of a criminal trial likely be revealed. After all, the defense is entitled to know the evidence that the government will use in its case, including the identity of the sources and how the information was collected. As a result, informants or other valuable sources may no longer be usable, and the techniques favored for gaining information about terrorist activities may lose their value if the terrorists learn about them and can take evasive measures. Second, as just noted, in ordinary criminal cases the prosecution recognizes that it must divulge to the defense any evidence it has that may be favorable to the defense, if it is material in any way to the charges. In most cases, the prosecution simply turns over its files. Failure to turn over material could lead to reversal of a conviction, if one is obtained. Sometimes, however, the prosecution will hesitate to provide the defendants with access to evidence if doing so might undermine national security.

Congress addressed this problem in the Classified Information Procedures Act (CIPA). CIPA allows the government to withhold classified information if it provides a suitable summary of the information that will suffice to provide a fair trial. What constitutes classified information can be determined by statute, by presidential order, or by regulation. If a summary is submitted by the government, the judge must decide whether it provides the accused with substantially the same ability to make his defense as would disclosure of the original. Two other problems also confound terrorism prosecutions in the United States. First, because of the willingness in the United States to impose the death penalty for some serious terrorism-related offenses, some foreign governments have refused to cooperate in any U.S. prosecution where the death penalty could result. These governments also decline to render or extradite suspects to the United States under such circumstances.

Second, obtaining jurisdiction—the authority to bring the criminal case—over suspects outside the United States is legally and practically complicated by unclear though evolving theories of extending jurisdiction beyond the borders of the United States and by the diplomatic and political complexities of cooperation with nations that may have as much or more to lose than gain by cooperating with the United States in a terrorism prosecution. The case of Saudi Arabia after the 1996 suicide truck bombing of the Khobar Towers complex that housed U.S. Air Force personnel near Dhahran Air Base is emblematic. The Clinton administration suspected that Hezbollah and perhaps even Iran were involved in the attack. Even though the United States and Saudi Arabia shared some intelligence before the attacks that indicated an increasing threat to U.S. installations there, the Saudi government was only secretly cooperative with U.S. investigators after the attack, no doubt because of its concerns that being seen working too closely with the United States would spur terrorist strikes against the Saudi government. Although the

Saudis arrested some suspects within days of the attack, they would not let the suspects be interrogated by U.S. investigators. Nor did the Saudis want the United States to strike Iran if proof of its involvement in the bombing was discovered. Saudi Arabia had been carefully balancing its relations with Iran and Iraq, and it feared that a U.S. strike against Iran, based on law enforcement and intelligence cooperation supplied by Saudi Arabia, would undermine Saudi Arabia's and Iran's positions in the region and possibly destabilize the Middle East.

CASE STUDY 5.1

A Tale of Two Terrorists

Ramzi Yousef

Ramzi Yousef's life began in either Kuwait or Pakistan. The nephew of the al Qaeda mastermind of the September 11 attacks, Khalid Sheikh Mohammed, Yousef was a bright student. He excelled in math and languages and studied engineering at what is now known as the Swansea Institute of Higher Education in Wales. There, Yousef joined the Egyptian Muslim Brotherhood.

In the late 1980s and early 1990s, Yousef began taking trips to Pakistan and Afghanistan and training at terrorist camps. Using a fake Iraqi passport, Yousef entered the United States on September 1, 1992, and, after being held in an overcrowded Immigration and Naturalization Service (INS) holding cell and given a hearing, he successfully claimed asylum.

Once free, Yousef settled in Jersey City and began networking with militant Muslims, including Sheikh Omar Abdel Rahman. In this New Jersey residence Yousef, with the help of Mohammed Salameh and Mahmud Abouhalima, began assembling a twelve-hundred-pound bomb made of urea nitrate and fuel oil. The crude bomb was made for less than $200. Their plan was to detonate the bomb in a rented van parked underneath one of the World Trade Center towers. If their plan was successful, after the bomb was detonated Tower One would collapse onto Tower Two.

In letters mailed immediately before the attack, Yousef demanded that the United States cease its aid of the state of Israel and end its interference with all Middle Eastern affairs. Otherwise, the attack would merely be the first of many to come.

At lunchtime on February 26, 1993, the bomb exploded in the underground garage beneath the World Trade Center, creating a thirty-meter-wide hole through four of the tower's sublevels. Six people were killed, and over a thousand were injured. Hours after the attack, Yousef was on a plane to Pakistan.

Almost two years later, in January 1995, Philippine police followed up on an earlier report of a fire in a Manila apartment complex and discovered a bomb-making laboratory, along with a computer hard drive that incriminated a local suspect. That suspect, in turn, named Ramzi Yousef as his leader, and told investigators that Yousef planned to bomb eleven or twelve airliners simultaneously over the Pacific, as well as kill the pope, who was due in the Philippines in January.

Yousef's trail was then lost for a month until South African student Istaique Parker, who was working for Yousef in Pakistan, read in *Newsweek* magazine that a $2 million reward was being offered for information leading to Yousef's capture. Parker had been trained by Yousef to place explosives-laden suitcases on United Airlines trans-Pacific flights originating in Bangkok, but instead he sought the reward and led officials to an Islamabad guest house where Pakistani and American officials arrested Yousef.

When he finally appeared in a New York City court, Yousef declared, "I am a terrorist, and I am proud of it." In November 1997, a jury found Yousef guilty of masterminding the World Trade Center bombing and sentenced him to life in prison plus 240 years, without parole. The judge also recommended that Yousef spend his sentence in solitary confinement at the SuperMax prison in Florence, Colorado. "Mr. Yousef, you are a virus that must be locked away," said the judge at the sentencing.

Mir Aimal Kansi

On January 25, 1993, at about 8 a.m., a line of passenger cars were stopped in two northbound, left-turn lanes on Route 123 in Fairfax County, Virginia, at the main entrance to the headquarters of the Central Intelligence Agency. The drivers of the cars, who had stopped for a red light, were waiting to turn into the entrance. Meanwhile, a lone gunman emerged from one of the cars in line. Armed with an AK-47 assault rifle, Mir Aimal Kansi moved among the cars, firing his weapon into each of them. Within a few seconds, two drivers were killed and three were injured, all CIA employees. Kansi fled the scene and later flew to Pakistan.

Kansi had entered the United States in 1991, using a fake passport purchased in Karachi, Pakistan. He found work at a courier service, and his deliveries included occasional stops at CIA headquarters. At the time of the attack, Kansi lived with a friend in a rented apartment in Reston, Virginia. Two days after the shootings, his roommate reported Kansi to the local police as a missing person. In searching the apartment, the police found the AK-47 used in the shootings. Kansi was later indicted for murder and other offenses in Virginia.

Four years later, some men in Kansi's inner circle in Pakistan learned about the $2 million reward being offered for information leading to his capture, and they approached the U.S. embassy in Karachi with an offer to reveal Kansi's location. Pakistani officials then raided the hotel where Kansi was hiding, and a few days later, on June 15, 1997, Kansi was flown to the United States to stand trial.

Yousef and Kansi have more in common than their Pakistani descent and place of capture. Both were well educated; both adopted a violent, radical form of Islam; and both directed their anger and resentment toward the United States. In addition, Yousef and Kansi found it relatively easy to enter the United States using fake papers. Their terrorist acts also reflect important differences. Whereas Kansi was a "lone wolf" terrorist, apparently unaffiliated with any international organization, Yousef was closely aligned with al Qaeda and radical Egyptian Muslim cleric Sheikh Omar Abdel Rahman. Kansi perpetrated a single, heinous act, while Yousef embarked on an ongoing campaign of terror. Both men ended up on the FBI's Ten Most Wanted Fugitives list, however, and both were betrayed by associates in Pakistan who were motivated by the offer of a $2 million reward.

Some policy makers have proposed that more stringent immigration measures and tougher border controls be adopted to make it less likely that terrorists could gain entry to the United States. Even with existing immigration and border standards, however, it is fair to say that the criminal justice system succeeded in combating terrorism by convicting these terrorists. ∎

The Growth in Criminal Laws Directed at Terrorism

The United States has combated terrorism since President George Washington dealt with the domestic terrorists who perpetrated the 1794 Whiskey Rebellion and President Thomas Jefferson used naval forces to fight the Barbary pirates. However, the use of law enforcement techniques and processes to counter terrorism is a modern phenomenon. In part, the late entry of the criminal law as a means of fighting terrorism is explained by the absence of terrorism directed at Americans on U.S. soil until the 1990s. Those attacks that did occur against the United States or its citizens or interests generally were carried out abroad or aboard airliners or ships. The state-sponsored terrorism that predominated until the 1990s was subject to sanctions and embargoes imposed by the president as part of presidential emergency powers enabled by legislation. A World War I–era law known as the Trading With the Enemy Act (TWEA) criminalized the conduct of certain commercial activities with enemies of the United States during wartime, and it permitted the president to stop or regulate a range of other economic transactions with enemies and allies. Between the world wars, Congress amended the act to permit the president to exercise its authorities whenever an "emergency" arose, whether in war or in peace.

During the Cold War, presidents often invoked the TWEA to impose sanctions on other nations. By the mid-1970s, Congress was seeking to rein in what it then viewed as expansive executive discretion to wield emergency economic powers, and it cut back on the TWEA, set forth new procedures for utilizing emergency powers, and modernized the authorities in the International Emergency Economic Powers Act (IEEPA). The IEEPA allows the president to impose economic sanctions during emergencies, which are defined as "any unusual and extraordinary threat" originating from outside the United States to the national security, foreign policy, or economy of the United States. President Ronald Reagan relied on his IEEPA authority many times, often to impose sanctions on Libya for its sponsorship of terrorist attacks targeting the United States.

One high-profile criminal prosecution spawned by the first World Trade Center bombing in 1993 illustrates another law enforcement tool for prosecutors. Sheikh Omar Abdel Rahman, a blind Islamic scholar and cleric, was alleged, on the basis of a decades-old criminal law, to be the leader of a "seditious conspiracy" for the purpose of fomenting jihad, or a struggle against the enemies of Islam. Rahman and his codefendants allegedly were responsible for attempting to murder Egyptian president Hosni Mubarak, providing assistance in the bombing of the World Trade Center in 1993, and undertaking a campaign of attempted bombings in 1993 of buildings and tunnels in New York City. The government charged that Rahman urged his followers to "do jihad with the sword, with the cannon, with the grenades, with the missile . . . against God's enemies." [1] Although Rahman did not participate in carrying out any of the completed or attempted violent acts, he provided overall supervision and direction to those with whom he conspired.

Sheikh Rahman was convicted and sentenced to life in prison for engaging in a "seditious conspiracy" intended "to overthrow, put down or to destroy by force the Government of the United States." [2] Thus, at least in this setting, terrorism crimes could be prosecuted under laws written for a different time and a different purpose. Rahman argued on appeal that the seditious conspiracy statute actually makes treason against the government criminal, and that, because the Treason Clause of the Constitution states that "[n]o person shall be convicted of Treason unless on the Testimony of two Witnesses to the same overt Act, or on Confession in open Court," the seditious conspiracy statute is unconstitutional. The court rejected that argument. It found that treason charges are reserved for persons who express a betrayal of allegiance to the United States and that the facts indicated that Sheikh Rahman's utterances were not treasonous by such a standard.

The current criminal laws on terrorism are an outgrowth of these earlier sources of executive discretion to punish state sponsors of terrorism. However, there is no single or uniform crime of "being a terrorist" or "engaging in terrorist activities." Instead, terrorism crimes have developed piecemeal, following policy makers' determinations of what specific activities should be forbidden or controlled—determinations usually made following a terrorist attack or series of attacks. For example, in 1979 the United States became a signatory to the United Nations International Convention against the Taking of Hostages. One article of the treaty gives signatory nations the discretion to assert law enforcement jurisdiction when their nationals are taken hostage, wherever the hostage taking occurs. After a series of terrorist attacks in which Americans were taken hostage (including the seizure of the U.S. embassy in Tehran in 1979 and the seizure of diplomatic personnel as hostages), President Reagan introduced a legislative proposal that would "send a strong and vigorous message to friend and foe alike that the United States will not tolerate terrorist activity against its citizens within its borders." Enacted in 1984, the Comprehensive Crime Control Act authorized federal prosecution of the taking of hostages in the United States or abroad when the seizure or detention of the person is coupled with threats to kill or injure if certain conditions are not met.

Omnibus Diplomatic Security and Antiterrorism Act

In the decade between 1975 and 1985, 2,500 terrorist acts were directed at Americans or U.S. interests abroad, a stunning increase in violence targeting the United States. In 1986 the Omnibus Diplomatic Security and Antiterrorism Act was the nation's first effort at comprehensive terrorism legislation. For the first time, the act made it a crime to harm Americans abroad. The focus of the act was on international terrorism, defined as violent acts, or acts dangerous to human life, intended to intimidate a civilian population. Among other things, the act sought to protect diplomatic missions and provide maritime security. It also authorized the offering of rewards for information that could lead to the arrest of a suspected terrorist, and it provided a mechanism, for the first time, to compensate the victims of terrorism. That terrorism might be directed at the United States on its own shores was not considered a serious problem at the time.

Antiterrorism and Effective Death Penalty Act

More comprehensive legislation was enacted in 1996, largely in response to the 1993 World Trade Center attack, the 1995 bombing of a U.S. training center in Riyadh, Saudi Arabia, and the 1995 bombing of the Oklahoma City federal building. The Antiterrorism and Effective Death Penalty Act of 1996 (AEDPA) expanded considerably the number and scope of federal crimes directed at terrorism, and it increased the penalties for some existing offenses. Perhaps more important, the AEDPA represented the first real sign that the United States would use legal mechanisms to anticipate and prevent terrorist acts, as well as prosecute and punish any terrorist acts actually carried out.

In part, then, the AEDPA goes beyond the traditional criminal law mechanisms and authorizes the use of various financial devices, such as freezing and forfeiture of assets, prohibiting financial transactions with state supporters of terrorism, and designating terrorist groups as foreign terrorist organizations. (See Chapter 4.) After a foreign group is designated an FTO, its members, as authorized by Congress, are denied entry to the United States and the group's assets in the United States are frozen.

The single most widely used and, perhaps inevitably, most controversial component of the AEDPA has been its provision making it a crime to provide terrorists or designated FTOs with "material support." The material support crimes have become central to combating terrorism, particularly since the attacks of September 11, 2001, as part of the Bush administration's strategy aimed at preventing terrorist attacks. However, as suggested in Chapter 4, strategies that seek to anticipate terrorism by regulating or proscribing conduct that could lead to or support terrorism run the risk of sweeping wholly innocent activities into the dragnet, including expressive conduct by individuals that may by constitutionally protected. As those accused of material support crimes have challenged the constitutionality of the statute as it is applied to their specific activities and more generally, the courts and Congress have revised and updated this central piece of the law enforcement strategy to combat terrorism several times since 1996.

One group that has wandered into this murky area is the Humanitarian Law Project (HLP). The HLP describes itself as "a non-profit organization founded in 1985, dedicated to protecting human rights and promoting the peaceful resolution of conflict by using established international human rights laws and humanitarian law." Some of the groups it supports, however, have been viewed with suspicion by the U.S. government. In fact, some officials have wondered whether the HLP should be criminally charged with lending material support to two designated FTOs—the Kurdistan Workers Party (PKK) and the Liberation Tigers of Tamil Eelam (LTTE).

The HLP claimed to provide only nonviolent humanitarian and political aid to the two organizations, but correctly feared that any such support would be deemed a violation of the Antiterrorism and Effective Death Penalty Act. In a 2000 decision, a court rejected claims by the HLP that its support was protected by the First Amendment. The HLP maintained that the statute amendment in effect imposes guilt by association, such that by supporting these groups the HLP is presumed to be engaging in activities pursued by only the supported group. In addition, the HLP argued that the First Amendment protects the HLP's advocacy of the political claims advanced by the LTTE and PKK. And yet the court rejected these claims and reasoned that the goal of the HLP in lending support was not important, because "material support given to a terrorist organization can be used to promote the organization's unlawful activities, regardless of the donor's intent. Once the support is given, the donor has no control over how it is used." [3]

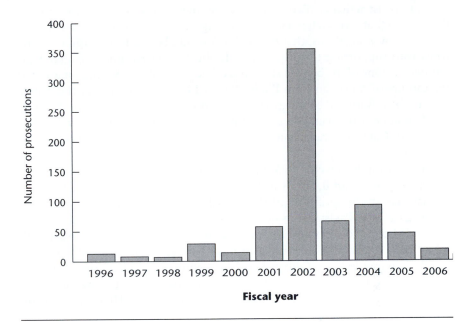

Figure 5.1 Federal Criminal Prosecutions for International
Terrorism Offenses, 1996–2006

SOURCE: "Criminal Terrorism Enforcement in the United States during the Five Years since the 9/11/01 Attacks," TRAC Reports, Transactional Records Analysis Center, Syracuse University, Syracuse, N.Y., April 17, 2007, http://trac.syr.edu/tracreports/terrorism/169.

Three years later, another court reaffirmed the 2000 decision with some modification. It still was not important how the HLP intended its support to be used, but if it knew that it was lending support to an organization designated as an FTO or knew of the unlawful activities undertaken by the organization that would lead to such a designation, then it was guilty of providing material support to the groups.

Despite the broad authority to bring "material support" prosecutions, data show that even though the prosecution of individuals classified by the government as international terrorists surged soon after the September 11 attacks, it returned to pre–September 11 numbers five years later. (See Figure 5.1.) Although the threat of international terrorism is usually characterized as higher today than six or seven years ago, the rate of prosecution does not match the threat perception.

One indicator of the breadth of the AEDPA is its special provisions for removing alien terrorist suspects from the United States. The act created a special Alien Terrorist Removal Court (ATRC) to hear removal applications filed by the attorney general against any alien accused by the government of engaging in terrorist activities. Parallel procedures may be invoked to deny entry to the United States of such persons, including those associated with FTOs.

If there was any doubt that the AEDPA would be used to charge U.S. citizens with supporting terrorism, that doubt was erased not long after September 11. One of the biggest stories to come out of the U.S.-Afghan war was the capture of American John Philip Walker Lindh, also known as the American Taliban. Born and baptized a Catholic in Washington, D.C., Lindh developed an interest in Islam as a teen while watching the film *Malcolm X*. After moving to California, he began attending services at a mosque and converted to Islam.

In 1998 Lindh traveled to Yemen for eight months to study Arabic, and returned again in 2000, after which he journeyed to Pakistan before reaching Afghanistan in the spring of 2001. In mid-2001, Lindh attended a military training camp in Pakistan run by Harakat ul-Mujahedin (HUM), a terrorist group dedicated to an extremist view of Islam. After receiving training, Lindh told HUM leaders that he wished to fight with the Taliban in Afghanistan. Lindh then traveled to a Taliban recruiting center in Kabul, presented a letter of introduction from HUM, and told Taliban personnel that he was an American and that he wanted to go to the front lines to fight. They agreed to his request.

After the attacks of September 11, 2001, Lindh remained with his fighting group on the front lines even after he was told about the September 11 attacks and that al Qaeda was responsible for them. In November 2001, Lindh was captured by the Afghan Northern Alliance and questioned by CIA agents. During an uprising that resulted in the death of one CIA agent, Lindh was shot. He then hid in a bunker, where he was found a week later after an irrigation stream was diverted in his direction. After his capture, he signed a confession in which he admitted being a member of al Qaeda.

At the time of his confession, Lindh had been without medical treatment for his wounds, and he had received only limited food and water. Allegedly, Lindh also received rough and abusive treatment by his captors. Once brought to the United States, Lindh entered a plea of not guilty to numerous charges, including providing material support to a terrorist organization and conspiring to murder Americans.

Eventually, prosecutors offered Lindh a deal in which the government agreed to drop eight of the ten charges levied against him. Lindh, in exchange, agreed to plead guilty both to serving in the Taliban army and to carrying weapons. Lindh also dropped his claims of mistreatment by U.S. military personnel, and agreed to a gag order for the duration of his twenty-year sentence without parole, which he began serving in January 2003. In his statement before the court, Lindh apologized, saying, "had I realized then what I know now . . . I would never would have joined [the Taliban]." [4]

The public response to the Lindh trial ran the gamut. Some people called for charges of treason and the death penalty, while others saw him merely as a confused and lost teenager who got caught up with the wrong crowd and was ultimately an innocent bystander.

This case raises the question: if there had been no plea agreement, what elements of "material support" could Lindh have been convicted of providing to al Qaeda or the Taliban? The court that decided the pre-agreement motions in the Lindh case found that he "willfully and unlawfully supplied and attempted to supply services to the Taliban." [5] But is providing "services" in this way a violation of the material support law? Alternatively, could Lindh have been successfully prosecuted for treason? As noted, Article III, section 3, of the U.S. Constitution states: "Treason against the United States, shall consist only in levying War against them, or in adhering to their Enemies, giving them Aid and Comfort. No person shall be convicted of Treason unless on the Testimony of two Witnesses to the same over Act, or on Confession in open Court."

USA PATRIOT Act

Within weeks of the September 11 terrorist attacks, Congress enacted and President Bush signed into law the USA PATRIOT Act (Uniting and Strengthening America by Providing Appropriate Tools Required to Intercept and Obstruct Terrorism). Although the legislation is lengthy (342 pages) and complex, it suffers from considerable lack of clarity and unresolved issues, because, in the rush to take some demonstrative action after the attacks, Congress engaged in only limited debate on and consideration of many of the act's provisions.

By and large, the Patriot Act sought to enhance the tools needed to investigate both terrorist and other criminal activities and to update the technological means for keeping track of terrorist activities. To the extent that the Patriot Act added to the criminal laws that are now employed to combat terrorism, it did so by expanding and clarifying some of the definitions of terrorist activity, by adding variations to existing crimes, and by adding a few new crimes, including terrorist acts against mass transit, harboring terrorists, and acts of "domestic terrorism."

Despite the fact that enactment of the Patriot Act made only modest substantive additions to the criminal laws, the act became a lightning rod for criticism and the center of the controversy over the Bush administration's conduct of the war on terrorism. Remarkably, in the two years after enactment of the Patriot Act, three states and over 150 cities passed resolutions criticizing the act or portions of it. Civil liberties organizations took aim at the law; the Electronic Frontier Foundation, the American Civil Liberties Union, and others asserted that the civil liberties of ordinary Americans were significantly compromised by the new law. Elsewhere, the *Washington Post* editorial staff characterized the Patriot Act as "panicky legislation" that "reduced the healthy oversight of the courts." [6]

Most of those Americans who expressed a view about the Patriot Act may have feared its provisions because they had difficulty understanding them—a situation perhaps attributable to the relative haste that attended enactment of the legislation. In fact, the Patriot Act's 342 pages contained only a small number of controversial changes in the law, and nearly all of those referenced expanded investigative authorities, some of which were discussed in Chapter 4. Congress also subjected these controversial authorities to sunset provisions, so that they would expire on December 31, 2005, unless extended by subsequent legislation. After a concerted effort by Bush administration officials, nearly all of the provisions subject to sunset were made permanent by new legislation in 2006, while two of them were extended to the end of 2009.

Homeland Security Act

Another piece of major legislation that uses law enforcement to combat terrorism is the Homeland Security Act of 2002 (HSA). The act was yet another lengthy and complex legislative package, principally because of the challenge of writing the charter for the transfer of seventeen agencies and 170,000 personnel to a new cabinet department, the Department of Homeland Security.

Although the criminal laws were not expanded much by the HSA, the institutional changes wrought by creation of the new department were designed to and indeed do have a considerable effect on law enforcement to combat terrorism. For example, post–September 11 finger pointing placed blame on the Immigration and Naturalization Service for failing to stop the September 11 hijackers when they entered the country or to find and detain them for visa overstays or other violations while they lived in the United States and prepared for their mission. The HSA abolished INS and assigned immigration functions to a new bureau of U.S. Citizenship and Immigration Services (USCIS) and a new enforcement agency, Immigration and Customs Enforcement (ICE). Meanwhile, the reorganization has been a difficult one, because personnel have complained about being separated from former colleagues in INS and the agency's subordinated role to the FBI in some kinds of investigations. The HSA also enhanced existing criminal provisions proscribing cyberterrorism, and it provided new authorities to encourage law enforcement and intelligence agencies to cooperate in their investigations and to share information about terrorist activities.

Intelligence Reform and Terrorism Prevention Act

The Intelligence Reform and Terrorism Prevention Act of 2004 (IRTPA) was enacted in response to the report and recommendations of the National Commission on Terrorist Attacks upon the United States. Like the HSA, the IRTPA is structural legislation, designed principally to reform the way in which the intelligence function is organized and managed within the government.

Also like the HSA, the IRTPA amends a range of criminal laws to increase penalties, strengthens denial of entry and removal provisions for aliens associated with terrorist activities, enhances money-laundering crime provisions, adds to information-sharing authorities, amends the material support crime provision, and expands federal authorities to detain terrorism suspects pretrial.

All of these legislative packages have been reactive in one way or another to major terrorist incidents or to the reports produced in response to those incidents. That commonality raises the question of whether the reactive approach actually produces legislation that is effective in combating terrorism.

Universal Jurisdiction for Terrorism Crimes

In addition to expanding the array of criminal laws written to deter and to provide the means for punishing terrorists, Congress and the courts have joined together to extend the authority of these laws to include conduct beyond U.S. territory. For example, in the trials of those accused of involvement in the 1993 bombing of the World Trade Center and the 1994 conspiracy to bomb U.S. commercial airliners in Southeast Asia, the convicted defendants argued on appeal that Congress lacks the authority to legislate conduct outside the United States because of principles of international law that limit any nation's sovereign right to enforce its laws inside the boundaries of another nation. But the reviewing court in *United States v. Yousef* (1996) easily concluded that Congress intended its criminal laws at issue in the case to apply outside the borders of the United States. (See the account in Chapter 1 of Ramzi Yousef's role in the 1993 World Trade Center bombing.)

The more difficult question was whether the criminal laws of the United States could be applied to an alleged terrorist for a crime of terrorism that occurred outside the United States when customary international law had no consensus norm or rule proscribing terrorism. The court took the position that U.S. law could be applied to the defendants even if it conflicted with customary international law or even with treaty-based international law. The court was of the view, shared by most American courts, that customary international law may inform the judgment of U.S. courts, but that it cannot limit legislative policies made by the Congress that are within its constitutional limits. As applied by U.S. courts, customary international law is part of the law of the United States to the extent that "where there is no treaty, and no controlling executive or legislative act or judicial decision, resort must be had to the customs and usage of civilized nations." [7]

In December 2001, Richard Reid, a citizen of the United Kingdom, sought unsuccessfully to destroy an American Airlines flight from Paris to Miami using explosives he had hidden in his shoes. The fuses that protruded from his tennis shoes raised suspicion among the flight crew once he boarded the flight, and he was apprehended and guarded by airline security personnel for the duration of the flight. At his trial in the United States, Reid pleaded guilty to attempted use of a weapon of mass destruction, attempted homicide, placing an explosive device aboard an aircraft, and various other offenses.

At his sentencing hearing where he received a life sentence, Reid declared, "I am at war with your country," and he vowed his "allegiance to Sheik Asama bin Laden." [8] His trial raises the questions of whether the United States was justified in applying its criminal laws to Reid's conduct and on what basis U.S. courts had the jurisdiction to prosecute Reid.

In the setting of airline-related terrorism, the Hague Convention for the Suppression of Unlawful Seizure of Aircraft and the Montreal Convention for the Suppression of Unlawful Acts Against the Safety of Civil Aviation provide a means for criminal jurisdiction over those who commit terrorist acts within the territory or airspace of states contracting to the treaties. The states agree either to try the suspect or to return the suspect to trial in the charging state, in this case the United States.

For example, after Ramzi Yousef, one of the planners of the 1993 World Trade Center bombing, was arrested in Pakistan in 1995 and transferred to the United States, he was tried and convicted for his role in planning an unsuccessful plot to blow up civilian airliners over the Pacific. Even without the treaties, the court found authority to try Yousef on the basis of the customary principles of jurisdiction that, for example, reach the accused because the plot to bomb aircraft included U.S.-bound airliners, or because the purpose of the attack was to influence U.S. foreign policy. The Yousef court joined others that have held that for a few especially heinous offenses universally regarded as such by the nations of the world universal jurisdiction exists to try and punish the violators. "Crimes against humanity" are one such category, including genocide. However, the court was unable to conclude that the term *terrorism* had a sufficiently clear meaning and application across the globe to permit jurisdiction based on the universality principle.[9] To further minimize the chance that such reasoning will not stand in the way of U.S. courts having authority to try those accused of terrorism crimes against the United States or its citizens, Congress has increasingly made explicit in the criminal laws jurisdictional provisions for dealing with conduct that occurs outside of the United States:

Acts of Terrorism Transcending National Boundaries

(a) Prohibited acts.

(1) Offenses. Whoever, involving conducting transcending national boundaries and in a circumstance described in subsection (b)

(A) kills, kidnaps, maims, commits an assault resulting in serious bodily injury, or assaults with a dangerous weapon any person within the United States; or

(B) creates a substantial risk of serious bodily injury [by destroying or damaging property within the United States]

in violation of the laws of any state, or the United States, shall be punished. . . .

(b) Jurisdictional bases.

(1) Circumstances. The circumstances referred to in subsection (a) are

(A) . . . any facility in interstate or foreign commerce is used in furtherance of the offense;

(B) the offense . . . affects interstate or foreign commerce. . . .

(C) the victim, or intended victim, is the United States government [or any member of the armed forces or an employee of the United States]. . . .

(E) the offense is committed in the territorial sea . . . of the United States. . . . [10]

Law enforcement and its processes are part of almost every nation's toolkit in combating terrorism. The possibility that one nation's criminal courts might purport to try persons or even high-ranking government officials of another nation for terrorism-related crimes has created some controversy in the United States, however. On November 30, 2004, the Center for Constitutional Rights and four Iraqi citizens filed a criminal complaint with the German Federal Prosecutor's Office at Karlsruhe Court in Karlsruhe, Germany. The four Iraqis claimed that they were victims of gruesome crimes, including severe beatings, sleep and food deprivation, hooding, and sexual abuse at Abu Ghraib prison in Iraq while it was being run by U.S. Department of Defense personnel. Their complaint sought an investigation into war crimes allegedly carried out by high-ranking U.S. civilian and military officials, including Secretary of Defense Donald Rumsfeld, who is accused of failing to prevent the abuses that occurred under his command. The charges include violations of the German criminal code, which outlaws torture, cruel and inhumane treatment, sexual coercion, and forcible transfers. The code holds responsible those who commit these acts as well as those who condone, induce, or order the acts. The code also makes liable commanders who fail to prevent their subordinates from committing such acts.

The German code obligates the prosecutor to investigate all crimes that constitute violations of the code, regardless of the location of the person or the nationality of the persons involved. The German code thus adopts the doctrine of universal jurisdiction—providing a legal basis for the German court to try Americans for crimes allegedly committed in Iraq. Similar criminal charges have been made in Germany and Italy against U.S. CIA operatives who allegedly abducted and then oversaw the coercive interrogation of a suspected terrorist.

That said, obtaining actual jurisdiction over these U.S. officials in a German or Italian court is highly unlikely, and most nations, including the United States, do not recognize or practice the doctrine of universal jurisdiction. Still, these examples reveal one of the risks when U.S. officials engage in conduct that might be viewed as criminal in some other nation.

Rendition

Rendition is generally understood to be the surrender of a person from one state to another state that has requested that person, typically pursuant to a criminal prosecution. Rendition ranges from informal, ad hoc circumstances, as described shortly, to a formal process (in the form of an extradition treaty), to an extraordinary situation in which, for example, the United States has transferred detainees to foreign countries in circumstances in which it is more likely than not that the individuals will be subjected to torture or to cruel, inhuman, or degrading treatment. (See Case Studies 5.2 and 5.3 for examples of rendition.)

On June 11, 1985, Fawaz Yunis and four other men boarded Royal Jordanian Airlines Flight 402 shortly before its scheduled departure from Beirut, Lebanon. They wore civilian clothes and carried military assault rifles, ammunition bandoleers, and hand grenades. Yunis took control of the cockpit and forced the pilot to take off. The other hijackers tied up Jordanian air marshals and held the civilian passengers, including two Americans, captive in their seats. The hijackers announced that they wanted the plane to fly to Tunis, where an ongoing meeting of the Arab League was under way. The hijackers sought a meeting with the delegates and stated that their goal was the removal of all Palestinians from Lebanon.

After a refueling stop in Cyprus, the flight headed for Tunis, but it was turned away when local officials blocked the runway. Following a refueling stop in Palermo, Sicily, another attempt was made to land in Tunis. After this attempt failed, the plane returned to Beirut, picked up reinforcements from the Amal Militia, made another attempt to land, this time in Syria, but failed again and returned again to Beirut, where the passengers were released. After holding a press conference reiterating their demand that Palestinians leave Lebanon, the hijackers then blew up the plane and fled.

After a U.S. investigation identified Yunis as the leader of the plot, the FBI issued a warrant for his arrest. In September 1987, FBI agents lured Yunis onto a yacht in the eastern Mediterranean Sea with promises of a drug deal, and arrested him once the vessel entered international waters. The agents then transferred Yunis to a U.S. Navy ship, interrogated him there for several days, transferred him again to a naval aircraft carrier, and then transported him by military aircraft to Washington. There, he was indicted and charged with air piracy, hostage taking, and aircraft damage.

CASE STUDY 5.2

The Abduction of Humberto Álvarez-Machaín

Humberto Álvarez-Machaín, a Mexican citizen and resident, was indicted in 1990 for participating in the kidnapping and murder of a U.S. Drug Enforcement Agency (DEA) agent and a Mexican pilot working with the DEA agent. The DEA alleged that Álvarez-Machaín, a physician, prolonged the agent's life so that others could further interrogate and torture him.

In 1990 Álvarez-Machaín had been forcibly kidnapped from his medical office in Guadalajara, Mexico, and flown by private plane to El Paso, Texas, where he was arrested by DEA agents and officials. (Although DEA officials were later determined to be responsible for the abduction, they did not carry out the kidnapping themselves.) The United States and Mexico had a formal extradition treaty that provided for a mechanism to send persons from one country to the other to stand trial. However, the treaty did not state explicitly that its terms were understood to be the exclusive means for rendering suspects from one country to the other. ■

In contrast to the extradition of Álvarez-Machaín, "extraordinary rendition" fits only loosely into the category of law enforcement mechanisms to combat terrorism. The objective in these instances is not to bring a suspect to stand trial in the United States, nor to bring him to the United States at all. Instead, the rendition is directed to a third country, where the United States may seek to detain the suspect and then have the suspect interrogated, unaffected by the legal limits that would be imposed on U.S. interrogators operating in the United States.

CASE STUDY 5.3

The Extraordinary Rendition of Maher Arar

Maher Arar, a dual citizen of Canada and Syria, was detained by U.S. officials in September 2002 while he was transiting through John F. Kennedy International Airport in New York City to a connecting flight to Montreal. He had lived in Ottawa with his family since he was a teenager. Arar had been vacationing with his family in Tunisia, when he was called back to work by his employer to consult with a prospective client.

While in transit at Kennedy Airport, Arar presented his passport to an immigration inspector. A few moments later, he was identified as "the subject of a lookout as being a member of a known terrorist organization." Arar was interrogated by various officials for about eight hours. They asked him if he had contacts with terrorist groups, which he categorically denied. Arar was then transported to another location at Kennedy Airport, where he was placed in solitary confinement. After holding Arar for thirteen days under harsh conditions in the United States, interrogating him for hours on end and depriving him of contact with his family, his consulate, and his lawyer, federal officials rushed Arar off in a private jet to Jordan and then, through Jordanian officials, to

Syria, even though Syria has long been on the State Department list of state sponsors of terrorism.

Federal officials apparently removed Arar to Syria because of Arar's casual acquaintance with individuals thought to be involved in terrorist activity. However, the Canadian officials who informed their U.S. counterparts of their suspicions about Arar were mistaken, based on a surveillance error. Indeed, there was no evidence to indicate that Arar was involved in any terrorist activity.

For ten months, Arar was detained by Syrian military intelligence officials and coercively interrogated and tortured. To minimize the torture, after some time Arar falsely confessed to having trained with terrorists. Syrians carried out the interrogations and torture, although U.S. officials may have briefed them on areas of interest and on their interrogations at Kennedy Airport.

After Canadian embassy officials in Syria inquired about Arar in October 2003, the beatings and interrogation stopped. Arar was thereafter released into the custody of Canadian officials in Damascus and then flew home to his family in Ottawa. Syria's highest diplomat in Washington reportedly told U.S. officials that every link and relationship was investigated to connect Arar to al Qaeda, but that no such connection could be found.

A Canadian government commission convened to look into the affair later concluded that Arar never posed a risk to Canadian security, and that he was mistakenly placed on a terrorist watch list that was, in turn, forwarded to U.S. officials. Although Arar received a formal apology from Canadian officials, he did not receive one from the United States. Indeed, in January 2007, U.S. officials decided to retain Arar on its terrorist watch list. Arar has sued the United States for the harm suffered during his ordeal.

Although the outcome of Arar's lawsuit against the United States has not yet been determined, the assertions in his claim and the conclusions of the Canadian government commission underscore that extraordinary rendition can subject the transferred person to harsh and degrading treatment. Although it may be possible to outline the justifications for a program of extraordinary rendition, crafting a program that meets the requirements of human rights law is especially challenging in view of the uncertainties of the practices of the eventual host state. ■

Sleeper Cell Prosecutions

In sleeper cell prosecutions, the suspect has not been linked to any specific terrorist plot or other harmful act. Instead, the government is made aware of some terrorist threat, but it has no suspect. This section will show that evolving laws allow for the prosecution of sleeper cells and other forms of inchoate terrorist activity. However, the use of these new laws is controversial. Does the prosecution of sleeper cells amount to criminalizing evil thoughts as opposed to evil deeds?

The Material Support Statutes

The first material support statute was enacted in 1994, not long after the first World Trade Center bombing. This provision, often known simply as section 2339A, reads as follows:

Providing Material Support to Terrorists

(a) Offense. Whoever, within the United States, provides material support or resources or conceals or disguises the nature, location, source, or ownership of material support or resources, knowing or intending that they are to be used in preparation for, or in carrying out, a violation of [specified federal crimes] . . . shall be fined . . . imprisoned, or both.

(b) Definitions. As used in the section

(1) the term "material support or resources" means any property, tangible or intangible, or service, including currency or monetary instruments or financial securities, financial services, lodging, training, expert advice or assistance, safehouses, false documentation or identification, communications equipment, facilities, weapons, lethal substances, explosives, personnel (1 or more individuals who may be or include oneself), and transportation, except medicine or religious materials. . . .[11]

From the prosecutors' point of view, this statute was of limited value, because it required that the government prove beyond a reasonable doubt that the donor (the accused) intended or knew that the assistance he or she provided would support the commission of one of the listed crimes. Anyone could provide support to a known terrorist organization—Hezbollah, for example—and so long as donors believed that their gifts were going to support services for the needy or a political campaign in Lebanon no crimes were committed.

Particularly because section 2339A did not forbid fund raising inside the United States by foreign terrorist organizations, absent the specific intent to support a particular terrorist act, the Clinton administration and members of Congress sponsored new legislation in 1995 that would proscribe such fund raising regardless of whether the funds were intended for humanitarian or other nonviolent purposes. After the bombing of the Alfred P. Murrah Federal Building in Oklahoma City in April 1995, a sense of urgency accompanied consideration of the proposal, although critics continued to charge that the new legislation would stifle peaceful expression of political views, which, under the First Amendment, included the right to contribute financially to favored causes. Eventually, section 2339B became part of the Antiterrorism and Effective Death Penalty Act in April 1996. It reads: "... Whoever know-ingly provides material support or resources to a foreign terrorist organization, or attempts or conspires to do so, shall be fined ... or imprisoned ... or both." [12] To violate this paragraph, a person must have knowledge that the organization is a designated terrorist organization, or that the organization has engaged or engages in terrorism.

As enacted, section 2339B applies only to support given to a "designated foreign terrorist organization"—that is, those so identified publicly by the sec-retary of state after a prescribed administrative review process. In this respect, section 2339B is narrower than section 2339A, which applied to support given to anyone. And yet section 2339B, as written, prohibits aid without regard to the donor's intentions or any understanding about the use of the support. The donor must only intend that the support knowingly go to a des-ignated organization. Although the main objective of the two provisions is to curtail the supply of money and other resources to terrorists, they also are used to prosecute participants in terrorist activities and those who would be partic-ipants. As a package, sections 2339A and 2339B have enabled prosecution of those providing support for terrorist activities, although both statutes contain limits that stood in the way of unfettered prosecution.

Material Support and Sleeper Cells

Before September 11, only a few prosecutions were based on the material sup-port laws, and the cases that were brought were not controversial—support for designated groups was charged, and convictions were obtained. Since Sep-tember 11, material support crimes have become the central vehicle for pros-ecutors who are charged with working to prevent additional terrorist attacks. As such, the material support provisions are employed by the Department of Justice not simply to prosecute terrorists in the way most people think of pros-ecution—investigating to find those who have violated the law and bringing them to trial—but also to prosecute inchoate crimes—that is, the activities of persons who belong to "sleeper cells." This change in orientation by the Jus-tice Department has resulted in the widespread use of the material support laws, along with convictions in which the accused argued unsuccessfully that their activities were constitutionally protected and did not constitute terror-ism at all.

One such case revolved around the "Lackawanna Six"—six Yemeni Amer-icans from the Buffalo area who traveled to Afghanistan in the spring of 2001 to attend an al Qaeda "training camp" and who were then charged with pro-viding material support to terrorists. The convicting judge provided the fol-lowing summary of the activities of defendants:

Both Alwan and Al-Bakri have admitted to traveling to a "training camp" some distance from Kandahar, Afghanistan. Both of these defendants have stated that while at the training camp, they saw and interacted with the defendants Goba, Mosed, Taher and Galab who were there all at the same time. Al-Bakri further stated that "while in the Kandahar guest house he was given a uniform" which he "wore at the al-Farooq camp on every day but Friday." Al-Bakri also "indicated that while he was at the al-Farooq training camp, he considered himself to be a member of al-Qaida." Both defendants Alwan and Al-Bakri also stated that while all six defendants were at the al-Farooq training camp, Usama bin Laden spoke to the attendees at the camp.

Alwan states that Usama bin Laden gave his speech "on approximately the eighth day of the Taseesy camp" and that bin Laden spoke about an "alliance of the Islamic Jihad and al-Qaida" and that he "mentioned how important it is to train and fight for the cause of Islam." Alwan stated that bin Laden also "espoused anti-American and anti-Israeli statements."

Al-Bakri has stated that in the speech given by bin Laden at the al-Farooq camp which he attended along with the other five defendants, bin Laden spoke "about the need to prepare and train" because "there was going to be a fight against Americans."

Based on the statements of Alwan and Al-Bakri, I find that the "training period" at the al-Farooq camp was to be for five weeks and that with the exception of Alwan, all the defendants remained at that camp for the five week period.

While at the al-Farooq training camp, all of the defendants were given code names and were given training in the use of explosives. The al-Farooq training camp was "dedicated to producing and training terrorist fighters for the al-Qaida cause."

The defendant Alwan has also "admitted being lectured by several people at the Kandahar guest house on topics such as jihad and the justification for using suicide as a weapon."

One of the documents seized from a residence of the defendant Taher pursuant to a search warrant issued by this Court, consists of a lengthy dissertation on the justification of suicide as a form of "martyrdom" under Islam. Counsel for the defendant Taher argues that the document was obtained and retained as an educational reference and consists of nothing more than a comparison of differing theological or philosophical views on the validity of suicide as a means of supporting a cause. Although that may very well be the case, the document contains some disturbing statements. There is an interchange between the words "suicide" and "martyrdom" and self-destruction is valid if done as an act of "martyrdom" and may not be such if it is defined as "suicide." [13]

The FBI began surveillance of the group after receiving an anonymous letter that described the Lackawanna recruiting apparently being conducted by one of the men and identified those who traveled to Afghanistan. Eventually, FBI director Robert S. Mueller received twice-daily reports about the men, and President Bush was briefed frequently by Mueller about the surveillance. During the summer of 2002, FBI and CIA analysts debated the seriousness of the threat, if any, posed by the Lackawanna Six. Many inside the FBI wanted to continue surveillance, and the CIA determined that the six men were a terrorist cell and that they were dangerous. When senior administration officials asked whether the FBI could assure them that the six would not cause harm while they were subject to surveillance, the FBI responded that it was 99 percent confident that it could prevent the men from causing harm. Administration officials decided that such an assurance was not good enough, and a debate ensued on how to interdict what was assumed to be a sleeper cell.

Some senior leaders recommended that the six be detained by the Defense Department and classified as enemy combatants. Others, including Attorney General Ashcroft, argued that the criminal justice system could accommodate prosecution of the six. Yet there was no criminal conspiracy that could be charged, no basis for holding any of them as material witnesses, and, because the men were citizens, no basis for immigration detention on the basis of collateral crimes. In a then-creative interpretation of the material support law, the government charged the six with receiving training and providing themselves as personnel in provision of "material support or resources" to al Qaeda. In other words, the six men became the material support by their participation in the training camp.

Preventive Charging and Detention

In traditional law enforcement, the government could do little in a sleeper cell situation other than to intensify surveillance of potential targets and suspicious groups or individuals, if known. Under the prevention strategy practiced by the Department of Justice since September 11, however, additional options can be pursued. Foreign-based threats may be deterred by more stringent enforcement of existing immigration laws, denying entry to those who lack a proper visa or whose names appear on a watch list of terrorist suspects, and removing those who have overstayed a visa. Document fraud and financial transfer fraud enforcement also might deter would-be terrorists. Most significantly, prosecutors can now use the material support laws to prosecute those who provide support to terrorists, even when the donor has no intention of supporting any particular terrorist act, or even terrorism in general. Although prosecuting supporters of terrorism may not thwart a planned attack, in theory at least a diminished level of support will prevent harm from terrorist attacks.

The prevention approach would be more effective, of course, if those persons identified as potentially dangerous but who have not committed any terrorism-related crime could be detained or otherwise neutralized as a threat. One technique utilized by the Justice Department, "preventive charging," appears to accomplish the desired end. Attorney General Ashcroft issued this statement in October 2001: "We have waged a deliberate campaign of arrest and detention to remove suspected terrorists who violate the law from our streets. If you violate a local law, you will be put in jail and kept in custody as long as possible. We will use every available statute. We will seek every prosecutorial advantage." [14]

Justice Department officials defended this preventive charging strategy as distinct from the program of preventive detention practiced in some European countries. Instead, the U.S. strategy engages in prosecution, not detention, based on actual law violations, albeit violations far removed, typically, from the terrorism threats that officials are seeking to interdict. Sometimes referred to as the "Al Capone approach" (for the Chicago gangster who was responsible for a litany of murders, extortion, and other violent crimes in the 1920s and 1930s, but who was eventually charged and convicted of income tax evasion when evidence problems compromised his prosecution for the violent crimes), or the "spitting on the sidewalk approach" (prosecute for violating an innocuous municipal ordinance), preventive prosecution is harmless at first glance: if crimes are committed and prosecuting the violators takes dangerous persons off the street, all the better. However, implementation of the preventive prosecution strategy spurred controversy in the wake of September 11 when it was implemented primarily against noncitizens who were detained for minor immigration violations. Critics of the strategy wondered whether the government was, in effect, profiling Middle Eastern men and rounding them up for preventive detention, using immigration status questions or minor violations as a pretext.

Whatever its promises and pitfalls, preventive prosecution requires a violation of the law. What can government do to meet its prevention strategy when the suspicious person or group has not violated the law, even in a minor way? One solution pursued periodically since September 11 is the use of a statute that permits the detention of a "material witness" to assure his or her availability to testify in a pending criminal prosecution. If the government asserts that someone suspected of involvement in terrorist activities may have testimony that could be material to a criminal prosecution of terrorists, the material witness may be detained, indefinitely, so long as a supervising judge agrees that biweekly reports made by the government justify the continued detention of the potential witness.

Assuming that the government uses the material witness option to detain suspected persons, the detention is for a limited period—it buys time. A more durable alternative was first exercised in 2002 when the government detained suspected al Qaeda operative José Padilla as he entered the United States on an international flight. Although Padilla was first held as a material witness in connection with grand jury proceedings investigating the September 11 attacks, two days before a judge was expected to rule on a motion from Padilla's lawyer that her client must be released because material witness warrants may not be used in support of grand jury proceedings, President Bush declared Padilla an enemy combatant and ordered him transferred to military custody, where he remained for more than three years. (Padilla eventually was transferred back to civilian custody, where he was tried on terrorism charges unrelated to the attacks of September 11.)

Material Support Law: Is It Appropriate?

Is the material support law an appropriate tool for combating terrorism? On the one hand, it is difficult or perhaps impossible to know when sleeper cells may become operational. The material support law permits removing such threats before they may cause harm. On the other hand, the persons charged may never intend to cause any harm. Perhaps the Lackawanna Six described earlier were curiosity seekers, or perhaps they were temporarily taken in by the rhetoric of the local recruiter. Others may be similarly innocent. This kind of law does then raise many questions: Does material support prosecution threaten freedom of expression or the associational liberties of groups, large or small? Are its provisions so vague that an average person would not know whether he is violating them? As for whether it is an effective instrument in countering emerging forms of terrorism, if the traditional organizations no longer engage in most terrorist acts and they are carried out instead by loosely structured cells or even unaffiliated individuals, the FTO prerequisite for a section 2339B prosecution may miss many of the desired targets of the law. When coupled with the intent requirement of section 2339A, the two provisions may insufficiently mark out the kinds of terrorist support activities of greatest concern to the government.

International Cooperation and International Criminal Law

Nations can cooperate in enforcing their criminal laws by rendering alleged offenders from one state to the state that wishes to prosecute the suspect. Although rendition may be informal or pursuant to bilateral or multilateral agreements between nations, extradition treaties or agreements often form part of broader formalized arrangements between nations to cooperate in defining terrorism crimes and in detecting, apprehending, and prosecuting suspected terrorists. These agreements are central to the success of extradition, because, absent an ad hoc informal deal to render a suspect from one state to the requesting state, extradition requires that there be "dual criminality"—that is, the conduct subject to prosecution in the requesting state also must be criminal in the state that would extradite the suspect.

Many of the problems associated with any individual nation trying in its courts a terrorism-related crime that is really transnational in nature could be alleviated by an agreed body of international criminal law and one or more international courts that could decide such cases. In theory, the task of coming up with the international criminal law is made easier by the fact that some terrorism crimes have historically been treated as violations of the laws of armed conflict. Thus in general, such crimes have customary application among nations. In practice, however, except for crimes as grievous as genocide, it has been difficult to achieve an international consensus on the norms that would be criminally charged and enforced, much less on a court that would have jurisdiction to decide the cases.

Nevertheless, an International Criminal Court (ICC) was proposed in statutory form at the conclusion of a conference in Rome in 1998. The ICC was created as a permanent court that would handle a range of cases and would be patterned in part on the more limited-jurisdiction courts created earlier in the Balkans and in Africa after the Rwanda genocide. Although the United States signed the Statute of the International Criminal Court on December 31, 2000, during the last days of the Clinton administration, it withdrew its consent to the ICC early in the Bush administration and expressly notified the UN in 2002 that it did not intend to become a party to the agreement or to the ICC's jurisdiction. Ironically, the United States opposed efforts to include terrorism in the ICC's jurisdiction on the grounds that so doing might undermine other counterterrorism efforts. More particularly, the United States worried that the ICC would not be able to undertake important longer-term investigations or employ sophisticated intelligence sources and methods, much less meet the demands for protection of such sensitive materials in criminal trials. In the view of the United States, domestic courts are better equipped to perform the law enforcement function in combating terrorism.

Despite these misgivings by the United States and some other nations, the Statute of the International Criminal Court went into effect in July 2002, supported by 139 signatory nations. Among the crimes it may adjudicate are aggression, war crimes, crimes against humanity, and genocide. Some definitional detail is included in the statute, and other applicable law is to be derived from treaties and customary international law and the laws of armed conflict. It is too early to evaluate the success of the ICC. Little activity of note has occurred thus far.

Conclusion

There is little doubt that the criminal law remains a mainstay in countering terrorism. Even though deterrence theory may have limited application to terrorism crimes, and perhaps no application to terrorists who show no reluctance to give their own life for their cause, governments continue to amend their approaches to law enforcement to keep up with the evolving nature of terrorism. As shown in this chapter, the most noteworthy trend in the use of law enforcement to counter terrorism is the development of legislation that allow for the prosecution of anticipatory terrorism. This venture toward "pre-crime" conduct carries its own risks, but the trends toward preventive law enforcement and toward the aggressive use of the material support provisions are undeniable. Along the way, controversial programs to bring terrorist suspects to interrogation or to stand trial have emerged, as have new laws that target the indirect support network of terrorist activities. But in this field the risks to human rights protections are pervasive, as this chapter has shown.

FOR FURTHER READING

Abrams, Norman. *Anti-Terrorism and Criminal Enforcement.* 2d ed. St. Paul, Minn.: Thomson/West, 2005.

Chesney, Robert M. "The Sleeper Cell: Terrorism-Support Laws and the Demands of Prevention." *Harvard Journal on Legislation* 42, no. 1 (2005).

Chapter 6 **Planning for Homeland Security**

A t 9:02 a.m. on Wednesday, April 19, 1995, a rented truck parked on the street-front side of the Alfred P. Murrah Federal Building in Oklahoma City exploded. The truck contained, among other things, two tons of ammonium nitrate, and, when detonated, it destroyed the front half of the nine-story building. One hundred and sixty-eight people were killed, including nineteen children, and over five hundred were injured in the deadliest domestic terrorist attack ever carried out by an American citizen.

At first, law enforcement officials and media outlets assumed that the bombing was the work of foreign terrorists; the attack two years earlier on the World Trade Center made this assumption highly plausible. Naturalized U.S. citizen Abraham Ahmad had left his Oklahoma City home shortly after the bombing on April 19, planning to fly to Jordan via Rome. When he landed in Chicago, agents detained him and searched his carry-on baggage. After missing his flight, Ahmad was questioned by the FBI for several hours before agents released him. Ahmad then returned to Oklahoma City, only to find that his wife and daughters had fled their house under intense media scrutiny and abuse from passersby. As media-enhanced anti-Islamic sentiments grew, rescuers and investigators began to piece together the events leading up to the disaster.

After locating a partial vehicle identification number among the rubble of the explosion, FBI agents traced the vehicle to a rental agency in Junction City, Kansas. Based on a description of the men that rented the truck, the FBI made composite drawings. A motel manager in Junction City recognized the composite drawing as a guest who was driving a truck from that agency; he had registered under the name Timothy McVeigh. On April 21, investigators searched the National Crime Information Center database for mention of McVeigh and learned that he was jailed for a traffic violation in Noble County, Oklahoma, only an hour and twenty minutes after the bombing. The FBI then contacted the jail where McVeigh was being held and notified the district attorney not to release the prisoner on bail.

Investigators believed that McVeigh had pulled the rental truck into a parking area outside the Murrah Building and then casually walked away. He detonated the bomb by remote control while wearing earplugs to protect his hearing from the blast. The day of his bail hearing, the FBI took custody of McVeigh to question him about the bombing. The presence of law enforcement helicopters attracted crowds and the media, and the broadcast images of an expressionless McVeigh being led away by FBI agents from the courthouse through the angry crowd signaled to the world that officials had indeed quickly found a lead in the bombing.

McVeigh's trial, one of the country's most expensive and well publicized, opened on April 24, 1997. At the trial, prosecutors asserted that the motivation for the attack was to avenge the federal government's violent clashes with white separatist Randy Weaver at Ruby Ridge, Idaho, in 1992 and with David Koresh and the Branch Davidian cult at Waco, Texas, in 1993. Prosecutors also argued that McVeigh had been inspired by *The Turner Diaries,* a white supremacist novel that is a manifesto for many U.S. right-wing militia groups. Prosecutors argued that McVeigh had attempted to use the truck bomb to punish the U.S. Bureau of Alcohol, Tobacco and Firearms, whose agents he (wrongly) believed were working in the Murrah Building.

In carrying out their scheme, McVeigh and his accomplice, Terry Nichols, consulted various bomb-building manuals. They followed a recipe and stockpiled their materials, which they purchased using aliases, in rented storage sheds. The recipe also called for ingredients such as blasting caps and liquid nitromethane, which they stole. To fund the large quantities of materials they had to purchase, McVeigh and Nichols robbed a gun collector at gunpoint. The phone cards McVeigh had purchased under an alias consistently tracked his location. Fingerprints on receipts proved his purchase of the bomb's ingredients. Explosives residue on his clothing and earplugs confirmed his involvement.

In May 1997, the prosecution in the McVeigh trial rested its case after calling 137 witnesses in eighteen days. After four hours of deliberation, the jury found McVeigh guilty and sentenced him to death. He later insisted that all appeals on his behalf be dropped, and he asked to be executed. After some procedural delays, Timothy McVeigh was executed by lethal injection on June 11, 2001. McVeigh's execution was the first federal execution in thirty-eight years.

McVeigh's co-conspirator, Terry Nichols, was convicted of eight counts of manslaughter in a U.S. District Court and sentenced to life in prison. The state of Oklahoma then charged him with capital murder, and his trial began on March 1, 2004. Terry Nichols was convicted on August 9, 2004, of 161 counts of first-degree murder. The presiding judge found there was no credible or legally admissible evidence of any persons other than McVeigh and Nichols having directly participated in the bombing of the Murrah Building. As in the federal trial, the jury spared him the death penalty, and he was sentenced to life in prison without parole.

In 1995 interviews with journalists and authors, McVeigh publicly admitted to the bombing and verified facts related to it. Although this confession should have put an end to conspiracy theories about whether McVeigh and Nichols acted alone, numerous theories persist.

Carried out only two years after a terrorist attack on the World Trade Center, the Oklahoma City bombing forced Americans to confront the reality that the terrorist threat could be both homegrown and of international origins. Whatever its source, it was now clear that terrorism could happen within the United States and that the government would have to take steps to anticipate and prevent terrorism in the homeland.

But the task of planning for homeland security is complicated. Not only does it require much work to ensure an effective response to an attack, but also each step taken to make the nation and its communities safer inevitably raises the question of whether the incrementally greater security is worth the loss of liberties that often accompanies each new security measure.

The decision makers responsible for homeland security planning must consider strategy, operational implementation of security measures, and ensuring accountability for the homeland security mission. Deciding how to balance the risks of harm against the benefits of protection is also a central requirement, because many of the measures taken to enhance security could compromise the civil liberties promised in the U.S. Constitution.

This chapter explores the efforts by the United States to plan for domestic security. First, it reviews the uneven but inexorable trend toward greater homeland security planning and preparedness efforts before and after September 11. Then it assesses the principal governmental agency for homeland security planning, the Department of Homeland Security—its structure and mission, its effectiveness, and its early efforts at implementation and reform. Case studies involving domestic terrorism, homegrown international terrorism, and biological terrorism will reveal the difficulties that DHS, other federal, state, and local government agencies, and the private sector have as they confront homeland security planning. Finally, the chapter considers continuing efforts to shape the principal emergency preparedness plans in the United States—the National Response Plan (NRP) and its National Incident Management System (NIMS), along with efforts to keep the public informed during a crisis—in order to better understand just how challenging the task of homeland security is, particularly when balanced against the government's commitment to ensuring civil liberties and an open society.

Early Planning for Homeland Security

From 1950, when the Soviet Union tested its first atomic weapon, until the end of the Cold War, the American people lived in constant fear of a nuclear attack. For more than forty years, the Federal Civil Defense Act of 1950 directed a program intended to minimize the effects of such an attack on the civilian population and to deal with the emergency conditions produced by it. Included in the program were planning for continuity of government, recruitment of emergency personnel, stockpiling of critical materials, and provision of warning systems and shelters. The civil defense program, administered since

1979 by the Federal Emergency Management Agency (FEMA), was supposed to convince the American people and the Soviet leadership that the United States could not only survive a nuclear war, but also win one.

Among the plans developed by FEMA under the Federal Civil Defense Act was "Crisis Relocation." [1] If a nuclear attack appeared likely, the plan called for the evacuation to the countryside of 145 million Americans living in big cities or near key military bases. In each of four hundred target areas, the exodus would be guided by instructions printed in local telephone directories. Under the plan, evacuees would be welcomed by their rural hosts and housed in schools, churches, and other public buildings until the trouble blew over. As recently as 1981, FEMA asserted that a "moderate-cost, balanced civil defense program . . . could enable survival of roughly 80 percent of the U.S. population in a heavy attack." [2] Critics of the plan were numerous, some warning that as soon as word of an impending attack got out, target populations would most likely evacuate spontaneously and chaotically.

The Federal Civil Defense Act also provided for federal responses to natural disasters, such as floods and hurricanes. It was augmented in 1974 by the Robert T. Stafford Disaster Relief and Emergency Assistance Act (Stafford Act), which provides broadly for federal assistance to states affected by various disasters. The Stafford Act can be invoked in the event of a presidentially declared major disaster or emergency, including "any natural catastrophe . . . or, regardless of cause, any fire, flood, or explosion," or on "any occasion for which, in the determination of the President, Federal assistance is needed to supplement State and local efforts and capabilities to save lives and to protect property and public health and safety, or to lessen or avert the threat of a catastrophe." Although the president's declaration is usually based on a state governor's request for help, the president may act without such a request when "the primary responsibility for response rests with the United States." Moreover, the president may direct the Department of Defense to perform any emergency work "essential for the preservation of life and property" for up to ten days.[3]

In the 1990s, most Americans were riveted on, at least for a time, the first World Trade Center bombing and the Oklahoma City attacks, as well as anarchist Ted Kaczynski's campaign of mail bombs, which killed three and wounded twenty-three between the late 1970s and early 1990s. On April 19, 1995, President Bill Clinton declared an emergency under the Stafford Act in response to the Oklahoma City terrorist bombing and directed FEMA to direct and coordinate responses by other federal agencies and provide needed federal assistance.

Outside the spotlight of the mainstream media, small towns and suburban neighborhoods were suffering a significant increase in bombings and attempted bombings. For example, in July 1996, FBI agents arrested members of the Arizona Vipers, a paramilitary group, on charges of conspiring to blow up government buildings after an undercover agent infiltrated the group and recorded some conversations between members. At about the same time, the federal government indicted nine persons, including a leader of the Washington State Militia in Seattle, on federal charges of conspiring to make bombs for use against the U.S. government and the United Nations. Members of the Washington group included a chimney sweep, a mason, workers at the Boeing Company, a religion teacher, and a television repairman. An FBI agent infiltrated this group, recording some of its meetings. The group possessed pipe bombs, an increasingly popular weapon among terrorists. And yet despite these incidents and the higher profile attacks in New York City and Oklahoma City, public opinion polls showed relatively little fear of terrorism among Americans, and governments did not place high priority on homeland security planning or preparedness. (See Case Study 6.1.)

Meanwhile, the threat to the homeland from international terrorism was growing, unbeknownst to most Americans. The relative notoriety obtained by Ramzi Yousef as the mastermind of the 1993 World Trade Center bombing inspired other radical Islamists to participate in planning attacks against the United States. Khalid Sheikh Mohammed (KSM), uncle of Yousef and later architect of the September 11, 2001, attacks, based his hatred of the United States on its support for Israel. KSM joined Yousef on a 1994 trip to the Philippines, where they began planning the bombing of twelve U.S. commercial airliners over the Pacific in a two-day period. They also acquired bomb-making materials while in the Philippines and targeted other U.S. flights, cargo planes, and even President Clinton himself during his November 1994 trip to Manila. After Yousef was arrested in Pakistan in 1995, KSM moved to Afghanistan, where in 1996 he met with Osama bin Laden and his lieutenant Mohammed Atef and presented a proposal for a plan that involved training pilots who would intentionally crash airliners into U.S. buildings. The KSM proposal became the September 11 plot.

CASE STUDY 6.1

Homegrown Terrorism: Azzam the American

Adam Gadahn, an American who was born in Oregon and raised in California, converted to Islam at age seventeen. Since he joined the jihad in the late 1990s, Gadahn has become one of Osama bin Laden's senior operatives, and he serves as a spokesperson for al Qaeda. Gadahn, who is also known as Azzam al-Amriki (Azzam the American), preaches militant Islamist theory and has often threatened the United States. In a 2006 videotape, he refers to the United States as "enemy soil," and he proclaims that the September 11 hijackers were "dedicated, strong-willed, highly motivated individuals."

In another 2006 videotape "An Invitation to Islam," Gadahn urges the people of the United States to "join the winning side" and convert to an uncompromising form of Islam. He also exhorts U.S. soldiers to "surrender to the truth" and "escape from the unbelieving Army." Earlier, in 2005, Gadahn observed the fourth anniversary of the September 11 attacks by speaking in an al Qaeda videotape that was broadcast on the ABC news program *Good Morning America*. After criticizing U.S. foreign policy and military operations in Iraq and Afghanistan, Gadahn suggested additional terrorist attacks would be carried out in Los Angeles and Melbourne, Australia.

Gadahn represents the kind of homegrown terrorist threat that is particularly worrisome to government officials—the convert to a violent, radical form of Islam. Like Richard Reid, the shoe bomber, and José Padilla, the alleged dirty bomber, Gadahn is not a second- or third-generation Muslim, but a convert, who found Islam as a teenager through a fascination with cults. Gadahn's parents were counterculture nomads in California and Oregon, and Gadahn's father converted to Christianity after a beachside epiphany in the 1970s. Their son Adam, who was homeschooled and who participated in Christian homeschool support groups, was a quiet, shy kid, enthralled with death metal, an offshoot of heavy metal rock music.

From death metal, Adam learned about the occult, and he began exploring alternative religious communities and ideas as he learned how to navigate the Internet. There, he was captivated by what he saw and read about Islam, and he began to attend Islamic Society meetings. At age seventeen, he converted to Islam. After witnessing the victimization of Muslims in the wars that broke out in the Balkans and in Chechnya in the 1990s, Gadahn came to believe that, beyond those wars, followers of his new faith were under threat in many places: Algeria, Afghanistan, Tajikistan, and in the ongoing struggles between Palestinians and Israelis in the Middle East.

As Gadahn learned that supporting Muslims in their struggles was considered to be an honorable following, he identified with the growing use of the term *jihad* to signify a struggle for peace and justice. Meanwhile, he was increasingly influenced by those who dismissed nonviolent jihad as weak and who insisted that only violent struggle was truly reflective of Islam. By 1997 Gadahn was radicalized, and he made his first trip to Pakistan. There, he met and identified with the mujahideen fighters in Afghanistan, and he encountered al Qaeda leaders. At first, he worked as a low-level functionary in their organization, but after September 11 he was encouraged to use his persuasive skills (and his mother tongue) in promoting al Qaeda messages around the world.

Soon after his 2006 videotaped statements, Gadahn became the first American to be charged with treason in more than fifty years. In addition to his indictment for treason and for providing material support to al Qaeda, Gadahn's name is on the list of the government's most-wanted terrorists, and a $1 million reward has been offered for information leading to his capture.

No one knows how or why Adam Gadahn converted to a violent, radical view of Islam. Nor is it clear what could so radicalize an otherwise mainstream American. The Gadahn example surely underscores that homegrown terrorists exist, whether they are radicalized at home or abroad. Their activities may or may not directly target their homeland, but these terrorists surely present a threat to homeland security.   ■

Creation of the Department of Homeland Security

Within a matter of days after the September 11 attacks, President George W. Bush announced the creation of a White House Office of Homeland Security, headed by Pennsylvania governor Tom Ridge. Resisting proposals by some experts and members of Congress to create a significant new cabinet-level department with considerable powers to direct and control the activities of agencies that most affect homeland security, the president opted for a White House office, a small staff under the leadership of Ridge, and a charge to coordinate the activities of the existing homeland security agencies. After all, the president had campaigned on the promise that he would not increase the size of the federal government. Instead, he would seek coordination of the existing assets in government. In the words of President Bush, Governor Ridge and his staff would "connect the dots" that did not get connected before September 11.

The challenge of connecting the dots was and is still considerable. The integral role of the intelligence agencies and their failure to connect the pre–September 11 dots are illustrative. At least since the immediate post–World War II era, a variety of agencies have shared responsibility for intelligence functions that affect homeland security. Since the 1920s, the FBI, which is within the Department of Justice, has investigated internal security threats, and that role continues today. The CIA, created at the same time as, but independent of, the Department of Defense in 1947, investigates foreign-based threats to the United States. Inside the Pentagon, the National Security Agency (NSA) collects intelligence using technical means, including intelligence that affects homeland security. In addition, the Department of State has its own intelligence service, as does the Secret Service, which before the creation of DHS was in the Department of the Treasury. All of these intelligence agencies are supposed to provide intelligence information to the National Security Council, which, in turn, presents that information to the president. In the best of times, coordination of these divergent agencies has been difficult. Each agency has had its own methods, its own operational culture, and a natural tendency to protect its role from encroachment by outsiders, even natural allies in the intelligence community.

While the September 11 hijackers were making plans to travel to the United States, the CIA and NSA were tracking their movements, and the State and Treasury Departments were trying to persuade foreign governments to arrest their al Qaeda partners and to encourage foreign banks to freeze their al Qaeda accounts. When the hijackers arrived in the United States, they were subject to immigration and customs controls and screening. After they moved to U.S. communities and neighborhoods, the FBI was trying to keep track of them. Even on the day of the attacks, the FAA subjected all nineteen to routine pre-flight screening. And yet with all of this intelligence collection, the dots were not connected, and all nineteen hijackers evaded detection.

This propensity of the U.S. intelligence community to cling to stovepipe intelligence collection and analysis—separating collection and analysis for each government agency and program into discrete agencies and reporting systems—had already been recognized as a major downfall of homeland security preparedness even before it was so dramatically demonstrated by the failure to share intelligence that could have led to the September 11 hijackers before the event. After September 11, the government was determined to break down the barriers to sharing, and the USA PATRIOT Act, enacted in October 2001, unleashed greater intelligence collection powers and provided the legal means for greater sharing of intelligence information. The institutional stovepipes remained, however, and the White House was soon forced to recognize that its small coordination team for homeland security could not break down the barriers.

It was not just intelligence collection and information sharing that lacked coordination and overall direction; many agencies and bureaus had overlapping mandates. For example, the Immigration and Naturalization Service within the Justice Department was charged with keeping would-be terrorists from entering the country, while the Coast Guard protected the nation's coastline. The Customs Service, part of the Transportation Department, monitored dangerous goods, while the Department of Agriculture had two offices charged with protecting the public from harmful food, plants, and animals. The Centers for Disease Control (CDC) in the Department of Health and Human Services monitored potential threats from biological terrorism and disease, while the Nuclear Regulatory Commission (NRC) kept watch over nuclear power plants, and the Department of Energy protected nuclear weapons and stockpiles facilities.

In the event of a domestic attack, the agencies of the Department of Health and Human Services (HHS), including the CDC and the U.S. Public Health Service, would respond to the public health dimensions of a crisis. FEMA was charged with responding to natural disasters, in addition to terrorism-induced crises. The FAA and the Federal Highway Administration had crews trained to respond to damage to those critical infrastructures, and the Environmental Protection Agency (EPA) could respond with experts in the event of a radiological or chemical attack. In addition, the Department of Energy had Nuclear

Emergency Support Teams (NESTs) that could be sent to the scene of a nuclear incident. Although the military had no command structure for the homeland in 2001, it had specialized teams trained to respond to attacks with WMD, and the state-controlled National Guard could deploy its personnel in the event of a terrorist attack. In short, the federal government had access to considerable counterterrorism expertise on September 11, 2001, but it was fragmented, compartmentalized, and not well coordinated. The challenge was one of coordination and cooperation.

By the spring of 2002, the White House realized that entrenched bureaucracies in the affected agencies and departments, and the limited authority that Governor Ridge had to command the attention of those players, meant that the White House Office could not get the coordination job done. In July 2002, the White House Office of Homeland Security issued its National Strategy for Homeland Security. In line with earlier recommendations, this strategy recognized the need to "clarify lines of responsibility for homeland security in the executive branch, . . . mobilize our entire society, . . . and manage risk and allocate resources judiciously." [4] It called for planning to defend against terrorist attacks using conventional weapons as well as WMD and against cyberattacks and new or unexpected tactics.

To accomplish these goals, the White House proposed the establishment of a new Department of Homeland Security, which would assume primary responsibility for intelligence and warning of a domestic attack, border and transportation security, domestic counterterrorism, protection of critical infrastructure, and response and recovery from any future terrorist attack. DHS also would respond to natural disasters and consolidate emergency activities into one "genuinely all-discipline, all-hazards plan." [5]

While the shape and structure of a new entity was being debated in Congress, the White House assembled a team of policy advisers to work on the homeland security project. They were told that everything was on the table for discussion, meaning that any part of government that should be part of the homeland security apparatus could be considered for relocation to a new department. During these discussions, agencies proposed for inclusion but eventually dropped, largely for political reasons, included the FBI, National Guard, Drug Enforcement Agency, and Federal Aviation Administration. Those personnel who would be affected by the transfer of agencies to the new department were not made part of the White House discussions. Nor were they briefed until the day before President Bush announced his support for the creation of DHS. Cabinet secretaries and other senior officials in the Departments of Health and Human Services, Energy, and Treasury worked behind the scenes to scuttle some of the reassignments, but their efforts were to no avail. White House cybersecurity chief Richard A. Clarke warned Tom Ridge's White House Office of Homeland Security that the forced merger of many disparate agencies, some of which had been traditional rivals, would lead to chaos, and that the reorganization contained no effective mechanisms to control the fiefdoms that would be simply moved from one department to another.

One foundational component of DHS was expected to be the Office for National Preparedness (ONP). Inside DHS, FEMA director Joe M. Allbaugh anticipated a greatly expanded role for FEMA, as it effectively absorbed new personnel as part of the ONP. The linchpin to transferring domestic preparedness authorities to DHS and an invigorated FEMA was the dismantling of the Office of Domestic Preparedness (ODP), a small office inside the Department of Justice. But the Justice Department successfully fought off ODP being absorbed into ONP and FEMA, and it instead became part of the DHS border directorate, which had nothing to do with preparedness. Without ODP, FEMA still intended to become the new DHS Emergency Preparedness and Response directorate, but incoming FEMA director Michael Brown sought to keep FEMA outside the DHS framework and to acquire the significant ODP grant program as part of FEMA so that it would have additional clout over planning and response activities with state and local governments. Instead, ODP grants were held inside the secretary's office and FEMA languished inside DHS as a response and recovery agency, with little responsibility for planning and preparedness.

A similar series of bureaucratic struggles surrounded the location and use of the National Disaster Medical System (NDMS), an office designed to deploy and coordinate volunteer teams of medical personnel during a public health crisis. NDMS had been located inside the Department of Health and Human Services, but during the negotiations in shaping the new DHS, NDMS was transferred from HHS to DHS. HHS secretary Tommy Thompson was outraged, and he argued with Secretary Ridge that NDMS should remain inside the department that had expertise and overarching responsibility for the public health. Ridge, however, decided that NDMS would stay inside DHS, under the supervision of FEMA, but then he approved a set of crisis response mechanisms that involved complex, coordinated decision making and oversight of the NDMS response by DHS and HHS. An already complex system was made more complex.

The new department was created later the same year with passage of the Homeland Security Act of 2002. (See Figure 6.1.) The act merges all or portions of twenty-two federal agencies and 170,000 employees into the Department of Homeland Security. (See Table 6.1.) Included are the U.S. Coast Guard, U.S. Customs Service, Transportation Security Administration, FEMA, U.S. Secret Service, parts of the U.S. Immigration and Naturalization Service, and a long list of less well-known federal entities.

One of the principal goals of DHS is to oversee federal homeland security planning. In addition, DHS is charged with providing a unified federal response to a terrorism incident as well as to natural disasters. DHS is now the focal point for communications among federal, state, and local agencies, and

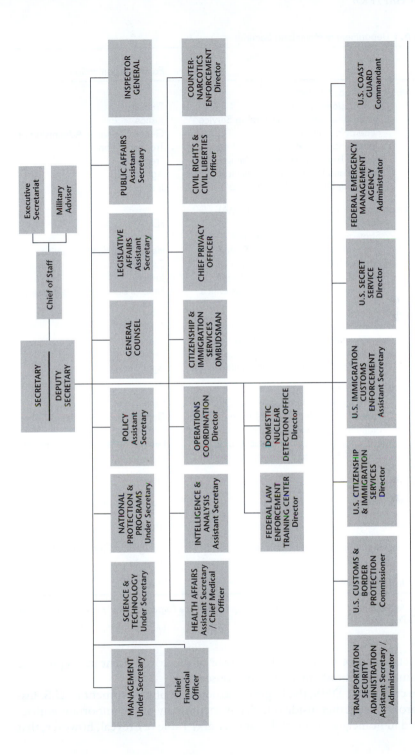

Figure 6.1 Department of Homeland Security, as of 2007

SOURCE: U.S. Department of Homeland Security, www.dhs.gov/xabout/structure/editorial_0644.shtm.

Table 6.1 Department of Homeland Security

Major division	Agency	Former organization
U.S. Customs and Border Protection		
	U.S. Customs Service	Treasury
	Immigration and Naturalization Service	Justice
	Federal Protective Service	General Services Administration
	Transportation Security Administration	Transportation
	Federal Law Enforcement Training Center	Treasury
	Animal and Plant Health Inspection Service	Agriculture
	Office for Domestic Preparedness	Justice
Federal Emergency Management Agency (FEMA)		
	FEMA	FEMA
	Strategic National Stockpile and National Disaster Medical System	Health and Human Services
	Nuclear Incident Response Team	Energy
	Domestic Emergency Support Teams	Justice
	National Domestic Preparedness Office	Federal Bureau of Investigation
Science and Technology		
	CBRN Countermeasures Programs	Energy
	Environmental Measurements Laboratory	Energy
	National BW Defense Analysis Center	Defense
	Plum Island Animal Disease Center	Agriculture
National Protection and Programs		
	Critical Infrastructure Assurance Office	Commerce
	Federal Computer Incident Response Center	General Services Administration
	National Communications System	Defense
	National Infrastructure Protection Center	Federal Bureau of Investigation
	Energy Security and Assurance Program	Energy
Management		New
U.S. Coast Guard		Transportation, Defense
U.S. Secret Service		Treasury
U.S. Citizenship and Immigration Services		Immigration and Naturalization Services
Office of Inspector General		New

SOURCE: Adapted from Steven H. Hook, *U.S. Foreign Policy: The Paradox of World Power* (Washington, D.C.: CQ Press, 2007), table 6.3.

it is intended to be the authoritative voice of the government in keeping the public informed about emergency responses.

The creation of DHS, the largest restructuring of government in U.S. history, brought together inside one department many of the important entities involved in homeland security. Figure 6.1 and Table 6.1 reveal, however, that some homeland security-related agencies are *not* part of DHS—the CIA and the National Security Agency, the HHS response entities (the CDC and the U.S. Public Health Service), the FBI, and the FAA. The Department of Defense and its homeland defense and homeland security components also remain independent.

The 2002 National Strategy for Homeland Security defines the task of homeland security as "a concerted national effort to prevent terrorist attacks within the United States, reduce America's vulnerability to terrorism and minimize the damage and recover from attacks that do occur." [6] Over time, the term *homeland security*, based wholly on terrorism and its effects, has become more or less interchangeable with national preparedness, a concept that focuses on any emergency, including natural disasters. As such, the mission of DHS has become broader and encompassed all-hazards preparedness to respond to terrorists, disasters, or any other emergency. The mission has also broadened to incorporate efforts made by the private sector and citizens to enhance homeland security.

The National Strategy defines mission areas that are designed to meet the overarching prevention, vulnerability reduction, and response and recovery goals:

- Intelligence and warning, to interdict an attack before it can do harm
- Border and transportation security, to prevent terrorism that uses modes of transportation to deliver terrorist means
- Domestic counterterrorism, to stop terrorism inside the United States through intelligence and law enforcement
- Protection of critical infrastructure, to assess vulnerable assets and then protect them
- Defense against catastrophic threats, to counter WMD terrorism
- Emergency preparedness and response, to design and implement an integrated national system for responding rapidly and effectively to a crisis.[7]

In addition to the mission areas, the National Strategy organizes the United States into fourteen functional sectors, and assigns to each sector a federal agency responsible for determining and protecting the assets and infrastructures that are critical to that sector's continued operation:

Agriculture—Department of Agriculture

Food—Agriculture (for meat and poultry) and HHS for all other products

Water—EPA

Public health—HHS

Emergency services—DHS

Continuity of government operations—DHS

Defense industrial base—Department of Defense

Information and telecommunications—DHS

Energy—Department of Energy

Transportation—DHS

Banking and finance—Department of the Treasury

Chemical industry and hazardous materials—EPA

Postal and shipping—DHS

National monuments and icons—Department of the Interior.

The set of mission assignments was complemented by a series of strategy documents issued by the Bush administration in 2002 and 2003, each of which outlines in broad strokes the elements of a security plan that overlaps with the National Strategy for Homeland Security. The strategy statements have been followed by presidential directives and executive orders that develop in more detail the operational responsibilities of government entities that have some responsibility for homeland security.

At least in part because of legal limits, the federal government may not compel state and local governments to implement and enforce federal programs, at least not directly. Consequently, the National Strategy and its implementing mechanisms urge state and local governments to enact legislation and complementary plans to better combat terrorism, and then include extensive financial incentives for state and local governments to participate fully in the federal processes.

Meanwhile, states and many cities have undertaken reviews of their legal authorities and plans related to homeland security preparedness and response. Measures that have been considered and revised or adopted include improved security standards for issuance of state driver's licenses, an enhanced market capacity for terrorism insurance, improved state and local capacity to withstand cyberattacks, new efforts to thwart money laundering activities in support of terrorism, and reviews of state and local public health authorities, including quarantine.

The National Strategy also recognizes that private sector firms possess the expertise and means to protect the infrastructure they control, and that the firms should conduct their own risk assessments and then invest in systems to protect critical assets. However, the strategy also urges the development of public-private networks to protect critical infrastructure assets. The Homeland Security Presidential Directive (HSPD-7) on protecting critical infrastructure issued by President Bush in 2003 facilitated these partnerships. It contemplates the development of industry-specific Information Sharing and Analysis Centers (ISACs) that would allow private companies to share security information in a secure environment and would permit a comprehensive review of systemic vulnerabilities, threats, and any countermeasures that might be undertaken by the networked partners to forestall the effects of a terrorist incident. In addition, each federal agency is charged with assessing the vulnerabilities of its own critical infrastructures and taking appropriate precautions.

Planning for a Terrorism Incident

The November 2002 Homeland Security Act directed the secretary of homeland security to improve the nation's emergency response capabilities by building a comprehensive national incident management system and by consolidating existing federal emergency response plans into a single, coordinated national response plan. In February 2003, the White House issued the Homeland Security Presidential Directive (HSPD-5), entitled Management of Domestic Incidents.[8] It was meant to "ensure that all levels of the government across the Nation have the capability to work efficiently and effectively together, using a national approach to domestic incident management," and it declared the secretary of homeland security to be the "principal Federal official for domestic incident management."

And yet under the directive the secretary of health and human services is to share responsibility with DHS for biological incidents, and the attorney general is given lead responsibility for criminal investigations of terrorist threats or acts within the United States, and is directed to "coordinate the activities of other members of the law enforcement community to detect, prevent, preempt, and disrupt terrorist attacks against the United States." In addition, the Defense Department may provide military support to civil authorities in a domestic incident, but always under the command of the secretary of defense. DHS responsibilities are triggered when a federal agency acting under its own authority requests DHS assistance with an incident, when state and local resources are overwhelmed and federal assistance has been requested by state and local authorities, when more than one federal agency has become involved in responding to the incident, or when the president directs the secretary of homeland security to assume management of the incident.

HSPD-5 also ordered the creation of a National Incident Management System to provide a flexible national framework within which governments at all levels and private entities could work together to manage domestic incidents. The NIMS, which became a reality in 2004, must, according to HSPD-5, be adopted by all federal departments and agencies for use in their "individual domestic incident management and emergency prevention, preparedness, response, recovery, and mitigation programs and activities, as well as in support of all actions taken to assist State, local, or tribal entities." Because the NIMS is thought to integrate best practices that have proven effective in preparedness and response, it is envisaged as an all-hazards, all-jurisdictions, all-disciplines system, suitable for terrorist attacks, natural disasters, and other emergencies.

HSPD-5 also called for development of a National Response Plan to replace existing national emergency response plans. The NRP, issued in January 2005, provides for a coordinated, all-hazards approach to "incident management," spelling out in broad terms the roles of all relevant elements of the national government and calling for communications and operational coordination by offices within DHS. But the NRP does not purport to supply the roadmap for responses to minor incidents—that is, those that can be routinely managed by a local or state government. Instead, the NRP focuses on "Incidents of National Significance," or "those high-impact events that require a coordinated and effective response by an appropriate combination of Federal, state, local, tribal, private sector, and nongovernmental entities in order to save lives, minimize damage, and provide the basis for long-term community recovery and mitigation activities."

Soon after releasing HSPD-5, the president issued HSPD-8, a companion directive that identifies the procedures to be followed by federal agencies in preparing for a terrorist incident or natural disaster. HSPD-8 directed the DHS secretary to develop a national preparedness goal applicable to all hazards and to establish readiness priorities and targets that balance the risk of the threats against the resources required to interdict or respond to the incidents. The directive also specified that the national preparedness goal include assessment measures so that planners could measure progress toward the goal.

The NRP sets out a framework for federal interaction with state, local, and tribal governments and with the private sector in an emergency. In addition, it includes twelve Emergency Support Functions (ESFs), described in annexes to the NRP that supply details on the mission, policies, and concept of operations of the federal agencies involved in support to state and local agencies.

Together, the NRP and NIMS describe the component parts of a planning and response system that is designed to work together for homeland security:

- *Incident command and management.* The NIMS calls for an Incident Command System (ICS) that defines operating characteristics, interactive management components, and the structure of incident management and emergency response organizations actually involved in an incident. It also includes Multiagency Coordination Systems, established to define the interactive structures and relationships of ICS entities through mutual aid or other agreements, and Public Information Systems, created to establish processes and systems for communicating effectively with the public during an emergency.
- *Preparedness.* Preparedness activities include integration of planning, training, multijurisdictional exercises, qualification and training of personnel, acquisition and certification of equipment, mutual aid agreements, and standardization and management of publications.
- *Resource management.* The NIMS standardizes mechanisms and requirements to inventory, mobilize, dispatch, track, and recover resources throughout the cycles of an incident.

- *Communications and information management.* The NIMS standardizes a framework for public communications, and for the collection, analysis, and dissemination of information generally, as well as mechanisms for information sharing across levels of government during an incident.
- *Support technologies.* The NIMS anticipates that the relevant agencies will provide support for voice and data communication systems, information management systems, and other technologies that facilitate operations and ongoing management activities during an incident.
- *Ongoing management and maintenance.* The NIMS anticipates direction and oversight of NIMS activities associated with any covered incident throughout planning, response, and recovery.

Under the National Response Plan, DHS would coordinate the response to a terrorism incident or natural disaster, and the secretary of homeland security would become the president's principal adviser in directing other federal agencies to respond to a crisis. The NRP and its accompanying Incident Command System and National Incident Management System were reshaped and refined in 2005 to take into account the president's decision directives and to move forward with an all-hazards response system that would ensure coordinated protection and response to any homeland crisis. The NRP anticipates that federal support to states and cities will be requested rather than launched without such a request, and that the default response will remain within the purview of state and local first responders and decision makers.

Protecting Critical Infrastructure

What do homeland security planners mean by "critical infrastructure?" In 1997 the President's Commission on Critical Infrastructure Protection defined critical infrastructure (CI) to include the networks, processes, synergy, and continuity needed "to produce and distribute a continuous flow of essential goods and services." So defined, critical infrastructure encompasses transportation, energy, water, environmental services such as waste disposal, and telecommunications. The 1998 Presidential Decision Directive/NSC 63 defined critical infrastructure as "those physical and cyber-based systems essential to the minimum operations of the economy and government." A few years later, in 2001, the USA PATRIOT Act defined such infrastructure as "systems and assets, whether physical or virtual, so vital to the nation that the incapacity or destruction of such systems would have a debilitating impact on security, national economic security, [or] national public health and safety." The planning documents that have been developed since 2001 have both expanded the breadth of what is considered critical infrastructure and focused on its detailed components, now including at least these categories: agriculture, banking, hazardous chemicals, defense, emergency services, energy, mail and shipping, public health and health care, telecommunications, transportation, water, along with national monuments, commerce and manufacturing, dams, nuclear power plants, and the government. Perhaps it would have been easier to list what is NOT critical infrastructure.

On a more practical level, it is easy to appreciate and understand what critical infrastructure is, because it threads its way through people's daily routines. The energy infrastructure is responsible for the alarm clock that goes off thirty minutes before the first class, while the shower and the breakfast gulped down are courtesy of the local public water service and the nation's vast agriculture and food distribution systems. Commuters may use mass transit or electronically controlled traffic systems. Those checking e-mail and instant messages, surfing the Web, or engaging in online research are using computerized databases that may be hosted anywhere in the world. Likewise, a visit to the ATM at the local bank or picking up a care package of baked goods from home also depends on critical communications networks. The point is obvious—some services and goods are critical for the conduct of everyday lives.

The overwhelming majority of the nation's critical infrastructure is in private, state, or local hands. Obviously, business owners have always had an incentive to protect their infrastructure assets, and they have invested in measures to mitigate risks to those assets. Indeed, many businesses had their own versions of CI protection plans long before homeland security became part of the national consciousness. The question, then, is how those responsible for homeland security planning can learn about CI vulnerabilities and protection in the private sector. How should companies share their information, and what assurances can the government give that information that reveals vulnerabilities or details about security measures will not fall into the wrong hands and undermine the objectives of CI protection?

CI Preparedness and Response

The National Infrastructure Protection Plan promulgated by DHS includes a comprehensive risk management framework that defines the roles and responsibilities of the various actors, private and government, entrusted with protecting critical infrastructure. Clearly, then, DHS has assumed a leadership role in managing the CI protection planning process, which requires the participation and cooperation of all levels of government and private sector leaders. During the department's first two to three years, turf battles and coordination problems inside DHS hampered efforts to protect critical infrastructure. Those efforts are fragmented not only within DHS (see Figure 6.1), but also outside, where the department's important planning partners include the Departments of Agriculture, Defense, Energy, Health and Human Services, and Treasury, the FBI, and state and local government agencies.

In other countries, CI assets have been targeted by terrorists on several occasions. For example, as noted in earlier chapters the group Aum Shinrikyo spread sarin gas in three subway lines in Tokyo in 1995. The target may have been Japanese government officials, but the critical component of infrastructure was clearly vulnerable. Also in 1995, terrorists bombed a Paris subway car and subways. In 2004 trains were bombed in Moscow and Madrid, resulting in hundreds of deaths. Once again, governments may have been the targets of these attacks and the objectives may have been to sway public opinion, but the infrastructure bore the brunt of the attacks. Although the September 11, 2001, attack targeted major U.S. landmarks and symbols, the hijackers also sought to damage the U.S. government and the country's financial infrastructure. The attacks damaged the subway system in New York City as well.

In the United States, oil and gas pipelines have been terrorist targets on several occasions, as has the electric power grid. In 2002 cyberattacks were reported by 70 percent of U.S. energy and power companies. And break-ins have occurred at water system facilities throughout the United States.

Contributing to the difficulties in tracing and assessing vulnerabilities, much of the U.S. critical infrastructure is interconnected. In fact, some CI systems are interdependent and thus depend on one another for operations or functions. Interdependence may be physical, geographic, functional, or financial. As a result, much of the U.S. critical infrastructure is heavily centralized, particularly water and utility systems, petroleum refineries, transit systems, and waste treatment facilities. In addition, the virtual explosion of information technology has had dramatic effects on critical infrastructure. Information technology includes the computing and communications of CI systems, and it often operates or is somehow involved in many other aspects of CI activities. Although innovations in information technology greatly enhance CI capabilities (such as cell phones, the Internet, and wireless technologies), vulnerabilities are increased when the technology breaks down or when terrorists attack information technology systems.

State and Local Government Planning

There is considerable truth to the adage "all terrorist incidents are local." For the firefighter or emergency medical technician who is first on the scene of a terrorist incident, the federal plans, systems, and directives are not of much consequence, because many cities and all states have their own homeland security plans. To the extent that the local or state authorities have adopted and implemented the federal National Incident Management System and National Response Plan, the processes and structures described in previous sections may be mirrored at the state and local levels.

And yet the National Strategy anticipates that a host of federal agencies will provide guidance and support, including financial and technical, for virtually all facets of state and local homeland security planning. In addition, the federal plans promote cooperation among state, local, and private sector plans, and they seek to identify and propose solutions to the gaps and overlaps between them. The common insertion of federal coordination and suggestions reflects the legal and political realities of the U.S. federal system: the states retain the fundamental and independent power to make and implement the key policy choices in protecting their security.

Because governors and state legislatures, mayors and city councils retain the authority to make and implement homeland security plans and protocols for their jurisdictions, there is the potential for conflict and confusion if a major incident affects more than one jurisdiction, or if an incident overwhelms the capacity of state and local resources and personnel and necessarily involves a federal response role. To forestall just such conflicts, many states and counties have entered into mutual aid agreements or emergency assistance compacts in which states prearrange the sharing of resources, including personnel and equipment, so that emergencies can be addressed by responders from more than one jurisdiction.

In fact, many states have developed homeland security plans that rival the federal plans in sophistication and complexity. The costs of planning and preparedness do, however, place a significant drain on state taxpayers, and there is ongoing tension over the need to exercise and train those in the state homeland security sector in the face of financial shortfalls in state budgets. That said, the opportunities for regional cooperation and governance mechanisms may alleviate some of the pressure on the states, and a greater willingness to involve private sector firms in homeland security planning and response may further spread the responsibility for readiness.

Although providing for the security of the citizenry is a quintessential government function, and is, indeed, the reason that the states came together as a union, the federal government has never found it easy to issue commands to state and local governments. Typically, the federal government cajoles state and local governments to implement federal policies by providing conditional grants or other financial inducements.

For example, after the September 11 attacks it was revealed that the hijackers easily obtained driver's licenses from various states—thirteen of them from Florida, which required no proof of residence. Those licenses, in turn, permitted the hijackers to pass airport screening identification requirements. As a matter of policy, the knowledge gained in the aftermath of the September 11 attacks provided a sound basis for requiring some uniform set of standards for issuing driver's licenses, standards that would ensure that the applicant has a verifiable residence and identity, among other things. Still, the Bush administration insisted in 2002 that driver's license requirements should be settled by the states. When in 2004 the 9-11 Commission urged federal action to set standards for driver's licenses, the administration balked at forced national standards and instead compromised with Congress the same year to provide time for the administration to negotiate licensing standards with state leaders.

The badly bungled federal response to Hurricane Katrina also illustrates the vagaries of the federal dynamics in ensuring preparedness for emergencies, whether caused by terrorists or by nature. Even though the National Response

Plan was designed to showcase a rational crisis response, major exercises that tested its premises revealed "confusion at all levels" and a "fundamental lack of understanding" about how the plan was supposed to operate. When Katrina made landfall in late August 2005, the NRP was incomplete. Worse still, DHS did not activate the critical components of the NRP until four days after the U.S. National Hurricane Center warned of Katrina's path and its power.

Instead of the unified command anticipated by the NRP in which agencies at all levels coordinate their efforts through their own structures and leadership, during the Katrina crisis officials at all levels sought without success to find central leadership. The unity of command could not be found because officials at various levels of government were confused about NRP and NIMS procedures, and because communications and coordination problems and shortfalls left any form of leadership in short supply. Political problems between federal and Louisiana officials exacerbated these tendencies, and FEMA and its leadership were simply not up to the task of managing the federal response, albeit one they were charged to manage so late that their task was not achievable realistically under the circumstances.

The Perils of Implementation

Since its creation in 2002 in the largest government reorganization since the Department of Defense came into being in 1947, the Department of Homeland Security has struggled with its apparently haphazard design, its ongoing bureaucratic warfare, and a series of unfulfilled promises. Although its initial assignments were to synthesize intelligence, secure borders, protect infrastructure, and prepare for the next crisis, DHS has, for the most part, failed to accomplish any of these tasks. It was not given the authority to force cooperation from the CIA, FBI, or Pentagon, all of whom resisted facilitating DHS missions. Indeed, until he could see that Congress was moving toward creation of DHS, whether or not the administration joined in the effort, President Bush was opposed to creation of the new department. He maintained that his White House Office of Homeland Security, under the leadership of Gov. Tom Ridge, could successfully coordinate the necessary homeland security preparedness.

While attending the State of the Union address four days after being sworn in as secretary of homeland security, Ridge learned that one of the cornerstones of the supposed DHS mission—an intelligence fusion center charged with connecting the intelligence dots—would instead be placed outside DHS, not subject to the secretary's direction or control. Ridge had understood that the new intelligence coordination and fusion center, designed to prevent the kind of coordination lapses that had helped the September 11 hijackers elude detection, would be located inside DHS, so that he could ensure that all the intelligence agencies with raw product and analysis would have their work shared to protect the homeland. Instead, the intelligence agencies won their fight to remain outside the new department, and so the intelligence directorate at DHS began with no under secretary, no assistant secretary, and only ten or so on a staff that was to have included about three hundred experts.

Even though in the wake of September 11 the people and members of Congress showed great support for the president and his strategy for ensuring homeland security, the first six post–September 11 years were characterized by inconsistent, relatively disorganized, and sometimes plainly ineffective homeland security preparedness. Part of the problem was the sheer size of the undertaking and the traditional reluctance to expand the reach of the federal government into areas traditionally under the purview of state and local authorities.

As for congressional oversight, because of the massive restructuring, which saw the consolidation of formerly independent agencies into one department, DHS found itself responsible for reporting to eighty-four different congressional committees and subcommittees. Early on, DHS was besieged with congressional inquiries, new responsibilities, a huge shortfall in personnel at all levels, and significant difficulties in sustaining leadership at the top. Secretary Ridge lost his chief of staff after seven months, and his deputy secretary left shortly after that. The secretary's authorities were not clearly mapped out in the legislation creating the department, and the homeland security tasks entrusted to DHS and to the secretary were often shared with other departments and agencies, each of which had its own legal authorities and presidential directives.

One example of the ambivalence of national leaders toward expanding the federal role in homeland security is the experience of the Transportation Security Agency (TSA). Well before the September 11 attacks, critics were lamenting the weaknesses of contractor-run passenger and baggage screening at U.S. airports. The Clinton administration opted not to reform the system, citing opposition from the aviation industry. After September 11, the screening system was federalized in a hurry, and the contract workers were replaced by TSA employees. The agency was given early deadlines for improving the screening procedures.

Even after TSA took this initiative, the Bush administration, having recommended that the private sector continue to provide airport screening, opposed the agency-run screeners, and Congress imposed a cap on the number of screeners that TSA could hire. After security heads at major airports complained that the cap was unrealistically low and would imperil safety, Congress lowered the cap even further. Moreover, pay and working conditions for screeners remained so poor that attrition and turnover significantly impaired training efforts, experiments with new screening methods, and the deployment of new baggage screening technologies.

After a 2005 General Accountability Office (GAO) study found that funding shortages were the primary obstacle to improving detection systems for explosives in checked baggage and that other technological improvements could not be implemented without higher federal funding, Congress and the administration did not commit the funds. In August 2006, British counter-terrorism agencies, in a widely reported success, stopped a terrorist plot to destroy ten cross-Atlantic flights using liquid explosives that cannot be detected by existing screening technologies. U.S. officials already knew about the prospects of liquid explosives bombs on U.S. airliners; a 1995 scheme to bring down transoceanic airliners would have used the same materials. Even so, DHS and TSA cut TSA's research and development budget to cover competing priorities.

An Implementation Example: Planning for Airline Security

The U.S. commercial aviation industry consists of hundreds of airports, thousands of planes, and tens of thousands of daily flights that carry more than half a billion passengers each year. As first noted in Chapter 4, the United States and some other nations began to consider policies to provide for airline security in the 1960s, after a spate of airline hijackings. Although the earliest U.S. security programs subjected only those who fit a "skyjacker" profile to frisking and a metal detector, by 1973 all passengers were required by presidential order and the rules of the Federal Aviation Administration to go through a metal detector and to submit to a search and usually an X-ray scan of all carry-on items. This security program continued, more or less unaltered, until the September 11 attacks. Private companies supplied the personnel to implement the screening,

The failure of this airline screening process to detect, much less stop, the September 11 hijackers was described at the outset of Chapter 4. That the hijackers were able to board the four flights carrying dangerous weapons and then were able to turn the airplanes into massive weapons illustrated tragically the failure of the airline security system; it was in serious need of repair. The box cutters were, inexplicably, well within the FAA rule forbidding knives with blades more than four inches long, and the hijackers had studied the planes and their protocols well—they knew that the cockpit doors could be opened using moderate force.

In the immediate aftermath of September 11, many Americans were afraid to fly. Airline passenger traffic dropped off considerably, exacerbated by stringent new security measures that generated long lines and countless delays at the nation's airports. As airlines lost revenue and related business suffered from the effects, planners faced a classic policy maker's dilemma: How should the government invest in airline security? How intrusive and comprehensive could the security measures be in light of the costs in passenger satisfaction, personal liberties, and economic well-being? How much vulnerability to another terrorist attack could the United States permit, knowing that terrorists might well change their tactics and their targets? (See Case Study 6.2.)

Aviation security planners had known for some time that terrorists might use aircraft as weapons. Indeed, al Qaeda had already used truck and boat bombs in attacking the United States, and so the notion of using airplanes was not a stark departure for the terrorists. In 1995 officials thwarted a plot crafted by Ramzi Yousef to blow up a dozen or more airliners over the Pacific, and one of Yousef's accomplices told investigators that they also planned to crash a plane into the CIA's Virginia headquarters. The next year, the Clinton administration's counterterrorism czar, Richard Clarke, sought to create an air defense component for the security plan for the 1996 Summer Olympic Games in Atlanta. Although the Treasury Department and its Secret Service cooperated with Clarke, the Pentagon declined to participate.

In 1996 TWA Flight 800 crashed soon after takeoff from Kennedy Airport in New York City; 230 were killed. Initial suspicions were that the plane was attacked by terrorists. In response, President Clinton asked Vice President Al Gore to chair a commission to report on shortfalls in aviation security. The Gore Commission's lengthy report focused on the danger of placing bombs on airliners rather than using suicide hijackers or airliners as weapons.[9] The commission also emphasized the problems of insufficient screening of passengers and their carry-on items.

At least since 1998, threat reports from U.S. intelligence agencies have mentioned terrorist threats to hijack planes and to take hostages in hijacking them. One briefing for President Clinton noted a bin Laden plan to hijack a plane in an effort to free imprisoned Sheikh Omar Abdel Rahman. (See Chapter 5.) Another one discussed a possible terrorist plan to fly an explosives-laden airplane into a U.S. city. And yet another briefing reported that a group of Libyans might crash a plane into New York City's World Trade Center.

Richard Clarke continued to encourage more airline security planning, but he met with little success. An exercise he created out of the failed attempts to develop an air defense plan for the Atlanta Olympics involved a stolen Learjet, loaded with explosives and routed to a target in Washington, D.C. Officials from the Defense Department, FAA, and Secret Service participated, but they did not resolve the security issue, nor did they pursue any planning initiative as a result of Clarke's work. Clarke continued to raise airline security concerns with his Counterterrorism Security Group inside the White House in 1999 and 2000, but, again, nothing came of his efforts.[10] And then, famously, in President Bush's Daily Brief for August 6, 2001, intelligence officials included a section entitled "Bin Ladin Determined to Strike in US." It pointed to "suspicious activity in this country consistent with preparations for hijackings" by bin Laden.[11]

Other agencies showed interest as well in aviation security before September 11. A Justice Department lawyer wrote an analysis of the legal issues involved in shooting down a U.S. airliner in an aircraft terrorist plot, and the North American Aerospace Defense Command (NORAD) wrote a series of exercises to counter the threat posed by aircraft as weapons. Still, taken together, the pre–September 11 planners did not analyze how an aircraft might be used as a weapon, even though suicide terrorism had become an important means of attack by terrorists. Nor did officials pursue, much less monitor, the indicators that the planning for such attacks was under way. Officials also declined to pursue work on how to strengthen the nation's defenses against aircraft hijackings or suicide attackers from the air.

Implementing Airline Security

Early on after the September 11 attacks, uniformed military personnel, mostly National Guard and reservists, patrolled the perimeters and even inside the terminals of major airports. The FAA had been particularly weak in its pre–September 11 security planning role. What changes would it encourage now—expanded "no-fly" lists? Searching suspicious passengers as identified by a computer-based screening system? Deploying air marshals in planes? Hardening cockpit doors? More training for crew and attendants and other staff on the changing face of terrorism?

Before September 11, airlines performed the passenger screening services, largely by contracting with private security companies. Although there was widespread agreement that the private security firms could not be trusted to continue the screening task, there was considerable disagreement about what to do in their stead. The result was that dozens of new aviation security plans were brought forward in the days and weeks after September 11. In November 2001, Congress enacted the Aviation and Transportation Security Act, which created the Transportation Security Administration. As part of a White House compromise with members of Congress and interested industry groups, the act federalized the checkpoint security screeners and mandated the security methods and technologies already in use in the nation's airports. Although the new TSA screeners would have to be to trained before fully taking over passenger screening in the nation's airports, the effect of the change was to increase air travel, slowly at first, to its pre–September 11 levels.

And yet, despite the issuance of federal standards for screeners and screening and the infusion of considerable taxpayer dollars, no comprehensive strategic plan is in place to assess the risks and the attendant costs and benefits of improved airline security. Commercial aviation is still beset with inadequate screening and access measures, and security for checked baggage and for air cargo is rudimentary at best.

What kind of security system makes the most sense in light of limited resources and competing demands for homeland security spending? Different mechanisms might be appropriate for different problems, such as suicide bombers, hijackers, insider threats, and attacks on planes from the ground or air. Watch lists for aviation, or "no-fly" lists, might be one layer of security. But policy makers must decide which agencies would perform these tasks and who would control them and monitor them for updates and changes.

Computer-assisted screening might be an additional layer, but it is difficult to know what kind of computer-assisted screening system can identify potentially dangerous passengers without significant numbers of mistakes, and without unduly compromising personal privacy. Special scrutiny for explosives, in any form, might act as another layer of screening. But it is unclear who should manage and implement the technologies and whether they can be applied to checked and carry-on baggage and cargo.

TSA has continued to struggle with screening and its mechanisms. The shoe rule is illustrative. Even after shoe makers advertised "security friendly" shoes that would not set off the metal detectors, TSA screeners continued to insist that all passengers remove their shoes, whatever their type. Experienced travelers who posed little or no security threat were inconvenienced with long lines and cumbersome processes and were asked to put up with a system that was designed not to let dangerous people board planes. Meanwhile, TSA tinkered with the rules and their implementation frequently, seeking to speed up the process, to reduce passenger complaints, and to please its congressional overseers.

The Computer-Assisted Passenger Prescreening System (eventually called CAPPSII) used computer-generated profiles of passengers to select those who should be subjected to additional screening. It relied on commercial data to calculate "scores" for passengers. But privacy concerns were highlighted when at least four airlines and two travel agencies confessed that they had given the personal information of millions of travelers to a private company working on a Pentagon contract to develop an improved computer-assisted screening program, and to the government itself. Although the airlines and agencies violated their own policies when they turned over the information and they apologized to their passengers, there was no assurance that the release of private information would not be repeated. In 2005 Congress prohibited the use of appropriated funds for CAPPSII or its successor, Secure Flight, until the government could certify that privacy requirements were being met, largely those related to false positives and the sharing of private information.

By early 2007, veteran American Airlines pilot Kiernan O'Dwyer had been detained by U.S. customs agents about eighty times since 2003, apparently because his birth date and name are similar to those of an IRA leader whose name is on a U.S. watch list. Even though officials concede that O'Dwyer is no threat to the United States, the database continues to flag him whenever he enters the United States. The customs watch list problems mirror those of TSA and their false positives under CAPPS. Both agencies may manually remove names from their lists, but the problems associated with false positives continue to compromise the effectiveness of the screening mechanisms—and highly frustrate travelers.

Screening for airline and airport employees, and for the screeners themselves, presents another set of concerns. Standards for security at the perimeters of airports are also set by federal guidelines, but an industry group claims that most airports do not meet them. Construction workers come and go; airport employees may need to show only some form of identification to enter their work area; and they may not have been screened prior to employment.

CASE STUDY 6.2

The Shoe Bomber

As if air travelers were not nervous enough, on December 22, 2001, passenger Richard Reid, en route from Paris to Miami on an American Airlines flight, attempted to use matches to light fuses that protruded from his sneakers. After flight attendants and passengers restrained and then subdued Reid using drugs from the first-aid kit, the flight diverted to Boston, accompanied by U.S. military jets. Once the plane was on the ground, FBI agents took custody of Reid and found that his sneakers were stuffed with explosives, enough to blow a hole in the fuselage of the plane, causing it to crash. Investigators soon found connections between Reid and al Qaeda and evidence that al Qaeda had developed shoe bombs before Reid resorted to the tactic using his sneakers. Almost immediately, new security regulations were adopted that forced passengers to remove their shoes and send them through the same X-ray screening used for other carry-on items.

In January 2003, Reid was convicted on terrorism charges and was sentenced to consecutive life sentences. During his sentencing hearing, Reid affirmed his affiliation with al Qaeda and declared himself an enemy of the United States. Reid was apparently converted to a radical form of Islam while serving time for a string of petty crimes in a London youth offenders' prison. From there, Reid frequented the same south London mosque attended by other radical Muslim former prisoners. Before his ill-fated flight from Paris to Miami, authorities believe that Reid traveled in Europe and South Asia, testing airline security arrangements and scouting targets for al Qaeda. Whether the shoe removal rule still in effect in the United States is an effective response to terrorism remains an open question. ■

Public Health Infrastructure

A range of public health professionals, from epidemiologists and administrators to laboratory experts, are among the "first responders" who would have management responsibilities in the event of a terrorist attack with biological weapons, also known as bioterrorism. (See Case Study 6.3.) However, for several reasons the demands on the nation's public health infrastructure imposed by preparedness for a biological attack far outstrip its capabilities. First, there is no national "system" for public health in any meaningful sense. Instead, some 2,800 local health departments cooperate and communicate with one another in various ways. Second, the federal government has no clear national public health mission related to terrorism preparedness. Third, the existing public health departments are overburdened. Fourth, the new capabilities that exist for responding to terrorism are still in their infancy, lacking training and practice. Finally, the U.S. federal system augers against the imposition of national standards on local systems that are used to respond to local needs.

Local public health departments do not, for the most part, have trained first responders able to act in an attack with biological weapons. A tradition of responding to vulnerable populations and specific local needs has resulted in a series of unique local structures that are not well situated to respond and cooperate across jurisdictions to a large-scale outbreak. Further complicating any effort to organize and plan on a national basis are the diverse public health laws in the states. Some state laws, particularly those enacted after September 11, prescribe the command and control relationships and the roles of the federal, state, and local players that would be involved in a public health emergency. Other states retain decades-old authorities that offer little guidance to officials who must make quick decisions in an emergency.

Despite considerable funding and federal efforts since September 11, the basic public health infrastructure remains unprepared for bioterrorism. Moreover, a bioterrorism attack will require significant medical resources well in excess of what cities can provide. Beyond those who may be affected by an agent or be in close contact with someone who has been exposed to a contagious disease, those who panic and fear the effects of an outbreak (the "worried well") will flood local hospitals, as will the uninsured who regularly go to emergency rooms for primary care. In short, the "surge capacity"—that is, the excess medical and public health resources that can respond to a crisis—is limited.

CASE STUDY 6.3

Anticipating an Attack with Weapons of Mass Destruction: The Case of Bioterrorism

One common approach to emergency planning is to study the worst-case scenarios. By working hard to create effective preparedness and response mechanisms for such scenarios, planners can use the lessons and resources gained from the worst-case planning effort to better prepare for a range of potential emergencies. Particularly in view of federal planners' determination since 2003 that preparedness and response activities be geared toward an "all-hazards" approach, the worst-case scenarios will help prepare responders for all kinds of terrorist threats, as well as for natural disasters and other emergencies.

The worst case would be an attack with a weapon of mass destruction such as a nuclear detonation in a major city, or the detonation of simultaneous radiological dispersion devices (dirty bombs) in urban areas, or the release of chemicals in mass transit systems, or an attack with deadly germs. The latter, and especially a biological weapons attack with a contagious agent such as pneumonic plague, is the nightmare scenario for most planners.

Plague is a bacterium that usually results in death in untreated cases and can become an epidemic. It is best known as the cause of Justinian's Plague (in the mid-sixth century) and the Black Death (in the mid-fourteenth century), two pandemics that killed millions. A third, lesser-known pandemic began in China in the late 1800s and spread to all inhabited continents, leading to nearly thirty million cases and more than twelve million deaths in the period from 1896 to 1930. This third, or Modern Pandemic, prompted an intensive multinational research effort to identify the causative agent of plague (it was *Yersinia pestis,* a bacterium). This effort also produced conclusive evidence that rat fleas transmit the disease to humans during epidemics. Later studies indicated that smaller numbers of cases also arise from bites by wild rodent fleas, from handling infected animals, or from inhaling the infectious respiratory droplets exuded in the cough of persons with plague pneumonia. Other studies demonstrated that plague bacteria are maintained in nature through transmission cycles involving wild rodent hosts and flea vectors. Armed with this knowledge, public health workers were able to design and implement prevention measures that reduced the incidence and spread of plague in many regions.

In this hypothetical bioterrorism attack scenario, members of the Universal Adversary (UA) release pneumonic plague in three main areas of a major metropolitan city using small fluid canisters with spray nozzles. At approximately 7 a.m., five members of the UA discharge canisters in bathrooms at the city's major airport. Fifty persons are exposed to these releases, including thirty-five passengers on a flight between Canadian and U.S. cities. That afternoon, the terrorists make a similar release in twenty-five bathrooms in the city's major sports arena during a playoff hockey game. Three thousand people are exposed, including 750 international travelers. Among the international travelers, 250 fly home to Canada the day after the game; ten others fly to destinations in Europe, Asia, South America, and the Middle East. Finally, between 5:30 p.m. and 6 p.m., the terrorists discharge canisters in bathrooms in the city's major train station, exposing an additional fifty persons.

The first cases arrive in emergency rooms about thirty-six hours after the releases, with rapid progression of symptoms and fatalities in untreated (or inappropriately treated) patients. The rapidly escalating number of previously healthy persons with severe respiratory symptoms quickly triggers alarms within hospitals and at the local health department. Observed incubation periods, which vary significantly between individuals, range from one to six days after exposure. It is estimated that the some eighty hospitals in the major city's metropolitan area can make room for as many as three thousand additional patients on fairly short notice, with total capacity in the state exceeding eight thousand beds. It is not known precisely how many patients requiring intensive care can be absorbed, but the number is significantly less than three thousand, possibly on the order of a couple of hundred. Intensive care bed capacity could be increased fairly rapidly by temporarily lodging patients with pneumonic plague in post-anesthesia care units.

The situation in the hospitals is complicated by the fact that the symptoms of pneumonic plague are relatively nonspecific and by the need to initiate definitive therapy rapidly once symptoms begin. It is expected that large numbers of worried patients, including many with fever and upper respiratory symptoms, will crowd emergency rooms. Distinguishing patients with pneumonic plague from those with more benign illnesses will require the promulgation of clear-cut definitions and guidance. Physician uncertainty will result in low thresholds for admission and administration of available countermeasures, producing severe strains on commercially available supplies of ciprofloxacin and doxycycline (among other medications) and exacerbating the surge-capacity problem.

Pneumonic plague is transmissible from person to person, and the public will want to know quickly whether it is safe to remain in the city and surrounding regions. Because of the large number of persons initially exposed and the escalating nature of the epidemic, it is likely that state and federal public health officials will recommend a modified form of sheltering-in-place or voluntary "snow day" restrictions as a self-protective measure for the general public and as a way of facilitating the delivery of medical countermeasures and prophylaxis to those at risk of contracting pneumonic plague. Some people may flee regardless of the public health guidance provided.

Support of critical infrastructure and the maintenance of supply chains during this period will pose significant logistical and human resource challenges. The public may place pressure on pharmacies to dispense medical countermeasures directly, particularly if there are delays in setting up official points of distribution. Public health guidance must be provided in several languages. The number of visitors and commuters at or passing through the major city's airport, the sports arena, and the train station on the morning of the attack will complicate the identification of patients and the distribution of antibiotics, because cases will present over a wide geographic area, and the timing of the attacks will not be known within a timeframe relevant to the provision of postexposure prophylaxis.

Within the first two days of the attack, physicians in both the United States and Canada will become alarmed at the volume of patients with similar and increasingly severe symptoms. Hospital staff, medical examiner office personnel, and local officials will recognize the scope of the current incident. Public health officials will face the task of defining and managing the crisis. By the third and fourth days, the plague will worsen in the major city and nearby Canadian cities and will have already spread across both the Pacific and Atlantic Oceans to encircle the globe. By the end of the first week, more than eight thousand cases of plague will be confirmed, along with more than two thousand deaths.

It is not difficult to imagine other forms of terrorist attack on the nation's cities or infrastructure. Some would be less complex to manage, even if just as devastating, such as using civilian airliners to deliver conventional explosives. Others could be even more sinister than this scenario, such as a series of covert attacks with contagious biological agents in which the symptoms do not become apparent for several days. From the description of the key players identified in this chapter, it is apparent that many parts of government—federal, state, and local—would be part of the response to an outbreak like this one. It is much less clear who would be in charge of the response and which agencies would coordinate the critical response activities. Although all levels of government have conducted exercises and training in anticipation of an emergency of this scale, many facets of the preparedness and response work continue to present serious challenges.

SOURCE: This case study is adapted from National Planning Scenarios, Scenario 4: Biological Attack—Pneumonic Plague, Department of Homeland Security/Homeland Security Council, Version 20.1, Draft, April 2005, www.media.washingtonpost.com/wp-srv/nation/nationalsecurity/earlywarning/NationalPlanningScenariosApril2005.pdf. ■

Post–September 11: A Fragmented Bureaucracy and a Role for a Resilient Citizenry

Even before the post–September 11 critiques of the U.S. government's readiness for domestic terrorism began to appear, the 2001 report of the U.S. Commission on National Security/21st Century, also known as the Hart-Rudman Commission for its cochairs Senators Gary Hart and Warren Rudman, complained about the disarray within the executive branch and urged a reshaping of the homeland security bureaucracy so that it was "coherent and integrated." [12] In large part, the commission and other such study groups complained that it was not clear who was in charge of the domestic preparedness mission or of the response. In a time of crisis, it would be essential to know who is in charge.

A 2004 report from the Heritage Foundation and the Center for Strategic and International Studies concluded that DHS had essentially failed in breaking down old barriers, categories, and jurisdictions to reshape an effective homeland security apparatus.[13] Instead, DHS was "rife with turf warfare." Battles inside DHS threatened or derailed several initiatives. For example, Immigration and Customs Enforcement (ICE), responsible for compliance with immigration and customs laws inside the United States, fought to gain the hundreds of millions of dollars that it claimed should have been moved from Customs and Border Protection (CBP), which was responsible for enforcement of the border itself. Only after a three-year struggle and ICE's decision to impose a hiring freeze and release illegal aliens with criminal convictions who could no longer be detained because of the shortfall in the ICE budget did ICE gain the promised resources.

Unsurprisingly, the muddled DHS reorganization produced morale problems. A worker survey in 2005 found that DHS had the worst working conditions of any federal department, and that most DHS workers reported that they did not know how their work related to the overall DHS mission. Structural problems inside the DHS organization made it impossible for senior administrators to force cooperation from lower-level counterparts in other parts of the department. And, inevitably, the inexperience and turnover of new political appointees harmed the reorganization. By 2005 DHS had lost a secretary and deputy secretary, three under and six assistant secretaries, the chief security officer, the chief and deputy information officer, the cybersecurity director and his deputy, and dozens of other key personnel. Fully two-thirds of the senior DHS staff had left by 2006.

Nor did Congress contribute to an effective reorganization when it failed to streamline its oversight of homeland security. Twenty-six committees and sixty subcommittees in Congress share jurisdiction over homeland security affairs. When the 9-11 Commission added its weight to mounting criticism of the cronyism of continuing fragmented oversight, the House created a standing committee on homeland security, although its authority was limited. The Senate then took similar steps, but the overall reform of oversight has been minimal to date.

To be sure, DHS can point to some successes in implementation. Commercial airliners now have hardened cockpit doors, thanks to DHS/TSA; interstate truck drivers now undergo background checks; and the nation's ports have radiation detectors. DHS has also managed to absorb eight payroll providers into one system, and it has melded twenty-two human resources offices into seven. Most notably, there has not been another major terrorist attack on the homeland since September 11.

And what role might the citizenry play in this post–September 11 world? It has long been assumed that, in the event of a terrorist attack, the affected communities of people would require protection and that any efforts by the public to participate in a response effort would only get in the way. Indeed, it has been feared that, instead of contributing to an effective response to a terrorist attack, the public would panic and only create social disruption, especially in the event of a major strike or a bioterrorism incident that threatens widespread sickness or death. However, even in the worst situation—a catastrophic epidemic caused by a bioterrorist attack—decision makers have come to realize that a resilient community may react and respond effectively in crisis circumstances, and that a positive role for members of the public as volunteers and in shielding themselves from the panic that might otherwise overtake a community should be seriously considered in planning for homeland security. From a planning perspective, it may be essential for the success of preparedness to involve members of the affected communities in the planning process, so that the public has a stake in the preparedness objectives. So viewed, the public may be an ally in countering an attack, and in practice citizens may assist as parts of voluntary organizations or from their homes or places of work. Citizens may also assist in communicating with others during a crisis.

Conclusion

It is tempting to ridicule the massive scale of the government reorganization that produced DHS and its spin-off agencies. To be sure, there have been plenty of failures of management, leadership, organization, and imagination to go around. And yet it is too early to give final grades to the homeland security planning side of DHS and its reorganization. The Department of Defense, the only real analog to DHS in government in terms of its size, was hardly a well-oiled bureaucratic machine in its early years, and the department has had sixty years of experience during which to build its effective organization.

In 2006 Congress revisited in some significant ways the structure and approaches to homeland security planning and emergency preparedness. It was driven to do so primarily by the critiques supplied after Hurricane Katrina. Although Secretary Michael Chertoff had already launched emergency management system reforms at DHS on the basis of his authority as secretary, the Katrina experience suggested to Congress that DHS was not well structured or organized for emergency responses, and particularly FEMA. Congress learned that the agency had deteriorated since its incorporation into DHS, because its weaknesses were very much on display in the Katrina episode. Accordingly, new legislation has reorganized DHS with a reconfigured FEMA, designed to elevate FEMA's stature and authority to plan for and manage emergencies. The details of these reforms will be considered in the next chapter.

FOR FURTHER READING

Ervin, Clark Kent. *Open Target: Where America Is Vulnerable to Attack*. Basingstoke, Hampshire, UK: Palgrave Macmillan, 2006.

Kean, Thomas H., Lee Hamilton, and Benjamin Rhodes. *Without Precedent: The Inside Story of the 9/11 Commission*. New York: Knopf, 2006.

National Commission on Terrorist Attacks upon the United States. *Final Report*. Washington, D.C.: Government Printing Office, 2004, http://www.gpoaccess.gov/911/index.html.

Rosner, David, and Gerald E. Markowitz. *Are We Ready? Public Health Since 9/11*. Berkeley: University of California Press, 2006.

Chapter 7 **Incident Response**

What happens when, despite the best efforts of planners and intelligence experts and others involved in homeland security, the worst happens? Before September 11, 2001, many Americans thought that planning in advance to anticipate such a crisis was ill-advised, because it would be costly and time-consuming to make such plans, and because a catastrophic attack on the homeland seemed unlikely. Now the investment in incident response preparedness is heavy, and its pace remains rapid, spurred by natural disasters such as Hurricane Katrina in 2005 and the specter of pandemic flu. The incident response plans that have been developed are intergovernmental, across federal agencies and between layers of government, and yet they offer relatively little operational detail. Because of the complexities of the task and the lack of details in preparedness, it is not clear how incident response will work in practice.

Crisis decision making and crisis response constitute the supreme test of a government and its leaders. Large-scale crises also present formidable challenges for the citizenry. They must decide what measures can be taken in advance of a crisis—such as participating in incident response planning or learning how to protect themselves during a terrorist incident.

This chapter builds on the planning themes and issues addressed in Chapter 6. When a terrorist or natural event does occur, the atmosphere of crisis, threatened or real, greatly complicates rational and systematic response plans. In addition to exploring the implications of this heightened tension, this chapter revisits the complications raised by having so many constituencies involved in making decisions and contributing to a crisis response. These constituencies include federal departments and agencies, as well as the military, state and local agencies, first responders, and nongovernmental and private sector interests.

The first section of this chapter traces the current state of incident response preparedness by reviewing the evolution of federal plans, including the National Response Plan, and the exercises undertaken to test those plans. A separate segment examines in greater detail federal public health preparedness, arguably the hardest sector to prepare. Then added to the mix is a brief review of state and local incident response plans and mechanisms, along with the possibilities for regional responses. These parts of the chapter are interspersed with case studies—one returning to the plague case study in Chapter 6—that illustrate how the preparedness mechanisms fare in times of crisis. Another major section of the chapter examines the military role in a crisis response, including the special capabilities offered by the nation's citizen soldier, the

National Guard. It also features a brief look at the first military command created expressly for homeland defense and homeland security, Northern Command or NORTHCOM. The final section examines the controls on people (such as quarantines and evaluations) that must be undertaken in a crisis.

Federal Incident Response Plans and Exercises

The plans and mechanisms designed to ensure national preparedness for all the hazards assessed in Chapter 6 are commonly referred to as the comprehensive emergency management (CEM) system. The institutional responsibility for CEM tasks was exercised by the Federal Emergency Management Agency before enactment of the Homeland Security Act of 2002. After passage of the act and the creation of the Department of Homeland Security, the tasks were fragmented within the Department of Homeland Security among FEMA, the Border and Transportation Security Directorate (BTS), and the Preparedness Directorate (PD). The debacle of anticipating and then responding to Hurricane Katrina in 2005 prompted Congress to reshape CEM and vest responsibility for the federal CEM role squarely in FEMA.

Under the Post-Katrina Act, as of March 31, 2007, FEMA inherited the Preparedness Directorate, and the director of FEMA became an under secretary of DHS. The act also permits the president to designate the FEMA director as a member of the cabinet in the event of a crisis. It created a regional FEMA system, with ten regions and ten regional directors, and a National Integration Center (NIC), which is charged with overseeing the National Incident Management System. In addition to maintaining the NIMS and NRP, the NIC will revise and release revisions and updates to the NRP.

During the period the NRP, NIMS, and other components of federal preparedness took shape before and after the 2002 legislation, major federal exercises directed at terrorist attacks, dubbed Top Officials (TOPOFF), were carried out in Denver (plague), Portsmouth, New Hampshire (a chemical weapon), and Washington, D.C. (a radiological weapon), beginning in 2000. Attacks with different kinds of WMD (including, it is now known, civilian airliners) pose different threats to the population. But the challenges they present to the nation's public health and law enforcement systems (and perhaps the military) have much in common. In varying degrees, they raise the same issues of leadership, authority, and ability to plan for inherently unpredictable developments. Because it is impossible to know in advance what form a terrorist attack might take, the issues raised by each possible threat must be considered. These initial TOPOFF exercises indicated that state and local public health capabilities were not nearly sufficient to respond to a large-scale outbreak. The exercises also revealed unreliable communications among local, state, and federal officials, as well as cumbersome decision-making processes and widespread perceptions that no one was in charge.

A subsequent exercise, TOPOFF 2 in May 2003, featured a simulated radiological attack in Seattle, a dispersal of plague bacilli in Chicago, a cyber-attack, and terrorist threats in other locations. Unlike in the earlier TOPOFF exercises, however, in TOPOFF 2 participants were notified of the exercises well in advance. Thus the resulting lack of unpredictability and spontaneity may have reduced its value as either a test of preparedness or an aid in planning. A similar TOPOFF 3 exercise was conducted in early 2005. When the results of these exercises struck supervising DHS officials as very much like those from the earlier TOPOFF exercises, the Department of Homeland Security deferred further applications of its TOPOFF exercise module until additional work is done to reform response plans and implementation mechanisms.

Decision Making in a Crisis: Triggering the NRP

The centerpiece of federal homeland security planning is the National Response Plan. As described in Chapter 6, the NRP covers all hazards, from terrorism to natural disasters, and provides the template for the assistance and operations of all federal agencies in the event of an actual or potential Incident of National Significance (INS). Although the NRP is designed to be flexible, along with the accompanying NIMS, and is capable of selective implementation with specific components as needed in any appropriate circumstance, the specific triggering circumstances and decisions are not so clear.

Under Homeland Security Presidential Directive (HSPD-5), the DHS secretary is supposed to coordinate the federal response under the National Response Plan whenever one of four conditions applies:

1. A federal department or agency acting under its own authority has requested the assistance of the secretary

2. The resources of state and local authorities are overwhelmed, and the appropriate state and local authorities have requested federal assistance

3. More than one federal department or agency has become substantially involved in responding to the incident

4. The president has directed the secretary to assume responsibility for managing the domestic incident.

Unfortunately, the NRP does not state clearly what circumstances prompt a threatened or actual event to become an INS. It could be that satisfaction of one of the criteria just listed triggers an INS and thus initiates the federal role under the NRP. Or it could be that the secretary of homeland security or the president has to declare an INS. In 2005 this ambiguity was showcased in the worst way when DHS secretary Michael Chertoff declared an INS two days after two of the four criteria had been satisfied with the arrival of Hurricane Katrina along the Gulf Coast. By the time the INS was declared, the federal response was for the most part too little, too late. It is unclear whether senior federal officials, including Secretary Chertoff, were simply caught off guard by the intensity and size of the storm, or whether the response mechanisms themselves had been insufficiently fine-tuned or had not been tested in an event the magnitude of Hurricane Katrina.

As the Katrina experience demonstrated, the NRP does not say what specific actions should be taken and which parts of government should take them once an INS is clearly under way, however declared. For example, in the first two days after Hurricane Katrina made landfall, some NRP-related response activities were undertaken, in relatively uncoordinated fashion, even in the absence of declaration of an INS. In short, the NRP continues to lack a clear "concept of operations"—that is, how the multiple federal departments and agencies will coordinate their work with state, local, and tribal responders and officials, nongovernmental and private sector organizations, and any other entities involved in response and recovery. In theory, the NRP provides for the secretary's appointment of a principal federal officer (PFO), who would work alongside a federal coordinating officer (FCO) at the helm of a Joint Field Office (JFO). The FCO, a position created earlier by the Stafford Act, manages the federal resource activities and coordinates delivery of federal aid to affected communities and persons.

One of the frequent criticisms of the federal response mechanisms raised during the TOPOFF exercises was ignorance about who is in charge during a crisis. In one leadership model, *unity of command,* each person or entity reports to one designated leader. Like a military chain of command, unity of command ensures unity of effort under one responsible commander. By contrast, under the *unified command,* contemplated by the Incident Command System for incidents affecting multiple agencies or multiple jurisdictions, the multiple agencies and entities from different governments or private sector entities work through designated leaders from each such entity to determine unified objectives and unified command through collaboration and cooperation. The NRP, HSPD-5, and NIMS assume a unified command structure. But unified command in theory is not necessarily unified command in fact. During the federal government's response to Hurricane Katrina, it was unclear for the first few days, particularly in New Orleans, which parts of the government were in charge.

Apart from the activities in the field, the Homeland Security Operations Center (HSOC) at DHS headquarters is supposed to coordinate information sharing, operational planning, and further deployment of federal resources once an INS has occurred. The Interagency Incident Management Group (IIMG) is made up of managers below senior leadership who are responsible for undertaking detailed coordination activities and resolving any conflicts that emerge among agencies or others in the early response to an INS. (See Figure 7.1.)

The NRP includes twelve Emergency Support Functions (ESFs), set out in annexes to the NRP. (See Table 7.1.) Field, regional, and local coordination activities are expected to occur within ESF systems and frameworks. The ESFs

Figure 7.1 National Response Plan

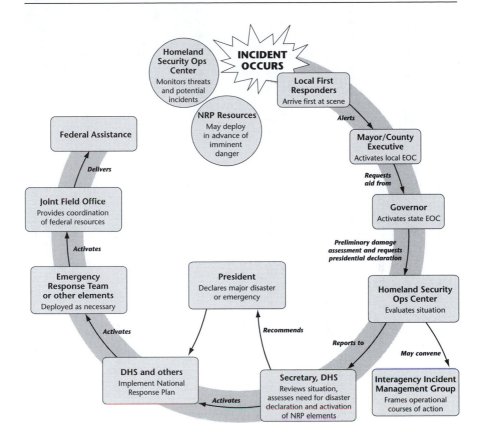

SOURCE: U.S. Department of Homeland Security.
NOTE: EOC refers to Emergency Operations Center.

combine government and private sector experts in an emergency response. They are charged with ensuring that the appropriate mix of response assets and expertise are delivered where it is needed. Together, the ESFs supply details on the mission, policies, concepts of operations, and responsibilities of the federal agencies involved in support of state and local agencies in an Incident of National Significance. For example, the Biological Incident Annex (described in greater detail in the next section) and the Public Health and Medical Services Annex prescribe what federal responders should do in support of state and local activities in the event of an attack with germs. The Catastrophic Incident Annex and its Supplement provide federal and state officials with additional detailed guidance on the roles and missions of federal agencies in the event of a catastrophic incident, whatever its cause.

Table 7.1 Emergency Support Functions (ESFs)

ESF	Description	Lead agency
1. Transportation	Assists federal agencies, state and local government entities, and volunteer organizations requiring transportation capacity to perform response missions after a major disaster or emergency. Also serves as a coordination point between response operations and restoration of the transportation infrastructure.	U.S. Department of Transportation
2. Communications	Ensures the provision of federal telecommunications support to federal, state, and local response efforts after a presidentially declared major disaster, emergency, or extraordinary situation under the National Response Plan (NRP). This ESF supplements the provisions of the National Plan for Telecommunications Support in Non-Wartime Emergencies.	National Communications System
3. Public Works and Engineering	Provides technical advice and evaluation, engineering services, contracting for construction management and inspection, contracting for the emergency repair of water and wastewater treatment facilities, potable water and ice, emergency power, and real estate support to assist the state(s) in meeting goals related to lifesaving and life-sustaining actions, damage mitigation, and recovery activities after a major disaster or emergency.	U.S. Department of Defense, U.S. Army Corps of Engineers
4. Firefighting	Detects and suppresses wild land, rural, and urban fires resulting from, or occurring coincidentally with, a major disaster or emergency requiring federal response assistance.	U.S. Department of Agriculture
5. Information and Planning	Collects, analyzes, processes, and disseminates information about a potential or actual disaster or emergency to facilitate the overall activities of the federal government in providing assistance to one or more affected states. Fulfilling this mission supports planning and decision making at both the field/regional operations and headquarters levels.	Federal Emergency Management Agency
6. Mass Care	Coordinates federal assistance in support of state and local efforts to meet the mass care needs of victims of a disaster. This federal assistance supports the delivery of mass care services of shelter, feeding, and emergency first aid to disaster victims; the establishment of systems to provide the bulk distribution of emergency relief supplies to disaster victims; and the collection of information to	American Red Cross

ESF	Description	Agency
7. Resource Support	operate a Disaster Welfare Information (DWI) system for the purpose of reporting victim status and assisting in family unification. Provides logistical and resource support to other organizations through purchasing, contracting, or renting and leasing equipment and supplies in a potential or actual presidentially declared major disaster or emergency.	General Services Administration
8. Public Health and Medical Services	Provides coordinated federal assistance to supplement state and local resources in response to public health and medical care needs after a major disaster or emergency, or during a developing medical situation. Resources are furnished when state and local resources are overwhelmed and public health or medical assistance is requested from the federal government.	U.S. Department of Health and Human Services
9. Urban Search and Rescue	Rapidly deploys components of the National Urban Search and Rescue (US&R) Response System to provide specialized lifesaving assistance to state and local authorities in the event of a major disaster or emergency. US&R operational activities include locating, extricating, and providing on-site medical treatment to victims trapped in collapsed structures.	Federal Emergency Management Agency
10. Hazardous Materials/ Environmental Protection	Provides federal support to state and local governments in response to an actual or potential discharge or release of hazardous materials after a major disaster or emergency.	U.S. Environmental Protection Agency
11. Food and Water	Identifies, secures, and arranges for the transportation of bulk food, water, and ice to affected areas after a major disaster or emergency or other event requiring a federal response.	U.S. Department of Agriculture
12. Energy	Helps restore the nation's energy systems after a major disaster, emergency, or other significant event requiring federal response assistance.	U.S. Department of Energy

SOURCE: U.S. Department of Homeland Security, http://www.dhs.gov/xlibrary/assets/NRP_Quick_Reference_Guide_5-22-06.pdf.

NOTE: Three additional ESFs are being developed in draft revisions to the NRP: public safety and security, long-term community recovery, and external affairs.

In the aftermath of a terrorism incident involving WMD, coordination among agencies and levels of government may become highly confused. Although federal laws supply authority for federal personnel, civilian and military, to take various actions in such an instance, including some law enforcement tasks, the laws do not authorize federal control over state and local personnel. It is at least conceivable that a governor could disagree with or have different objectives about the provision of federal support in a domestic terrorism crisis. Coordination becomes even more complex and potentially politically charged when personal liberties may be restricted, and when military personnel become part of the response to an incident.

The Federal Public Health and Medical Services Response

The most challenging aspect of most terrorism incidents is likely to be public health. Hospitals and other parts of the public health infrastructure will be severely tested; it may not be possible to provide medical services at the same levels they are provided during nonemergency circumstances; and insufficient trained personnel and equipment may be on hand to meet the needs of the emergency. All of these factors would be greatly exacerbated in an event involving a communicable disease or agent.

ESF 8, Public Health and Medical Services, provides the general mechanism for coordinating federal assistance in support of state, local, and tribal resources in a public health emergency. (The support functions are described in Table 7.1, and the public documents pertaining to them may be found at http://www.dhs.gov.) The Biological Incident Annex to ESF 8 supplies an additional layer of detailed guidance in the event of a disease outbreak. The Department of Health and Human Services is in charge of ESF 8 operations, and the Department of Homeland Security is charged with coordinating ESF 8 efforts through an assistant secretary assigned to public health emergency preparedness. This shared HHS/DHS leadership in a crisis has been criticized as a recipe for a failed response to a crisis, although the departments have sought to outline how their cooperation in such an instance would unfold. Within ESF 8, fifteen federal departments and agencies and the American Red Cross provide support in needs assessment, public health surveillance, and the provision of medical care personnel and equipment and supplies. The Biological Incident Annex further develops these functions and details specific roles and actions in threat assessment notification procedures, laboratory testing, joint investigative and response procedures, and activities related to recovery. As described in these documents, the federal role in responding to biological terrorism may be summarized in this way:

- Detection through surveillance and monitoring
- Identification of at-risk populations

- Determination of the source of the outbreak
- Assessment and analysis of the public health and law enforcement implications
- Containment or assistance to state and local governments in containing any epidemic
- Provision of assets to augment the surge in the demand for public health and medical services
- Monitoring and interdiction of potential resurgence or follow-on outbreaks
- Determination of contamination and decontamination of the area.

A disease outbreak may not be noticed initially, and, when it is, it may not be possible to pinpoint its cause, much less its source. Because a biological weapon attack may not be apparent at the time of dissemination of the agent, it may not be discovered for up to several days. Exposure to anthrax, for example, would not be apparent to the victim until symptoms appear, which may be several hours or even one or two days after exposure, when treatment may be too late. This problem of latent discovery of the attack affects the efficacy of the federal response mechanisms.

The Catastrophic Incident Annex (CIA) to ESF 8 is designed to provide additional federal support for essential activities in an especially significant crisis in which, for example, large-scale evacuations may be required at the same time that public health considerations demand isolation of victims or of those who are contagious. As was learned in the aftermath of Hurricane Katrina, however, the federal response tends to be reactive, at least during natural disasters, and the catastrophic nature of the storm did not prompt Secretary Chertoff to invoke the CIA.

One of the continuing ambiguities in the entire NRP structure that is especially noticeable in the CIA is who or what conditions trigger the federal role, whatever its nature. In the federal system, the traditional expectation has been that federal support is part of a "pull" system in which state or local officials "pull" the federal support to their jurisdictions by making a request. However, the NRP and the INS may be triggered when state and local officials are "overwhelmed," and obviously "overwhelmed" states or cities may not be in a position to request federal help. The "push" model would trigger the federal response when a particular set of conditions develop and after a declaration by the secretary of homeland security or the president. The CIA is designed to be part of the "push." Its assets may be proactively sent directly to the incident site, where further decisions on what to do and under whose leadership can be determined after deployment. But the recurring problem remains: How will officials know when to operate a "push" system as opposed to a "pull" system? Should these judgments be made by the FCO (federal coordinating officer) or the PFO (principal federal officer), or by on-site officials, such as state and local leaders and their first responders?

State and Local Incident Responses

Despite the relative sophistication and the simple bulk of the federal emergency response plans and implementation schemes, emergency response remains a state and local responsibility. Indeed, until state and local resources are overwhelmed or exhausted, there is no denying that terrorism incidents are local. Ensuring the public's health, safety, and welfare has always been an area of government responsibility reserved to the states in the federal system. And yet during a terrorism crisis, when the powers of state officials are correspondingly at their highest, those responsibilities may be severely tested.

Typically, state constitutions and other laws give governors broad powers during emergency circumstances, and some states extend similar authority to public health agency heads within their spheres of authority. For example, some states permit public health officials to issue orders isolating those who have an infectious disease to prevent its spread. Following some declaration of emergency, governors may invoke emergency powers, thereby waiving or exempting state laws that would otherwise apply. These declarations, which take the form of executive orders or decrees, are often accompanied by statewide plans and procedures for responding to emergency incidents.

Inevitably, invoking emergency powers requires careful attention to striking a proper balance between individual and communal interests. Although the laws that enable the emergency declarations themselves include processes to ensure that decision makers take into account how addressing community-based needs affects individual rights, the affected individuals may still object to emergency measures. For example, some people may complain that a forced evacuation should not occur without establishing a demonstrable need to leave. Or people who suffer from disabilities may claim with justification that the general evacuation order cannot be applied to all groups in the affected communities. Still others might demand that the government provide vaccines or medicines when resource allocation decisions have been made on the basis of finite supplies.

In a terrorist attack involving a contagious biological agent or radiation, state officials may decide either to restrict or to force the movement of persons in order to limit the spread of the contagion and to preserve order. An attack with a nuclear device would create such physical devastation, such a high number of casualties, and such widespread contamination that some areas would become uninhabitable on a long-term basis. Public health management would be a critically important function of government in such situations. But which level of government is responsible for making and enforcing the decisions? The decision to evacuate, quarantine, or otherwise restrict the movement of persons for public health reasons is a creature of state law in the federal system. Some states have revised state public health and emergency management authorities in response to the threats of a biological weapons attack. However, states generally are not well prepared for such a contingency, and the federal support authorities are inadequate as well.

The one-two punch of the September 11 attacks and the anthrax letters prompted the Center for Law and the Public's Health of Georgetown University and the Johns Hopkins University to draft the Model State Emergency Health Powers Act (MSEHPA) in the fall of 2001. The idea in developing the MSEHPA was to provide state and local governments with a template for legislative reform of existing public health and emergency response laws in light of the preparedness challenges posed by terrorism. Over the course of five years, more than thirty-five states have enacted some portion of the MSEHPA as law, varying in content across the states.

The model defines a public health emergency as an occurrence or imminent threat of an illness or health condition that, first, is believed to be caused by any of the following: (1) bioterrorism, (2) the appearance of a novel or previously controlled or eradicated infectious agent or biological toxin, (3) a natural disaster, (4) a chemical attack or accidental release, or (5) a nuclear attack or accident; and, second, poses a high probability of any of the following harms: (1) a large number of deaths in the affected population, (2) a large number of serious or long-term disabilities in the affected population, or (3) widespread exposure to an infectious or toxic agent that poses a significant risk for substantial future harm to a large number of people in the affected population.

If these criteria trigger declaration of a public health emergency, MSEHPA grants public health agencies a series of powers not possessed in ordinary times. In fact, existing legal requirements are suspended for the specific purposes identified in the emergency declaration. Among other things, officials could waive professional licensing and related certification requirements, as well as liability protections, as applied to volunteers joining emergency response efforts. They could also expedite the acquisition of essential supplies and personnel and suspend other regulatory requirements for the conduct of state or local business.

Public health or emergency management officials also could designate any government property needed for emergency use related to the public health emergency, as well as a private facility, such as a hotel or private meeting place, if it is needed as a place to provide emergency public health services, such as vaccinations or shelter. Similarly, private property (such as medicines or medical equipment) may be taken by the government during the emergency, subject to the requirement that the owners be compensated fairly for the loss after the emergency has subsided.

Among the biggest challenges facing public health and other state or local decision makers when a public health crisis is imminent is handling the medical surge—that is, the demand for services and protection that so far outstrips day-to-day capacities. Triage conditions may exist, and criteria may be developed, even ad hoc, to strictly ration care. Thus the capacity to waive licensing and certification requirements to permit widespread use of volunteers may be essential, as would be the need to provide waivers for liability for those volunteers. Neither MSEHPA nor most existing state and local laws provide expressly for the possibility of networked responses to public health crises, in which existing response structures and institutions are enhanced by others inside government and from the private sector and nongovernmental organizations. Networks have successfully been employed in crisis situations in other settings—such as fighting forest fires in California. Stripping away the legal and institutional impediments to such networked solutions could go a long way toward enhancing preparedness for a public health crisis.

Inevitably, the structure and the politics of federalism complicate an emergency response. Even inside each state, it is not always clear where local government authority ends and state authority begins. Some states have rules that presume that local governments have only those authorities expressly assigned by the state constitution or another state law. Other states follow a "home rule" approach, in which local governments may do anything within their geographic limits absent contrary instructions in state law. Regardless of legal authorities, limited expertise and finite resources often stand in the way of effective local government preparedness for an emergency response, leaving most cities dependent on the beneficence and leadership of their state government.

Between the states and federal government, the Hurricane Katrina experience showcased just how dysfunctional the federal-state relationship can be, especially when politics enter a crisis-burdened decision environment. The "push" versus "pull" response also underscores the unresolved tensions. Because the federal and state governments share responsibility for homeland security, conflict and confusion are an expected by-product of the crisis response experience. Yet when the stakes are especially high, as they are when dealing with an Incident of National Significance, the uncertain locus of decision authority and relatively untested efforts at coordination of leadership and unified command continue to bedevil the emergency response. In response, emergency response experts have increasingly recommended that governments adopt networks of government and private sector responders, even where the network mechanisms are not expressly provided for by law or recognized in the NRP or NIMS. (See Box 7.1.)

Regional Responses

In between the conventional "pull" system, in which states request federal assistance when needed, and the "push" model, in which a federal role is inserted proactively in a crisis, cooperation among affected states in a crisis may afford a sort of middle ground between push and pull. Some emergencies affect more than one state, but they do not necessarily require the full panoply of federal resources in support. For example, during a terrorist attack on an industrial facility in New Jersey the released chemical vapors would affect New Yorkers. Even where federal support is surely required, regional mechanisms can supplement the federal assets.

Box 7.1   **Incident Response Network**

Networks and informal relationships are an approach to incident response that contrasts with the traditional hierarchical structures and strict rules for who does what. Participants in a networked response focus not so much on the structure of their network, as is commonly done in bureaucratic institutions. Instead, participants focus on the common purposes of those in the network. Just as terrorist organizations have learned to use carefully coordinated networks to carry out terrorist attacks, emergency response officials have begun to develop network approaches to supplement the NRP, NIMS, and other more hierarchical arrangements.

- An important concern in utilizing networks to perform government functions, including incident response, is accountability. To whom are networks accountable?

- Which parts of government manage and take responsibility for networked responses?

Although mutual aid agreements for emergency management have been a feature of U.S. law and practice since the early Civil Defense Act days of the 1950s, the Emergency Management Assistance Compact (EMAC) was ratified by Congress only in 1996. After Hurricane Andrew devastated southern Florida in 1992, southern governors formed a compact, which in 1995 grew to include any state that wished to join, before Congress codified the arrangement the next year. Although the EMAC legislation contemplates regional plans and the sharing of resources and information in an all-hazards range of crises, its mechanisms urge decentralization of the emergency response tasks. EMAC plans and procedures are recognized as legitimate response mechanisms in the HSPD-5, the NRP, and NIMS. EMAC arrangements also worked relatively well in the response to Hurricane Katrina, one of the few government institutions that received high marks in the follow-on studies.

CASE STUDY 7.1

Responding to the Plague Attack

The scenario described in Case Study 6.3 in Chapter 6 raises some important questions about how and to what extent the existing institutions in any major city would be able to handle a bioterrorism crisis. Who would be the first responders to the release of the plague? And how would they be protected from the disease? What measures would they take to protect those who have not been exposed? What steps would they take to investigate and apprehend the terrorists? How would they work to forestall the panic that could ensue once it is widely known what has happened?

Persons affected by primary aerosol exposure to plague must receive antibiotic therapy within twenty-four hours in order to avoid near certain death. Preventing secondary, person-to-person spread by fleeing victims is another challenge, along with the required epidemiological assessments, including contact investigation and notification. Public health officials on-site after the attack must identify the hazard and establish control of the site, set up and operate the Incident Command System (the federal mechanism for organizing a response to a major disaster, described in Chapter 6), isolate and treat the exposed victims (self-quarantine through shelter-in-place may be instituted), initiate mitigation efforts, obtain personal protective equipment (PPE) and prophylaxis for responders, initiate site remediation and monitoring, notify airlines and other transportation providers, provide the public with information about the incident, and initiate effective coordination with national and international public health and government agencies.

After such an attack, tens of thousands of people will require treatment or prophylaxis with ventilators and antibiotics, and thousands will seek care at hospitals, with many needing advanced critical care because of the pneumonia caused by plague. Steps also must be taken to mobilize the Strategic National Stockpile (SNS), a federally supported program for the rapid dissemination of medicines during a crisis. This program is coordinated by HHS/DHS. Finally, anyone exposed to plague must be informed of the signs and symptoms suggestive of plague as well as measures to prevent person-to-person spread. Mortuary requirements, animal-based surveillance to monitor potential spread of plague via natural methods, and veterinary services also must be considered. Because this scenario involves an international incident, the U.S. Department of State's Bureau of Consular Affairs will have to be contacted in order to assist foreign populations residing in the United States, foreign nationals in the United States, or U.S. citizens exposed or ill abroad.

Within the metropolitan area, the 911 system may be flooded with calls from both the sick and the "worried well." As fear spreads in the city and other areas, calls to hospitals, doctor's offices, emergency call centers, and public health offices could increase drastically. Responding to the medical transport needs of casualties may overwhelm emergency service representatives. Hospital beds will fill rapidly, and staff will have to work longer hours. With the high demands on pharmacies, persons who use medications for chronic health conditions may have difficulty obtaining refills.

Because the biological agent is known to be contagious and readily transmitted from one individual to another, closing or restricting modes of transportation may be necessary to reduce the spread of the disease. The local transit authority operates mass transit rail and bus service throughout the city and its thirty-eight suburbs, carrying 1.5 million passengers on a typical business weekday. Because the city in which the attack occurred is one of the major air transport nodes in the United States, the closure or restricted use of the airport would create large perturbations in the passenger and cargo aviation system worldwide.

In the weeks after the attacks, food prices in the city area are likely to soar because of the threat of reduced supplies. However, any transportation restrictions that might be implemented are not likely to cause serious shortages in the first week after the incident. Moreover, many people may be afraid to venture out, thus averting (at least initially) any hoarding or panic shopping.

As the financial world in the city and elsewhere begins to realize the likelihood of an epidemic, a sell-off will occur in the financial markets. Banks, other financial institutions, and major corporations will be hit by high absentee rates. But bank and other financial customers also may be staying home, afraid to venture into public places and trying instead to conduct business on the phone. As a result, the phone systems at financial institutions may become completely tied up, and automatic teller machines (ATMs), especially drive-up machines, may run out of cash before they can be replenished. Recalling the anthrax incidents of 2001, many citizens may also be afraid to open their mail.

This scenario underscores the complexities and importance of preparing to respond to a major incident in which the public health is threatened. The interaction of federal, state, and local decision makers and responders will require considerable coordination and cooperation, some of which has yet to be demonstrated in practice. At the same time, states and some cities are working to update their legal authorities and plans in anticipation of a major threat to public health.

SOURCE: This case study is adapted from National Planning Scenarios, Scenario 4: Biological Attack— Pneumonic Plague, Department of Homeland Security/Homeland Security Council, Version 20.1, Draft, April 2005, www.media.washingtonpost.com/wp-srv/nation/nationalsecurity/earlywarning/NationalPlanningScenariosApril2005.pdf.

First Response: Who Provides It?

The hypothetical plague attack introduced in Case Study 6.3 in Chapter 6 and continued in Case Study 7.1 illustrates many of the challenges in responding to a significant terrorist attack. If terrorists launch an attack in the United States using chemical, biological, or nuclear weapons or high-yield powerful explosives, local police, emergency medical technicians (EMTs), hospital and other public health personnel, firefighters, and HAZ-

MAT teams will be the first responders, seeking to contain the damage, minister to the injured, and collect evidence for a criminal prosecution. Some of those first responders may well become victims, further complicating the response. The federal role will, in most circumstances, be secondary and supportive of the state and local responders. Overarching guidance may or may not be provided by the federal leadership, depending on whether an incident is designated an Incident of National Significance by the secretary of homeland security or a governor seeks federal leadership. Two incidents, presented here as case studies, frame this consideration of the roles and challenges faced by first responders. The 2001 anthrax attacks were the first significant act of bioterrorism against the United States. (See Case Study 7.2.) Although the attack consisted of as few as four or five letters containing the anthrax bacteria, the incident tested the nation's preparedness and provided important lessons for future planning. Only days earlier, the attack on the Pentagon in the Washington, D.C., area, using American Airlines Flight 77 as the weapon, had been overshadowed by the more dramatic calamity the same morning at the World Trade Center in New York City. Nevertheless, it demonstrated that intergovernmental planning and cooperation can pay off during a crisis. (See Case Study 7.3.)

CASE STUDY 7.2

Lessons from the Anthrax Attacks:
Implications for U.S. Bioterrorism Preparedness, by David Heyman

On October 2, 2001, a 63-year-old photo editor employed by America Media Inc. (AMI) in Florida was admitted to a Palm Beach community hospital emergency department with fever, vomiting, muscle aches, and confusion. He was initially treated for bacterial meningitis. On the basis of preliminary tests, a diagnosis of anthrax was considered within six hours, and penicillin was added to the treatment regime. Upon suspicion of anthrax, the case was reported to local public health authorities. At this point, however, new treatment could not reverse the course of the disease, and the man died. His autopsy on October 6 confirmed that he had died of anthrax. The progression of disease from the onset of symptoms to death took only six days. Until this case, there had been only 18 incidents of human inhalation anthrax in the United States since 1900—the most recent case in 1976.

Within a week after this case, a 38-year-old woman employed by NBC in New York was diagnosed with cutaneous anthrax (contracted through exposure to the skin). She had presented symptoms at the end of September, but it was not clear until after the first case was publicized that anthrax might be indicated. It was subsequently determined that she had handled a letter that contained a suspicious powder.

On October 15, the offices of Senate Majority Leader Tom Daschle (D-S.D.) received a letter containing a powder that tested positive for the bacteria that causes anthrax. The letter was opened, and the powder was released into the air. As a result, initially one corner of the Hart Senate Office Building in the U.S. Capitol was closed; eventually the whole building had to be shut down. Individuals who were exposed or possibly exposed to the powder were given a course of antibiotics as prophylaxis.

On October 21, a postal worker employed at the mail facility that serviced the Senate offices was diagnosed with inhalation anthrax. He and one of his colleagues both died from inhalation anthrax the following day. Two other postal employees from the same facility were also treated for inhalational anthrax, and survived. A fifth individual in the Washington, D.C., region—a federal government mailroom employee—was hospitalized with inhalation anthrax and also survived. The Brentwood postal facility and other downstream mail-handling facilities were subsequently shut down.

Small amounts of *Bacillus anthracis* were also later found in numerous buildings in the Washington, D.C., area—the Supreme Court, the Walter Reed Army Institute of Research, the Department of Health and Human Services, and the main State Department building. These buildings were believed to have been contaminated from letters that came in direct contact with the Daschle letter or passed through sorting equipment at the postal facility that sorted the Daschle letter. A letter addressed to Senator Patrick Leahy (D-Vt.), found by hazardous materials experts sorting through 250 barrels of mail quarantined after the discovery of the Daschle letter, also tested positive for anthrax on November 16.

Two other states—New Jersey and Connecticut—were affected through probable cross-contamination of mail routed through the postal system. In total, 18 individuals contracted anthrax (11 inhalational, 7 cutaneous) in five states (Florida, New York, the District of Columbia, New Jersey, and Connecticut). More than 33,000 people required post-exposure prophylaxis. Five of the individuals who contracted anthrax died. All of the anthrax associated with these attacks was found to have come from the same stream of *Bacillus anthracis* bacteria.

These attacks were the first significant acts of bioterrorism in the United States. . . .

The Actual Response

From the medical and public health communities, the direct response to these attacks involved more than 1,000 physicians, epidemiologists, public health officials, and clinicians. These officials and medical practitioners came from both the private and public sectors and from all levels of government—local, state, and federal. The Centers for Disease Control (CDC) and local public health communities had to investigate the index case and each additional case, establish or expand surveillance, confirm additional cases, find the source of the attacks, define exposure, and recommend treatment. They also assisted with clinical evaluations of patients, counseling, the provision of antibiotics, data collection, and environmental sampling. The CDC ran 200 sorties to deploy antibiotics from the National Pharmaceutical Stockpile and responded to 280 requests for advice from foreign countries. The District of Columbia initiated the largest ever mass-medication program in the United States, dispensing medication to more than 17,000 individuals. When the number of hoaxes plus the scared but healthy individuals (the "worried well") who required medical attention are considered, the number of medical and public health professionals involved in the response was much higher.

From law enforcement, thousands of police officers, FBI agents, and government officials have contributed to the ongoing investigation. In calendar year 2000, the FBI responded to 257 cases potentially involving weapons of mass destruction (WMD), of which 200 were anthrax matters. (All turned out to be hoaxes.) By comparison, between October and December 2001, the FBI launched more than 8,000 WMD investigations. Previously, hoaxes were considered relatively harmless, requiring limited resources for response. After October 15, this changed, and law enforcement officials in New York City, for example, chose to close off three square blocks to respond to their first anthrax threat.

To date, 47 people have been indicted in anthrax-related cases (though none of these individuals has been linked to the anthrax attacks in the District of Columbia, Florida, New York, New Jersey, or Connecticut). More than 10,000 samples have been provided to the U.S. Army Medical Research Institute of Infectious Diseases (USAMRIID) from the U.S. Capitol complex for testing, and more than 30,000 individual assays have been performed on these samples. At its peak, USAMRIID was receiving more than 700 samples a day. Each of the samples had to be treated with appropriated evidentiary procedures to maintain proper chain of custody to ensure its viability in court. For every sample, a 25-page document must be prepared. The overall level of activity at USAMRIID during the peak of the response far exceeded normal operating diagnostic capacity.

The specific response at the U.S. Capitol required establishing an incident command system and overseeing logistics support (e.g., establishing and maintaining trailers and tents, sealing buildings, and dispensing meals), security, public affairs, environmental sampling and agent characterization, and remediation. More than 400 contractors were brought in to support these operations, and approximately 400 additional federal and local liaisons were also credentialed for on-site activities. Total costs for the operation will exceed $24 million.

Beyond the public health and law enforcement efforts, local, state, and national elected officials, civil servants, postal workers, contractors, and private citizens have been pulled into the crisis in one way or another, whether as part of the overall response, as part of the recovery process, or, more likely, as unintended casualties. As a direct result of the terrorist attacks, for example, the U.S. Postal Service estimates it will incur costs of more than $3 billion. The U.S. Postal Service also had to reassign the vast majority of its 1,900 inspectors and 1,400 postal police officers to respond to the anthrax threat.

Apart from the extensive public health and law enforcement activities, one of the most heavily stressed segments of the crisis response was public affairs—communicating with the public. From the first reports in Florida, officials responsible for keeping the public informed provided incomplete and sometimes inconsistent information and advice to the public. Instead of one voice and a single government message, there were multiple spokespersons and many different messages. Even the postal service contributed to the shortcomings in notifying the public— patrons whose mail was sorted at the Brentwood postal facility were told little about how to handle their mail other than a notice *sent through the mail* about reporting suspicious packages and letters.

Although the public affairs function was poorly managed during the anthrax crisis, the harm to the public and the potential for widespread panic could have been far worse if a communicable agent, such as small-pox, had been weaponized. Still, anthrax is an extremely dangerous substance and, as the letters demonstrated, it is relatively easy to disperse it widely.

SOURCE: This case study is adapted from a portion of an unclassified report of a National Forum on Biodefense, organized by the Center for Strategic and International Studies and the Defense Threat Reduction Agency (DTRA) and written under contract with DTRA. The report was released by the U.S. Department of Defense nearly two years after its completion in 2002. The full report can be found at Federation of American Scientists, www.fas.org/irp/threat/cbw/dtra02.pdf.

■

CASE STUDY 7.3

The Attack on the Pentagon, as Reported in the 9-11 Commission Report

If it had happened on any other day, the disaster at the Pentagon would be remembered as a singular challenge and an extraordinary national story. Yet the calamity at the World Trade Center that same morning included catastrophic damage 1,000 feet above the ground that instantly imperiled tens of thousands of people. The two experiences are not comparable. . . .

The emergency response at the Pentagon represented a mix of local, state, and federal jurisdictions and was generally effective. It overcame the inherent complications of a response across jurisdictions because the Incident Command System, a formalized management structure for emergency response, was in place in the National Capital Region on 9/11. Because of the nature of the event—a plane crash, fire, and partial building collapse—the Arlington County Fire Department served as incident commander.

Different agencies had different roles. The incident required a major rescue, fire, and medical response from Arlington County at the U.S. military's headquarters—a facility under the control of the secretary of defense. Since it was a terrorist attack, the Department of Justice was the lead federal agency in charge (with authority delegated to the FBI for operational response). Additionally, the terrorist attack affected the daily operations and emergency management requirements of Arlington County and all bordering and surrounding jurisdictions.

At 9:37, the west wall of the Pentagon was hit by hijacked American Airlines Flight 77, a Boeing 757. The crash caused immediate and catastrophic damage. All 64 people aboard the airliner were killed, as were 125 people inside the Pentagon (70 civilians and 55 military service members). One hundred six people were seriously injured and transported to area hospitals. . . .

Local, regional, state, and federal agencies immediately responded to the Pentagon attack. In addition to county fire, police, and sheriffs' departments, the response was assisted by the Metropolitan Washington Airports Authority, Ronald Reagan Washington National Airport Fire Department, Fort Myer Fire Department, the Virginia State Police, the Virginia Department of Emergency Management, the FBI, FEMA, a National Medical Response Team, the Bureau of Alcohol, Tobacco, and Firearms, and numerous military personnel within the Military District of Washington. Command was established at 9:41. At the same time, the Arlington County Emergency Communications Center contacted the fire departments of Fairfax County, Alexandria, and the District of Columbia to request mutual aid. The incident command post provided a clear view of and access to the crash site, allowing the incident commander to assess the situation at all times.

At 9:55, the incident commander ordered an evacuation of the Pentagon impact area because a partial collapse was imminent; it occurred at 9:57 and no first responder was injured. At 10:15, the incident commander ordered a full evacuation of the command post because of the warning of an approaching hijacked aircraft passed along by the FBI. This was the first of three evacuations caused by reports of incoming aircraft, and the evacuation order was well communicated and well coordinated.

Several factors facilitated the response to this incident, and distinguish it from the far more difficult task in New York. There was a single incident, and it was not 1,000 feet above ground. The incident site was relatively easy to secure and contain, and there were no other buildings in the immediate area. There was no collateral damage beyond the Pentagon. Yet the Pentagon response encountered difficulties that echo those experienced in New York. As the "Arlington County: After-Action Report" notes, there were significant problems with both self-dispatching and communications: "Organizations, response units, and individuals proceeding on their own initiative directly to an incident site, without the knowledge and permission of the host jurisdiction and the Incident Commander, complicate the exercise of command, increase the risks faced by bonafide responders, and exacerbate the challenge of accountability." With respect to communications, the report concludes: "Almost all aspects of communications continue to be problematic, from initial notification to tactical operations. Cellular telephones were of little value. . . . Radio channels were initially oversaturated. . . . Pagers seemed to be the most reliable means of notification when available and used, but most firefighters are not issued pagers."

It is a fair inference in view of the differing situations in New York City and Northern Virginia that the problems in command, control, and communications that occurred at both sites will likely recur in any emergency of similar scale. The task looking forward is to enable first responders to respond in a coordinated manner with the greatest possible awareness of the situation.

SOURCE: National Commission on Terrorist Attacks upon the United States, *Final Report* (Washington, D.C.: Government Printing Office, 2004).

The anthrax attacks consisted of as few as four or five mailed letters, and yet the attacks temporarily shut down parts of Congress, the Supreme Court, and other government offices, and scattered postal operations. The response and recovery activities were huge relative to the number of attacks, and the recovery costs exceeded several billion dollars.

The use of hijacked commercial airliners as weapons on September 11, 2001, was also an innovation by the terrorists. Again, a small group with modest resources caused enormous harm. The response task at the Pentagon was limited by the finite size of the blast site and its effects, and the responders were more effective overall than those responding to the anthrax letters.

Because of the complexities of the two kinds of attacks and their consequences, coordinating the response was of critical importance. Although the Pentagon responders had prior experience working together in various settings and benefited from an adopted Incident Command Center, arguably the regional coordination was most beneficial to the Pentagon response. Mutual aid agreements had been executed, allowing most of the first responders to share a common radio frequency. Thus they received response assignments by radio and went to work immediately upon arrival at the crash site.

The Military Role in Incident Response

September 11 and the war on terrorism that followed generated an array of new plans, policies, and laws that affect the military's possible role in responding to a domestic terrorism incident. Within days of the World Trade Center and Pentagon attacks, Congress passed a joint resolution authorizing the president to "use all necessary and appropriate force" against those responsible for the events of September 11 "in order to prevent any future acts of international terrorism against the United States by such . . . persons." No geographic or time limit was placed on the authority granted, and the authorization to "prevent any future acts" raised the possibility that the military could undertake domestic activities for the foreseeable future. Indeed, by implication the resolution contemplated new law enforcement roles for the military incident to the use of force against terrorists or in mitigating a terrorist attack on the homeland.

A few weeks later, Congress enacted the USA PATRIOT Act. Among other enhancements to authorities to combat terrorism in the homeland, the Patriot Act ensured that the military would respond to requests for assistance involving actual or threatened attacks with WMD.

The Role of the Federal Military

In 2002 President Bush announced the National Security Strategy of the United States of America and the National Strategy for Homeland Security, both of which emphasized the increasingly important role of the military in protecting the homeland from terrorism. The National Strategy for Homeland Security calls for "a concerted national effort to prevent terrorist attacks within the United States . . . and minimize the damage and recovery from attacks that do occur." However, the strategy documents do not further specify military roles and missions. Nor do they distinguish between possible war fighting and support to civil authorities.

As part of the implementation of the Homeland Security Act of 2002, the secretary of defense created the position of assistant secretary for homeland defense (ASD/HD), whose principal duty is the overall supervision of the homeland defense activities of the Department of Defense. In effect, the

ASD/HD is the Pentagon's domestic crisis manager, and the advent of the position transfers from military to civilian control the department's policy oversight of military support for homeland defense.

If military personnel and equipment were utilized in a domestic terrorism incident, substantial coordination and cooperation would be required among federal agencies and between civilian and military officials. During a crisis with public health consequences, the Departments of Homeland Security and Health and Human Services would share coordination of the federal response. DHS would coordinate any military role, except where military assets might be deployed in support of public health or medical needs. In that case, HHS would coordinate the military's involvement. If DHS officials determined that military personnel could provide technical support to law enforcement or crisis response personnel or that the military could interdict the terrorist event and apprehend the terrorists, the on-site DHS commander could request military support from the senior defense official at the site after the attorney general requested Department of Defense assistance in enforcing the laws. As indicated in Figure 7.2, the coordination also includes state officials, including the governor and adjutant general of the state.

The new arrangements and authorities are exceptions to the traditional presumption against using the armed forces to enforce laws inside the United States. Since 1876, the Posse Comitatus Act has codified the presumption in a statute that may be overcome only by an explicit statutory authorization for a military role in law enforcement, or by an exercise of the constitutional powers of the president. One long-standing such statutory exception is the Insurrection Act, which permits the president to use the armed forces to quell civil disturbances either upon the request of a governor or on his own initiative after an order that those causing the disruption cease and desist. Use of the military in response to Stafford Act declarations of an emergency is not considered such an exception, because the activities performed in response to a Stafford Act deployment do not involve enforcing the laws.

Acting pursuant to its special legal authority for responding to WMD terrorism, the Department of Defense may supply technical assistance in the form of equipment, facilities, or personnel. The same statutes permit the Department of Defense to provide direct operational law enforcement assistance. Once approved by the secretary of defense, military units plan and implement their support, subject to military command. If a tactical military force were deployed to respond to a domestic terrorism crisis, the deployment decision would be based on a determination that public safety cannot be assured by civilian law enforcement capabilities, or that a hostile attack threatens the continuity of government. The president could decide to make available military units to the Department of Homeland Security's on-site leadership through DHS's Homeland Security Operations Center as part of an Interagency Incident Management Group.

Figure 7.2 Calling the Cavalry: How the Process Is Designed to Work

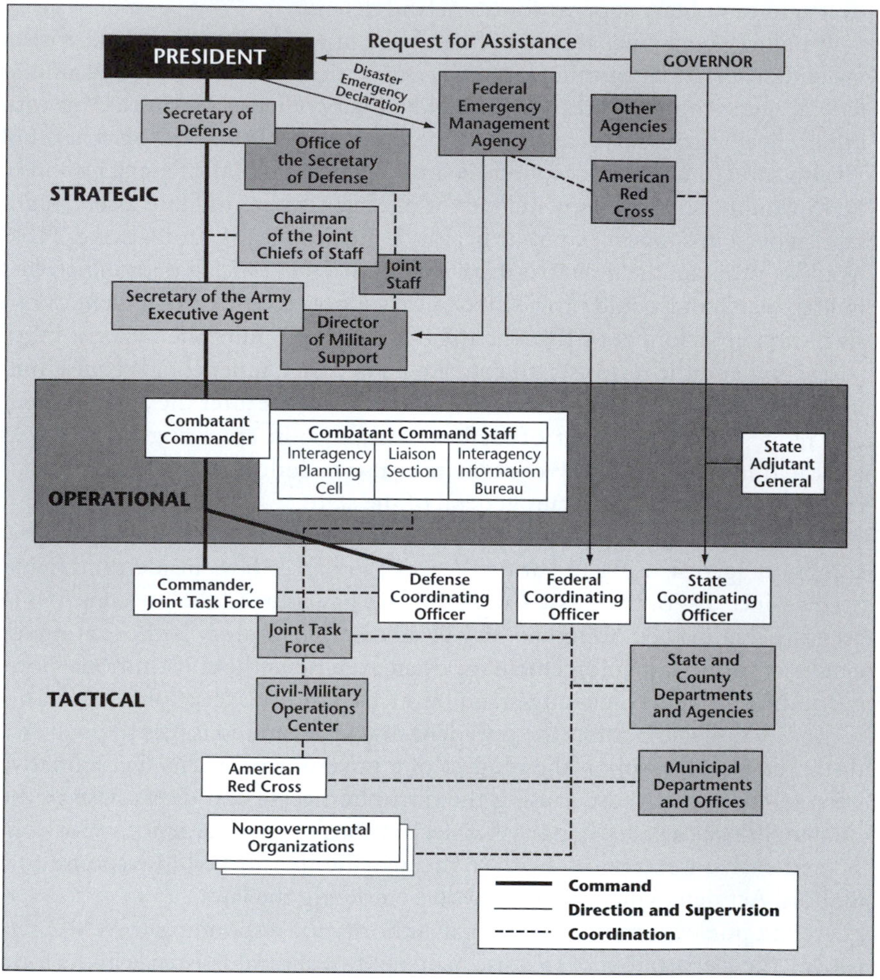

SOURCE: Globalsecurity.org, www.globalsecurity.org/military/library/policy/army/fm/3-05-401/fig2-6.jpg.

One of the most difficult and contentious issues surrounding any future role for the military in law enforcement during a domestic terrorism crisis is the rules of engagement that would govern the actions taken by armed members of the military. On the one hand, the prospect of calling in the military to supplement or to supplant traditional civilian law enforcement in a crisis indicates that law enforcement is not up to the task, because, for example, a terrorist organization armed with lethal WMD has overwhelmed civilian capabilities. Or a spreading disease outbreak could prompt panicked citizens to disruption and looting. Civilian law enforcement capabilities are not designed to match a paramilitary assault on the homeland, especially one that employs WMD.

On the other hand, unless otherwise trained and equipped, soldiers deployed in such situations will be used as they have traditionally been trained—that is, under military rules of engagement (and a tradition of shooting to kill) rather than law enforcement rules, in which deadly force may be used only in self-defense or in defense of other agents in imminent danger of death or serious bodily harm. Military personnel will be obligated to sort combatants from others, likely on the spur of the moment, to make assessments about the use of deadly force on the same basis, and to treat the provocation as an act of war, with attendant consequences. Even if trained in law enforcement rules and techniques, in the heat of the moment military personnel may default to their base training orientation and culture.

After riots erupted in response to the verdict in the Rodney King trial in Los Angeles in 1992, the Joint Task Force Los Angeles implemented for the first time the Department of Defense Civil Disturbance Plan (GARDEN PLOT). Among its rules of engagement, minimum force must be used at all times when responding to civil disturbances; warning shots are not permitted; and deadly force may be used only if lesser means have been exhausted or are unavailable, the risk of harm to bystanders is not significantly increased, and the purpose is self-defense, to prevent serious crime or destruction of vital public health or safety, or to prevent the escape of a person who is a serious threat to persons or property. The rules of engagement emphasize that military personnel should merely support civilian officials, leaving law enforcement tasks to state and local authorities whenever possible.

The Role of the National Guard and Reserves

In one respect, the National Guard "solves" the problems presented by assigning federal armed forces to respond to a domestic terrorist attack. Particularly to the extent that a terrorist incident is local, within one state, state-deployed National Guard can provide military-type law enforcement support to enforce a quarantine, other area restrictions, or curfews, and to distribute health or other emergency supplies in support of civilian authorities. As a state entity that is not part of the armed forces of the United States, the Guard is not restricted by the Posse Comitatus Act, and the tradition of keeping the armed forces out of civilian law enforcement would not include state National Guard personnel. Thus the National Guardsman may be a citizen soldier, subject to local control, or a trained supplement to the regular military, prepared to wage combat.

In 1933 Congress created the National Guard of the states and the National Guard of the United States. Members belong both to the state Guard and to the federal Guard, and are civilians when not having military status. Later, Congress created a separate Air National Guard of the United

States and limited the original federal Guard to the U.S. Army component. Even when called into federal service, members of the National Guard are not on "active duty," a status limited to full-time, active, federal military service personnel. Particularly since the end of the Cold War, the Guard has become an ever more frequent source of combat support. Once federalized, National Guard personnel serve as reserves of the army.

State laws typically authorize the adjutant general, directed by the governor, to call up National Guard units in an emergency. National Guard personnel also provide support to civil authorities after natural disasters, including cleaning up after floods or storms, assisting in fighting fires, and helping with evacuations and managing supplies. The authority to order such support was transferred in 2003 from the secretary of the army to the new assistant secretary for homeland defense.

It is thus logically assumed that Guard personnel would be well positioned to become involved in the event of a significant terrorist attack in the United States. In 1998 Secretary of Defense William Cohen expressly added response to chemical and biological weapons terrorism as a new mission for the Guard. This mission began in 1999 with the development of Rapid Assessment and Initial Detection (RAID) teams, configured to assist state and local personnel in response to a terrorist attack. The specific missions of the RAID teams were to identify a suspected chemical or biological agent associated with a terrorist event, to track dispersal patterns and evacuate victims, to control access to the site, to assist in bringing other federal and state assets to the site, and to advise civilian leaders. After delays in training the RAID teams, the program was modified and renamed the Weapons of Mass Destruction Civil Support Teams (WMD-CSTs) in 2000.

By late 2006, the Department of Defense had certified more than sixty WMD-CSTs as ready to assist in a WMD incident. Each team consists of twenty-two full-time National Guard personnel, who assess a WMD event, advise civilian first responders on appropriate responses, and facilitate introducing follow-on military support into the affected area. The primary function of the teams is to identify the weapon/agent and to supply communications with other federal, state, and local agencies.

However, uncertainty about the roles of and legal restrictions on the National Guard in homeland defense is growing. For example, state-deployed National Guard units could be charged with enforcing a quarantine. However, the regular Guard units (that is, those in federal or state service who are not part of the WMD-CSTs) are trained for combat, not law enforcement. In addition, it is conceivable that, in a germ or radiation attack that affects more than one state, the governor in State A could ask for federal military intervention, while the governor in State B wishes to rely on state-deployed National Guard units, or even no military personnel. Or one or both governors could dispute the president's judgment that federalized National Guard personnel should enforce quarantine or curfew or border and travel restrictions.

The president could federalize the Guard for the purposes of enforcing the quarantine, but only if a state makes the request because of the lack of federal quarantine authority. The president could, however, decide to rely on the Insurrection Act provision that permits unilateral presidential orders of military deployment in the event of a breakdown of civil authorities in a state. Otherwise, the federalized Guard units would also be subject to the Posse Comitatus Act and its presumption against federal military involvement in civilian law enforcement, and the operation would require a different independent legal justification. Although the absence of federal legal restrictions would afford more discretion for state officials to deploy National Guard units, in the event of a significant deployment cost factors may favor federal activation, because the federal government would pay for the operation once the force is federalized. The difficult dynamics of the federal versus state National Guard status are illustrated by the experience in responding to Hurricane Katrina in August 2005 and described in Box 7.2.

Even more difficult legal questions could arise if a state adjacent to one suffering from a WMD terrorist attack decided to close its borders to those flee-

---

Box 7.2   Responding to Hurricane Katrina

Local responders were overwhelmed when Hurricane Katrina hit New Orleans and the surrounding communities and states in August 2005. Trying to grapple with the situation, Louisiana governor Kathleen Blanco sent an urgent request to the White House to supply forty thousand military personnel to help in the response and recovery operation. The White House, however, delayed sending active-duty military forces for five days, and when President George W. Bush did send troops, sometime after he flew over the affected areas in *Air Force One*, he sent only 7,200. The president had been advised that to exercise federal authority he would have to federalize Louisiana National Guard forces, invoke the Insurrection Act, and then use the federal forces to enforce the laws in the face of looting and disruption.

When Governor Blanco balked at relinquishing control over Louisiana National Guard personnel, the president was told he could federalize those troops despite the governor's objection. But President Bush sought to avoid the perception that he was seizing control from a female southern governor from the other major party. The eventual deployment of thirty thousand troops, federal and state, was the largest of the military domestically since the Civil War. In the aftermath of the crisis, President Bush suggested that Congress consider creating the legal mechanisms needed to permit the military to be the lead federal agency in responding to a terrorist incident or a natural disaster.

- Should the military take the lead in responding to a terrorist incident?
- What advantages and disadvantages might be associated with having the military take on a large share of the homeland security response?

ing a contagion. Although the states retain police powers to protect their citizens, a wholesale border closure might treat unfairly those unaffected by the terrorists who seek refuge in an uncontaminated state. It is unclear whether federal officials, civilian or military, could force the adjacent state to accept contaminated persons or persons exposed to the disease.

Some experts have warned that freighting the military role for homeland defense onto the Guard could create a worst-case scenario, in which the Guard becomes a quasi-federal, domestic constabulary with a singular focus that diminishes its role as the primary reserve for the army's fighting force. The army could then become a purely federal force of unprecedented size, threatening the economic, social, and political traditions of the country. Ironically, assuming that policy preferences are to utilize Guard forces with state active-duty status, a state's funding priorities may drive a decision to federalize any large-scale or expensive military deployment in response to a terrorist incident in order to force the transfer of the costs of the deployment to the federal government. Although any federalized National Guard force would be subject to the Posse Comitatus Act, other express terrorism-related authorities would permit the Guard to act—even to engage in direct law enforcement—in response to a domestic terrorism incident.

Other experts see the Guard as the component of the armed forces best situated to be the lead military agency for homeland security. Because the Guard is scattered throughout the nation, representing every community, Guard units are arguably well positioned to assist first responders or to respond otherwise to attacks on the homeland.

Northern Command (NORTHCOM) and Civilian Controls

Explicitly assigning to the military a national security mission of protecting the homeland complicates further the military role in providing support to civil authorities. When the new Unified Combatant Command, the U.S. Northern Command (NORTHCOM), commenced operations on October 1, 2002, it became the first ever command authority for homeland defense. NORTHCOM will provide support to civilian authorities in managing the consequences of natural and terrorism-related disasters, but it will also deter, prevent, and defeat external threats against the American homeland.

The assignment of homeland defense responsibility ensures that NORTHCOM would be responsible for enforcing a quarantine or a similar restriction on personal liberties once the Insurrection Act or some other emergency authority of the president is invoked. No permanent forces are assigned to NORTHCOM. However, in the event of a terrorist attack on the United States the Joint Task Force–Civil Support (JTF-CS) teams operate under NORTHCOM to support civil authorities.

Potential implementation problems remain, however. The JTF-CS has been placed in the critical position of being asked to translate requests for assistance from civilian officials, almost always from state or local officials, into requirements that military personnel can meet. It is a considerable challenge for military officers to identify which units trained and equipped for war fighting can be adapted to meet the requirements of the civilian requesters. Another challenge is that the authorization to perform the requested tasks must pass from the state or local officials through the Federal Emergency Management Agency and the Department of Homeland Security, to the secretary of defense, and then to the JTF-CS. The likely first military responders are the federally trained and funded Civil Support Teams (CSTs). The teams serve under the command of state governors unless they are federalized by the president, when they would be subject to the command of the Joint Task Force–Civil Support.

Even assuming that authorities are clarified for making and enforcing quarantine and related measures with some military support, nettlesome issues remain about the rules for the use of force. At present, state law enforcement agencies, federal agencies that may be involved in a terrorist incident, and the branches of the military all have different and sometimes inconsistent rules for the use of force, which is the term often substituted for "rules of engagement" in domestic operations. When Insurrection Act conditions exist and the applicable procedures are followed, the Department of Defense Civil Disturbance Plan (GARDEN PLOT) rules of engagement govern U.S. military involvement. Although the Insurrection Act invocation permits armed military forces to enforce the law directly and to exercise authority over civilians, GARDEN PLOT rules presume that civilian authorities would exercise such authority if possible, including searches of persons and property. State National Guard and law enforcement agency rules may differ from these rules, however, and each of those rules may vary from state to state.

If a federal military presence follows a Stafford Act request, federal forces would instead follow rules of engagement prescribed by the incident-specific executive order. There is a presumption that military units deployed in a terrorism incident pursuant to the Stafford Act will not carry arms, although weapons may be deployed to the site in storage. But this presumption can be overcome on the say-so of the secretary of defense, in consultation with the attorney general.

Legislation enacted in October 2006 gives the president new authority to call up National Guard troops and reserves. For the first time, reservists who have full-time duty status in the National Guard are authorized to perform assigned duties upon the potential or actual intentional or unintentional release of toxic or poisonous material that does or might result in catastrophic losses. The same legislation amends the Insurrection Act to enable the president to use the National Guard to restore public order if a "natural disaster, epidemic, or other serious public health emergency, terrorist attack or incident" prevents state authorities from maintaining public order.

Controlling People: Enforcing Quarantine, Evacuation Orders, Vaccination Programs, and Related Disorder

In a terrorist attack involving a contagious biological agent or radiation, state officials may decide either to restrict or to force the movement of persons in order to limit the spread of the contagion and to preserve order. An attack with a nuclear device would create such physical devastation, such a high number of casualties, and such widespread contamination that some areas would become uninhabitable on a long-term basis. Public health management would be a critically important function of government in such situations. As noted earlier, a terrorist attack involving a contagious biological agent or radiation may force officials to quarantine or otherwise restrict the movement of persons for public health reasons. Because such a decision is made at the state level in the federal system, some states have revised state public health and emergency management authorities in response to the threats of a biological weapons attack.

The surgeon general is authorized to and has promulgated regulations "necessary to prevent the introduction, transmission, or spread of communicable diseases" from foreign nations into states, or from one state to another. In turn, the president specifies by executive order the diseases that could trigger this limited quarantine authority. Assuming a terrorist attack with biological weapons, federal authorities may be invoked if the agent transmits one of the communicable diseases covered by existing regulations. Plague is covered. Any person "reasonably believed to be infected with a communicable disease in a communicable stage" may be stopped and examined if he is moving or is about to move from state to state, or if he is "a probable source" of infection to others who will be so moving. However, no existing federal regulations permit the detention or other regulation of persons once identified as communicable to prevent the spread of a disease. Nor are there federal regulations authorizing the imposition of quarantine after an attack by chemical, radiological, or nuclear weapons. Thus, unless domestic quarantine regulations are promulgated, no federal quarantine may be lawfully imposed except at the international borders. Moreover, principles of federalism and constitutional limits on the exercise of federal regulatory authority may not permit a federal quarantine within a single state.

Even if quarantine regulations were promulgated, the surgeon general, the Department of Health and Human Services, and the Centers for Disease Control do not have any police forces that could enforce a quarantine. One analysis of a federal exercise involving a fictional biological weapons attack in Denver offered a sobering assessment of the quarantine enforcement problem:

> Local officials . . . believed that the public would probably not cooperate with compulsory orders to commandeer property, restrict movement of people, or forcibly remove them to designated locations. . . . [C]itizens get angry at forced evacuations for such visible calamities as hurri-

canes, floods, and wildfires, not to mention a stay-at-home order for a microscopic killer that they may doubt is in their midst. Police also questioned whether their colleagues would recognize the authority of the public health officer to declare a quarantine or would even stick around to enforce the order. . . . [S]ome wondered whether there were enough local and state police to quarantine a large metropolitan area in the first place. . . . [One police captain stated] if police officers knew that a biological agent had been released, 99 percent of the cops would not be here. They would grab their families and leave.[1]

Depending on the level of force required to enforce the quarantine, an armed military may be necessary for law enforcement purposes.

States may apply quarantine restrictions incident to their generic police power, so long as they do not exceed what is necessary for the state to protect itself. The state quarantine could restrict any individual's constitutional right to travel on the basis of finding that the quarantine is reasonably related to the goal of protecting the public health. However, civilian law enforcement personnel may not be able to enforce the quarantine. A range of military assets could be deployed to enforce a quarantine, but it is far from clear what would be the appropriate military role and force configuration for quarantine enforcement. The potential for disagreement between civilian and military officials and between federal and state or local decision makers in such situations is high. Vaccination, like quarantine, is a public health policy also reserved to the states and their police powers. Also like quarantine, even mandatory vaccination programs are lawful so long as any risk to the individual is outweighed by the risk to the community of not completing the vaccination program. However, like some other facets of a massive biological weapons attack, the potential military roles in mass vaccination have not been set out or even recommended, and thus there are no federal plans or guidelines for evacuation planning or implementation. And yet part of the Post-Katrina Act does authorize DHS to approve state and local governments' use of DHS grants to fund evacuation programs and plans and to conduct exercises to implement those programs and plans. The act also authorizes FEMA to set evacuation standards and requirements and, upon request from state or local governments, to assist in evacuation planning for institutions that house individuals with special needs.

Another incident response reform enacted in the wake of Hurricane Katrina was creation of a Surge Capacity Force to be deployed by the FEMA director to disaster sites, including those designated as catastrophic incidents. Those deployed would be trained and sent under Stafford Act authorization. In general, DHS employees other than those working for FEMA and employees of other federal departments and agencies would be designated to serve on the Surge Capacity Force. The same legislation authorized FEMA to support the development of new mutual aid agreements within the states, to award grants to administer provisions of existing EMAC arrangements, and to consult with the EMAC administrator to enhance coordination in the event that federal support is requested.

Conclusion

By any measure, national preparations for a crisis response in the event of a terrorist attack are a work in progress. Because of the range of potential targets, vulnerabilities, and means of attack (see Chapter 2), coupled with the relative ease with which potential terrorists can live and move about freely in an open society, the magnitude of the incident response assignment is overwhelming. As described in this chapter, the federal government has stepped up its incident response preparedness considerably since the September 11 attacks. Even though it is widely acknowledged that incidents will occur and that no response system can be perfect, the all-hazards NRP and NIMS, the HSPD implementing instructions, the ESFs, and the annexes to the NRP together constitute a comprehensive scheme for coordinating and managing responses to major incidents.

At the same time, the complexity of the task of managing and coordinating even the federal department and agency players in incident response continues to present obstacles to effective response, judging from the experience with federal exercises and expert evaluation of the plans. And, as if orchestrating the federal scheme does not present enough of a challenge, state and local groups and sometimes tribal players and institutions must be folded into incident response, along with critical private sector interests and the affected citizenry. Indeed, one lesson of this chapter is that the default response to a terrorist incident is provided by state and local first responders, directed by state and local agencies and officials. Federalism further complicates incident response. Critical decisions must be made at the state level about whether federal support should be sought, and whether the federal role should follow a "pull" from the governor or be a "push" from the president or secretary of homeland security. The federalism questions are more political than legal, but their resolution may be the single most important component to an effective crisis response.

Finally, this chapter has revealed that military personnel can play an integral role in responding to a terrorism incident in the homeland. And yet the traditional military training and orientation geared to fighting a war is not well suited to support for a homeland security crisis response. The National Guard force is, however, well suited; no other government resource is as widely dispersed across the nation or as well organized or resourced as the Guard. The result is that the traditional antipathy in American culture to military involvement in civilian law enforcement is now being refined, and National Guard and some active-duty units, under NORTHCOM direction, will likely be at the forefront of incident response in the future.

FOR FURTHER READING

Carafano, James Jay, and David Heyman, *DHS 2.0: Rethinking the Department of Homeland Security*. Washington, D.C.: Heritage Foundation, 2004.

Kettl, Donald F. *The Transformation of Governance: Public Administration for Twenty-First Century America*. Baltimore: Johns Hopkins Press, 2002.

Lasker, Roz. *Redefining Readiness: Terrorism Planning Through the Eyes of the Public*. New York: Center for the Advancement of Collaborative Strategies in Health, New York Academy of Medicine, 2004.

Model State Emergency Health Powers Act, 2001. www.publichealthlaw. net/MSEHPA/MSEHPA2.pdf.

National Commission on Terrorist Attacks upon the United States. *Final Report*. Washington, D.C.: Government Printing Office, 2004.

U.S. Department of Defense. *Strategy for Homeland Defense and Civil Support*. Washington, D.C.: U.S. Department of Defense, 2005.

Chapter 8 International Cooperation

In December 1994, a small bomb exploded on a Philippines Airlines plane en route from Manila to Tokyo, killing one passenger and injuring ten others. Although the control cables to the wing flaps on one side of the plane were damaged by the bomb, the flight crew was able to land the plane safely an hour later. The bomb had been planted by Ramzi Yousef, one of the masterminds of the World Trade Center bombing in New York City in 1993. After boarding the plane in Manila, he had put the bomb together in the plane's lavatory and then hid it in the airliner. His work done, he disembarked in Cebu, a connecting stop in the Philippines before Tokyo.

The Cebu bombing was a test run for a much larger terrorist attack that Yousef planned in January 1995. He and his accomplices hoped to blow up more or less simultaneously eleven U.S. airliners traveling from Bangkok, Thailand, to the United States, in an attack they referred to as "Bojinka." However, the plan was foiled, primarily by luck. The chemicals being mixed for the bombs caused a fire in Yousef's Manila apartment, but he and his partners were able to flee before the police arrived, leaving behind chemicals, timers, an instruction manual on how to build a liquid bomb, and a computer containing details of the bomb designs and the plan on its hard drive. The police also caught Abdul Hakim Murad, one of the plotters, and during interrogation he divulged details of the plot. But Yousef and another accomplice, Wali Khan Amin Shah, escaped from the Philippines shortly after Murad was arrested.

When Philippines police discovered the plot, they shared what they knew with U.S. investigators. A global manhunt ensued, and in February 1995 authorities in Pakistan arrested Yousef. Shah was arrested in Malaysia in December 1995. Both men were extradited to the United States, where, along with Murad, they were convicted of plotting to kill thousands of people and given life sentences. Yousef received an additional sentence for his participation in the 1993 bombing of the World Trade Center in New York City. Links between the airliner bomb plotters and al Qaeda were discovered only after another plotter, Khalid Sheikh Mohammed, was captured in Pakistan in 2003.

The Importance of International Approaches to Combating Terrorism

U.S. efforts to protect against terrorism cannot be limited to America's shores because the terrorist threat is global. Indeed, much of the planning for the

September 11 attacks took place outside the United States. Terrorists have demonstrated their abilities to exploit the ease of international travel and international financial transactions. Moreover, at least twenty thousand people from a wide range of countries—including the United States and Western Europe—trained in al Qaeda's terrorist training camps in Afghanistan before 2001. Even after the U.S. intervention in Afghanistan, the majority of these would-be terrorists remain at large. Many are thought to have returned to their home countries, where they may be planning further terrorist attacks. Today, it is believed that al Qaeda cells exist in more than sixty countries.

Terrorism poses threats to many different countries. Some of these threats are rooted in deep-seated internal conflicts, such as the ongoing struggle between Israel and Palestine and the Tamil Tigers' fight against the government of Sri Lanka. Other threats have been carried out by groups either associated with or sympathetic to al Qaeda. For example, Jemaah Islamiya (JI), an extremist Islamic organization in Indonesia, is believed to be responsible for terrorist attacks in Bali and Jakarta in 2002 and 2003. The problem presented by such groups is one that transcends borders; JI is believed to operate from bases in the lawless territories of the southern Philippines and possibly Malaysia. (See Table 1.2 in Chapter 1 for a list of major terrorist attacks in the 1990s and Table 8.1 for those since September 11, 2001.)

Because the threat is global, terrorism demands a global response. Combating international terrorism requires cooperation in a wide range of areas among different countries and international organizations. Diplomatic efforts are needed to maintain and strengthen international prohibitions against terrorist acts and to encourage more states to endorse international treaties against terrorism. Economic cooperation is needed to eliminate sources of terrorist financing and to ensure that economic tools can be used effectively to punish states and actors that continue to support terrorists, actively or passively. Security cooperation is needed to ensure that states share intelligence on terrorists, a particularly critical element of the fight against terrorism, and that law enforcement agencies work together across borders.

International cooperation is especially critical to addressing the danger of terrorists obtaining WMD. The United States is particularly concerned that terrorist groups will seek to use such weapons to carry out attacks more devastating and dramatic than those already experienced. Recent revelations that A. Q. Khan, a prominent Pakistani physicist involved in Pakistan's nuclear weapons program, had an extensive illicit international network that provided weapons-related materials to Iran, Libya, and North Korea has increased fears that non-state groups such as al Qaeda might also be able to purchase the materials necessary to build a crude nuclear, biological, or chemical weapon. The international nature of Khan's illicit network, which included companies in countries in Europe, Africa, and Asia, reinforces the need for international cooperation to prevent the spread of nuclear weapons and materials.

Table 8.1 Major Terrorist Attacks since September 11, 2001

Year	Location	Incident	Terrorist organization/individuals	Fatalities and injuries
2001	India	Car bombing	Jaish-e-Mohammed suspected	35 killed, 40 injured
	India	Attack on Indian Parliament	Kashmiri terrorists	12 killed, 22 injured
2002	Tunisia	Truck bombing of synagogue	Al Qaeda blamed	21 killed, over 30 injured
	Pakistan	Car bomb in Karachi	Al Qaeda sympathizer	13 killed
	Russia	Bomb explosion during Victory Day ceremony in Dagestan	Chechen rebels	42 killed, over 130 injured
	Pakistan	Car bomb at U.S. consulate, Karachi	Al Qaeda-linked group	12 killed
	Colombia	Mortar attack at presidential inauguration	FARC	13 killed, 50 injured
	India	Attack on temple complex in Ahmedabad	Jaish-e-Mohammed	30 killed, many injured
	Indonesia	Bombing in tourist district	Jemaah Islamiya	202 killed
	Russia	Hostage crisis in Moscow theater	Chechen militants	120 hostages and 40 terrorists killed
	Russia (Chechnya)	Truck bomb at Chechen Parliament	Chechen militants	83 killed
2003	Colombia	El Nogal club bombing	FARC blamed, deny	36 killed, 150 injured
	Philippines	Bomb attack in Davao Airport	unknown	21 killed
	Saudi Arabia	Riyadh compound bombings	Al Qaeda blamed	34 killed, 160 injured
	Morocco	Casablanca attacks on Western and Jewish targets	Al Qaeda-linked group	43 killed, over 100 injured
	Russia (Chechnya)	Truck bomb in Znamenskoye	unknown	59 killed
	Russia	Bomb attacks at Moscow rock festival	unknown	15 killed, 40 injured
	Indonesia	Hotel bombing in Jakarta	Jemaah Islamiya	12 killed, 150 injured
	Russia	Explosion at Russian hospital	unknown	50 killed, 76 injured
	India	Two bombs in Mumbai	unknown	48 killed, 150 injured

	Country	Event	Attribution	Casualties
	Colombia	Motorcycle bombings in Florencia	FARC	10 killed, 54 injured
	Saudi Arabia	Truck bomb in Riyadh housing compound	unknown	18 killed, 120 injured
	Turkey	Istanbul bombings, four truck bombs	unknown	57 killed, up to 700 injured
	Pakistan	Two assassination attempts on president	Amjad Farooqi suspected	15 killed
	Russia	Attack on a train in southern Russia	unknown	45 killed
2004	Philippines	Superferry bombed in Manila Bay	Abu Sayyaf	116 killed
	Russia	Bomb in Moscow metro	unknown	41 killed
	Pakistan	Attack on Shia Muslims associated with Ashura holiday	unknown	43 killed, 160 injured
	Spain	Madrid commuter trains bombed	Al Qaeda–linked group	190 killed, 1,800 injured
	Saudi Arabia	Al Khobar massacre at oil compound	Islamic militants	22 killed
	Russia	Attacks on government in Nazran	Chechens blamed	90 killed
	Russia	Suicide bomb near Moscow metro	unknown	11 killed, 33 injured
	Russia	Airliners bombed	Chechens blamed	89 killed
	Russia	Beslan school hostage crisis	Chechen separatists	335 killed
	Egypt	Sinai bombings of hotels in Taba and Ras Shitan	Palestinian group	34 killed, 171 injured
	Philippines	Bombing at Christmas market	unknown	15 killed
2005	Myanmar	Multiple bombs in Myanmar	unknown	19 killed, 160 injured
	Iran	Bombs explode in Ahvaz and Tehran	unknown	10 killed, 80 injured
	United Kingdom	London bombings	Indigenous al Qaeda–linked group	37 killed, over 700 injured
	Egypt	Sharm el-Sheikh attacks	Abdullah Azzam Brigades	88 killed, 200 injured
	India	Jaunpur train bombing	Attributed to Islamists	13 killed
	Indonesia	Suicide bomb attacks in Bali	Possibly Jemaah Islamiya	20 killed, 129 injured
	Russia	Attacks on government in Nalchik	Chechen rebels	137 killed
	India	Bomb attacks on Delhi markets	Islamic Inquilab Mahaz	61 killed, over 200 injured
	Jordan	Explosions at three Amman hotels	Al Qaeda in Iraq	57 killed, over 100 injured

continues . . . .

Table 8.1 Major Terrorist Attacks since September 11, 2001 (continued)

Year	Location	Incident	Terrorist organization/individuals	Fatalities and injuries
2006	India	Bombings in Varanasi	Lashkar-e-Tayyiba	28 killed, 100 injured
	Egypt	Hotel bomb attacks in Dahab	Jama'at al-Tawhid wal-Jihad	23 killed, 84 injured
	Pakistan	Suicide bomb attack in Karachi	unknown	57 killed
	Sri Lanka	Mines targeting a bus	LTTE	64 killed, 86 injured
	India	Explosions on commuter trains in Mumbai	Lashkar-e-Tayyiba	209 killed, 714 injured
	Russia	Moscow market bombing	Racially motivated	13 killed
	Somalia	Assassination attempt on president	Islamic Courts Union blamed	11 killed
	Sri Lanka	Pottuvil massacre	LTTE blamed	10 killed
	Sri Lanka	Suicide attack on navy convoy	LTTE	At least 92 killed, over 150 injured
2007	Sri Lanka	Sri Lankan bus bombings	LTTE suspected	22 killed, 100 injured
	Pakistan	Suicide bomb in Peshawar	unknown	14 killed, 30 injured
	Pakistan	Suicide bomb inside a courtroom	Taliban suspected	15 killed
	India-Pakistan	Samjhauta Express train bombed	unknown	68 killed, at least 30 injured
	Iran	Zahedan bombings	Jundallah	18 killed, 31 injured
	Colombia	Bomb attack in Buenaventura	FARC blamed	16 killed, 16 injured
	Algeria	Algiers bombings	Al Qaeda	33 killed, 222 injured
	Pakistan	Suicide bombing	unknown	28 killed, 35 injured
	Colombia	Two roadside bombs	FARC blamed	19 killed
	Pakistan	Restaurant bombing in Peshawar	unknown	24 killed
	Lebanon	Car bomb in Beirut	unknown	10 killed

NOTE: This table includes only those attacks in which ten or more people were killed. It excludes attacks in Afghanistan, Iraq, and Israel, where terrorist attacks are endemic.
SOURCE: The authors.

Despite the gravity and scope of the terrorist threat, international cooperation can be problematic for a variety of reasons. First, states have different perspectives on the nature of the terrorism problem. One element of these different perspectives is definitional, as discussed in Chapter 1. The international community has been unable to agree on how to define terrorism, and views differ on whether terrorist acts can be justified under certain circumstances. The debate about whether terrorist acts are appropriate in fighting political oppression, or whether they are simply criminal acts against innocent civilians, remains unresolved in some parts of the world. Public support for terrorist acts has declined significantly in most countries in the last few years, including in the Muslim world. But populations in some countries remain conflicted about whether terrorism is legitimate in the struggle against oppression, or in defense of Islam.[1]

Second, different states face different kinds of terrorist threats. As a result, these states have diverging views of the appropriate response to terrorism and of what the priorities should be. The United States, which is largely fighting an external threat, is seeking to confront terrorists abroad if at all possible. Many other states are facing primarily a domestic threat from homegrown terrorist groups, which may or may not have links to outside groups. Some states do not see themselves as particularly threatened by terrorism, which makes them less concerned about closing loopholes that terrorists might exploit to attack others. This lack of concern is problematic, however, because groups such as al Qaeda have shown their ability to adapt and innovate, and the "weak links" in global efforts to fight terrorism are those most likely to be exploited by such groups.

Third, states bring very different capabilities to the struggle against terrorism. Indeed, some states have proven powerless to prevent terrorist groups from using their territory as sanctuary or seeking to gain internal support within their borders. States with weak governing structures may also be incapable of strengthening their legal systems or financial networks, and they may not have the resources to enforce existing laws or patrol their national borders.

This situation is complicated by a fourth factor: the growing links between terrorists and international criminal networks that are adept at exploiting state weakness. As a result, an important tool of international cooperation is capacity building in order to help states enhance their abilities to address terrorism.

Fifth, the U.S. intervention in Iraq and its ongoing presence there have created some serious problems in the global fight against terrorism. To begin with, preparations for the invasion of Iraq in 2002–2003 diverted resources from efforts to track Osama bin Laden and al Qaeda in Afghanistan. The 2003 invasion also opened fissures between the United States and key allies in Europe, which will take time and effort to heal. Meanwhile, the evidence of prisoner abuse by some U.S. personnel at Abu Ghraib prison in Iraq and elsewhere caused significant and lasting damage to the U.S. image in the Muslim world and beyond. Moreover, the U.S. troop presence in Iraq has raised fears in the Muslim world about U.S. intentions and whether the United States is seeking a permanent presence there. It is commonly believed that Iraq has become a "training ground" for foreign terrorists and insurgents, who may take their newly acquired skills elsewhere with devastating effect.

Finally, concerned about safeguarding their sovereignty, some states may be hesitant to engage in intensive cooperation with the United States or others in confronting terrorism. Because the threat of terrorism is global in nature, some states may be asked to allow foreign troops or intelligence services to operate on their territory. Many governments worry not only that such a request infringes on their sovereign control over their territory, but also that local populations would react negatively to such cooperation. Governments may experience opposition from anti-American groups at home and retribution from terrorist groups if they appear to be cooperating too closely with the United States.

These difficulties notwithstanding, international cooperation against terrorism is extensive and growing. Cooperation takes multiple forms. Much of it is bilateral, as states work to address specific problems. International organizations are playing a role in setting standards and in providing technical assistance to states that want to improve their capacities to confront terrorism. And then informal coalitions of states are working together both in the areas of intelligence sharing and law enforcement and in efforts to prevent the spread of WMD.

This chapter examines how different forms of international cooperation are contributing to the fight against terrorism. It looks first at the political strategies being used to confront terrorism, including international law and efforts to develop conventions prohibiting terrorism, along with attempts to quell the spread of WMD. Next, it examines economic strategies to block terrorist financing and to protect international trade. A range of different tools is investigated, including controlling global money flows, sanctions, capacity building, and efforts to enhance the security of the global trading system. Finally, the chapter takes a closer look at the security policies used to combat terrorism, including law enforcement and intelligence sharing, paying special attention to the experiences of Europe and Southeast Asia.

Political Strategies: International Laws and Conventions

International conventions are an important framework for addressing the problem of international terrorism. International treaties set standards for domestic laws. When states ratify international treaties, they commit to harmonizing their national laws with the international legal obligations they have established. This process gives the international community an important tool in seeking to create global standards. Those states that have signed on to international legal obligations can then legitimately put pressure on those states whose domestic laws do not do more to live up to treaty conventions. International conventions can also help to shape international public opinion on important issues. One of the key goals in combating terrorism is to ensure that terrorism is viewed as illegitimate around the world, and international conventions help to delegitimize terrorist actions.

International efforts to prohibit terrorism date from the 1960s. They then gained momentum during the 1970s and 1980s in response to the rash of terrorist attacks in Europe and the Middle East. Twelve international conventions were established between 1963 and 1999 to address different aspects of terrorism. Because of ongoing disagreements about how to define terrorism and about which groups should be considered terrorists as opposed to revolutionary movements, no convention outlawing terrorism altogether was adopted. Instead, agreements tended to outlaw specific terrorist acts. For example, in response to the rash of airplane hijackings that began in the 1960s, many of which were carried out by members of terrorist groups, an international treaty outlawing hijacking was established in 1970. Other treaties banned the taking of hostages and attacks on diplomats, among other things.

By the late 1990s, this collection of agreements had evolved into a relatively comprehensive body of treaties, which could be said to make up an antiterrorism regime with broad international support. The sticking point, however, was that many states failed to sign and ratify these treaties, which limited their international scope and hindered efforts to encourage states to enforce their provisions. Differences in definitions notwithstanding, several regional organizations adopted conventions proscribing international terrorism, an indication that attacks against innocent civilians were widely viewed as reprehensible. To be sure, state leaders were also motivated by the goal of securing themselves against potential revolutionary groups. (See Table 8.2 for a list of international and regional conventions against terrorism.)

The UN Security Council has also sought to constrain state sponsorship of terrorism by imposing sanctions on states believed to be supporting or harboring terrorists. Largely at the urging of the United States, the Security Council imposed sanctions on states such as Sudan, Iran, Iraq, and Libya for their support of terrorist groups during the 1980s and 1990s. (See Case Study 8.1.) The Security Council also passed, at U.S. urging, several resolutions in response to the emerging threat posed by Osama bin Laden and al Qaeda in the 1990s. The 1993 attack on the World Trade Center, committed by militants associated with al Qaeda, the bombing of the Khobar Towers army barracks in Saudi Arabia in 1996, and the 1998 bombings of the U.S. embassies in Kenya and Tanzania revealed clearly that al Qaeda posed a serious international threat. In 1999 and 2000, the Security Council passed resolutions demanding that the Taliban regime in Afghanistan turn over Osama bin Laden to international authorities for trial and that it close the terrorist training camps that al Qaeda had established in the country. UN Security Council Resolution 1267, passed in 1999, placed limited sanctions on the Taliban if it failed to comply. (Table 8.3 lists the main UN Security Council resolutions on terrorism.)

Table 8.2 International and Regional Conventions on Terrorism

Convention	Date
International conventions	
Convention on Offences and Certain Other Acts Committed on Board Aircraft	September 1963
Convention for the Suppression of Unlawful Seizure of Aircraft	December 1970
Convention for the Suppression of Unlawful Acts against the Safety of Civil Aviation	September 1971
Convention on the Prevention and Punishment of Crimes against Internationally Protected Persons, Including Diplomatic Agents	December 1973
International Convention against the Taking of Hostages	December 1979
Convention on the Physical Protection of Nuclear Material	March 1980
Protocol on the Suppression of Unlawful Acts of Violence at Airports Serving International Civil Aviation, supplementary to the Convention for the Suppression of Unlawful Acts against the Safety of Civil Aviation	February 1988
Convention for the Suppression of Unlawful Acts against the Safety of Maritime Navigation	March 1988
Protocol for the Suppression of Unlawful Acts against the Safety of Fixed Platforms Located on the Continental Shelf	March 1988
Convention on the Marking of Plastic Explosives for the Purpose of Detection	March 1991
International Convention for the Suppression of Terrorist Bombings	December 1997
International Convention for the Suppression of the Financing of Terrorism	December 1999
International Convention for the Suppression of Acts of Nuclear Terrorism	September 2005
Regional conventions	
Organization of American States: OAS Convention to Prevent and Punish Acts of Terrorism Taking the Form of Crimes against Persons and Related Extortion that are of International Significance	February 1971
Council of Europe: European Convention on the Suppression of Terrorism	January 1977
South Asian Association for Regional Cooperation: SAARC Regional Convention on Suppression of Terrorism	November 1987
League of Arab States: Arab Convention on the Suppression of Terrorism	April 1998
Organization of the Islamic Conference: Convention of the Organization of the Islamic Conference on Combating International Terrorism	July 1999
Organization of African Unity: OAU Convention on the Prevention and Combating of Terrorism	July 1999
Commonwealth of Independent States: Treaty on Cooperation among States Members of the Commonwealth of Independent States in Combating Terrorism	June 1999

SOURCE: United Nations Treaty Collection: Conventions on Terrorism, http://untreaty.un.org/English/Terrorism.asp.

CASE STUDY 8.1

Sanctioning Libya

U.S. relations with Libya were strained by Muammar al-Qaddafi's sei-zure of power in Libya in 1969. Although the United States sought to maintain strong ties with Libya, Qaddafi's nationalization of several U.S.-owned oil facilities and his growing alignment with the Soviet Union led to worsening relations. Libya's support for terrorist groups, notably the Palestine Liberation Organization, finally cemented U.S. hostility toward Qaddafi. As a result, by 1979 Libya was included on the U.S. State Department's first list of state sponsors of terrorism. Libya's support for terrorist groups continued, nevertheless, and the U.S. gov-ernment placed additional sanctions on trade and travel to Libya. It also sought to gain multilateral support for sanctions against Libya, but, at first, with little success.

After Libyan agents detonated a bomb in a Berlin discotheque fre-quented by U.S. soldiers in 1986, killing three people and wounding at least 150 others, the United States attacked targets in Libya associated with its efforts to support terrorism, including the intelligence service's headquarters, along with Qaddafi himself. The attack appeared to quell Qaddafi's support for terrorism, at least temporarily. In 1989, however, bombs brought down two airplanes: France's UTA Flight 772, travel-ing from Brazzaville, Congo, to Paris, which exploded over Niger on September 9, and Pan Am Flight 103, traveling from London to New York, which exploded over Lockerbie, Scotland, on December 21. Libyan agents were pinpointed as the likely suspects in each of these bombings.

When Libya refused to hand over the suspects to British and French authorities, the UN Security Council imposed sanctions against the country in April 1992. The sanctions included an embargo on arms sales and air travel to Libya, and it constrained the number of diplomats that Libya could send abroad. Additional UN sanctions imposed in 1993 banned sales of equipment for Libya's oil and gas industries and froze Libyan assets overseas. The UN made clear that its sanctions would be lifted if Libya handed over the bombing suspects for trial.

In 1999 Libya finally complied with UN sanctions demands and turned over the suspects in the Lockerbie case to a court in The Hague for trial. This action led to a suspension of UN sanctions. One of the two suspects tried was convicted in 2001. In 1999 France convicted six Libyan agents in absentia for the UTA Flight 772 attack. In 2004 Libya agreed to settle a lawsuit brought in U.S. courts by the victims of UTA Flight 772.

After Libya agreed to compensate the relatives of the victims of Pan Am Flight 103 in 2003, the UN sanctions were formally lifted. The U.S. sanctions were formally lifted in May 2006. In addition to renouncing support for terrorism, in 2004 Libya officially gave up its effort to buy or build nuclear, chemical, and biological weapons, which made the lifting of the remaining U.S. sanctions possible.

This case highlights three points about the use of international sanctions to address terrorism. First, unilateral U.S. efforts to sanction Libya failed to change its behavior. Only after several major states supported stronger action against Libya did sanctions have a greater effect. Second, UN sanctions can be an effective tool for changing the behavior of state sponsors of terrorism. Such sanctions may take years to bring about the desired changes, however, and their success depends on the international community's willingness to sustain punitive sanctions. Third, it is often difficult to determine the precise effects of sanctions, because many other issues may influence a sanctioned state's decisions. Not only did Libya lose superpower backing after the collapse of the Soviet Union, but it also had to take into account the stronger U.S. resolve to punish state sponsors of terrorism after the September 11 attacks. Along with the sanctions, these changes may have influenced Libya's decision to renounce support for terrorism.   ■

Both the UN Security Council and the UN General Assembly condemned the September 11, 2001, terrorist attacks the day after the attacks took place. On September 28, the Security Council passed Resolution 1373, which called on all states to deny financial or other support for terrorist groups, to deny them safe haven, to share information and to assist other states in tracking down terrorists, to criminalize in their domestic laws both active and passive assistance for terrorists, and to enforce these laws. It also called on states to become parties to the relevant international conventions relating to terrorism. Notably, Resolution 1373 was passed under Chapter VII of the UN Charter, which makes compliance with its provisions binding on all member states. The resolution also mandated the creation of the Counter-Terrorism Committee (CTC) to monitor states' compliance with their obligations under Resolution 1373.

This effort by the Security Council reflects U.S. recognition of the importance of multilateral support to combat terrorism. As with many of the earlier sanctions against state sponsors of terrorism, U.S. officials helped to shape the provisions of Resolution 1373, and they worked hard to ensure its adoption.

The initial response to Resolution 1373 was positive, indicating both widespread international outrage at the September 11 attacks and recognition that global collaboration was essential to address the problem. The CTC set up a reporting system for states, which obliged them to submit initial statements

Table 8.3 Key UN Security Council Resolutions Proscribing Terrorism, 1970–2005

Resolution number	Resolution date	Purpose
286	1970	To call on states to prevent further hijackings; first Security Council resolution on terrorism
579	1985	To condemn acts of hostage taking and abduction (post–*Achille Lauro*ᵃ)
635	1989	To condemn all acts of unlawful interference with security of civil aviation
638	1989	To condemn all acts of hostage taking and abduction
731	1992	To call on Libya to hand over terrorist suspects
748	1992	To impose aviation, arms, and diplomatic sanctions on Libya
883	1993	To freeze Libyan assets
1054	1996	To restrict Sudanese diplomats because of Sudan's refusal to hand over those believed responsible for a plot to assassinate Egyptian president Hosni Mubarak
1267	1999	To demand that the Taliban turn over Osama bin Laden to the appropriate authorities so he can be brought to justice
1269	1999	To unequivocally condemn all acts of terrorism as criminal and unjustifiable and to call on member states to adopt specific measures
1333	2000	To demand that Afghanistan's Taliban authorities close all camps where terrorists were trained
1368	2001	To condemn the September 11 attacks
1373	2001	To require states not to help terrorists in any way; established a counterterrorism committee
1506	2003	To lift sanctions imposed on Libya by the UN
1526	2004	To revise sanctions in UN Resolution 1267 to target al Qaeda and Taliban, but not Afghanistan
1540	2004	To require all states to punish terrorists or other non-state actors who acquire or sell weapons of mass destruction or related materials
1566	2004	To require all states to act against terrorist groups not covered by UN Resolution 1267
1624	2005	To condemn all terrorist acts and incitement of terrorist acts and to call for their prohibition

SOURCE: Security Council Actions to Counter Terrorism, www.un.org/terrorism/securitycouncil.html.

ᵃ In October 1985, terrorists hijacked the Italian cruise ship *Achille Lauro* near Egypt and demanded that Israel release fifty Palestinian prisoners. The terrorists killed one passenger, Leon Klinghoffer, and fled the ship after two days. The United States sought to capture the hijackers so they would stand trial in the United States, but the plane they were escaping on landed in Sicily, and the Italian government insisted on trying them instead.

assessing how closely their legal systems complied with 1373's requirements and where they stood in terms of ratification of international treaties on terrorism. Almost all states in the international system met this initial reporting requirement, achieving a higher level of initial compliance than that for virtually any other UN treaty or resolution. After the first reports, CTC staff initiated dialogues with states by requesting further information or elaboration of areas in which states needed assistance to meet their obligations. Although states are obliged under Resolution 1373 to ensure that their legal and financial systems are not conducive to terrorist operations, many states do not have the capacity either to establish the appropriate legal framework or to enforce laws on the books.

To address this problem, the CTC established a clearinghouse of information about technical assistance. The CTC has interpreted its role as a facilitating one, helping to link states that need help improving their capacity to fight terrorism with states that have the capacity to aid them. The CTC itself is not in a position to offer such assistance. The CTC also established working relations with other international organizations, such as the World Bank and the International Monetary Fund, and it has encouraged these organizations to consider how their aid programs can contribute to efforts to prevent terrorists from operating freely around the globe. The CTC does not have "teeth," however; although it can demand that states take steps to prevent terrorism, it does not have the means to enforce their compliance. This situation raises two important questions. How can the UN encourage states to cooperate with counterterrorism measures? And what can the United States do to encourage other states to comply with UN obligations?

U.S. concern about the threat of WMD terrorism has also shaped international efforts to address the problem of terrorism. As U.S. senator Richard Lugar has noted, expressing a widely shared sentiment, the war on terrorism will not be effective unless all materials that can be used to build WMD are completely under control.[2] This view has been reinforced by evidence that al Qaeda sought to acquire WMD capabilities and by Osama bin Laden's insistence that the use of such weapons against the United States and the West was a "religious duty." Evidence that several important states of concern both for their support of terrorists and for their desire to acquire WMD—namely, North Korea, Iran, and Libya—had been aided by A. Q. Khan's illicit nuclear supply network has only increased worries about WMD terrorism. U.S. concerns about the spread of WMD led it to urge stronger measures to prevent the spread of materials that might enable terrorists to build such weapons. One diplomatic step was to gain passage of UN Security Council Resolution 1540 in April 2004. It criminalizes the spread of WMD, particularly to terrorist groups. Like Resolution 1373, it was adopted under Chapter VII of the UN Charter, which makes compliance with its provisions binding for all states, including those that had not signed on to the Nuclear Non-Proliferation Treaty (NPT), the core international treaty supporting global efforts to prevent the spread of nuclear weapons. Thus states such as India, Pakistan, and Israel that have not signed the NPT are expected to comply with Resolution 1540.

Resolution 1540 obliges states to adopt laws criminalizing the spread of WMD, to ensure that they have strong export controls in place to prevent the spread of such weapons or related materials, and to secure sensitive materials such as nuclear fuel within their borders. As it did for Resolution 1373, the Security Council established a committee (the 1540 Committee) to oversee compliance with the resolution's provisions and to aid states in meeting their obligations. Such committees under Security Council auspices are uncommon. They have been established to deal with two issues: enforcing sanctions imposed by the Security Council and terrorism. Its efforts to establish greater coordination among the different committees addressing terrorism demonstrate that the United States considers their activities important to the international effort to combat terrorism.

Resolution 1540 has had relatively broad support from the United States, the European Union (EU), and the UN General Assembly in recognition of the shared threat of WMD. But some states have pointed out that the only way to guarantee completely that such weapons will not be used is to achieve their total elimination, including by the five nuclear powers recognized under the NPT. So long as this double standard exists, they point out, it will be difficult to prevent other states from seeking to acquire these kinds of weapons.

Like their approach to Resolution 1373, most states have sought to meet their reporting obligations under Resolution 1540, but these reports have differed in quality. The United Kingdom not only submitted its draft report, but also shared it with other states as a possible model in order to encourage other states to comply. The central question is whether this process will succeed in pushing states to adopt further measures. The resolution's text is ambiguous both in defining its terms and in spelling out exactly what states are expected to do. This situation is not surprising, because the compromises that must be made to reach agreement among the fifteen Security Council members, and, in particular, among the five veto-wielding states—China, France, Russia, the United Kingdom, and the United States—can often lead to vague terminology.

In addition to the problems of language, many states do not have the capacity to fulfill the export control requirements mandated by the resolution, and they will need help from other states to build this capacity. Voluntary export control regimes that have long been in place as part of the nonproliferation regime, such as the Nuclear Suppliers Group or the Wassenaar Arrangement, primarily include countries with advanced economies that were able to establish export control mechanisms or to develop them over time. The United States and other members of existing export control regimes have a big role to play in helping other states to put export controls in place. Although U.S. encouragement can be useful, it also can be counterproductive at times because of suspicions about U.S. motivations or resistance to some of its policies, such as support for Israel. International bodies such as the International

Atomic Energy Agency (IAEA), which oversees compliance with many features of the NPT, can also play an important role. The IAEA is generally perceived to be a neutral body and not a tool of U.S. policy.

The effort to prevent nuclear terrorism was bolstered by the UN General Assembly's adoption of the International Convention for the Suppression of Acts of Nuclear Terrorism, which was passed by consensus in April 2005 and opened for signature in September of that year. Discussions of a treaty to ban nuclear terrorism began in 1998, at Russia's request. Little progress was made for years because of the concern by some states that the treaty would implicitly define terrorism. But when the treaty was narrowed to focus on prohibiting terrorist *acts* using nuclear materials, agreement was reached relatively quickly. The treaty criminalizes acts of terrorism using radiological devices, as well as the possession of radioactive material by non-state actors. It also requires states to improve their information sharing about terrorists. Although this treaty is regarded as a significant addition to efforts to prohibit terrorism, its narrow focus on non-state actors but not states has appeared to some observers to be furthering the double standard on nuclear weapons noted earlier.

Despite its noteworthy successes in proscribing terrorist acts, the international community remains unable to reach agreement on outlawing terrorism altogether, primarily because of ongoing differences over the definition of terrorism (see Chapter 1) and the dispute over whether terrorism is simply always unacceptable or whether acts of terrorism can be a legitimate response to repression or occupation. UN Secretary General Kofi Annan unsuccessfully sought to break the deadlock by proposing in 2005 that terrorism be defined as "any action . . . intended to cause death or serious bodily harm to civilians or non-combatants with the purpose of intimidating a population or compelling a government or an international organization to do or abstain from doing any act." [3] But the questions remain: Can a general treaty prohibiting terrorism gain broad international support if the debate over definitions is not resolved? And what are the major obstacles to reaching agreement on a definition of terrorism?

Economic Strategies: Blocking Terrorist Finances and Securing International Trade

In another effort to inhibit terrorist activities, the international community has sought to block funding that supports terrorist groups. Terrorist acts are not expensive, but they are not cost-free; some funding is required. For example, it has been estimated that the 2002 Bali bombings cost less than $50,000 to carry out. The 2004 Madrid attacks cost between $10,000 and $15,000, and the price tag put on execution of the London attacks in July 2005 is about $2,000. Even carrying out the attacks of September 11, by far the most dramatic, is believed to have cost less that $500,000.

Today, terrorist funding has three main sources. The first is charities. For devout Muslims, charitable giving is a pillar of their religious beliefs, and Islamic terrorist groups have successfully exploited the practice of charitable giving as a means to fund violent acts. Although most Islamic charities are just what they claim to be, organizations that support the requirements in the Qur'an to help the poor, a few charities are fraudulent and specifically designed to fund terrorist groups. Reliance on charities to divert money to terrorists is not new; groups ranging from the Irish Republican Army to Basque separatists to communist revolutionary groups in the Philippines have long relied on charities for funds. Finally, some quite legitimate charitable organizations may have unknowingly hired employees who seek to divert funds to terrorist groups.

An additional problem in determining whether particular groups are truly charitable organizations lies in the difference in views on what constitutes terrorism and what constitutes revolutionary activities. Hamas, for example, is a militant Palestinian nationalist movement that has refused to accept Israel's right to exist. Best known in the United States as a terrorist organization that has launched attacks against Israelis for decades, Hamas also maintains a network of social service organizations that is widely regarded as the most effective in the Palestinian-controlled territories. Indeed, most observers believe that widespread appreciation of the social services provided by Hamas and its apparent lack of corruption led to Hamas's victory in the January 2006 elections in which it gained control of the Palestinian parliament.

Because it has maintained separate "militant" and "social" wings, many governments and charitable institutions regard financial support for Hamas's social wings as legitimate. The EU did not drop the distinction between these two wings and designate Hamas as a terrorist group until 2003, and it did so then only after extensive U.S. urging.

A second source of terrorist funding is criminal activities, including money laundering, trading in drugs, and counterfeiting. The 2004 Madrid bombings are believed to have been funded by drug trafficking, and apparently members of the group that carried out the attacks conducted counterfeiting operations. Islamic groups in France and Canada have relied on armed robbery to fund terrorist acts, and other groups rely on trade in stolen goods and drugs to finance operations. Al Qaeda is believed to have laundered many of its funds by converting them into untraceable goods such as diamonds through middlemen in Liberia during Charles Taylor's rule.

Terrorist groups and organized crime were long seen as distinct and unlikely to cooperate because of their different motivations. Terrorists are largely driven by an ideology or religion, whereas criminal groups are motivated by profits. And terrorist groups seek to destroy a particular political system through dramatic public acts, whereas criminal groups and networks want to exploit the system to their advantage and to operate without drawing undue attention to themselves.

Recent evidence suggests, however, that, these differences notwithstanding, terrorist groups and organized criminal groups are increasingly working together to their mutual advantage. Terrorists buy weapons from organized crime groups, and criminal groups can turn to terrorists for training in the use of weapons and explosives. Moreover, as authorities have made progress in squeezing other forms of terrorist finances, the criminal angle has grown. Both terrorist and criminal groups tend to rely on the drug trade because it is so lucrative that it is hard to resist. Profits from the marijuana trade in Europe alone are estimated at $12 billion a year.

Reliance on crime is widespread. The Irish Republican Army, for example, has long been involved in organized crime. Initially, the IRA justified its criminal activities as a means of funding its political activities, but its later criminal activities, which included counterfeiting and tobacco smuggling, were undertaken simply for profits. The IRA was also linked to the Revolutionary Armed Forces in Colombia, and it may have trained FARC members in the use of explosives. FARC itself relies heavily on the drug trade to finance its activities.

The third source of terrorist funding is the front companies established by terrorist groups. Such legitimate businesses allow terrorist groups to gain profits through the sale of goods and to launder money. Al Qaeda's Osama bin Laden owned a chain of retail honey shops throughout the Middle East when the September 11 attacks occurred, and India's rogue nuclear merchant A. Q. Khan used front companies set up by a businessman based in Dubai, Buhary Syed Abu Tahir, to arrange the transfer of various components of nuclear weapons from countries such as Malaysia to Libya and North Korea.

Many challenges face those seeking to block funding for terrorists. For one thing, charitable giving, a major source of funding for terrorist groups, is difficult to regulate. Moreover, not all states have been willing to coordinate their efforts to monitor and limit charities. Most European states and some Asian countries are cooperating with the United States in setting standards, with the goal of closing loopholes on legitimate versus illegitimate charities. It has been harder to convince Arab and Muslim governments to cooperate for two reasons: the Muslim tradition of charitable giving and the perception in much of the Muslim world that money laundering is a problem associated with the drug trade, and therefore is not one common in Muslim countries. However, of the forty charities worldwide the United States has designated as supporters of terrorism, many have strong ties to states such as Saudi Arabia.

Another challenge is that money laundering is an enormous problem globally. Money laundering is undertaken to conceal the origins of assets obtained through illegal acts, so that money can be moved from the illicit underground economy to the formal economy. Although money laundering is generally associated with crime and the drug trade, the scope of this problem has made it easier for terrorists to fund transactions. It has been especially easy for terrorist groups to launder money in Southeast Asia, because there law enforcement is relatively weak and large amounts of drug money already move

Box 8.1 **The Hawala Remittance System**

Hawala is an underground banking system that existed long before formal banking was developed. It has been traced as far back as the eleventh century, when it was used by merchants on the Silk Road from China to the Middle East to avoid robbers and to transmit funds home. *Hawala* means "reference" in Urdu, one of Pakistan's main languages, and "trust" in Arabic. It has also been interpreted as "transactions in the air"—"hawa" means "air" or "wind" in Hindi. Widely used by Muslim and Hindu diasporas, hawala networks make it possible to transfer money to remote locations without actually moving money across international borders.

Hawala operators in one country have counterparts in other countries. An individual wishing to use the system pays a hawala operator in his or her own country. The operator contacts another hawala operator in the destination country, who then distributes money as requested by the person paying. Hawala operators are often in the import-export business, which both enables them to establish relationships with operators in different countries and gives them a way to account for the financial transactions they incur without moving money. Operators in the United States and India can adjust the amounts they charge on invoices for imported and exported goods, for example, as a way to balance their accounts for money received in one country and paid out in another. In this way, no money must move across borders. The system is based on trust, both between hawala operators and between clients and the operators they pay.

Why use hawala rather than legal wire transfers? Millions of Asian and South Asian emigrants use hawala to send remittances home, despite the fact that this unregulated form of money transfer is illegal in many states. For one thing, hawala operators often offer better exchange rates than banks, so those using the system view it as a more cost-effective way to send money home. Conventional banks and wire transfers also tend to charge high commissions on their transfers, whereas hawala operators charge generally lower fees. Because there is no formal record of a transaction and no money crosses borders, hawala transfers also avoid taxes. Finally, hawala operators are able to transfer money quickly and reliably to remote areas, which conventional banks and wire transfers generally do not serve.

The volume of money moved through hawala networks is huge. By one estimate, between $2 and $5 billion moves through this system to Pakistan alone on an annual basis. The World Bank estimates that 9 percent of all private income transfers to the Philippines were transmitted through hawala operators between 1981 and 2000; the corresponding figure for Indonesia is 23 percent and for Pakistan 55 percent.[a]

Although most of those who use hawala do so for legitimate purposes—to send money home to relatives—this unregulated system of money transfer

continues . . .

raises concerns because funds moved this way are virtually untraceable. Generally, there is no paper record of money paid or dispersed, and most transactions are conducted using code words. The money itself rarely crosses an international border. Moreover, there is evidence that hawala mechanisms have been exploited by drug dealers, militants, and terrorists to transmit funds without leaving traces. But this possibility is very hard to prove because of the nature of the transactions.

- Can governments do more to regulate hawala?

- How would efforts to limit the use of such methods affect the economies of countries on the receiving end of the system?

- What does the widespread use of hawala networks suggest for efforts to track and freeze terrorist financing?

---

[a] Douglas Frantz, "The Financing: Ancient Secret System Moves Money Globally," *New York Times*, October 3, 2001; Mohammed El Qorchi, Samuel Munzele Maimbo, and John F. Wilson, "Informal Funds Transfer Systems: An Analysis of the Informal Hawala System," International Monetary Fund and World Bank, Washington, D.C., March 24, 2003, www.johnfwilson.net/resources/Hawala+Occasional+Paper+_3.24.03_.pdf.

through some states such as Thailand. In the Philippines and Indonesia, money laundering was not even illegal before 2001. Informal banking mechanisms known as hawala further complicate efforts to trace or block terrorist funding. (See Box 8.1.) Money laundering and funding for terrorism and militants are a very small part of the total funds transmitted this way, but the situation is worrisome, nevertheless.

A final challenge associated with efforts to block terrorist funds is that terrorist groups have proven to be good innovators. They have responded to early successes in blocking financing by developing new mechanisms—indeed, bin Laden's shifting of resources to diamonds followed the successful freezing of Taliban assets in the United States after the 1998 embassy bombings in Kenya and Tanzania. The scattering of terrorist groups affiliated with al Qaeda further complicates efforts to trace funds, making it harder for authorities to keep up with terrorists in this area.

Two overarching goals are underlying efforts to block terrorist financing. The first is to prevent questionable money from moving through the legitimate international financial system by standardizing regulatory mechanisms and laws. Central tasks in achieving this goal are to remove loopholes both within different states' regulatory systems and in the international regulatory system more broadly and to enhance states' abilities to detect illicit funds by increasing the transparency of financial transactions.

The second broad goal is to crack down on individuals, groups, and states known to support terrorists in order to make it more difficult for the terrorists to do business. The tools available for this purpose are freezing assets, imposing economic sanctions, designating groups or states as supporters of terrorism, and criminalizing support for terrorism and terrorist acts.

How should these different tools be used? Should the top priority be to freeze the assets of groups associated with terrorism, for example, or to "follow the money" in order to learn more about how terrorist networks operate? The latter approach might make it possible to break up terrorist networks rather than merely blocking their access to assets. In their final report published in 2004, the National Commission on Terrorist Attacks upon the United States argued in favor of tracking finances.[4] This stance was partly in recognition of the fact that, although the initial efforts to freeze funds after September 2001 had been relatively successful, progress slowed significantly as terrorists found other ways to finance their operations. Roughly $125 million in terrorist assets was frozen between 2001 and 2002, but the total amount of assets frozen had risen to only $140 million in 2004, indicating that it was becoming harder to find and freeze terrorist assets. By 2005 the United States had adopted a two-pronged strategy of both attacking the sources of financing and following the money to discover terrorist groups.

Successful cooperation to limit money laundering and terrorist finance is particularly challenging because it requires both cooperation among states and cooperation with and among private actors such as banks. States must work together to set international standards and to close any loopholes that might compromise legitimate international transactions. At the same time, cooperation with the financial services industry and banks is needed both vertically, with governments, and horizontally, among different companies, to ensure that questionable transactions are spotted and blocked. The USA PATRIOT Act, passed in October 2001, makes both forms of information sharing mandatory for banks operating within the United States.

Controlling Money Flows and Closing Loopholes

Money laundering is not a new problem, but it became particularly acute as the international drug trade exploded in the 1980s. The scope and severity of the problem led to the 1988 UN Convention Against Illicit Traffic in Narcotic Drugs and Psychotropic Substances, known as the Vienna Convention, which sought to constrain drug trafficking, associated money laundering, and trade in "precursor" chemicals that could be made into illicit drugs. During the 1990s, efforts to quell both the drug trade and terrorism focused on money-laundering activities. In 1997 the UN expanded its effort to enforce the Vienna Convention and made recommendations for intensifying international efforts to constrain the drug trade and resultant money laundering. The same year, it established the UN Office on Drugs and Crime (UNODC). The UNODC was also given the task of helping states to constrain terrorism—an indication of the growing concern about the threat posed by international terrorist groups and their reliance on criminal activities. In 1999 the UN also adopted the International Convention for the Suppression of the Financing of Terrorism. This convention requires states to make funding of terrorist acts a criminal offense, to identify and seize funds suspected of being used by terrorists, to prosecute or extradite suspected terrorists, and to ensure that their domestic laws require financial institutions to track potential terrorist funding. The convention entered into force in April 2002, as more states were energized by the September 11 attacks to ratify the treaty.

The Financial Action Task Force (FATF), another international body established to address money laundering, was created in 1989 by the Group of Seven (G7) industrialized nations. Its mission is to track money-laundering activities and to make recommendations to governments on ways to make their banking systems more resistant to use by those seeking to launder money. After September 11, FATF was also given the mission of finding ways to deter terrorist financing. In addition to the forty recommendations FATF urges members to adopt on money laundering in general, in October 2001 the organization added nine special recommendations on ways to protect against terrorists' use of financial networks:

- Take immediate steps to ratify and implement the relevant United Nations Instruments
- Criminalize the financing of terrorism, terrorist acts, and terrorist organizations
- Freeze and confiscate terrorist assets
- Report suspicious transactions linked to terrorism
- Provide the widest possible range of assistance to other countries' law enforcement and regulatory authorities for terrorist financing investigations
- Impose anti-money laundering requirements on alternative remittance systems
- Strengthen customer identification measures in international and domestic wire transfers
- Ensure that entities, in particular non-profit organizations, cannot be misused to finance terrorism
- Do more to control the movement of currency or other instruments of exchange carried by couriers across borders.[5]

A fundamental problem with FATF's efforts, however, is that the task force is far from universal—it has only thirty-three member states. To help address this limitation, both the International Monetary Fund (IMF) and the World Bank are working with FATF to encourage states to adopt FATF's recommendations. The United States and the EU also have sought to cooperate in promoting FATF's recommendations. They have established a regular dialogue on terrorist financing and worked to improve cooperation in information sharing, enforcement, and monitoring borders to protect against illegal transactions.

One recent regional effort to address money laundering and terrorist financing was the creation in November 2004 of the Middle East and North Africa Financial Action Task Force (MENAFATF), with headquarters in Bahrain. This is the first tentative step by states in the region to address what they now recognize is a serious regional problem. The ASEAN Regional Forum (ARF), a group of ten members of the Association of Southeast Asian Nations (ASEAN) along with other states from the region that joined together to establish a security dialogue in Southeast Asia, agreed in July 2002 to several steps intended to prevent terrorist financing in the region. The ARF also reinforced members' commitment to UN measures against terrorist financing. Although efforts to quell terrorist financing are far from global, these regional efforts indicate that states far and wide are recognizing the problem and seeking forms of cooperation to address it.

The United States has also sought to use domestic laws to pressure private companies, including foreign banks, to do more to prevent terrorists from laundering money. The USA PATRIOT Act authorizes the Treasury Department to block foreign banks from doing business in the United States if they do not meet U.S. and international transparency standards, or if they are operating in ways that raise concern that they may be tolerating money laundering. Banks remain excluded from the U.S. financial system until they can prove they have fixed the problems. Under the Patriot Act, in 2004–2005 the Treasury blocked a Syrian bank from operating in the United States and ordered U.S. commercial banks to sever their ties with it. The Treasury Department also established the Office of Terrorism Finance Intelligence (TFI), which works at both the domestic and international levels to expand intelligence about terrorist financing and money laundering.

Efforts to block terrorist financing illustrate one of the central difficulties confronting international cooperation to combat terrorism—enforcement. Although most international treaties impose binding obligations on their members to bring their domestic laws into alignment with their international commitments, it is very difficult to make states do so in practice. International lending organizations have been encouraged to push states to do more in this area as a precondition for assistance, but some organizations see this as outside their mandate of promoting development or helping the poor. The United States and other advanced countries have some leverage, because they can withhold access to their lucrative domestic markets if states do not comply with their treaty obligations. But the question remains: how much priority should lending organizations give to efforts to stop terrorist financing in view of competing priorities?

Designations and Sanctions

Individuals and groups identified and designated by the United States and other countries as supporting terrorism are denied access to the U.S. financial system and, if possible, the international financial system as well. Beginning with the Export Administration Act of 1979, the United States sought to use a combination of designations and sanctions against states believed to be sponsors of terrorism. This decision was based on the assumption that terrorist groups could not operate internationally without state backing, and so the key to hindering their activities was to punish the states that helped them. Since 1979, the State Department has published annually a list of states believed to be supporting terrorist groups. (See Table 8.4.) Mandatory sanctions against these states include banning U.S. foreign aid and sales of military items and a U.S. vote against international lending to the designated countries. The United States also maintains lists of individuals and groups identified as terrorists or key supporters (see Table 4.1 in Chapter 4), as does the EU. It makes these designations in cooperation with other governments and international organizations.

The UN also identifies and sanctions states believed to be sponsoring terrorism. UN Security Council Resolution 1267, passed in 1999, built on and expanded U.S. efforts to pressure the Taliban regime ruling Afghanistan to hand over Osama bin Laden and other al Qaeda leaders for prosecution or face sanctions. Resolution 1267 also established a committee to monitor international compliance with the sanctions leveled against the Taliban regime if it refused to cooperate. Similar sanctions were adopted against Libya in 1992 and 1993 and against Sudan in 1996. The sanctions imposed on the Taliban regime under Resolution 1267 were revised and strengthened in January 2004, and the focus was shifted from Afghanistan to al Qaeda and remnants of the Taliban, as well as any properties and resources they own. The revised resolution, 1526, also requires states to cut the flow of funds from nonprofit organizations and informal remittance systems (such as the hawala networks described earlier) to terrorists.

Although sanctions can be effective in changing state behavior, as the Libyan example discussed earlier shows, questions have been raised about what makes sanctions "work." When are sanctions an appropriate tool? When are they counterproductive? Some scholars argue that sanctions are used primarily when states cannot agree on better policy options. This economic tool became controversial in the 1990s, when critics charged that sanctions meant to compel Saddam Hussein to comply with UN resolutions demanding that he give up his WMD programs instead hurt the Iraqi population. This situation stirred a debate about whether it is possible to impose "smart" sanctions designed to punish leaders but not the populations of target states. An example of a "smart" sanction is the travel ban imposed on the leaders of Sudan, who are suspected of complicity in war crimes in the Darfur region. Another example is the ban imposed in 2006 on exporting luxury items—from cognac to yachts—to North Korea, as a way to punish leader Kim Jong-il but not the North Korean population.

Sanctions are effective only to the extent that the most important trading partners of the targeted state are willing to comply with them. Some states,

Table 8.4 U.S.-Designated State Sponsors of Terrorism

Current state sponsors

Country	Date designated as a sponsor of terrorism
Syria	December 29, 1979
Cuba	March 1, 1982
Sudan	August 12, 1983
Iran	January 19, 1984
North Korea	January 20, 1988

States recently removed from the list

Country	Date of removal of terrorism sponsor designation
Iraq	September 25, 2004[a]
Libya	May 15, 2006[b]

SOURCES: U.S. Department of State and U.S. Department of Defense.

[a] Iraq was on the first list of state sponsors of terrorism, but it was removed in 1982, when the United States supported it in the Iran-Iraq War. Iraq was redesignated a state sponsor of terrorism in 1990, and it remained on the list until 2004, after Iraq's new transitional government was in place. Most sanctions had already been lifted, however—after Saddam Hussein was removed from power in 2003.
[b] On this date, U.S. Secretary of State Condoleezza Rice announced that Libya would be removed from the list after a forty-five-day waiting period.

however, may be unwilling to enforce sanctions if they have significant financial interests in a particular state that would make supporting sanctions painful at home. When faced with such conflicts of interest, combined with doubts about the effectiveness of sanctions or concerns about whom sanctions will actually hurt, some important trading states may decide to ignore sanctions, thereby rendering them an ineffective tool for changing state behavior.

One reason that many states fail to bring domestic structures in line with their international treaty obligations is that they simply lack the capacity to do so. This problem is important because international efforts to prevent terrorism are only as strong as the weakest global link in efforts to block terrorist movements or finances. Thus assistance with capacity building is an important element of the struggle against terrorism. This need is evident in legal, economic, and security areas, including helping states to update their laws and the legal institutions to enforce them, to expand their intelligence collection capabilities, and to strengthen rules for banking systems so that terrorists cannot exploit weaker systems. The broader goal is to convince more states to criminalize terrorist financing and to meet multilateral standards in regulating banking systems.

Both the United States and the Group of Eight (G8) industrialized countries provide technical assistance to countries seeking to revise their laws (Russia joined the G7 in 1998). This assistance has been extensive; by April 2006, the G8 had provided technical assistance on terrorist financing to 120 countries. Both the UN's Counter-Terrorism Committee and the 1540 Committee are seeking to facilitate capacity building by linking states in need of assistance with those that can offer help.

Securing International Trade against WMD

Roughly nine million shipping containers arrive in the United States each year. Many experts fear that these shipping containers would be the easiest way to bring nuclear materials into the United States, but these shipments would be especially hard to detect because of the enormous volume of international trade. Moreover, these containers pose a threat well before U.S. Customs has a chance to examine them; a nuclear explosion in a busy port before a ship reached U.S. Customs could be catastrophic. This concern has led to a series of efforts intended to prevent nuclear materials from entering the United States through commercial shipping. Three initiatives deserve mention because they depend on cooperation with global trading partners: the Container Security Initiative, the Megaports Initiative, and the Customs–Trade Partnership against Terrorism. (Also see Box 8.2.) Notably, all of these initiatives rely on the development of sophisticated screening technology and its placement in ports worldwide. Even though the initial goal has been to safeguard the continental United States rather than all global trade—a goal that makes sense at a time when the United States perceives itself to be the primary target of international terrorism—over time other states are likely to want similar protections for containers entering their territory.

Under its Container Security Initiative (CSI), U.S. Customs and Border Protection is developing means to ensure that shipping containers can be screened and certified as safe in ways that do not impose significant delays on international trade and are tamper-proof from terrorists or criminal groups. The CSI is based on four core elements: (1) using intelligence and automated information to identify and target containers that pose a risk for terrorism; (2) prescreening containers believed to pose a risk at their port of departure rather than waiting until they arrive at U.S. ports; (3) using detection technology to quickly prescreen these containers; and (4) using smarter, "tamper-evident" (that is, the use of a sealing device or process that makes any tampering easily apparent) containers to ensure that once a container has been screened, it remains unopened with its contents unchanged until it reaches its final destination. The United States has placed customs personnel at forty-four overseas ports to coordinate these screening efforts. So far, these efforts have focused only on protecting the United States. Japan and Canada have accepted the U.S. offer of reciprocal arrangements to states that might wish to examine exports from the United States to their territory. The EU also plans to adopt a model along the lines of the CSI for its ports in order to protect the EU states from the threat of nuclear terrorism.

Box 8.2 **The Proliferation Security Initiative (PSI)**

The PSI is an "activity" intended to prevent WMD, their delivery systems, and related materials from entering or leaving states that are viewed as potential buyers or sellers of nuclear weapons–related materials, or those that might transfer such materials to terrorist groups. Driven by its concern about the illicit transfer of nuclear materials, and the prospect that terrorists might seek to purchase them, the United States initiated discussions in 2003 with eleven close allies about new measures to interdict questionable transfers. These discussions led to the announcement in September 2003 of a set of "interdiction principles" on which the eleven core states agreed.

The PSI is intended to fill a gap in the existing nonproliferation architecture by ensuring that states within the Nuclear Non-Proliferation Treaty framework live up to their commitments not to acquire or aid in the acquisition of WMD. It also will help to halt questionable exports to states outside the NPT.

PSI activities include stopping and boarding ships, airplanes, or vehicles suspected of transporting questionable shipments of WMD or related materials to target countries. For example, a small group of states might agree to stopping and boarding a ship to determine whether its cargo was legitimate or should be seized to prevent proliferation to target states and terrorists. The states involved in any activity might include the state in whose waters interdiction would occur, the state whose vessels planned to stop the ship, and the state under whose flag the ship traveled, along with its owner's state.

About eighty countries have participated in either exercises or interdictions as part of the PSI. Of those, however, only about twenty have accepted the PSI's interdiction principles publicly, and the rest have expressed their support privately. It is unknown how many interdictions have taken place because the United States refuses to discuss them, other than to claim that there have been "a good number" of successful interdictions of materials of concern.

The United States favors the PSI because it prefers to work with small groups, or "coalitions of the willing," to ensure ease and speed of action and to avoid allowing other states to veto activities it wishes to undertake. It also views the PSI as a means of strengthening export control efforts without creating new layers of cumbersome international bureaucracy.

Questions have been raised, however, about the PSI's status under international law. Boarding ships at sea without their permission may violate the law of the sea. Indeed, the United States is negotiating treaties with the main states that provide shipping vessels with "flags of convenience" to ensure that it has a legitimate right to board vessels bearing their flags. The secrecy associated with the PSI also raises concerns about its claims of success: are these accurate, or are they overstated? It is hard to know. Moreover, the activity has little accountability. There is no legislation covering the PSI's activities in the United

continues . . .

States or elsewhere, and it is unclear how legal issues related to the seizure of goods might be handled. What if states or shipowners sue for reparations? Finally, some people have questioned how successful "coalitions of the willing" are likely to be over the long term, and suggest that formal means of cooperation might be more durable.

- Why might the United States wish to avoid institutionalizing the PSI? What factors affect this preference?

- What would be the benefits of greater institutionalization of this activity? What are the downsides?

- How does the PSI fit in with broader efforts to prevent the spread of WMD materials?

The Megaports Initiative is a supplement to the CSI. Working with its core trade partners, the United States has provided their major ports with radiation detection equipment so that more containers can be screened before they arrive in the United States. So far, detection equipment has been installed in about fourteen ports in Europe, Asia, South America, the Middle East, and the Caribbean. The ports targeted are, understandably, those with the highest volumes of trade.

Rather than focusing on ports themselves, the Customs–Trade Partnership against Terrorism (C-TPAT) is seeking to create secure supply chains, from factories overseas all the way to the U.S. market. Companies that choose to participate in the program must prove their ability to maintain the security of their products from production through the many steps that must be taken in transit until the products reach the United States. The security measures required include background checks on factory workers to protect against terrorist infiltration, secure storage, and tamper-proof shipping containers. Although these requirements are quite onerous, the advantage for companies that can meet them is expedited processing through U.S. Customs once their products reach the United States.

Security Policies: Law Enforcement and Intelligence Sharing

International cooperation to combat terrorism is essential in several areas: domestic law enforcement, intelligence sharing, and military operations. (See the earlier examinations of domestic interdiction and law enforcement in Chapters 4 and 5, and see Chapter 10 for a closer look at military operations.) In the United States, the FBI investigates crimes committed domestically and abroad, and it conducts intelligence investigations of domestic terrorist threats. The CIA collects foreign intelligence; it is not authorized to conduct domestic investigations except to the extent they involve collecting foreign intelligence. It is important, then, to ensure that law enforcement and intelligence agencies can work together in tracking terrorist activities that cross international borders.

Intelligence has been characterized as "the first line of defense" in the fight against terrorism. But the difficulties faced within the U.S. intelligence community in its efforts to improve cooperation since the September 11 attacks reveal just how hard achieving such cooperation can be. Cooperation is even more difficult across borders. Sensitive intelligence tends to be highly compartmentalized, and intelligence services fear sharing it with others—even their close counterparts—because they might put their sources at risk. In addition, different countries have different laws on the protection of individual privacy, which complicates sharing intelligence.

Most intelligence sharing is bilateral rather than multilateral. Intelligence cooperation takes place on a "need to know" basis, with little information offered that is not essential to a particular case. Trust tends to be based on individual ties between intelligence operatives through quid pro quo exchanges of information. This individual approach also complicates efforts to expand cooperation, because agents are likely to resist sharing information if they do not personally know who will receive it. The good news for the United States is that because it has by far the largest intelligence-gathering capabilities globally, other countries want to share intelligence with it so they can get intelligence back. The intelligence the United States receives through this cooperation is critical to its efforts to fight terrorism, because much of the U.S. intelligence effort is technologically driven, based on "signals intelligence" from satellites, drones, telephone intercepts, and other means. U.S. intelligence gathering is far weaker in the area of human intelligence—that is, old-fashioned spying by individuals on the ground with a deep knowledge of local customs and activities and language fluency, who are able to conduct investigations without raising suspicions. Notably, the broad range of partners with whom the United States cooperates in its efforts to track terrorists worldwide includes states believed to be sponsors of terrorism, such as Syria and Iran, and yet these states have provided valuable intelligence on al Qaeda and other groups.

Two regions of particular concern to the United States in the fight against terrorism are Europe and Southeast Asia. Both of these regions have experienced multiple attacks, and they have been used as staging areas for terrorist attacks elsewhere. Yet cooperation varies dramatically between and even within the two regions.

Europe

Because terrorism has a long history in Europe, police agencies there recognize the importance of cooperating with their counterparts in other countries to track terrorists and criminal groups slipping across state borders. As early as 1975, European police forces established the Trevi Group as a forum in which to discuss security problems related to terrorism, radicalism, and extremist violence. This Group contributed to the dismantling of Hezbollah's western European network in 1987.

As cooperation within the EU has deepened, police cooperation has become more established. For example, the Trevi Group was replaced in 1994 by Europol, an organization designed to facilitate law enforcement cooperation and criminal intelligence sharing within the EU. Initially, Europol focused on organized crime and drug trafficking, but in 2002 its mandate was broadened to ensure greater police cooperation against terrorist groups. Cooperation in sharing information also expanded dramatically after several EU members agreed to establish an EU "border" and to allow free passage within it as part of the Schengen Accord of 1985. This development led to the creation of the Schengen Information System (SIS), a database on border security and law enforcement available to all participating members, which enables them to allow the free movement of people and commerce across borders. Thirteen EU member states plus two non-EU countries, Norway and Iceland, have participated in the SIS since it went into effect in March 2001; the ten states that joined the EU in 2004 are scheduled to join the Schengen borders agreement in 2007. The United Kingdom and Ireland participate only in part in the agreement. From a counterterrorism perspective, the SIS includes data on extradition requests and whether particular individuals are considered "undesirable" by the participating states or have committed crimes in these states. It also monitors possession of firearms. The SIS is generally viewed as a success in facilitating police cooperation.

After the September 11 attacks, the EU took several additional steps to facilitate tracking criminals within its borders. One notable step was the creation of an EU-wide arrest warrant. In 2003 the EU also developed an EU-wide fingerprint ID database to aid police efforts. The purpose of the arrest warrant was to simplify the extradition process and to make it less time-consuming. Before the EU warrant was created, extradition from one European country to another could take almost a year—and in at least one case an Algerian suspect was held by British authorities for ten years before being extradited to France to stand trial. The EU arrest warrant went into effect throughout the EU in January 2004, and over three thousand warrants were issued that year, which led to over a thousand arrests. The EU warrant was used after both the Madrid train bombings in March 2004 and the London subway bombings of July 2005, and it led to the quick extradition of suspects in each case.

Europol also has contributed to better police cooperation among European states through joint training activities and the development of a network of intervention units in European police forces to aid in emergencies or hostage situations. Europol established a liaison with U.S. law enforcement in December 2001, which is intended to be the focal point of U.S.–EU data exchange on law enforcement.

Improving police cooperation has met some obstacles, however. In late 2005, a German court rejected the EU warrant as not in line with German laws, and it was unclear how the German stance would affect the efficacy of the warrant more broadly. Moreover, in spite of efforts to develop greater cooperation across the EU, along with greater integration, most police cooperation remains bilateral and operational, focused on particular problems. Although this situation is understandable and in many cases appropriate since most policing issues are local, it highlights the fact that law enforcement agencies continue to focus primarily on domestic threats rather than recognizing potential transnational dangers.

In Europe, it is critical that states cooperate in their intelligence-gathering activities, because there is no Europe-wide equivalent of the CIA seeking to identify threats to the EU countries. The Berne Group, an informal club of European intelligence organizations that has conducted joint training exercises and worked to build trust among intelligence agencies, has contributed to some notable successes in fighting terrorists. For example, there were indications that Osama bin Laden was planning a series of attacks in Europe, but the attacks were apparently thwarted in early 2001 by intelligence cooperation through the Berne Group, which aided several police operations across Europe, leading to arrests and in some cases to the seizure of the ingredients for explosives. One weakness of the Berne Group is that the United States is not a member. After the September 11 attacks, however, members of the Berne Group formed the Counterterrorist Group (CTG) as a forum for greater cooperation with non-EU countries. The United States, Switzerland, and Norway are members of this group, along with the EU states.

Since the September 11 attacks, the EU has strengthened its efforts to expand intelligence sharing for counterterrorism across its member states. A counterterrorism group was established, and the Secretariat of the European Council established a situation center to develop threat assessments. But the EU faces two obstacles in fostering wider cooperation in intelligence related to terrorism: member states have very different levels of intelligence capability with respect to terrorism, and they have very different perceptions of the terrorist threat. Within the EU, the "lowest common denominator" approach has tended to win out in official policy formation.

Before the September 11 attacks, only five states in the EU—those with the longest history of terrorist attacks—had counterterrorism legislation in place: France, Germany, Italy, Spain, and the United Kingdom. Not surprisingly, these states also have the best intelligence capabilities to address the terrorist threat. They began meeting informally in May 2003 to discuss counterterrorism, and they established a joint terrorist alert system, the G5, in March 2005, with the goal of creating a shared database to track individuals suspected of involvement in terrorist organizations. The rapid arrest of suspected terrorists in Italy after the Madrid and London bombings suggests that this intelligence cooperation is close and effective.

Even between the United States and its European allies, intelligence sharing takes place at different levels of cooperation. U.S. cooperation with the United Kingdom is the deepest. U.S. cooperation with other English-speaking countries (Australia, Canada, and New Zealand), takes place through the UKUSA network, and it is deeper than U.S. cooperation with other European allies, in part because the UKUSA alliance among intelligence agencies has been sustained since World War II. But the United States has worked out several important elements of cooperation with the EU, including an agreement to share information about passengers on transatlantic flights. Both sides are recognizing that they must develop faster means of sharing information on counterterrorism operations. Multilateral discussions about general threat assessments are seen as useful, to ensure that states have a shared sense of the threat. But the bulk of intelligence cooperation remains bilateral, because this way it is easier to control access to sensitive information. (See Case Study 8.2.)

CASE STUDY 8.2

International Cooperation and the Millennium Bomb Plot

Ahmed Ressam's efforts to attack the Los Angeles International Airport (detailed in Chapter 4) were halted in December 1999 through the alertness of a guard at the U.S.-Canada border. But because his activities had been monitored for years across several borders, French authorities were immediately able to provide the FBI with extensive information about his activities and associates. When Ressam went on trial in the United States, the French sent an official to testify in the proceedings.

The French had long been tracking the Armed Islamic Group (GIA), the Algerian terrorist organization responsible for a series of attacks in France, including the hijacking of an airplane that it hoped to fly into the Eiffel Tower, subway bombings in Paris, and an attempt to bomb a meeting of the G7 industrialized nations in Lille in 1996. The investigation by the French police of these attacks and plans revealed that the group's aims were international. They also discovered the connection to Ressam, who was then living in Montreal, Canada. The French notified the Canadian Security and Intelligence Service (CSIS) that the GIA appeared to have links or an active cell in Montreal, including Ressam. The CSIS then monitored the group for several years. In April 1999, French judge Jean-Louis Bruguière formally requested that Canadian officials issue a search warrant for Ressam as part of a French investigation of Algerian terrorists. Only after six months, however, did the Canadians approve this request.

This case points to the importance of international cooperation among intelligence and law enforcement officials. What is notable about the Ressam case was that French and Canadian authorities had been tracking Ressam, and French authorities provided important evidence to U.S. officials that enabled them to capture some of Ressam's associates and later to prosecute him. It also points to the difficulties of trust among intelligence organizations. Canadian authorities did not expedite France's search request on Ressam, and their cooperation with French efforts to conduct surveillance of the cell he had joined in Canada was limited. Similarly, in August 2001, the FBI contacted French intelligence to find out what information it had on Zacharias Moussaoui, who had raised suspicions. Although the French informed the United States that Moussaoui had long-standing links to radical Islamic organizations, including al Qaeda, the FBI did not trust this information enough to seek a search warrant for Moussaoui's computer. Only after the September 11 attacks did the FBI search the computer and discover links to Mohammed Atta, one of the leaders of the attacks.

SOURCE: This account draws heavily on Jeremy Shapiro and Benedicte Suzan, "The French Experience of Counter-terrorism," *Survival* 45 (Spring 2003): 67–98.

Southeast Asia

Al Qaeda has strong organizational links in Southeast Asia, fueling concerns about the spread of international terrorism in this region. Indonesia, the world's fourth largest state by population, has the world's largest Muslim population, and the terrorist bombings in Bali and Jakarta between 2002 and 2004 indicated clearly that al Qaeda's affiliates in the region shared its extremist goals. The Islamic extremist group Jemaah Islamiya is believed to have carried out many of the terrorist attacks in Indonesia, and its leader, Abu Bakar Bashir, appears to be linked to al Qaeda (some of its members trained in Afghanistan). Jemaah Islamiya may have cells throughout Southeast Asia. Another terrorist group, Abu Sayyaf, based in the Philippines, was set up by one of bin Laden's associates, Jamal Khalifa. The Moro Islamic Liberation Front (MILF) has also resorted to terrorist methods in its struggle against the Philippine government, and members of both Abu Sayyaf and MILF trained at al Qaeda camps in Afghanistan. Not only do these groups raise concern, but many states in the region have porous borders, with long sea coasts and many islands, as well as a weak state capacity to confront terrorist organizations.

For the nations of Southeast Asia, ongoing worries about the erosion of their hard-won sovereignty have complicated efforts to cooperate in the struggle against terrorism. The bitter legacy of colonialism has made some of these states wary of allowing a U.S. security presence in the region. Many states prefer to promote regional solutions to what are perceived as regional problems; moreover, there is concern that an expanded U.S. presence could exacerbate anti-American sentiment, making it only easier for domestic terrorist groups to recruit new members. Concerns about sovereignty are also complicating cooperation among regional states. One of the core principles of ASEAN, the main regional group which has as its central goals peace and prosperity, is non-interference in the domestic affairs of member states, and support for noninterference has limited options for coordination against terrorism. Moreover, some states, such as Malaysia and Indonesia, that face shared problems have had difficulty enhancing cooperation against criminals and terrorist groups because of ongoing territorial disputes over shared borders.

In spite of these handicaps, some limited regional cooperation is under way. In May 2002, Indonesia, Malaysia, and the Philippines signed an agreement to exchange information and improve communications procedures, which included provisions for cooperation against terrorism and other cross-border crimes, intelligence sharing, and joint training operations. Cambodia and Thailand later joined this agreement. The ASEAN Regional Forum has taken some steps to improve cooperation among police forces in the region, particularly to enhance their ability to prevent the movement of terrorists. The ARF also called on its member states to establish antiterrorism task forces, with the goal of aiding states affected by terrorist attacks. In August 2002, the United States and ASEAN established an agreement on cooperation against international terrorism, which includes measures for intelligence sharing and greater law enforcement to combat terrorism, along with capacity-building assistance from the United States in these areas. A similar agreement was reached between the EU and ASEAN in early 2003. It is not clear how much has happened since then, because the initial momentum for cooperation after the September 11 attacks has faded.

In addition to these multilateral initiatives, the United States, the EU, and Australia have sought to establish bilateral agreements with Southeast Asian states to expand counterterrorism activities. As in Europe, concern about terrorism varies among states in the region, because some face greater threats than others. Singapore and the Philippines have been particularly worried about the dangers they face from terrorism, and, not surprisingly, they have been most willing to work with the United States and others. In 2003 the United States and Malaysia agreed to establish a counterterrorism training center in Kuala Lumpur, and Australia has expanded its bilateral intelligence cooperation with Indonesia, the Philippines, and Thailand. India has also increased its security cooperation with Singapore, Indonesia, and Malaysia.

The Threat of Maritime Terror in Southeast Asia

An important shipping lane for much of the world's maritime commerce lies between Indonesia and Malaysia and Singapore in the Strait of Malacca. Of the two hundred and fifty ships that pass through this strait every day, about a third are oil tankers. Roughly ninety thousand ships pass through the strait

Map 8.1 Strait of Malacca

SOURCE: www.economist.com/images/20040612/CAS901.gif.

each year. The Strait of Malacca is considered a significant risk for terrorist attacks for several reasons: the huge volume of traffic that passes through it; the narrow shipping channel, which at one point measures 3.2 nautical miles across; and the high incidence of piracy that already plagues the strait.

A variety of factors make the strait particularly conducive to piracy. For one thing, the many small islands along its edge offer hiding places for pirates, who can exploit the international border between the states bordering on the strait to evade coastal police forces. Most large shipping boats, both container ships and tankers, tend to be unarmed, slow, and easy to spot. With their small fast boats and weapons, pirates generally can easily overwhelm ships' crews—and increasingly they appear willing to kill them. Because ships' crews are subject to few if any background checks, it is feared that many pirate groups may have an "inside man" tipping them off to a valuable cargo or a ship's location.

The scope of the piracy problem in the Malacca Strait is not known—shipping companies have little economic incentive to report piracy, because such attacks will raise their insurance rates. But the severity of the problem is evident in the fact that in July 2005 the London shipping insurance market classified the Malacca Strait as a war risk, which led to higher premiums for shipping there. This designation reflected not only concerns about piracy, but also about terrorism in the region. For example, on three different occasions in 2003 pirates took over chemical tankers and for several hours practiced steering them through the strait. These incidents raised concerns about the parallels between those incidents and the training the September 11 hijackers undertook to learn to fly airplanes—but not to land them. Experts worry that tankers could be turned into "floating bombs," used to destroy a port or to disrupt shipping in this narrow channel, either of which would have dramatic economic repercussions around the world. Osama bin Laden has claimed to have ten terrorist ships operating on the high seas, which increases this concern.

The coastal states bordering on the Strait of Malacca—Indonesia, Malaysia, and Singapore—have struggled to address the problem of piracy while they worry about the prospect of terrorism. In general, their coast guards are less well equipped than the pirates. Also, because the territorial jurisdiction of the strait is divided among these countries, pirates have easily evaded pursuers by crossing out of the territorial waters of those tracking them. These difficulties have led observers to argue, first, that the states in the region need to establish agreements allowing "hot pursuit" across international borders and to work more closely together to monitor the strait, and, second, that they should give priority to improving their coastal defense forces rather than maintaining the current preference for improving conventional naval forces. Conventional navies are ill-suited to deal with the problems presented by piracy and terrorism, but most states in the region favor these forces because of ongoing tensions over territorial waters, as well as resource disputes in the South China Sea, which has important fisheries and possibly oil deposits. For these countries, enhancing their coast guard capabilities would also be significantly cheaper than current efforts to expand conventional naval forces.

The concern about sovereignty noted earlier has been particularly apparent in the region's response to a U.S. suggestion that it could play a role in helping protect the Malacca Strait. In 2004 the United States proposed creating a Regional Maritime Security Initiative (RMSI), which would address the problems of piracy, terrorism, and trafficking in drugs and people in the region. The RMSI would seek to improve intelligence sharing with Southeast Asian states, as well as to allow the deployment of U.S. Marines and special forces to the region to help interdict pirates or terrorists. The prospect of U.S. troop deployments raised red flags for both Malaysia and Indonesia, and they argued that security in the strait was the responsibility of the coastal states. In response to such protests, the United States backed off its initial proposal, and instead offered to share expertise in how to police ships and encouraged greater dialogue among states in the region on patrolling the strait.

Partly in response to concerns that the United States might send troops to the region, in June 2004, Malaysia, Singapore, and Indonesia established the Trilateral Co-ordinated Patrols Malacca Straits (MALSINDO), which enables three-way maritime patrols by the coastal states. Indonesia and Singapore also created a joint naval monitoring system so that their patrols can share real-time data on what is happening in the strait. These are important first steps toward improving regional cooperation to prevent terrorist acts in the Strait of Malacca.

Conclusion

Expanding international cooperation is an essential part of any effort to defend against terrorism. Nevertheless, this effort will take hard work and patience. International political efforts to outlaw terrorism remain stalled by the ongoing debate over the definition of terrorism. Resolution of this debate may not be possible until progress is made on some of the chronic conflicts in the Middle East and elsewhere. Better economic cooperation to block terrorist financing and to improve the tools available to isolate or punish those who support terrorists will depend on a combination of capacity building and the sharing of ideas both about the nature of the problem terrorism poses and how it can best be addressed. Improvements in the security realm, in intelligence and law enforcement, rest on patient efforts to increase trust and experience working together. To carry out these efforts effectively, the United States must also pay attention to the concerns other states have about the threats they face to ensure that international measures to confront terrorism address the problems faced by both the United States and its allies.

FOR FURTHER READING

Boulden, Jane, and Thomas G. Weiss, eds. *Terrorism and the UN: Before and After September 11.* Bloomington: Indiana University Press, 2004.

Cirincione, Joseph, Jon B. Wolfsthal, and Miriam Rajkumar. *Deadly Arsenals: Nuclear, Biological, and Chemical Threats.* Washington, D.C.: Carnegie Endowment for International Peace, 2005.

Lilley, Peter. *Dirty Dealing: The Untold Truth about Global Money Laundering, International Crime, and Terrorism.* London: Kogan Page, 2006.

O'Sullivan, Meghan L. *Shrewd Sanctions: Statecraft and State Sponsors of Terrorism.* Washington, D.C.: Brookings, 2003.

Chapter 9   Media, Government, and Terrorism

Within hours of the first U.S. air strikes against the Taliban and al Qaeda targets in Afghanistan on October 7, 2001, Osama bin Laden appeared, AK-47 rifle in hand, in a prerecorded videotape broadcast around the world in which he declared war on the United States. Although this was not bin Laden's first declaration against the United States, its timing revealed the technical capabilities of terrorists and the extent to which the methods and outlets of the media have themselves become a central weapon of terrorists.

When Timothy McVeigh planned and then executed the fertilizer bomb attack on the Oklahoma City federal building in 1995 that killed 168 and injured several hundred more, he chose his target and timed his attack to receive as much attention as possible. McVeigh later stated that he selected the Alfred P. Murrah Federal Building because the open space around it allowed for the best news photos and television footage. The timing, around the anniversary of the federal government's ill-fated deadly siege of the Branch Davidian compound in Waco, Texas, was designed to capture the attention of Americans who were put off by the government's show of force in Waco. Although he never showed the slightest remorse for his actions, McVeigh said later that he regretted so many innocent children were killed, but only because their deaths overshadowed his overtly political message.

British terrorism expert Brian Jenkins famously opined that "terrorism is theater," and his prime minister, Margaret Thatcher, maintained that the media publicity "is the oxygen of terrorism." [1] Whatever else, in the age of mass electronic media terrorism is undoubtedly an act of communication. In many respects, the pervasiveness of the 24/7 news cycle makes the media one of the single most important components of the current dynamics of terrorism and counterterrorism. Today, many terrorists seek the spectacle that the electronic press and the Internet can bring to terrorist acts. Many of the same terrorists correctly view the media as an essential means of furthering their agendas through recruiting, spreading the message, and providing signals to operatives of impending plans.

Because terrorist organizations now have and use the most sophisticated communications technology, they are able to control the content, setting, and medium in getting the desired message out. Because the government-controlled and private mass media outlets are no longer the only or even the dominant voice in many places, terrorists' capabilities to create and disseminate their own messages greatly change the dynamic of terrorism and the media. Traditionally, terrorists viewed the conventional media as an enemy, to be pursued only when publicity was the desired end. Now, however, the criticism of terrorists often attributed to traditional media outlets can be overtaken by terrorists' distribution of their own message.

From another perspective, the media do in terrorism settings what they always do—report the news, for better or worse. From the government's point of view, terrorists' exploitation of the media must be controlled in order to control the terrorism. At the same time, censorship is anathema in a free society. In addition, the government may depend heavily on the free media to help spread a public affairs message when a terrorist crisis looms. Getting the word out, quickly and credibly, may require that government cooperate with the media in unprecedented ways.

This chapter first briefly reviews how the relationship between terrorism and the media has evolved over time. From the invention of the rotary printing press, to television and satellite transmission, and to the Internet and beyond, the dynamic of the relationship is fundamentally different today than it was even a few decades ago. From the perspective of the media, reporting the story has changed with the dynamics of international terrorism. From terrorists' point of view, the revolution in digital communications technology and the development of the 24/7 news cycle has created new opportunities to exploit the media for terrorist aims. The chapter then considers how terrorists employ the media to convey their messages. Included is an examination of the special role that the Internet plays in terrorist communications. The final sections assess the dynamic roles of government and the media in covering and combating terrorism—that is, how the government communicates the message it wants the public to receive; how the media get what they want from their coverage of terrorism; and how the government controls the content and mode of media reporting about terrorism.

The Media and the Terrorist: An Evolving Relationship

It is generally taken for granted that mass media outlets have profited from depictions of violence. Consumers seem to relish television violence, even as the same graphic scenes are shown over and over. In the media's depiction of terrorist violence, however, the relationship between the media and violence is especially stark. Terrorists want their violent acts broadcast as widely as possible. Indeed, the violence may sometimes appear to be simply the mechanism for communicating a message about the circumstances or the needs or demands of the terrorist group. Often, then, the "act of terrorism is in reality an act of communication." [2] The victims of the terrorist violence in these instances are instrumental; they are not normally targeted specifically. Indeed, the violence may be indiscriminate.

For example, in the mid-1990s the conflict between a newly independent Russia and an independence-minded group of separatists in the province of Chechnya demanded the attention of Russia and received the attention of the rest of the world only when Chechen leaders threatened to attack Russian nuclear power plants and bomb the Moscow subway. As the conflict dragged on, Chechen rebels utilized acts of terrorist violence to draw attention to their plight, and to their demands. Even though Russian television remained heavily subject to state influence and control in this early post-Soviet era, graphic car bombings, hijackings, and hostage takings by the most extreme Chechen separatists were routinely reported and their carnage broadcast on Russian television. Whatever the reason for the uncensored broadcasts, the Chechens had a stage, and they used it well.

Particularly in the West, the media cover every sensational event, whatever its origins or causes. Censorship is generally not practiced, and terrorist groups know that the more graphic and shocking their message, the more media attention it will receive. The press is free for a very good reason, of course— the people have a right to know what is going on around them. The extent to which the right to know might be conditioned by the government (or even by media owners) is a controversial issue, one considered later in this chapter in discussing the media's role in responding to a crisis.

In at least one respect, then, the media amplify the terrorists' acts. Because they reach a much larger audience than would have otherwise been possible, the media have been called "the terrorist's best friend." In more recent times, however, organized terrorist organizations have been capable of generating their own media message. Through the Internet, and using relatively inexpensive and portable video equipment and laptop computers, the multiplier effects of broadcast may be achieved even without coverage by the mainstream press. In 2006 al Qaeda leader Ayman al-Zawahiri maintained that "more than half [of] this battle is taking place in the battlefield of the media. . . . We are in a media battle in a race for the hearts and minds of [Muslims]." [3]

Hundreds of nontraditional media outlets are subject to control by terrorist organizations. But even without these new outlets, with the coming of age of CNN and other cable news networks worldwide, video reports are available all day every day within a few minutes of terrorism incidents anywhere. Indeed, there is such competition in the cable news industry that the media's rush to cover terrorism incidents and to determine the terrorists' objectives may place them in the role of unwitting accomplices.

Communication and thus the media's role in society changed over the course of the last two centuries. For most of modern history, terrorists could broadcast their message only by word of mouth, an exceedingly difficult task. When the established media came into existence, largely newspapers, most were controlled by the state or allied interests, and these mainstream media tended to criticize terrorists rather than promote or give additional voice to their message or demands.

In the nineteenth century, the invention of the rotary press revolutionized print communication. Not only could newspapers, pamphlets, and letters be mass-produced cheaply and relatively quickly, but the relatively low cost of at least obtaining the use of printing presses made it possible for terrorists to communicate with the masses. And many did. For example, Narodnaya Volya, or People's Will, a small group of Russians aligned against czarist rule, targeted selected individuals for assassination who were thought to be most responsible for the repressive policies of the Russian government. As part of their activities, and based on their alignment with other anarchist groups in Europe, Narodnaya Volya prepared and distributed widely the nineteenth-century equivalent of today's "how to" manuals for building bombs and carrying out assassinations.

In the twentieth century, television was an obvious boon to the media, and to the terrorists who could use the video image to convey a message. Yet it was the invention of remote television technology with the launching of the first television satellite in the 1960s that permitted the real-time broadcasting of terrorism incidents, and thus constituted the second media revolution most important to terrorists. Local stories could be transmitted to the television networks, where they could be used rapidly and with technical ease. Terrorists were quick to recognize the new worldwide audience for strikes against the United States and its interests, and the United States then became the target of choice for terrorists everywhere.

In addition to remote television technology, by the 1970s portable and lightweight video cameras had been developed, along with battery-powered video recorders and the time-base corrector, which converts video film into transmittable output that can be broadcast on television. These developments combined to make it possible for all facets of a broadcast to be brought directly from any remote location and then broadcast at a moment's notice to anywhere in the world. The 1972 Munich Summer Olympic Games are a first and memorable case in point. (See Case Study 9.1.)

CASE STUDY 9.1

Grabbing Attention: The 1972 Munich Summer Olympic Games and Black September

On September 5, 1972, eight terrorists claiming to be part of the Palestinian terrorist group the Black September Organization (BSO) kidnapped and murdered eleven Israeli athletes and coaches at the Summer Olympic Games in Munich, Germany. Munich was a watershed. Not only did it cement the strong antiterrorist alliance between the United States and Israel, but it also served to draw attention to the Palestinian cause, just as its planners and implementers had hoped. This event is known as well for launching a new era of security searches in airports and at public events, even in times of peace.

The BSO was named for the event Black September, in which King Hussein of Jordan expelled the Palestine Liberation Organization, an umbrella organization of groups advocating an independent Palestinian state, from his country in 1970. Established in 1971 to assassinate the king in retaliation for his policies, the BSO expanded its target from the Jordanian government to include Israeli and U.S. interests, as well as other Western targets. Recruits from groups such as the Popular Front for the Liberation of Palestine, a Marxist-Leninist group within the PLO, and the Syrian-controlled as-Sa'iqa also joined the BSO.

The 1972 Olympic Games were the first games to be held in Germany since the Nazis had hosted the games in 1936. Because the 1936 games were heavily propagandized by Adolf Hitler and because it wished to avoid appearing too militaristic, West German law enforcement did not have a strong presence at the 1972 games. Even though it was aware of the security situation, Israel did not provide additional security for its athletes.

After entering the Israeli athletes' quarters at 6 a.m. on September 5, the terrorist group killed two athletes and took nine hostages. The terrorists were identified as Palestinian refugees from camps in Lebanon, Syria, and Jordan. Two had previously worked in the Olympic Village, and the other six had arrived in Munich by train in the days prior to the attack. In exchange for the safe release of the nine hostages, the BSO demanded the release and safe passage to Egypt of 234 prisoners from Israeli prisons and two from German prisons by 9 a.m. that day. Although German negotiators were able to extend the deadline, the terrorists refused to back down on their demands, and Israel, led by Prime Minister Golda Meir, refused to deal with the terrorists. Israel did offer to send its special forces to assist German law enforcement, but the Germans declined. Germany was in a politically sensitive situation; the nation was shouldering the burden of having executed over six million Jews during World War II, and Jews the world over were carefully watching its response.

The standoff in the Olympic Village was filmed and broadcast on live television, which allowed the terrorists to watch the police as they prepared their rescue operations. The terrorists then foiled two attempts. Desperate to end the situation, the Germans agreed to supply the terrorists with two helicopters so that the group, hostages included, could go to an airport and take a plane to a new locale. The Germans had no intention, however, of permitting the terrorists to take the hostages out of the country, believing that such a move would ensure their deaths. The plan was to position six police officers, disguised as the flight crew, to overpower the terrorists who were to inspect the plane. The remaining terrorists were to be killed by five strategically placed snipers. However, the police officers, who had no prior training in hostage or terrorist situations, independently decided to abandon their mission. Chaos broke out when the terrorists discovered the set-up. As they sprinted back to the helicopter, the snipers shot and injured one of them, who escaped and was hunted down by dogs and killed in a gun battle later that night.

Because the Germans thought that there were only four or five hostage takers, they had positioned five snipers to shoot the terrorists as they walked from the helicopters to the plane. But most of the snipers were not trained as sharpshooters, and none of them was equipped with protective gear, two-way radios, or night-vision scopes. They were, however, able to kill the two terrorists who had been holding the helicopter pilots hostage. As the five remaining terrorists shot out all of the lights at the airport, the four helicopter pilots were able to flee to safety; the nine hostages, who were tied up, could not escape. Another stalemate ensued.

The stalemate was broken when four armored personnel carriers, summoned by the Germans only after their plan failed, pulled up and cornered the helicopters soon after midnight on September 6. The two terrorists in one helicopter responded by opening fire on the four hostages they were holding and releasing a hand grenade into the helicopter, thereby killing the hostages. Once they fled, both terrorists were shot and killed. There is some disagreement about what ensued in the second helicopter; the five remaining hostages were killed by gunfire either originating from one of the three remaining terrorists, or from misdirected sniper and police shots. These three terrorists were captured alive and imprisoned in Germany.

The international community was appalled by the Munich massacre, though King Hussein of Jordan was the only leader of an Arab nation to speak out publicly against it. Israeli prime minister Meir responded on September 9 by authorizing the bombing of Palestinian training camps in Lebanon and Syria. On October 29, other members of the BSO hijacked a German Lufthansa flight from Beirut to Ankara, Turkey. In response to the hijackers' demands, Germany quickly released the three imprisoned terrorists, who met with the hijackers in Libya, where they held an international press conference to relate their side of the story.

An estimated 500 million people watched these events unfold on their television screens. Without a doubt, the BSO succeeded in their goal of generating publicity for the Palestinian cause, and so, from the terrorists' point of view, the operation was enormously successful. And yet innocent Israeli athletes were brutally murdered. Is there any justification for targeting civilians with lethal force in order to gain publicity? At the same time, this case reveals the relative inexperience and lack of

> sophistication of the German government in anticipating and then responding to the terrorists' assault.　　　　　　　　　　　　■

Television news and its relationship to terrorism changed dramatically following these technological developments. For one thing, the technical capabilities led to an escalation of media competition to get the "scoop." Terrorists could only benefit from the rush to the scene. Instead of reflective editorial judgments about what to put on television or which interviews to air on the radio, crews on the ground rushed to obtain live footage and often bypassed much of what could pass for editorial control or discretion. This "breaking news" angle fed the terrorists' interests in keeping the story alive by producing supposedly new developments or new offers in hostage situations. In addition, "human interest" stories were dangled in front of live remote crews eager to continue their successful scoop, often with sound bites rather than thoughtfully presented news.

The Internet is almost surely the single most important development in communications for terrorists since the printing press. With the addition of the remote television technology, portable and inexpensive audio and video recording equipment, and wireless connections to the Internet, an organized terrorist group can either supplement or completely bypass the traditional media outlets in getting their messages out. The equipment needed for a satellite up-link can now easily be carried by one person in a suitcase or backpack.

Today, terrorists have their own television and radio stations. For terrorists, the advantages of these new communications capabilities are manifold. They are fast and can supply images in real time. The Internet is pervasive and inexpensive. Images and messages may be posted anonymously. Local issues can be made global issues with simply a few taps of a keyboard. Even more significantly, government control or censorship is entirely evaded, and the terrorists can control not only the content, but also the images and perception or context of their communications. The terrorists can repeat their desired communications as often and for as long as they like, and they can use these methods to seek financial contributions, new members, or simply sympathy for their causes or grievances. (See Box 9.1.)

The Internet "home" for a terrorist group is, of course, its Web site. Although fewer than half of designated foreign terrorist organizations had a Web site in 1998, all of them had developed such sites by the end of 1999. Some sites have grown increasingly sophisticated, and the most Web-advanced groups have multiple sites for a variety of purposes in different languages. By far, Islamic and Arab groups have the largest Web presence. Al Qaeda appeared on one Web site before September 11, 2001; now it has more than fifty. The sites are used by terrorist organizations to communicate, to propagandize, to recruit and raise funds, and sometimes to communicate opera-

Box 9.1 **The Zapatistas and the Internet**

The Zapatista National Liberation Army (EZLN), formed in 1994, is an insurgent group fighting the Mexican government. Operating from a remote rural location in the state of Chiapas in southern Mexico, the Zapatistas attacked the government in Chiapas, but they met a strong response from Mexican police and military forces. While holding their positions inside Chiapas, the Zapatistas and their charismatic leader, Subcomandante Marcos, developed a skillful set of external communications strategies that used the Internet to appeal to Mexican human rights and peace activists and to international human rights and other relief organizations to support their struggle against what they viewed as the repressive policies of the Mexican government. Reportedly, Marcos traveled with his laptop computer in a backpack, and he would simply plug in remotely and send electronic messages to supporters around the world. Eventually, the Zapatistas' strategy was successful in beating back the Mexican government's campaign against them, and by January 1995 the government had declared a truce in the struggle against the Zapatistas. (See Chapter 3.)

Although the Zapatistas were an insurgent group, not a terrorist organization, their successful use of the Internet served as a model for terrorists. Through the effective use of Internet strategies, the Zapatistas managed to so overwhelm the central government in Mexico City with e-mail and faxed communications that the government withdrew its operations against the insurgents.

- What accounts for the relative success of the Zapatistas' use of the Internet?
- What lessons should those who make policies to combat terrorism take away from the Zapatista example?

tional instructions to operatives through the technically sophisticated use of concealed messages in certain images, a technique called steganography. (See Box 9.4 later in this chapter.)

In this still-dynamic arena, a few developments stand out. First, the traditional news sources have been overtaken by other media. Most people in the world receive their news from nontraditional television or Internet sources. Second, the aspirations of those who foresaw the Internet as a bastion of enlightenment were in some ways overshadowed when it also became a distributor of crude conspiracy theories, graphic beheadings and other gratuitous violence, and false reporting. Third, the efforts of the United States and other Western nations to counter these images and messages have proven ineffectual, in part because they continue to rely on traditional media outlets and do not compete with or counter terrorist messages effectively in cyberspace.

Indeed, when the traditional media outlets compete with one another for market share and viewers, they may unwittingly become accomplices to terrorists in covering their violence. When the media devote considerable broadcast time or column space to violence, including terrorist violence, terrorists are able to spread their message of fear with ever greater success. One example is the September 11 attacks. Americans and many others around the world were glued to their televisions and computer screens on that day and for days and weeks afterward. On September 11, the CNN Web site was so swamped with visitors that its servers could not keep up with the demand—and crashed.

How Do Terrorists Employ Media Devices?

What do terrorists hope to achieve through the media? Most obviously, the media represent a source of free publicity. For some obscure terrorist groups, the publicity attracted by a terrorist act can give them instant recognition. For groups already recognized, publicity advances the cause of the organization, whatever it is. Sometimes, the publicity is for short-term needs, such as communicating demands in a hostage situation or a hijacking. Public awareness of tense standoffs between government and terrorists may fuel pressure on government decision makers to meet terrorist demands. At other times, the publicity serves longer-term objectives, helping to promote what the terrorists perceive as the virtue of their cause or the seriousness of their plight. (See Box 9.2.) Particularly for smaller or splinter terrorist groups, an act of violence, such as a bombing or assassination, might be carried out for the very purpose of establishing that group's separate identity or purpose.

At the same time that the media are providing a group of terrorists with publicity, the terrorist organization itself is currying the favor of the listening, reading, and viewing public toward its cause. For terrorist groups, then, part of the task is to have spokespersons who work hard to develop good relationships with reporters and broadcast crews. Meanwhile, the development and visibility of the best possible media image for the terrorist group are a central aspect of recruiting new adherents. If the message is out there and if it is clear and understandable, those who identify with the goals and means of the group are more likely to seek an affiliation with it.

At the core of the terrorists' objectives with the media is use of the media to spread fear, anxiety, and dread, along with sympathy, for their cause. In this respect, the media become an amplifier of what the terrorists want. If the amplification is especially successful, fear or panic among potentially affected people (by suicide bombings, for example) may cause economic loss and make people lose faith in their government and its ability to protect them. (See Case Study 9.2.) Governments may then overreact to the terrorist incident and impose restrictions on the people or take actions that further erode public trust in the government.

Box 9.2   **Al Qaeda and the Media**

Even before the spectacular media event it produced on September 11, 2001, al Qaeda had developed a sophisticated relationship with and presence in the media. In selecting targets for attack, al Qaeda has always held publicity to be a fundamental objective. The al Qaeda "Manual of the Afghan Jihad," which is used as a guide for training al Qaeda operatives, recommends targeting "sentimental landmarks" that "would generate intense publicity with minimal casualties." Examples listed include the Statue of Liberty, Big Ben in London, and the Eiffel Tower in Paris. The September 11 attack on the World Trade Center, timed as a two-stage strike, had the look of a "made for television" event. When the first plane struck one of the towers, it was attention grabbing, and so everyone was watching when the second plane struck.

When the traditional media do not meet the terrorists' demands for publicity, al Qaeda and other groups manufacture their own media. Al Qaeda has a committee for media affairs and highly sophisticated spokespersons, including an American convert to radical Islam who adds Western and popular culture language to some al Qaeda communications. (See Case Study 6.1 in Chapter 6.) When its varied Web sites are added to al Qaeda's capabilities to transmit video and audio messages through radio and television media sympathetic to its cause, the media presence of al Qaeda is significant and highly effective.

- What advantages do new media technologies and outlets provide for terrorist organizations?

- What are some effective ways in which governments might counter terrorists' use of the media?

CASE STUDY 9.2

Suicide Sympathy in Israel

On August 9, 2001, at about 2 p.m., twenty-two-year-old Izz al-Din Shuheil al-Masri, the son of a Palestinian restaurateur and wealthy landowner, entered the Sbarro Pizza restaurant in one of Jerusalem's busiest areas. Strapped to his body was a belt containing explosives, nails, and bolts. Detonating himself, the young man managed to kill another fifteen civilians and wound 130 more. Four of the victims were ten years old or younger, and another three were between the ages of fourteen and sixteen. After the bloody massacre, Palestinian students at An-Najah University in Nablus on the West Bank celebrated by opening an exhibition room that re-created the bombing with broken furniture covered in fake blood, body parts, and a portrait of al-Masri holding a Qur'an and a rifle.

In March 2002, in one of the many other suicide bombings that made up the so-called Passover massacre, a bomber entered the dining room of the Park Hotel in Netanya. The hotel was hosting a Passover dinner for 250 guests, mostly elderly Jews without families, some of them Holocaust survivors. Thirty of the dinner guests were killed, and another 140 were injured, many of them seriously.

Hamas was quick to claim responsibility for the bombing, and its spokespersons admitted that the attack was designed to derail a peace summit organized by the Saudi government. The Palestinian Authority had two reactions, one in English denouncing the attack and another in Arabic calling it *shahid*—a term used to glorify the bomber as a martyr. A year later, a memorial soccer championship was held in the bomber's name, and its seven top teams were named after bombers who "gave their lives to redeem the homeland." The bomber's brother distributed the trophies.

Suicide terrorism always draws widespread media attention because of the combination of indiscriminate violence and bloodshed. In this respect, it is an optimal form of violence from the terrorists' perspective. Since 1993, suicide bombing has been one of the most contentious issues of the Israeli-Palestinian conflict. It is difficult to imagine what could drive someone to kill himself or herself and seek, as is often the case, to kill as many others as possible. Yet for terrorist organizations suicide bombing makes perfect sense. For the most militant Palestinians, such as Hamas, the Palestinian Islamic Jihad, and the al-Aqsa Martyrs Brigade, suicide bombings have been an especially effective means of communicating terror. They are efficient; more people die in suicide attacks than other forms of terrorism. They are cheap, even when bombers' families are paid a sum after the fact. They are operationally simple—no escape plan is needed. And there is no shortage of volunteers; the potential pool of suicide bombers has grown to include men and women from different social strata.

Occasionally, the bombers strike at armed soldiers, but more often the targets have been random: commuters on a bus or the patrons of a café or nightclub. Suicide bombers typically kill without prejudice for their victims, whether children or the elderly. The Palestinian terrorist justification for this indiscriminateness is that all Israelis, no matter the age, are occupiers.

To a large extent, the more egregious the attack, the more sympathy is gained by the attacker. Although the initial reaction might be one of horror and outrage, almost inevitably the question eventually becomes one of motivation. As this question is asked, the focus is no longer on the victim but on the circumstances that led to the event. Suicide bombing has been employed in different countries, but it has been particularly effective in Israel and in raising sympathy for the Palestinian cause.

As demonstrated by the scenario described in the opening of this case study, in the Palestinian territories suicide bombers are often portrayed as heroes and martyrs of the resistance. Palestinian television stations air music videos glorifying the bombers and discuss the rewards that await the bombers for their acts. Saddam Hussein reportedly rewarded the families of bombers with checks for $25,000, further contributing to the hero status of the bombers. Some camps and programs in the Palestinian territories apparently teach young children to aspire to be martyrs, even to the extent of dressing the children in fake suicide belts.

Suicide bombing increased starkly after the 1993 Oslo accords, an agreement designed to bring about lasting peace between the two sides. Having already gained enough sympathy to bring about the accords, Palestinians designed the campaign of suicide bombing that followed to bring about even more sympathy and to improve their bargaining leverage with the Israeli government. In addition to their perceived effectiveness, suicide attacks surged during times when they were widely perceived as acceptable in the Palestinian community, when Muslim clerics offered religious justification for them, and when rivalries between Palestinian terrorist organizations spurred a macabre competition to see which group could mount the largest number of suicide bombings. Thus during the First Intifada, between 1987 and 1990, and the al-Aqsa or Second Intifada, beginning in 2000, the rate of suicide bombing increased, especially in 2002 during the peak of the Second Intifada.

In recent years, the bombings in Israel have almost completely stopped, in large measure because of the erection of a controversial security barrier by the Israeli government. Still, numerous attempted bombings are often deterred and go unnoticed by the international press, confirming that it is the destruction created by the bombings that generates the attention, not their prevention.

One of the most remarkable attributes of Palestinian suicide bombings is the extent to which they are accepted and even regarded positively by Palestinian communities. For the most militant Palestinian organizations, suicide bombing is viewed as one of the most effective instruments for waging war—that is, it is a way to win battles in an asymmetric war with a foe that is much stronger in conventional military terms. Although religious motivations are often important in recruiting bombers and in justifying the martyrdom for them, suicide terrorist attacks are predominantly a successful terrorist tactic in this long-term conflict in the Middle East. The attacks spread psychological fear, and they garner considerable attention.

Terrorists and the Internet

In a briefing given in late September 2001, the head of the U.S. National Infrastructure Protection Center told reporters that the September 11 hijackers had used the Internet, and "used it well." [4] After the attacks, federal agents issued subpoenas and warrants to just about every major Internet service provider. They found that the hijackers had booked online two to three weeks prior to the attacks at least nine of the airline tickets for the four doomed flights. After the arrest of al Qaeda leader Abu Zubaydah, reported mastermind of the September 11 attacks, a search of his computer revealed thousands of electronic messages that had been posted in a password-protected part of a Web site. Some messages included operational details of the attacks and were written and posted between May and September 9.

Why and how has the Internet been important to the terrorist phenomenon? Ironically, this network for communication that has enabled cultures to integrate their activities, showed a new way for businesses and consumers and governments to share information and ideas, and permitted the creation of a vast public forum around the globe has also provided terrorist organizations with a dazzling array of new tools to foment terrorism.

E-mail Communications and Web Site Networking

To preserve their anonymity, some of the hijackers used e-mail services that are largely anonymous, such as Hotmail, and created multiple temporary accounts. Some used public terminals, in libraries and elsewhere, and others used privately owned personal or laptop computers. The hijackers simply utilized code words to make their messages appear innocuous to eavesdroppers. For example, Mohammed Atta's apparent final message to his eighteen co-conspirators in the September 11 attacks read like this: "The semester begins in three more weeks. We've obtained 19 confirmations for studies in the faculty of law, the faculty of urban planning, the faculty of fine arts, and the faculty of engineering." [5]

Every terrorist organization today has an Internet presence through one or more Web sites, chat rooms, or online discussion groups of supporters and sympathizers. The Internet offers remarkable advantages to terrorist organizations, including:

- Rapid access to virtually real-time communication
- Pervasive and inexpensive access
- Enormous audiences across the globe
- Anonymity and ubiquity
- Access to a global audience for local issues
- Minimal regulation or opportunities for governmental control
- Capabilities to manage information
- Facilitation of recruitment and fund raising.

What does a terrorist Web site look like? Unsurprisingly, most sites provide a history of the organization and what it has accomplished. The sites typically include an elaborate narrative review of the organization's social and political background and points of view, its objectives in political or ideological terms, its critique of its enemies and oppressors, and sometimes even up-to-the-minute news. Most terrorist Web sites do not depict their violent activities, although they often include moral and political justifications for the use of violence in their background statements. In their recruitment and propaganda efforts on the Web, terrorist organizations feature catchy slogans and offer a range of items for sale, such as T-shirts and flags, audio and videotapes, all often in multiple languages.

How terrorist groups use the Internet has been the subject of intense study, especially since the revelations of the Web-based al Qaeda activities after September 11. Many groups use the Internet first and foremost to wage a form of psychological war, a sophisticated medium for the fear-based activities in which they engage outside the virtual world. For example, groups may disseminate threats to a government or a city or an event where many people will congregate. More graphic still, some groups do show images of violent acts, such as those featured after the beheading of American journalist Daniel Pearl in February 2002 in Pakistan. (See Box 9.3.)

That said, unleashed by the Internet from the editorial control and selection issues that limit their presence in the traditional media, terrorist Web sites can and do spread any message that portrays their organization and its cause in a favorable light. Often the sites will lament the fact that colleagues and sympathizers are the political prisoners of some supposedly repressive regime. The messages usually include a claim that violence is employed only because the group's enemies have left the organization no choice because of their acts of "murder" or the "slaughter" of innocents. Groups' enemies are regularly demonized on the groups' Web sites, and their violent acts are characterized as "brutality" and "inhumane," whereas the terrorists' message is generally one of moderation and nonviolence.

Apart from the organization-specific sites connected to organizations such as al Qaeda, Hamas, and Hezbollah, there are now many generic Muslim sites advocating radical jihadist terrorism. Some of these sites are run by groups that have more of a virtual than a real presence, although many are sophisticated and are linked with other such sites to provide attractive media emitting propaganda and radical Islamic ideology, recruitment and fund-raising activities, training manuals, and electronic bulletin boards and chat rooms.

The fund-raising and recruitment activities of terrorist organizations have been revolutionized by the Internet. Terrorist groups have always depended on donations to support their activities, and, before the Internet, many groups had effective informal networks through charitable organizations and other nongovernmental groups. Now, however, terrorists employ an integrated network of Web sites, chat rooms, and forums, all of which urge followers to sup-

Box 9.3   **Daniel Pearl**

Wall Street Journal reporter Daniel Pearl was kidnapped on January 23, 2002, while on his way to Karachi, Pakistan, for an interview with what he thought was a terrorist leader. A group calling itself the National Movement for the Restoration of Pakistani Sovereignty claimed responsibility for the kidnapping. Insisting that Pearl was a CIA agent, the group issued a series of demands to the United States, by e-mail, that included the freeing of Pakistani detainees and the release of a shipment of F-16 fighter jets from the United States to the Pakistani government. The messages included photos of Pearl with a gun being held at his head. The terrorists warned that, if their demands were not met, Pearl would be executed. Nine days later, Pearl was decapitated, and his body was found cut into ten pieces and buried in the outskirts of Karachi.

On February 21, 2002, a video entitled "The Slaughter of the Spy-Journalist, the Jew Daniel Pearl" began to appear on various jihadist Web sites. The video, which lasts over three minutes, shows, in this order, Pearl's mutilated body and then him stating his captors' demands, along with superimposed images of dead Muslims and of President George W. Bush shaking hands with Israeli prime minister Ariel Sharon. The video next shows Pearl with his throat slit and his beheading. These images are followed by those of the detainees at Guantánamo Bay, and then a scrolling of the terrorists' demands over an image of Pearl's disembodied head.

Four Pakistani suspects were arrested and charged with the kidnapping and murder of Pearl after the e-mail addresses of those who sent a ransom e-mail were traced by the FBI. All four were convicted, and the leader was executed. The Pakistani ringleader of the plot to kidnap Pearl stated during his trial that he wanted to "strike a blow at the United States and embarrass the Pakistani government."

- Does a grotesque spectacle like this one help or hinder the terrorists' cause?

- What advice might be offered to government officials on how to respond to this sort of atrocity and its glorification through media dissemination?

port the group. The sites include bank deposit information and some even permit credit card–based donations directly on the site.

Recruiting and Data-Sorting Techniques

Alternatively, terrorist fund raisers may use sophisticated data-sorting techniques to cull from Web sites and chat rooms lists of potential donors, who may then be solicited directly, often by e-mail. The solicitation will arrive from an organization other than the terrorist group, identified as supportive of the terrorists' aims but with no direct connection to the terrorists. In the United States, the government has frozen the assets of several "charities," such as the Holy Land Foundation for Relief and Development and the Benevolence International Foundation, on the grounds that they are raising funds to support terrorist organizations, in these instances Hamas and al Qaeda.

Even individuals in the United States who host a Web site to raise funds for terrorist organizations are vulnerable to criminal charges. A University of Idaho graduate student in computer science, studying in the United States on a visa from Saudi Arabia and sponsored by a National Security Agency scholarship, was charged with supporting terrorists when he created Web sites and an e-mail chat room that supported radical jihadist terrorists. After a jury trial, the student was acquitted of the charges, apparently because the jury did not believe that he knew that his technical support for the Web sites and chat room were being used to support terrorism.

Recruitment is also facilitated by the Internet. The Web site visuals and audio features themselves are attractive to many potential converts, but terrorist groups also often use more aggressive techniques, such as frequenting Internet cafés, roaming chat rooms, and scanning electronic bulletin boards and single-issue blogs or chat rooms in search of potential adherents. For example, terrorists launched an Internet-based drive after the U.S. invasion of Iraq in 2003 to recruit those willing to go to Iraq to fight against the U.S. and coalition forces. Web sites, chat rooms, and bulletin boards were blasted with anti-American propaganda, religious screeds, and instructions on how to get to Iraq, and how to fight once there.

Information and Resource Portal

An entirely different dimension of terrorists' use of the Internet relates to their operations and plans. The Internet is a library, one that has more than a billion pages of information, mostly available to anyone for free. Although governments, including the United States, have taken some countermeasures, terrorists can learn about targets on the Internet—such as the location and layout of airports and their infrastructure, the design and features of nuclear power plants, and the schematics of public buildings. Indeed, it is worth considering whether descriptions and discussions of the vulnerabilities of critical infrastructure facilities should be permitted on the Internet or in conventional media, even in a society that places a high value on free expression. Armed with the free software available on the Internet, terrorists can study structural weaknesses and predict the effects of an attack on other systems. Similarly, terrorist Web sites provide links to supposedly sensitive information inside the United States, such as the radio frequencies used by security agencies. And the sites provide tutorials on everything from building a bomb and spreading deadly viruses to hacking government computer databases and networks and sabotage techniques.

The Internet hosts a plethora of Web sites that provide how-to instructions for the aspiring terrorist. The most well known, "The Terrorist's Handbook" and "The Anarchist's Cookbook," contain guidance on how to construct chemical weapons and how to build an array of different kinds of bombs. The massive "Encyclopedia of Jihad," compiled by al Qaeda, offers detailed guidance on organizing a terrorist cell and carrying out an attack. The "Mujahideen Poisons Handbook," which can be found on Hamas Web sites, provides instructions for preparing poisons and poisonous gases. The guide "How to Make Bombs: Book Two" was read by a young man in London, who detonated nail bombs in scattered London locations in 1999, killing three people.

Organizing Platform

In operational terms, the Internet facilitates the decentralization of formerly more hierarchical terrorist organizations. For example, since the post–September 11 U.S. campaign against al Qaeda in Afghanistan and elsewhere, al Qaeda has apparently evolved into a series of quasi-independent cells that do not have a traditional hierarchy. Using the Internet, the cells can stay in touch with one another and with other terrorists or supporters, more or less in real time and with little cost. The Internet makes decentralization more attractive, and it overcomes one of decentralization's main disadvantages. By means of Internet communications, jihadist groups from across the Middle East, Asia, and Africa can exchange information and share ideas, such as how to carry out their attacks.

All of these operational activities carried out through the Internet can be disguised by steganography techniques in which messages may be hidden inside files. (See Box 9.4.) Or simple codes can be employed, such as those used by the September 11 hijackers.

What the Government Wants

When terrorism is in the news, particularly when a threatened or actual terrorist attack has occurred, the government wants to be part of the story. In some respects, government wants what the terrorists want—publicity. From the government's perspective, however, the media should report the story in ways designed to minimize the risk of danger or further harm to innocent people. The government also expects the media to reassure the public that the government has the terrorist situation under control in order to forestall panic or unrest. In addition, the government wants the media to present fully any public affairs messages it wishes to communicate, such as the closure of transit facilities or public buildings, restrictions on movement or a curfew, or where to go for medical screening or treatment.

Box 9.4   **Steganography**

This technique is used to conceal messages in certain images or other messages to prevent viewers from suspecting anything unusual. The message can be hidden in virtually any digital file. In this reconstruction of what such an image might look like, a secret message was "embedded" in a photograph of a tennis match. The "hidden" message is an actual plan for a thwarted 2002 terrorist attack on the Singapore subway system. Those who know how to look for the hidden message would be able to retrieve it from inside the digital file placed in the tennis ball in the middle of the racquet.

SOURCE: A similar recreation appears in Timothy L. Thomas, Information-Age "De-Terror-ence," *Military Review*, September–October 2001, http://leav-www.army.mil/fmso/documents/de-terror/de-terror.htm.

The Government and the Media: Competing Interests

Necessarily, the government's interests in how the media cover the terrorism story are at odds with what terrorists want. The government expects the media to emphasize the criminal nature of what terrorists do and, by its reporting, deny terrorists the platform they seek to spread their fear and communicate their grievances. Government officials also expect the media to provide them with information about the terrorist strike when the media have access in ways that the government does not, such as in a hostage situation. And the government expects the media not to present extensive coverage of the emotional reactions of families and friends of victims, particularly when a terrorist situation is ongoing and the portrayal of these losses could pressure the government to cave in to terrorist demands. In short, the government expects media cooperation in countering the terrorists. It also may ask the media not to reveal the operational details of an attack, hoping thereby to curtail copycat strikes, or it may even ask the media to misstate operational details or the effects of an attack in an effort to confuse the terrorists and to diffuse public anxiety and fear.

These competing interests for media attention and treatment are struggling with more than each other. The media interests may see these events as drama and spectacle, the kind of coverage that sells and builds market share. Before the September 11 attacks, many observers criticized the media for paying insufficient attention to the problems of terrorism. Even when the National Commission on Terrorism reported in 2000 that terrorists could be expected to strike the United States in lethal ways with highly sophisticated weapons and technology, the media barely covered the story.

September 11 changed the relative importance terrorism and its effects have received in the media. Yet the coverage was and is heavily tilted toward the graphic violence and its images, and does not tend to deal in depth with the policy and legal issues at the core of a range of anti- and counterterrorism approaches, strategies, and tactics undertaken by the United States and some other nations in response to the continuing terrorist threat.

Crisis Response and Public Affairs

From the government's perspective, one fortunate instinct of journalists in reporting on a crisis incident is that they tend to seek out those in authority to learn what is going on and to find out what the government wishes to communicate to the affected public. The government and its public affairs function thus have an initial opportunity in a terrorism crisis to shape public's perception of the crisis and of the government's response to it. One well-known example is New York City mayor Rudolph Giuliani and his actions after the September 11 attack on the World Trade Center. Whereas President George W. Bush followed his advisers' wishes and remained away from Washington temporarily before assuming a national role as manager of the crisis, Mayor Giuliani began immediately to use the media to communicate strong leadership and competent management of the crisis in New York.

About two hours after the first plane struck the North Tower of the World Trade Center, Giuliani spoke live on a New York cable television channel, urging people to remain calm and to evacuate lower Manhattan. He related that he had been in touch with the White House to ask for federal security around the city. He also reported regular communications with the governor. A few hours later, Giuliani gave a news conference, broadcast by local, national, and international media, in which he promised to save as many lives as possible and declared that New York and the United States were stronger and more resilient than any group of terrorists. In short, Giuliani was strong, tireless, compassionate, and grieving. He maintained his regular communication with the people through the media for months after September 11. Once he returned to the White House, President Bush similarly addressed the American people in more than fifty public statements designed to reassure people that the crisis was being managed effectively.

The government's public affairs function may also be viewed as a longer-term task, one that requires extensive public diplomacy to counter terrorism. So understood, public affairs is not so much about responding to the crisis of the moment as it is about seeking to educate publics in targeted areas about the harm that the terrorists cause and about the good that the countering government can do. (See Box 9.5.) These programs, such as those launched by the United States after September 11, utilize public presentations and television, radio, and print stories and interviews touting, for example, religious freedom and tolerance in the United States, or the beauty of Islam through the eyes of Americans. Ironically, these programs rely largely on the traditional media, which, in today's world, may be anachronistic or largely irrelevant in areas where the dominant media are cyber-based and not traditional broadcast or print outlets.

Box 9.5 **The Homeland Security Advisory System**

After being caught completely by surprise by the September 11 attacks, officials were determined to do a better job of threat detection and to connect the intelligence and threat warning dots in advance of an attack. And yet finding ways to gather and share terrorist threat information is one thing. Determining how and to what extent to communicate the threat information to the affected public is another. How should the government let the people know that they are at risk of being victims of a terrorist attack?

In the aftermath of September 11, warnings of additional attacks were legion. When the anthrax attacks followed in October and state and local officials' public affairs messages in Florida conflicted with the information being presented by federal officials (see Chapter 7), anxiety among the public and government officials only increased. Intelligence chatter suggested more attacks on bridges and tunnels and on airports and power plants, and some of these threats were communicated by officials, although not in any systematic or coordinated way. Those who might be affected by such attacks were not told what steps, if any, they should take to reduce their risk.

continues . . .

In March 2002, White House homeland security director Tom Ridge announced the implementation of a system to alert the public of potential threats. The Homeland Security Advisory System, a color-coded scale, consisted of five warnings:

- Red/severe—severe risk of terrorist attack
- Orange/high—high risk of terrorist attacks
- Yellow/elevated—significant risk of terrorist attacks
- Blue/guarded—general risk of terrorist attacks
- Green/low—low risk of terrorist attacks

Each color, in turn, called for different responses from affected citizens and government officials. Ridge launched the system on yellow alert, and the nation has largely been at the yellow or at an elevated level since. On only one occasion was the nation on red, or severe, alert. The alert level has never been lowered to either low or guarded.

In early 2003, Ridge, now secretary of homeland security, elevated the threat level from yellow to orange based on threats of an al Qaeda attack, particularly an attack with biological or chemical weapons. Secretary Ridge followed the threat level change with instructions to the public to have emergency kits on hand in case of a terrorist attack, including food, water, and plastic sheeting and duct tape to seal off rooms.

In response to Ridge's instructions, shoppers throughout the country made a run on duct tape and plastic sheeting, and some cities reported panicked consumers. At the same time, experts began to report that these precautions would have little if any effect, because such attacks could only be detected after they occur, and then the protections would be too late. Ridge was then forced to give a press conference in which he said, "God forbid, there may come a time when the local authorities or national authorities will tell you that you've got to use them. But for the time being, we just don't want folks sealing up their doors or sealing up their windows." Nevertheless, one man even went as far as wrapping his entire house in plastic.

An early major criticism of the system was that the threat warning was rarely accompanied by detailed information. Instead, vague generalities were broadcast that place citizens on edge, but gave them no opportunity to focus their diligence and thereby help to thwart a possible terrorist attack. Political pundits and comedians made quick work of the system with jokes about colors, high blood pressure, and unrequited anxiety.

The general warnings and sometimes questionable timing associated with the system have raised serious questions about how the president applies it. For example, in early August 2004, a major warning was issued for possible al Qaeda attacks on the financial institutions in New York City, Newark, and Washington. The administration claimed that the information leading to

continues . . .

the warning was fresh, obtained in the last two to three days, thereby giving a sense of immediacy to the threat. A day after issuing the warning, however, the administration clarified that, though recently obtained, most of the intelligence was years old.

Warnings are better understood when used in conjunction with some other tangible change in policies affecting Americans. The only time the system has been raised to a severe alert was in 2006 in response to the disruption of a reportedly major al Qaeda plot to blow up numerous planes en route from England to the United States. Accompanying the elevated threat level were heightened security measures at airports, such as banning all liquids and gels from flights and increased inspections. Although the new rules caused considerable inconvenience for travelers, the warning system helped to alert members of the public about the changed policies.

- How should the public warning system be reformed?

- Of course, terrorists do not advertise their attacks, and the information that U.S. intelligence and law enforcement agencies collect is usually fragmentary and does not include details about the nature and timing of any attack. Of what value is this incomplete information?

- If it is vague, what should citizens be expected to do with the information? If the government's advice appears ineffective or wrong, will it eventually be ignored in a situation in which the advice is most needed?

What the Media Want

Not surprisingly, the interests of the media in covering terrorism do not always coincide with what the government wants from the media. First, the media want the scoop, to be first with the story. They also want to be part of the drama by getting as close to the crisis as possible, especially during ongoing events such as hijacking incidents. At the same time, the media wish to remain independent and free to move about and to report as they wish, consistent with standards of professional journalism. Their independence thus ensures that their reporting will be accurate and fair, and newsworthy.

Part of being a professional journalist is protecting the public's "right to know"—that is, journalists feel obligated to present all aspects of the story that are newsworthy. At times, this obligation is understood by journalists to include reporting on the emotional reactions of the victims of terrorism and their families or friends and the views of witnesses or passersby. The "right to know" might also extend to reporting security information or other operational matters related to a terrorism incident that has been withheld by the government.

Within media outlets, some person or persons play a gatekeeping role, deciding what reporting is broadcast or aired or printed. These editors or decision makers are the ones to evaluate the newsworthiness of a terrorism story. For example, how long will it take for the story to unfold? Terrorism incidents that accommodate a news cycle are more likely to be covered or covered extensively. Bigger incidents receive more coverage, and those in which the purpose or message is clearest will be more likely to be covered more extensively. Obviously, surprise is a factor in newsworthiness, and the more unexpected the incident and the more it involves specific personal targets, the more coverage it will get. In addition, strikes against elite nations or persons will be covered more extensively than other attacks, and the more devastating the consequences of a strike, the more coverage it will receive. As is more fully shown by the example of the coverage of the bombing campaign of Ted Kaczynski (see Case Study 9.3), publishers and even the government may face difficult issues in deciding whether to publish the angry rant of a terrorist.

CASE STUDY 9.3

The Coverage Dilemma: The Unabomber

For more than a decade, Theodore (Ted) Kaczynski engaged in his own private campaign of terror, sending mail bombs to universities, the purveyors of technology, and airlines. Ultimately killing three and wounding twenty-three persons, Kaczynski—better known as the Unabomber—was driven by a hatred of modern technology, and eventually he chose to live beyond society's gaze in a secluded forest.

The young Kaczynski was a mathematical genius, excelling throughout his early school years and gaining admission to Harvard University at age sixteen. After graduating from Harvard in 1962, Kaczynski earned a Ph.D. in mathematics from the University of Michigan and began a research career there, specializing in highly advanced geometric function theory, understood by only a handful. He then became a member of the faculty at the University of California, Berkeley, but his aloof, awkward manner made him unpopular, and he resigned in 1969.

After he was rejected in his bid to immigrate to Canada, Kaczynski tried to reestablish contact with his family in Chicago. Kaczynski and his brother, David, purchased land near Lincoln, Montana, where Ted later built his remote cabin home. Until 1978, Kaczynski worked for David in a Chicago factory. But after David fired Ted for harassing a female employee, Ted moved to the remote cabin in Montana, where he lived alone on few means until his arrest in 1996.

In 1978 Kaczynski mailed his first bomb—to Prof. Buckley Crist at Northwestern University. Crist was suspicious of the package because the return address was his own, although he had not sent it. The campus policeman who opened the package was slightly injured by the explosion. The small bomb was poorly made of pieces of metal pipe and generally primitive in design. His later bombs would use batteries and heat-filament wire to ignite the explosives rather than rubber bands and matches.

After seriously injuring John Hauser, an air force captain and Berkeley graduate in 1985, Kaczynski achieved his first fatality in 1985. Hugh Scrutton, owner of a computer store in California, opened a package that was lying in his parking lot and was killed by a nail and splinter bomb. In 1987 Kaczynski launched a similar attack against a Salt Lake City computer store.

After a six-year break, Kaczynski resumed his attacks in 1993, targeting a professor of computer science, a geneticist, and an advertising executive. In 1995 Kaczynski began demanding through anonymous letters that his 35,000-word paper "Industrial Society and Its Future" (later known as the "Unabomber Manifesto") be published by a major newspaper. In return, he promised to stop his attacks. When his letters were ignored, Kaczynski sent another letter threatening to kill more people if it was not published. After much hand wringing and discussion inside government and the newspapers, Attorney General Janet Reno and the FBI recommended publication of Kaczynski's manifesto. The publishers justified their decision to do so by arguing that their actions might prevent another deadly bomb attack by an elusive terrorist. On September 19, 1995, both the *New York Times* and *Washington Post* published Kaczynski's manifesto in its entirety.

Although Kaczynski had not seen his younger brother, David, in a very long time, they occasionally corresponded by letter. When he read the manifesto, David grew suspicious, finding certain language strikingly reminiscent of his brother's. He and his wife spent days comparing letters they had received from Ted, and David struggled with the thought of turning in his brother. Eventually, David contacted the FBI, and told agents how to find Ted's secluded location in Montana, where in April 1996 he was arrested. Even though the FBI had promised David that his identity would remain secret, within hours of Kaczynski's arrest David's name and face were widely broadcast as the source leading to the arrest. Although many observers speculated that David turned his brother in for the reward money, David donated all of the reward proceeds to Ted's victims.

Kaczynski refused to enter an insanity plea in his defense. The examining physicians diagnosed Kaczynski with paranoid schizophrenia, but he was found to be competent to stand trial. After the government indicated that it would seek the death penalty, Kaczynski eventually agreed to plead guilty in return for a life sentence. Kaczynski is serving a life sentence without the possibility of parole in the Supermax prison in Florence, Colorado.

Meanwhile, *Time* magazine published a long interview with the Unabomber, in which interviewer Stephen J. Dubner reported Kaczynski's desire to create a movement of people who wish to get rid of technology. Had he been willing, Kaczynski could have had even more publicity. The leading broadcast news programs and several magazines sought interviews with the terrorist Kaczynski and essentially offered him a chance to explain his political agenda to a wider audience.

The decision to publish the Unabomber's manifesto was likely influenced heavily by the government, although the newspapers made the final decision. Bringing such influence to bear on a publication decision of the importance of this one is unusual, and it remains a controversial decision. As for Kaczynski's postconviction interview, any restraint on publication would be imposed by editors and publishers, not by the government.   ∎

Government Controls

The relationship between government and the media described so far in this chapter features cooperation and voluntary decisions about restraint or the direction of coverage. However, because of the differing interests of these two sides in this three-sided dynamic of government, terrorists, and the media, it should not be surprising that government has also sought to wield its authority to control how the media respond to terrorism. At one extreme, government might impose censorship, imposing prior controls on the content of what the media report. At what might be viewed as the least intrusive end, government might simply request continued voluntary cooperation with its requests in terrorism situations.

One of the strongest disincentives to the imposition of controls on the media, at least in societies in which the press is free, is that the controls might give terrorists the very kind of success that they seek, undermining liberties in a free society. The media also can glorify terrorism and terrorists and make media heroes out of those who bomb and kill and maim. Reporters' interviews with Timothy McVeigh and the Unabomber, noted earlier in this chapter, illustrate this phenomenon.

However, special circumstances can lead to special rules. Investigation of the September 11 attacks began before the last airliner crashed in Pennsylvania. Beyond simply attempting to find the perpetrators and their supporters, the government sought to anticipate the next attacks, and thus it waged a campaign to arrest and then detain anyone suspected of having ties to terrorist activities. Within weeks, the media reported that more than 1,100 persons had been or were being detained by law enforcement authorities. About 550 of these were detained by immigration officials for suspected immigration violations.

Eventually, a directive from U.S. immigration judge Michael Creppy outlined procedures that should be followed in "special interest" deportation hearings—that is, those for persons determined by the attorney general as possibly having connections to or knowledge of the September 11 attacks. Among the security procedures approved by Judge Creppy was closing the hearings to the public and to the press.

When family members, members of Congress, and members of the press challenged these secrecy rules, two courts came to different conclusions about their legality. In a case brought in New Jersey by a consortium of media groups, the court upheld the Creppy directive. The court conceded that the U.S. Constitution has long been interpreted to provide a right of access for the public and the press to criminal trials. However, reasoned the court, the same principle does not extend to executive branch proceedings because of the sensitive proceedings that may attend many hearings before administrative agencies.

Deportation hearings have frequently been closed to the public, the court stated, and in this situation, even if there were some benefit to opening the proceedings to the press, the risks in doing so outweighed the benefits. The court noted that public deportation hearings could reveal the sources and methods used by the government to locate and detain the detainee. When pressed to show how such information could be practically useful to terrorists, the court referred to the declaration of an FBI assistant director for counterterrorism, who asserted that such information, when assimilated with other information from other cases or sources, would allow the terrorist organization to build a picture of an investigation. The FBI official likened the investigative strategy to the creation of a mosaic. Even though isolated pieces and facts may seem unimportant, even to an immigration judge, the entire pattern of the mosaic, when assembled by the terrorists, could reveal important and sensitive security information.

The other case was filed in Detroit. There the court found that deportation hearings "walk, talk, and squawk" very much like a judicial proceeding and, as such, presumptively should remain open. The court opined that public and press access acts as a check on the executive by ensuring that proceedings are conducted fairly and properly. In addition, after the massive investigation that followed the September 11 attacks, having open deportation hearings would, said the court, serve a therapeutic purpose as outlets for community concern, hostility, and other emotions. In part, the court found that openness enhances the perception that the proceedings will be fair and honest. Finally, open proceedings help to inform the public about the affairs of government. According to the court, "[D]emocracies die behind closed doors. . . . When government begins closing doors, it selectively controls information rightfully belonging to the people. Selective information is misinformation." [6] These two opinions raise the question of which court got it right, and whether the interests of the press and of the public are separable in this setting.

In 1988, after a lengthy and debilitating struggle against the militant terrorism of the Irish Republic Army in Northern Ireland, Britain imposed a ban on television and radio broadcasts of interviews or any direct statements by members of the IRA and other organizations found to be collaborating in IRA terrorist activities. Critics contended that the ban did nothing to stop the terrorist bombing campaign and that it had the ironic effect of disabling the diplomatic efforts of the legal political party, Sinn Fein.

Conclusion

The relationship among the media, terrorists, and government is dynamic and complex. Now that the traditional news media have been overtaken by the Internet and nontraditional television and radio stations in terms of where the populations vulnerable to terrorism receive their news and entertainment, the relationship has become more challenging. The Internet, which was in its earliest days a beacon of enlightenment and education, now appears to many analysts to be the most effective vehicle for spreading terrorist propaganda and conspiracy theories. As demonstrated in this chapter, terrorists cannot survive without the attention of the media, and, for various reasons, the media are likely to provide it. As for the government and the media, what the government wants from the media and what the media are willing to provide are sometimes widely divergent, and the differences often play to the strength of terrorist organizations. In the end, governments that seek to counter terrorism may be learning that they need to counter the space most effectively occupied by the terrorists—cyberspace.

FOR FURTHER READING

Hoffman, Bruce. *Inside Terrorism*. Exp. and rev. ed. New York: Columbia University Press, 2006.
Nacos, Brigitte L. *Mass-Mediated Terrorism: The Central Role of the Media in Terrorism and Counterterrorism*. Lanham, Md.: Rowman and Littlefield, 2002.
Noll, A. Michael, ed. *Crisis Communications: Lessons from September 11*. Lanham, Md.: Rowman and Littlefield, 2003.
Paletz, David L., and Alex P. Schmid, eds. *Terrorism and the Media*. Thousand Oaks, Calif.: Sage Publications, 1992.

Chapter 10 Military Responses to Terrorism

On January 7, 2007, a U.S. Air Force AT-130 gunship launched an air strike on a convoy traveling near a remote coastal village in Somalia close to its border with Kenya. Although accounts varied, the attack appeared to have killed about twenty people in a convoy of fighters trying to escape from Ethiopian forces. The targets of the strike were said to be several senior al Qaeda officials who had been living in Somalia under the protection of Islamicist groups that had taken control of the country in 2006. Apparently, the al Qaeda leaders fled to the isolated fishing village after being driven out of Somalia's capital, Mogadishu, in December 2006 by Ethiopian military forces backing the transitional government. The strike was made possible after the CIA began making cash payments to a group of Somali warlords in return for their help in locating members of the al Qaeda cell. The CIA and military planners had found such targeted strikes hard to carry out against terrorists because of the difficulty in tracking their precise location and then delivering military force to it. On this occasion, however, they succeeded.

A Pentagon spokesman justified this attack and a follow-up attack a few weeks later by declaring, "We're going to go after al Qaeda and the global war on terror, wherever it takes us." [1] The targets were suspected of masterminding terrorist attacks in East Africa, including attacks on the U.S. embassies in Kenya and Tanzania in 1998 and an attack on an Israeli-owned hotel in Kenya in 2002. And yet after the air strikes, local residents claimed that dozens of civilians had been killed in the strikes, and anti-American anger spread throughout Mogadishu. Some of the locals claimed that the United States was seeking revenge for the infamous "Black Hawk Down" episode in 1993, when Somali warlord gunmen killed eighteen U.S. soldiers and downed two helicopters during a battle in Mogadishu.

The U.S. actions in Somalia in 2007 were part of a more aggressive effort by the Pentagon to confront terrorism in Africa. Apart from the continuing presence of al Qaeda cells in the Horn of Africa region, officials fear that an Algerian Islamic terrorist organization is working to unite radical Islamic groups across North Africa to wage jihad against Europe and the United States. The current U.S. plan to counter the threat of terrorism in Africa has included establishing a military base in Djibouti and dispatching an aircraft carrier to the Red Sea from the Persian Gulf to support intelligence-gathering efforts. The January 2007 U.S. attacks in Somalia, which were coordinated with Ethiopian forces on the ground, were based on shared intelligence. In the end, however, U.S. officials conceded that none of the targeted individuals was likely hit in the initial strike and that it remains unclear whether al Qaeda operatives were among those killed in the follow-up attack.

Force is an important and widely used tool in confronting the challenge of terrorism. But conventional military force is a blunt instrument that can easily provoke negative reactions, even if military means succeed in quelling terrorists. Military force can be employed in a variety of ways. For one thing, the military can be used to defend against prospective attacks, at home or abroad. Indeed, the U.S. military has made homeland defense a priority since the attacks of September 11, 2001, even establishing a new "Northern Command" to oversee the defense of the continental United States. In addition, military personnel may provide civilian authorities with support in the event of a terrorist attack.

At home or abroad, the use of military force to combat terrorism is complicated by the secretive nature of terrorist organizations and their goal of surprise. Conventional military operations to combat an enemy are a fixture of U.S. and other Western military training and orientation. But terrorist attacks are anything but conventional. Terrorists do not wear uniforms or the insignia of any state, nor do they follow the laws of armed conflict in waging their attacks. In fact, they usually attack without warning or attribution. They may infiltrate civilian populations and take up positions inside civilian homes. Likewise, they may attack innocent civilians, not military installations. A military counterattack may not be able to distinguish terrorists from civilians, and military means may not always be effective in thwarting the ability of the terrorists to mount the next attack.

In theory, military force can be used to deter terrorist attacks, either by making the costs too high for the terrorist group to absorb or by preempting its capacity to strike. The central issue, as noted in Chapter 1, is understanding the conditions under which terrorists are likely to be deterred from acting.

If terrorists have identifiable bases or other physical or economic assets that can be threatened, then they could be deterred by military means. Otherwise, they are more difficult to deter, especially if they hide among civilian populations. Deterring suicide attacks is virtually impossible, because threats are likely to be ineffective against terrorists who are already committed to dying while carrying out their attacks and who generally are undetectable until they detonate their deadly charge.

Military force can also be used in retaliation against a terrorist attack. Retaliatory attacks are often justified as self-defense, because the retaliating state may use force to protect against further attacks by the same group. The U.S. overthrow of the Taliban regime in Afghanistan after the September 11, 2001, terrorist attacks was justified as self-defense in order to eliminate the threat of further attacks by al Qaeda, particularly after the Taliban refused to give up Osama bin Laden and his compatriots, whom they were known to be sheltering. It was also a retaliatory response to the September 11 attacks. Using military force in self-defense against terrorists is complicated by the fact that such attacks may violate the sovereignty of the state in which the terrorists are attacked. Although Article 51 of the UN Charter allows states the use of military force in self-defense, unless a state is in some way supporting the terrorist group, such an attack may be condemned by the international community.

Another military response to terrorism is the preemptive or preventive use of force. The United States justified its invasion of Iraq as, in part, a measure needed to prevent Saddam Hussein from using WMD or giving them to terrorists. Preemptive attacks to quell terrorism have been justified as self-defense, and the U.S. government argued in its 2002 National Security Strategy of the United States that preemptive war may be necessary in the war on terrorism. There are some suggestions that this prospect has support in the international community. For example, NATO's strategy for addressing terrorism recognizes the possibility that preventive action may be necessary to address the threat posed by terrorism.

Regardless of the form it might take, using force in response to terrorism raises a range of policy, strategic, and tactical questions. To what extent, if any, does the use of military force to combat terrorism actually deter terrorists? How do states ensure that the use of force to combat terrorism is proportional to the attack and that such force does not harm civilians? In short, is the use of the military option to counter terrorism effective? Some countries such as the United States have responded to the upsurge in terrorist attacks by taking steps domestically to ensure their abilities to respond militarily should terrorist attacks occur.

Today, military operations to confront terrorism tend to fall into four categories: major military operations, special operations, targeted killings, and civil affairs operations in communities that might be potential havens for terrorists. This chapter begins by examining how states attempted to respond to terrorism militarily before the September 11 attacks. It will then review current military efforts, looking at domestic changes in the United States and the ways in which military forces have been deployed internationally to confront terrorism. The final section assesses the policy and strategy issues facing leaders who are considering the use of force to respond to terrorism.

Terrorism and Military Force before the September 11 Attacks

The use of military force in response to terrorism has long been an option for policy makers, although it has usually been viewed as an option of last resort. One example is from the earliest days of the Republic. From 1801 to 1804, Barbary pirates were attacking U.S. trade vessels in the Mediterranean. President Thomas Jefferson ordered the U.S. Navy to act to quell these attacks, and a marine expedition landed in Libya with orders to capture or kill the pirates. Similar short-term military operations were mounted to combat Mexican bandit Pancho Villa after his attack on a town in New Mexico in 1916, to capture Nicaraguan bandit leader Augusto César Sandino between 1928 and 1932, and to assist the Bolivian army in its campaign to capture or kill Ernesto "Che" Guevara in 1967.

As terrorist incidents grew in number in the twentieth century, more states responded to attacks with military means. Particularly after the Germans failed to rescue the Israeli athletes kidnapped by the Palestinian militant group Black September at the Olympic Summer Games in Munich in 1972 (see Chapter 9), some European states developed special commando forces in efforts to respond to airline hijackings or hostage taking. During this same period, Israel conducted military missions to stop cross-border incursions, and Britain deployed military troops in Northern Ireland to quell terrorist attacks there.

In addition to direct military operations against groups in neighboring states, after 1968 Israel also had to respond to a rise in airline hijackings targeting Israeli citizens. The Palestine Liberation Organization resorted to the hijackings, which garnered intense international media interest, to focus attention on the Palestinian cause and to free jailed Palestinians. Israel responded militarily to some of these attempts. Its most famous military action was a raid on Entebbe's airport in Uganda on the night of July 3, 1976. An Air France plane en route to Israel had been hijacked and diverted to Uganda, and the hijackers threatened to begin killing their more than one hundred hostages if Israel did not release forty Palestinian prisoners. They also demanded that additional prisoners be released by France, Germany, Kenya, and Switzerland. In their raid on the airport in Entebbe, Israeli special forces managed to free a hundred hostages and fly them safely out of the country. During the raid, two hostages died, along with forty-five Ugandan soldiers, all six hijackers, and one Israeli commando. Although Israel's actions provoked some criticism for violating Uganda's sovereignty, it was muted by Ugandan president Idi Amin's evident support for the hijackers. The raid dramatically illustrated the prowess of Israel's special forces and its determination to respond by any means necessary to terrorist acts.

The rash of hostage-taking incidents in Europe in the 1970s also pushed several European governments, including Germany, Britain, and France, to create special antiterrorist forces similar to Israel's to respond to these attacks. A German antiterrorist unit successfully rescued passengers flown to Somalia on a hijacked plane in 1977, and the British Special Air Services Regiment conducted a raid to rescue hostages held in the Iranian embassy in London in 1980, saving most of them.

Britain also confronted a protracted terrorist threat generated by the ongoing tensions in Northern Ireland between Protestant "unionist" forces, who desired to preserve the region's ties with Britain, and Catholic "republican" forces, who sought to unify Ireland. Although the Irish Republican Army was the best-known group in this struggle, groups on both sides resorted to terrorist acts, both in Northern Ireland and in Britain. The British army was deployed in Northern Ireland for over thirty-five years, beginning in 1969, to support the Northern Ireland Royal Ulster Constabulary police force in combating terrorism. It conducted routine patrols, guarded the province's border with Ireland, and provided specialized services such as bomb disposal. British military intelligence also conducted extensive operations in Northern Ireland in an effort to prevent terrorist attacks in both Northern Ireland and England by the IRA. Over seven hundred British soldiers were killed in terrorist attacks between 1969 and 2005. The size of Britain's military presence was reduced gradually after the Good Friday Accords of 1998 that led to a political solution to the conflict in Ireland, and the mission formally ended on August 1, 2007.

Iranian Hostage Crisis

Although U.S. citizens and interests were the targets of many attacks during the 1980s and 1990s, the United States made few attempts prior to the attacks of September 11 to respond to terrorist attacks with force. However, after the Carter administration failed in its attempt to rescue the U.S. diplomats taken hostage in November 1979 by Iranian militants in Tehran, the United States began to invest more systematically and strategically in a military capacity to respond to terrorism. Altogether, fifty-two U.S. embassy personnel were held hostage for 444 days. (See Case Study 10.1.)

In response to the military coordination problems that were at least partly responsible for the failed attempt to rescue the hostages in Tehran, the U.S. military developed what eventually became the Joint Special Operations Command (JSOC). Now part of the U.S. Special Operations Command (SOCOM), JSOC remains an important component of the U.S. military's capability to combat terrorism. The 1985 Palestinian terrorist attack on the Italian ocean liner *Achille Lauro* also served, in part, as the impetus for the establishment of maritime special forces capabilities in the U.S. Navy SEALS.

CASE STUDY 10.1

The Iranian Hostage Rescue Operation

On November 4, 1979, Iranian militants stormed the U.S. embassy in Tehran and took the Americans working there hostage. Within the first several weeks of the hostage seizure, diplomatic initiatives to gain the release of the hostages failed. While the Carter administration continued to explore diplomatic options, national security adviser Zbigniew Brzezinski, within days of November 4, began to consider military options, and planning continued until the mission was attempted. The chairman of the Joint Chiefs of Staff developed a plan for a rescue mission that involved a series of steps that were discrete, reversible, and yet complex and difficult.

The plan called for troops and materials to be pre-positioned in the Middle East and the Indian Ocean under cover of routinely scheduled activities. The actual rescue was to unfold in this way. Two nights before the rescue, eight helicopters and eight C-130 aircraft were to fly below Iranian radar coverage across five hundred miles of desert to a rendezvous inside Iran ("Desert One") for refueling and reloading of the helicopters. The helicopters would then proceed to a second mountain rendezvous, where they would remain concealed throughout the following day. On the second night, the rescue team would proceed to Tehran by local vehicles to undertake the actual rescue. Once the rescue was executed, the helicopters would reappear on the outskirts of Tehran just long enough to pick up the team and the hostages, and then fly to an abandoned airfield near Tehran to rendezvous again with the transport aircraft. Finally, the helicopters abandoned, the group would fly to safety under an umbrella of heavy U.S. air power.

Secretary of State Cyrus Vance opposed any military initiative, and he argued strenuously against the plan outlined by the Joint Chiefs. Vance reasoned that "the hostages would be freed only when [Ayatollah Ruhollah Mussaui] Khomeini was certain that all the institutions of the Islamic republic were in place. . . . The only realistic course was to keep up the pressure on Iran while the U.S. waited for Khomeini to determine that the revolution had accomplished its purpose, and that the hostages were of no further value."

President Jimmy Carter did not immediately approve the mission, preferring instead to exhaust all peaceful diplomatic means for obtaining release of the hostages. But U.S. allies refused to adopt meaningful sanctions against Iran, and by April 1980 hopes of a negotiated release had dimmed even further. On April 9, national security adviser Brzezinski told the president that, in his view, "a carefully planned and boldly executed rescue operation represents the only realistic prospect that the hostages—any of them—will be freed in the foreseeable future. . . . It is time for us to act now."

On April 11, during a National Security Council meeting from which Secretary of State Vance was absent, President Carter decided that a rescue mission should be launched on April 24. On his return, Vance objected vociferously and was permitted to present his case at another NSC meeting. Intelligence reports, he noted, indicated that the hostages were in no physical danger and in satisfactory health, and any rescue was almost certain to lead to deaths among them, as well as among the rescuers and the Iranians. He also predicted that the Iranians might react by taking American journalists hostage and turning toward the Soviet Union, and he reaffirmed his belief that time would lead to the release of the hostages. No one else supported his position, however, and the president confirmed his decision to go ahead with the rescue. On April 17,

Vance advised President Carter that he would have to resign if the mission went forward. He later did resign after the mission was made public.

On the night of April 23, President Carter met with Senate majority leader Robert Byrd to develop a short list for congressional notification concerning "possible military action." He did not inform Byrd that the rescue mission would be launched just hours later, at 10:30 a.m. EST on April 24, 1980.

The mission ran into difficulty almost immediately when several of the helicopters failed. Advised that there were too few helicopters to carry out the remainder of the mission, President Carter ordered it aborted. In the ensuing rush to evacuate "Desert One," a helicopter and a C-130 transport collided, killing eight persons; the dead were abandoned along with their equipment and sundry documents bearing on the mission. Only after the mission was aborted were other congressional leaders informed by telephone late in the evening of April 24 and during the following morning.

With the start of the Iran-Iraq War and the election of Ronald Reagan as president in the fall of 1980, the Iranians became more open to diplomatic negotiations. They wanted U.S.-imposed sanctions lifted so they could get needed military parts, and they feared that Reagan would take a harder line. Eventually, then, the United States and Iran negotiated the hostages' release on January 20, 1981, the day Ronald Reagan took the oath of office.

Several lessons can be drawn from this failed mission. One is the importance of consultation and reasoned debate of military options. Vance and Brzezinski did not get along, and their dislike for one another affected the Carter administration's ability to develop a consensus on policy. Moreover, during crises political leaders may "hunker down," as Carter did, whereas greater consultation with Congress or allies might have provided useful insights. Finally, great powers have more to lose than their smaller opponents in attempting to use force, and the failure of the military's ambitious plan made the "superpower" look weak and inept, while it handed the Iranian regime an unearned "victory."

SOURCES: This account is based on Gary Sick, *All Fall Down* (New York: Random House, 1985); Warren Christopher et al., *American Hostages in Iran: The Conduct of a Crisis* (New York: Council on Foreign Relations, 1985); Cyrus R. Vance, *Hard Choices* (New York: Simon and Schuster, 1983).

Military Retaliation for Terrorist Attacks

The United States has seldom used force in response to terrorist attacks. Ronald Reagan authorized the use of such force only once. On April 5, 1986, a Berlin nightclub frequented by American soldiers was bombed in an attack that was attributed to Libyan agents. In response, on April 15 the United States attacked several facilities believed to be integral to Libya's support for terrorists. (See Case Study 10.2.)

CASE STUDY 10.2

Raid on Libya

On April 5, 1986, a terrorist bomb exploded in a Berlin nightclub, killing one U.S. soldier and injuring sixty-four other Americans. On April 7, *CBS Evening News* reported administration officials as saying that there was hard evidence linking the Libyan People's Bureau in East Berlin to the bombing. These officials also acknowledged that detailed military contingency plans for retaliation were targeting five sites in Libya. The *Wall Street Journal* confirmed this account the next day, specifying the targets, and *CBS Evening News* reported that the administration had reached a consensus to retaliate. *ABC World News* made the same report the following day, and noted that "if it comes to that, seldom will U.S. military action have been so widely and publicly advertised in advance." [a]

President Ronald Reagan actually approved a raid on Libya after a National Security Council meeting on April 9. NSC officials then contacted their counterparts in the British cabinet to obtain approval for the use of Royal Air Force bases to launch the raid and to give specific information about the bombers that were to be used and the intended targets. The media reported on April 10 that President Reagan had approved a raid, and that the target options were all keyed to four missile batteries on the Libyan coast. *NBC Nightly News* also noted that aircraft carriers would be involved, as well as F-111s based in Britain.

On April 11, Oregon senator Mark Hatfield and other members of Congress telegraphed President Reagan, expressing the view that even though there had been ample time for a full and thorough consultation with Congress about the retaliatory raid on Libya, no consultation had been made. Because the Constitution lays out Congress's role in making war, Senator Hatfield argued that the president has a constitutional responsibility to consult with Congress in advance of any action.

Unknown to the press, on April 11, the United States asked France for permission to fly over its territory to reach the Libyan targets and was turned down. On April 12, the Italian premier told reporters that he did not believe that the retaliation would take place before Monday, April 14. Administration officials confirmed to the press that diplomatic lobbying would be complete by that date.

On April 13, an issue of *Newsweek* bearing the cover date April 21 carried a detailed and remarkably accurate analysis of the expected retaliatory raid based on accumulated leaks from administration officials.[b] It reported that Pentagon officials were determined to stick to the criterion of "proportionality" by limiting the attack to coastal military targets, but that they had been ordered back to the drawing board to consider airfield targets as well.

At 12:13 p.m. EST on April 14, eighteen U.S. F-111s departed from Britain. Four hours later, President Reagan contacted congressional leaders for the first time, advising them in a White House meeting that the raid was in progress. At 7 p.m. EST, U.S. planes dropped their bombs on suspected Libyan coastal targets, terrorist training facilities, and the residential compound of Libyan leader Muammar al-Qaddafi. Two hours later, President Reagan gave a nationally televised address about the raid. The United States argued that the raid had damaged Libya's ability to support terrorism, as intended, and stressed its effort to make the response proportional to the Berlin attack. The retaliatory raid was, however, generally condemned by the international community.

The fortuity of the clear intelligence connecting the Berlin bombing to Libya greatly supported the case for retaliation in this instance. Absent the clear Libyan "fingerprints," it is less clear what factors U.S. leaders would consider before deciding to respond with force.

---

[a] David Turndorf, "Note: The U.S. Raid on Libya: A Forceful Response to Terrorism," *Brooklyn Journal of International Law* 187 (1988): 144.
[b] "Targeting a 'Mad Dog,' " *Newsweek,* April 21, 1986, 20.

Reagan's successor in office, George H. W. Bush, did not resort to force against terrorists, and President Bill Clinton authorized force in response to terrorist attacks only twice. In June 1993, Clinton ordered the bombing of the headquarters of the Iraqi Intelligence Service in Baghdad in retaliation for an attempt to assassinate former president Bush during his visit to Kuwait earlier that year. In August 1998, the Clinton administration ordered cruise missile attacks on a suspected chemical weapons factory in Sudan believed to be owned by Osama bin Laden and on several al Qaeda training camps in Afghanistan. (See Case Study 10.3.) The attacks were in response to the August 7 al Qaeda attacks on U.S. embassies in Kenya and Tanzania that killed 301 people and wounded more than 5,000 others.

CASE STUDY 10.3

The 1998 Attacks on Sudan and Afghanistan

On August 7, 1998, truck bombs exploded at the U.S. embassies in Kenya and Tanzania, killing over three hundred people, including twelve Americans. Two weeks later, on August 20, the United States launched seventy-nine Tomahawk cruise missiles against terrorist training camps in Afghanistan and a Sudanese pharmaceutical plant that the United States alleged to be a chemical weapons facility. President Bill Clinton explained that he ordered the attacks because "we have convincing evidence that [Islamic terrorist groups, including that of Osama bin Laden] . . . played the key role in the Embassy bombings . . . and compelling information that they were planning additional terrorist attacks against our citizens." He had notified certain congressional leaders on August 19 that the attacks were coming, and he sent Congress a letter the day after the attacks reporting that "the United States acted in exercise of our inherent right of self-defense consistent with Article 51 of the United Nations Charter. These strikes were a necessary and proportionate response to the imminent threat of further terrorist attacks against U.S. personnel and facilities. These strikes were intended to prevent and deter additional attacks by a clearly identified terrorist threat."

Reports on the results of the attacks varied. A spokesman for bin Laden reported that twenty-eight people were killed in the attacks on the camps. Sudan reported that ten were injured in the attack on the pharmaceutical plant. The U.S. government subsequently asserted that a soil sample from the plant revealed the presence of a precursor chemical for the production of VX, a nerve agent. Other evidence suggested, however, that the plant was an unguarded pharmaceutical producer, which had often been visited by foreign dignitaries, and that the soil sample contained a chemical structure resembling an agricultural insecticide.

The U.S. attacks in Afghanistan and Sudan point to the difficulties of responding militarily against terrorist attacks. Terrorist groups can easily relocate, and they have the advantage of knowing about planned attacks in advance. Moreover, finding targets that reliably can be linked to terrorist groups or leaders is troublesome, particularly when these potential targets are thousands of miles from the United States in hostile countries.

SOURCES: Except as otherwise noted, background on the 1998 cruise missile attacks on Sudan and Afghanistan is drawn from Sara N. Scheideman, "Standards of Proof in Forcible Responses to Terrorism," *Syracuse Law Review* 50 (2000): 249; Sean Murphy, "Contemporary Practice of the United States Relating to International Law," *American Journal of International Law* 93 (1999): 161–166; Jules Lobel, "The Use of Force to Respond to Terrorist Attacks: The Bombing of Sudan and Afghanistan," *Yale Journal of International Law* 24 (1999): 537; Ruth Wedgwood, "Responding to Terrorism: The Strikes against bin Laden," *Yale Journal of International Law* 24 (1999): 559; William C. Banks, "To 'Prevent and Deter' International Terrorism: The U.S. Response to the Kenya and Tanzania Embassy Bombings," *National Security Studies*, CS 0699-12, 1999.

The U.S. use of force in these instances to combat terrorism was viewed by some observers as retaliatory, although both administrations argued that their military attacks on Libya, Sudan, and Afghanistan were intended to "prevent and deter" a potential future attack. These military operations shared certain qualities. For one thing, they were undertaken by the United States operating alone. Second, in each case there was clear evidence of which terrorists were responsible for the attack that prompted the response. This raises the question of whether the military option should be reserved for those situations in which attribution of the provocation attack can be clearly established. Third, in each instance precision weaponry allowed the intended objectives to be targeted narrowly to minimize civilian casualties as much as possible.

There was no significant military response to some of the most lethal terrorist attacks on U.S. targets, including the bombing of a U.S. Marine barracks in Beirut, Lebanon, in October 1983, in which 241 U.S. soldiers and one Lebanese were killed and sixty U.S. soldiers were injured; the Khobar Towers attack in Saudi Arabia in June 1996, which killed nineteen U.S. soldiers and one Saudi citizen and wounded 515 others; and the bombing of the USS *Cole* in the Yemeni port of Aden in October 2000, in which seventeen sailors died and thirty-nine were wounded. The French government retaliated against the bombing of a French military barracks in Beirut that occurred at the same time as the 1983 U.S. Marine barracks bombing. In the attack on the barracks, fifty-eight French paratroopers along with five Lebanese were killed, and fifteen others were wounded. The French air strike targeted Iranian Revolutionary Guard bases in Lebanon, because the Guards were believed to have supported the attacks.

Before the attacks of September 11, 2001, the United States seldom resorted to force for several reasons. First, it is usually difficult to determine with certainty who is responsible for an attack. Gathering forensic information and evidence takes time, and, even then, building a strong case against a known adversary terrorist organization can be next to impossible. The Libyan case in 1986 was a noteworthy exception because of the fortuity of a swift and sure intelligence report linking Libya to the attack. In addition, the investigators of an incident may find it difficult to gain access to evidence, suspects, and information because of the sensitivities of the governments in whose countries the attacks took place.

Second, finding good military targets against which to respond is often difficult. Absent clear state sponsors or the identification of operating bases, it is hard to identify military targets that are linked clearly to the perpetrators. The 1998 cruise missile attacks in Sudan exemplified this problem. Although the administration insisted that it had strong evidence that the plant targeted was owned by Osama bin Laden and had been used to make chemical weapons, the Sudanese government insisted it was a pharmaceutical plant making only medicines. In such instances, it is especially difficult to develop ironclad evidence of terrorist activities because such facilities may be dual-use facilities—

that is, they may be making medicines and chemical weapons, at different times.

Third, because of international law and concerns about sovereignty, the responding state may find it difficult to attack targets in neutral or friendly states, and such attacks may have negative repercussions for the responding state and for the region. Customary international law and the UN Charter forbid violations of the territorial integrity of any state. At the same time, international legal principles and the UN Charter recognize an inherent right of self-defense if an armed attack occurs against a state. Thus the debate and discussion on the propriety of using force against terrorism are ongoing. Is a military response an explicit violation of another state's sovereign borders, even when the state is providing sanctuary to a non-state terrorist group? Or is such a military strike better viewed as a defensive measure, designed to prevent and deter subsequent attacks by the terrorists?

Finally, other responses to terrorism may often appear more effective than the resort to force, such as the use of diplomacy and negotiation or the imposition of financial incentives or sanctions. Other approaches may seem more appropriate when policy makers weigh the security benefits to be gained from military actions against the political and diplomatic costs. One example is the ongoing efforts by the United States and other nations to prevent the development of nuclear weapons by North Korea and Iran.

Military Responses to Terrorism since the Attacks of September 11

The September 11 attacks led to a dramatic change in attitude about the use of force in response to terrorism, at least in the United States. The overriding goal of U.S. policy was then and continues to be to keep the fight as far from America's shores as possible. Thus, although steps have been taken to ensure that the military is better prepared to defend the continental United States, the U.S. military fight against terrorism is overseas. As the National Security Strategy of 2006 states in outlining U.S. policy, "The fight must be taken to the enemy."

Domestic Policy Changes

The most noteworthy step taken by the U.S. Department of Defense (DoD) in response to the September 11 attacks was to establish a new command structure within the military so that all U.S. military forces could work together promptly to protect the continental United States. The need for this new command was demonstrated, in part, by the fact that not a single fighter interceptor was able to reach any of the four airliners hijacked on September 11.

Established in October 2002, Northern Command, or NORTHCOM, is based in Colorado Springs, Colorado. It is located alongside the North American Aerospace Defense Command (NORAD), which has long been responsible for monitoring potential air or missile threats to the United States. NORTHCOM's commander is also head of NORAD. The new command's main goal is to lead DoD's homeland defense activities. NORTHCOM is also expected to help respond to terrorist attacks within the United States, including those involving the use of chemical, biological, radiological, or nuclear weapons. Few military forces are regularly assigned to NORTHCOM; rather, troops are assigned when they are deemed necessary for a particular mission. Since 2002, NORTHCOM has handled a range of domestic security issues, including providing defensive support at major public events, such as the Superbowl and State of the Union address, and coordinating efforts by a broad range of domestic agencies to begin considering the consequences of an epidemic outbreak of avian flu in the United States.

NORTHCOM is also tasked to support homeland security activities. If requested, the military can provide civilian authorities with support in an emergency. Because the federal troops deployed throughout the country would be critical to the response to any terrorist attack, U.S. base security has been improved to ensure that these troops will be able and ready to help if needed. Security at U.S. installations and embassies overseas has been increased as well. The attacks in the 1980s and 1990s on U.S. soldiers in Lebanon and Saudi Arabia indicate that overseas U.S. bases are likely targets, and the goal is to deter and defend against future attacks.

NORTHCOM is responsible for coordinating emergency teams to respond to any attack in the United States using mass-casualty weapons. The quick response Civil Support Teams of National Guard troops in place across the country are designated to aid in evaluating the nature of a suspected chemical or biological weapons attack and to assist in the response. Units from the U.S. Army, U.S. Marines, and Air National Guard also have significant detection and decontamination capabilities for use in responding to such attacks.

Major Military Operations

The United States is currently engaged in significant military operations in Afghanistan and Iraq. (See Table 10.1 for a list of U.S. military activities in response to terrorism.) Both Afghanistan and Iraq point to the difficulties of employing major military force to confront terrorists and the unintended consequences of the use of force.

Afghanistan

The U.S. intervention in Afghanistan that began in October 2001 was a direct response to al Qaeda's attacks in the United States a month earlier. Within hours of the attack, the September 11 hijackers had been linked to al Qaeda and Osama bin Laden. This military action had widespread support; the inter-

Table 10.1 U.S. Military Activities in the War on Terrorism

	Date	Activity
Domestic military operations		
Noble Eagle	September 15, 2001	Partial mobilization of U.S. reserves to assist in war on terrorism
Border support	September 15, 2001	Deployment of National Guard troops to improve homeland security at U.S. ports of entry
International military operations		
Enduring Freedom	October 7, 2001	Military intervention in Afghanistan in response to September 11 attacks by al Qaeda
Balikatan	January 1, 2002–	Annual military training exercise in the Philippines; ongoing special operations troop presence in south
Train and Equip Program	May 2002–April 2004	Aid to Georgian military
Security and Stability Operations	April 2004–April 2006	Assistance to Georgian military
Pan Sahel Initiative	November 2002–March 2004	Training of African militaries by U.S. special forces to improve border protection
African Coastal Security Initiative	March 2003–	Aid to improve regional naval and coastal capabilities through training and equipment
Trans-Sahara OEF	June 2005–	Military element of Trans-Sahara Counterterrorism Initiative; followed Pan Sahel Initiative
Air strikes	January 2007	Air strikes against suspected al Qaeda figures, Somalia

SOURCE: The authors.
NOTE: Some of these operations include partner countries.

national community had recoiled from the brutality of the September attacks, and it recognized the U.S. right to self-defense. The initial goal of the campaign was to capture or kill al Qaeda members in Afghanistan, along with members of the Taliban regime who had supported al Qaeda and refused to turn its leaders over to the United States for prosecution. Indeed, the Taliban and al Qaeda were held equally culpable in President George W. Bush's declaration of the war on terrorism, in which he held state sponsors equally responsible for terrorist acts. The president emphasized that "we will make no distinction between the terrorists who committed these acts and those who harbor them." [2]

The initial Afghan campaign was quite successful; the Taliban regime was overthrown in a matter of weeks. The largely improvised campaign served as a test of a model of warfare that supported Defense Secretary Donald Rumsfeld's goal of transforming the military into a lighter, more flexible force. This "Afghan model" rests on a combination of special forces deployed on the ground, precise and coordinated U.S. air power, and local allies able to conduct the bulk of the fighting. Some observers believe this model could be widely applied, thereby enhancing the ability of the United States to attack terrorist and insurgent forces without inserting a large U.S. military presence that might provoke a backlash. Others have argued that reliance on this model is risky; its success depends on the quality and dedication of the allies on the ground, and the degree of overlap between their goals and those of the United States.

The Afghan campaign bears out this concern. The initial U.S. military operations failed to capture or kill the leaders of al Qaeda and the Taliban. Instead, by the spring of 2002 they were able to flee into the mountainous border region between Afghanistan and Pakistan. Rather than sending additional troops in pursuit, however, the U.S. military began to shift its focus to the upcoming Iraq campaign. U.S. troops were thus withdrawn from Afghanistan, leaving the Afghan militias that were providing the local effort under the command of local warlords to conduct the bulk of the campaign against al Qaeda. However, compared with U.S. troops, these militias had far fewer skills, less equipment, and less motivation to confront al Qaeda once the Taliban had fallen. Although al Qaeda's leaders and significant forces were cornered in a region called Tora Bora, they were able to escape. Since then, the Taliban have regrouped, and they present a renewed threat to the Afghan government and U.S. and international forces in Afghanistan. There is evidence that al Qaeda also may have regrouped in the region, although less is known about its current operational condition.

Meanwhile, the international community has supported efforts to establish a government with popular support in Afghanistan. To this end, the International Security Assistance Force (ISAF) in Afghanistan, made up largely of NATO forces and troops from ten other countries, has worked with U.S. coalition troops since 2002 to provide security and stability in the capital, Kabul, and throughout the countryside. In 2007 about 35,000 international troops were in Afghanistan, including 27,000 U.S. troops and soldiers from thirty-five other countries. These troops were training the Afghan National Army, combating insurgents seeking to reassert the Taliban's authority in Afghanistan, conducting counterterrorism operations, and conducting counternarcotics

Map 10.1 Pakistan's Tribal Areas

SOURCE: *Asia Times*, February 8, 2006, www.atimes.com.

activities in response to the explosive increase in opium production in the Afghan countryside. The United States and the international community also appeared to recognize that in addition to ensuring the safety and security of the Afghan population, they must make good on promises of reconstruction and development assistance. Without proof that their lives had improved since the 2001 intervention, the Afghan population might abandon support for the central government and international efforts to defeat the Taliban.

Pakistan's role in the fight against al Qaeda and the Taliban is particularly complex. Immediately after the attacks of September 11, Pakistan's president,

Gen. Pervez Musharraf, was the first leader faced with the choice of being with or against the United States in combating terrorism. Pakistan was one of the few states that had backed the Taliban regime, and its cooperation was thought to be essential to the U.S. effort to overthrow the Taliban. In the end, Pakistan chose to support the United States, and, because of its geostrategic location, is considered one of its most important allies in the war against terrorism.

And yet strong support for the Taliban and Islamic extremism among members of Pakistan's intelligence service and military has made cooperation with the United States a risky strategy for Musharraf; by 2007 there had been at least three confirmed assassination attempts against him. Moreover, the central government has little authority in the tribal areas of western Pakistan that border Afghanistan. (See Map 10.1.) The government has been fighting militants in the region since 2004, and it ceded authority over these territories to tribal leaders in September 2006. Pakistan's military was supposed to be preventing incursions into Afghanistan by insurgents from these frontier provinces, but the Afghan government believed that Pakistani authorities were not doing enough to prevent Taliban and al Qaeda efforts to destabilize Afghanistan. By 2007 Pakistan's strategy was looking increasingly like a failed policy, and the Musharraf government was under mounting international pressure to take action against both the Taliban and al Qaeda, which had regrouped and rearmed for new attacks.

Somalia

Elements of the Afghan model were also present in the U.S. attacks against al Qaeda operatives in Somalia in January 2007. Somalia had been riven by conflict and ruled by rival warlords since its central government collapsed in 1991. In 2006 an Islamic fundamentalist group, the Islamic Courts Union (ICU), overran the capital city, Mogadishu, and the transitional government established in 2005 was forced to flee to the southwestern town of Baidoa. When the ICU threatened to take over Baidoa, Ethiopian troops backing the transitional government counterattacked, defeating the Islamic militia and reinstalling the transitional government. During its 2007 campaign, the United States conducted several air strikes against suspected al Qaeda bases in southern Somalia. Concurrent with the Afghan model, the United States is believed to have had some covert forces on the ground in Somalia to direct U.S. air strikes, but it did not have combat troops there; the fight against the ICU's forces was conducted by Ethiopian troops. Yet these troops withdrew from Mogadishu shortly after reinstating the transitional government, and internal fighting reintensified. Ethiopian troops remained in Somalia in mid-2007, along with initial elements of a UN peacekeeping force that was struggling to quell the violence between various factions.

Iraq

Whereas the 2001 Afghan campaign involved primarily U.S. special forces, the U.S. intervention in Iraq was a full-scale military operation. As in Afghanistan, the initial military campaign was successful; U.S. troops were in Baghdad within a matter of weeks, and Saddam Hussein had gone into hiding. The United States failed to sustain peace in Iraq, however; it was hampered by insufficient troops and questionable decisions about how to govern the newly liberated country.

Iraq's importance to the war on terrorism has been widely disputed. Although the Bush administration justified intervention primarily by highlighting Saddam Hussein's efforts to acquire WMD in defiance of UN censure, it also argued that the U.S. intervention to overthrow Hussein was central to the war on terrorism. Indeed, it attempted to link Saddam Hussein to al Qaeda and the September 11 attacks in the United States. Many critics, however, saw the intervention as a dangerous distraction from the war on terrorism. They argued that Saddam Hussein was deterred and contained by UN and U.S. sanctions, and that no credible evidence of ties between Iraq and al Qaeda existed. This lack of ties was later confirmed by the 2004 report of the National Commission on Terrorist Attacks upon the United States. Critics also warned that Hussein's overthrow could unleash sectarian and ethnic tensions that would destabilize the entire region. The debate about Iraq's role in the fight against terrorism has continued as U.S. and coalition troops have struggled to bring stability to Iraq in the face of increasing levels of violence aimed at both occupiers and the Iraqi population.

A full discussion of the military campaign in Iraq is beyond the scope of this chapter (see the "For Further Reading" section at the end of the chapter for a list of works that do address this topic), but a few points are worth noting here.

First, the U.S. military can easily defeat another state's armed forces in conventional force-on-force confrontations. This battlefield dominance, however, has spurred states and terrorist groups opposing the United States to resort to asymmetric means to attack U.S. forces, including in Iraq where insurgents have embraced the use of hidden improvised explosive devices (IEDs), suicide bombing attacks, and urban insurgent tactics, among other things. These techniques are also being used by terrorists and insurgents elsewhere, including in Afghanistan.

Second, those planning military interventions must pay proper attention to the aftermath of combat operations. U.S. forces proved unprepared to handle the occupation of Iraq, in part for political reasons and in part because of the military's own priorities. In response to the Bush administration's rejection of the idea that any kind of occupation of Iraq would be necessary, the military did not plan for a protracted stay in Iraq, nor did it have enough troops to ensure stability after the Iraqi government's overthrow. The military leaders who had argued prior to the invasion that the planned U.S. troop levels were

insufficient to maintain the peace were overridden by the Pentagon's civilian leadership. Further complicating the matter, the U.S. military has excellent capabilities for fighting wars, but it is less adept at handling the peacekeeping and stability operations that follow. The Pentagon is working to address this deficiency by improving troops' language and cultural training, and it now stresses the importance of having troops capable to handle the full spectrum of potential missions ranging from major combat operations to post-conflict and disaster relief.

The third and related point is that operations aimed at combating terrorist groups that hide in local populations must guarantee the security of that population, so that it will be an ally in the fight against terrorists.

Finally, the conflict in Iraq has shifted the military's assessment of the capabilities it needs for current and future operations. After the Bush administration took office in January 2001, Defense Secretary Rumsfeld determined that the U.S. military was in need of "transformation" to enable it to address new threats with greater speed and flexibility. The attacks of September 11 gave Rumsfeld greater leverage to implement his defense transformation plans, and the Iraq campaign in particular provided an opportunity to test his vision of warfare. At least initially, as noted earlier, the combination of the lighter, more mobile forces and the sophisticated information and surveillance technologies that Rumsfeld favored were highly successful in toppling the Iraqi regime. However, the ongoing operations in Iraq and Afghanistan have shown the limits of this model for addressing a counterinsurgency. Army forces in Iraq are now more heavily armored than the initial invasion force because of the ongoing threat they face from IEDs and other explosives.

Special Operations Activities

In another shift prompted by the September 11 terrorist attacks, the Department of Defense began increasingly to rely on special operations forces in combating terrorism. The military's Special Operations Command, based in Tampa, Florida, oversees the special operations forces of each branch of the U.S. military and acts as the unified combatant command for them.[3] U.S. military forces are currently grouped in six regional commands (see Map 10.2) and four functional combatant commands: SOCOM, STRATCOM (Strategic Command), TRANSCOM (Transportation Command), and JFCOM (Joint Forces Command).

The failure to rescue the hostages held in Iran in 1980 and the bombing of the U.S. Marine barracks in Lebanon in 1983 had pointed to a decline in special operations capabilities within the U.S. military. SOCOM was established in 1986 in response to that decline. The special operations forces were the first troops on the ground in Afghanistan in 2001, and they have been involved in every major action in Iraq and Afghanistan since then. In 2006 the special

Map 10.2 U.S. DoD Regional Commands

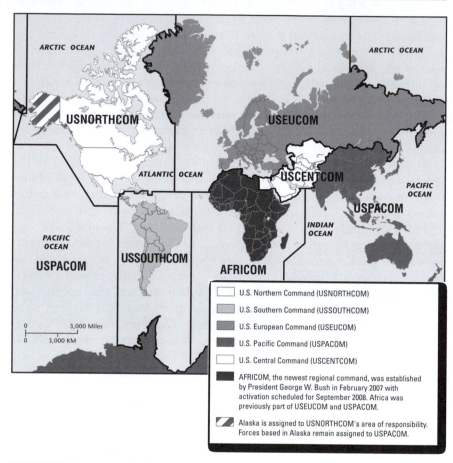

U.S. Northern Command (USNORTHCOM)

U.S. Southern Command (USSOUTHCOM)

U.S. European Command (USEUCOM)

U.S. Pacific Command (USPACOM)

U.S. Central Command (USCENTCOM)

AFRICOM, the newest regional command, was established by President George W. Bush in February 2007 with activation scheduled for September 2008. Africa was previously part of USEUCOM and USPACOM.

Alaska is assigned to USNORTHCOM's area of responsibility. Forces based in Alaska remain assigned to USPACOM.

SOURCE: U.S. Department of Defense, www.defenselink.mil/specials/unifiedcommand.

operations forces numbered about 47,000, of which over 7,000 were deployed in fifty-two countries. Ninety percent of them were in Iraq, Afghanistan, and other states in the region.

In 2004 SOCOM was designated as the lead combatant command in the global war on terrorism. Its central goals are to train special operations forces and to "detect, disrupt, and defeat terrorists" in a range of geographic locations. Reflecting its expanded role, SOCOM's budget increased dramatically between 2001 and 2006 (from $5.5 billion in 2002 to $8 billion in the fiscal year 2006 budget request), particularly after its designation as lead command. The DoD plans to increase the number of special operations forces by an additional 13,000 by 2011 and to expand SOCOM's capabilities in areas such as psychological operations. SOCOM also plans to develop its own unmanned aerial vehicle squad to support operations—an indication that it may want to avoid being dependent on other government agencies such as the CIA for support of politically sensitive missions.

Special operations forces have been used in a variety of ways to combat terrorism. In addition to participating in the military campaigns in Afghanistan and Iraq, such forces conduct joint training and other activities with the militaries of other countries, particularly in states confronting potential terrorist threats. Each year, SOCOM conducts over seventy training exercises in Asia alone. The U.S. military has been in the Philippines since 2002, helping the Philippine army to improve its ability to operate against insurgent groups in the southern islands. Although the Philippine constitution bars foreign troops from participating in combat operations on its territory, U.S. troops have been present in combat zones as advisers. Special operations forces also undertake humanitarian activities such as road building and medical aid as a way to gain greater support for U.S. efforts. The assistance of U.S. special operations forces has enabled the government of the Philippines to make considerable progress toward wiping out the Abu Sayyaf terrorist group, which had operated in the southern part of the country.

In recent years, the number of special operations devoted to military liaison operations overseas has grown, particularly in countries in which the United States may have to deal with terrorists in the future. In these operations, special operations forces working out of U.S. embassies report directly to the Pentagon, which has raised a range of concerns. For example, U.S. ambassadors have expressed concern about who has authority over these troops: the ambassador in the country in which they are operating or the regional military commanders? Several ambassadors have insisted that memos of understanding about the chain of command be signed before these troops start operations, arguing that it is important to clarify this authority before issues of control arise.

Finally, in Afghanistan and Iraq the United States has employed private contractors to augment special operations forces in meeting operational requirements. Private firms may quickly bring needed resources and expertise to an operation, and they may be able to develop operational capabilities more expediently and at less cost than developing the equivalent resources inside the U.S. government. At the same time, private firms may attract personnel by offering salaries higher than those paid by the U.S. military or by providing bonuses and other incentives. Such a policy does, however, raise some questions: Are there downside risks to employing private companies to take on some of the security tasks in Afghanistan or Iraq? How should the activities of private contractors be monitored and their accountability determined? For example, if a contract employee abuses a detainee, what kinds of sanctions can be imposed and by whom?

Targeted Killing

Another military response to terrorism since the attacks of September 11 is attempts to target and kill the individuals believed to be perpetrators of terrorism as a way to quell terrorist attacks. Israel is perhaps best known for conducting "targeted killings" of this sort. Since the 1970s, the Israeli government has relied on what it calls "extrajudicial punishment" to curb terrorist attacks. Israel's goal is to kill, in the name of prevention, those it regards as a threat to its security because they are believed to organize terrorist attacks or build the bombs used in suicide attacks. During the 1970s and 1980s, the main targets of such attacks were representatives of the Palestine Liberation Organization in states such as Egypt and Tunis, where the PLO was based. After the 1993 Oslo peace accords, Israel's focus shifted from the PLO to other Palestinian groups opposed to the peace process. Members of Hezbollah, Hamas, and Palestinian Islamic Jihad, all terrorist organizations that have stated their desire to destroy Israel, became prime targets of Israel's efforts to prevent terrorism.

In its own defense, the Israeli government has argued that it rarely resorts to extrajudicial killings, and only in exceptional cases. Since the beginning of the Palestinian intifada in September 2000, however, Israel appears to have increased its use of targeted killings in the Palestinian-controlled territories. The focus has shifted to suicide bombers and the leaders of military groups opposed to Israel. Israel has conducted such attacks using military forces and smaller, more specialized units and by launching missile attacks from planes or helicopters.

Israel's resort to this strategy has provoked significant debate and condemnation. But Israel argues that targeted killings are effective: they disrupt the leadership of groups planning attacks on Israel, and they force the leaders of terrorist groups to focus their attention on their own survival rather than on planning attacks against Israel. Those who might consider replacing current leaders also know that they will become targets by taking over these groups. Israel argues as well that if the Palestinian Authority will not detain militants and prevent suicide attacks, then Israel reserves the right to prevent attacks against its population by using targeted killings. The Israeli government claims it has asked the Palestinian Authority to arrest militants and, on occasion, has given the Palestinian Authority warning of potential raids, but that the Palestinian Authority has done nothing, or it has warned the militants.

As noted in Chapter 4, some observers question the effectiveness of a targeted killing policy. They argue that rather than preventing attacks, this policy provokes additional retaliatory attacks, which hardly helps to lessen the threat of terrorism. Legal scholars point out that targeted killings leave no room for the target to contest his culpability, which makes the practice look more like assassination than "extrajudicial punishment." They also argue that the practice is illegal, because many attacks have occurred within the territory of other states, thereby violating their sovereignty and international law. Israel has responded that international law requires states to prevent their territory from being used as a safe haven by terrorists to mount attacks against neighboring states, and terrorists are a common enemy. Therefore, Israel's neighbors have an obligation to prevent such attacks, as does the Palestinian Authority under the agreements it has signed since 1993. If these states and the Palestinian Authority will not stop these actions, Israel argues, then it is justified in defending itself.

The United States has, at least since a border war with Mexican bandits in 1916, also targeted individuals in combating terrorism and in other conflicts. But in response to perceived abuses by the CIA in supporting covert operations, particularly in Latin America during the 1970s, President Gerald R. Ford prohibited political assassinations by executive order in 1976. Subsequent presidents reaffirmed this ban.

The decision to target specific individuals with lethal force after September 11 was neither unprecedented nor surprising. In a time of war, subjecting individual combatants to lethal force has been a permitted and lawful instrument of waging war successfully. Moreover, this decision built on efforts during the 1990s to confront the threat posed by al Qaeda. Terrorists were first singled out by name as targets in a 1995 executive order by President Clinton that added the category "specially designated terrorists" to a list maintained by the secretary of state and the Treasury Office of Foreign Assets Control. The CIA has also been authorized since 1998 by presidential directive to use covert means to disrupt and preempt terrorist operations planned by Osama bin Laden. The Clinton administration directive was affirmed by President Bush in 2001 before the September 11 attacks, based on evidence linking al Qaeda to the August 1998 bombings of U.S. embassies in Africa. The directive stopped short of authorizing targeted killing, but it did authorize lethal force for self-defense.

In the weeks after September 11, President Bush signed an intelligence finding giving the CIA broad authority to pursue terrorists with lethal force around the world. The theater of the war on terrorism became worldwide rather than confined to Afghanistan as it had been previously. A finding, which contains the factual and policy predicates for the intelligence activities authorized in any significant operation, must be personally approved by the president. In the 2001 classified finding, the president also delegated targeting and operational authority to senior civilian and military officials. Although the details remain classified, the authority granted here is surely the most sweeping and most lethal since the founding of the CIA. The finding also assumes an unprecedented degree of cooperation between the CIA and special forces, as well as other military units. Reacting to the finding, one official implicitly warned the terrorists, "The gloves are off." [4]

Neither Clinton's 1998 directive nor the new one issued by President Bush after September 11 exempted the CIA and DoD from the executive order banning political assassination. But the 2001 finding broadened the class of potential targets of lethal force beyond bin Laden and his close circle and extended the boundaries beyond Afghanistan.

Resort to targeted killing became both more attractive to planners and a source of political controversy after September 11, 2001. The new technology at hand, pilotless drone aircraft (unmanned aerial vehicles, or UAVs) that were equipped both with sophisticated surveillance and targeting technology and with powerful Hellfire missiles capable of inflicting lethal force effectively from a safe distance (see Box 10.1), made targeted killing look like a promis-

---

Box 10.1 **The Predator**

The Predator, one of a growing number of unmanned aerial vehicles being used by military and civilian agencies, is an ungainly $40 million propeller-driven aircraft. Twenty-seven-feet long with a forty-nine-foot wingspan, it flies as slow as eighty miles per hour and is guided by an operator at a television monitor who may be hundreds of miles away. The drone can hover continuously for twenty-four hours or more at fifteen thousand feet above any battlefield, and it can send live video to AC-130 gunships or command posts around the world without putting any pilots in harm's way. The drone's radar, infrared sensors, and color video camera can track vehicles at night and through clouds, producing sharp enough images to see people on the ground from more than three miles away. Although designed primarily for surveillance functions, the Predator can be armed with two AGM-114 Hellfire missiles.

The Predator cannot fly in stormy weather; it has been prone to icing. The drone is also vulnerable to enemy anti-aircraft fire. The combat debut of the Predator came in 1995 in the skies over Bosnia, where it provided sharp real-time images of the battlefield.

One year before the September 11, 2001, attacks, an unarmed CIA drone captured video in Afghanistan of a man that intelligence officials believe was Osama bin Laden. In February 2002, a Predator patrolling thousands of feet above Afghanistan fed images to the CIA and military officers of a very tall man among a small group. After officials on the ground determined that the man could be Osama bin Laden, a request to launch a Hellfire missile was sent through the chain of command. The request was granted a few minutes later, but by then the group had disbanded. When the man and two others were spotted emerging from a wooded area shortly thereafter, the Hellfire was launched, and the three men were killed. Media reports later indicated that the three were local men who were scavenging for scrap metal. The Predator depends on reliable intelligence, but mistakes happen.

- What are the implications of using Predators to attack targets rather than to provide battlefield information?

- What are the advantages and disadvantages of using UAVs to combat terrorism?

ing tool in the war against terrorism. If targets as significant as Taliban leader Mullah Muhammad Omar or even Osama bin Laden could be dispatched effectively and with little or no risk to U.S. personnel, the objectives of the war on terrorism could be advanced dramatically. (See Case Study 10.4.)

CASE STUDY 10.4

Unleashing the Predator

In October 2001, on the first night of the campaign against al Qaeda and the Taliban in Afghanistan, the United States nearly had a major success. Officials believed they had pinpointed the location of the supreme leader of the Taliban, Mullah Muhammad Omar. While patrolling the roads near Kabul, an unmanned but armed CIA drone had trained its crosshairs on Omar in a convoy of cars fleeing the capital. Under the terms of an agreement, the CIA controllers did not have the authority to order a strike on the target. Likewise, the local Fifth Fleet commander in Bahrain lacked the requisite authority. Instead, following the agreement, the CIA sought approval from U.S. Central Command (CENTCOM) in Tampa to launch the Hellfire missile from the Predator drone positioned above Omar.

The Predator followed the convoy to a building where Omar and about one hundred guards sought cover. Some delay then ensued in securing the approval of Gen Tommy R. Franks, the commanding general of CENTCOM. One report indicated that a full-scale fighter bomber assault was requested, and that General Franks declined to approve the request on the basis of legal advice he received on the spot. Another report suggested that the magnitude of the target prompted General Franks to run the targeting by the White House. Media reports indicated that President George W. Bush personally approved the strike, although the delay gave Mullah Omar time to change his location. F-18s later targeted and destroyed the building to which he had been tracked, but Omar had escaped.

After the near miss on Mullah Omar, no verified intelligence reported seeing, much less targeting, either Omar or Osama bin Laden during the Afghanistan campaign. The senior leaders of al Qaeda, still at large in Afghanistan, were likely relocating early and often to elude detection, capture, or death. However, on November 3, 2001, a missile-carrying Predator drone killed Mohammed Atef, al Qaeda's chief of military operations, in a raid near Kabul. Then in early May 2002, the CIA tried but failed to kill an Afghan factional leader, Gulbuddin Hekmatyar, an Islamic fundamentalist who had vowed to topple the government of the newly installed president of Afghanistan, Hamid Karzai, and to attack U.S. forces.

The calculus for targeted killing changed dramatically on November 3, 2002, when an armed CIA drone fired a Hellfire missile and killed a senior al Qaeda leader and five low-level operatives traveling by car in a remote part of the Yemeni desert. In the first use of an armed Predator outside Afghanistan—indeed, the first military action in the war against terrorism outside Afghanistan—Qaed Salim Sinan al-Harethi was killed. Al-Harethi was described as the senior al Qaeda official in Yemen, one of the top ten to twelve al Qaeda operatives in the world, and a suspect in the October 2000 suicide bombing of the USS *Cole*. U.S. intelligence and law enforcement officials had been tracking his movements for months before the attack. The five al Qaeda operatives also killed included an American citizen of Yemeni descent, Kamal Derwish, who grew up in the Buffalo suburb of Tonawanda and who, according to FBI intelligence, recruited American Muslims to attend al Qaeda training camps.

The use of the Predator to target individual opponents illustrates how sophisticated military technology can contribute to the struggle against an elusive terrorist opponent. Yet by creating the temptation to attack individuals anywhere, this technology has been employed far beyond the purposes for which it was originally developed: to provide battlefield intelligence to military commanders.   ∎

But the Predator drones are a CIA tool, which has complicated their use on the battlefield. The idea of using the armed UAV in counterterrorism combat was not new. However, lingering disagreements over who should have the ultimate authority for firing the UAV's Hellfire missiles—the military or the CIA—slowed the development of the new counterterrorism weapon. Because the Predators are CIA aircraft, they are controlled by civilian leaders outside the chain of command. The civilian officials cooperate and share information and decision making with military commanders in a shared campaign against terrorism. Some questioned the use of the new weapon and its CIA links, as well as several more general short- and longer-term consequences of an invigorated policy of targeted killing.

The possibility that on the first night of the Afghan war a Predator missed a chance to strike a convoy that apparently included Mullah Omar finally settled the dispute over control of the Hellfires, at least for the time being, as described in Case Study 10.4. The missed opportunity, caused by traditional military chain-of-command reviews up to and apparently including the commander in chief, led to the CIA being given its first ever authority to strike beyond a narrow range of preselected counterterrorism targets.

Since 2001, Predators have been used to carry out targeted killings in Afghanistan, Yemen, and Pakistan. These attacks have not been without controversy, however, both because of the publicity surrounding them, which has created difficulties for the host governments, and because even precision attacks can kill innocent civilians.

When a CIA drone fired a Hellfire missile and killed the senior al Qaeda leader Qaed Salim Sinan al-Harethi and five low-level operatives traveling by car in a remote part of the Yemeni desert, there was little doubt among U.S. officials that the Predator strike had material benefits. An important al Qaeda leader was eliminated, and the world received a strong signal that there is no sanctuary for terrorists. Tactically, the strike against al-Harethi represented an escalation of the war on terrorism, and an expansion of the conflict beyond Afghanistan.

Four years later, use of the Predator once again spurred controversy. In the ongoing conflict inside Afghanistan, Pakistan had become a critical sanctuary for terrorists. Armed Predators have been used against targets in Pakistan at least twice: in May 2005 and in January 2006. In the 2006 attack, Hellfire missiles from an armed Predator struck three houses in the sparsely populated village of Damadola Burkanday in the North West Frontier Province of Pakistan. Their target was Ayman al-Zawahiri, the second in command of al Qaeda and allegedly the chief strategist for Osama bin Laden. Four children were among eighteen villagers who died in the attack, but al-Zawahiri was not among them. The Predator performed exactly as it was supposed to, but the intelligence that picked the targets and the timing of the strike was faulty.[5] Because the target in Pakistan this time was someone with the value of al-Zawahiri, the decision to strike was relatively easy, although protests were mounted in Pakistan and elsewhere against the United States and against the government of Pakistani president Pervez Musharraf.

As al Qaeda has become more diffuse and the Predator has had some successes, the operational difficulties and legal complexities embedded in use of UAVs have increased. Geographic expansion is one important consideration. Will the targeted killing program expand to Somalia, or to Indonesia, or to other new frontiers in the war on terrorism? Will the targeting reach beyond the leadership of al Qaeda and its affiliates to the rank and file?

One potentially positive outcome of the expanded program is the chance that the use of UAVs will deter governments and other groups that might provide sanctuary to terrorists. Yet the program could also foment anti-American sentiments and destabilize sensitive regimes. In addition, the program may open the field to additional foreign governments to conduct similar activities or be more overt about their intentions to do so. Israel now employs UAVs, and Iran is reportedly developing the capability.

One overarching issue—host state cooperation and the culpability of those who harbor terrorists—is legally murky, politically tricky, and largely dependent on case-specific personalities and circumstances. If the war against terrorists continues to expand, in part through these precise targeted killing technologies, what are its limits?

The Predator attacks in Yemen and Pakistan point to an additional challenge in confronting terrorism; many states do not want their support for U.S. policy to be public because of concerns about a popular backlash. For example, in Yemen the Predator attack appeared at the time to be a better option than a ground operation by U.S. troops because of fears that the ground operation might provoke a backlash by forces opposed to cooperation with the United States. However, the Yemeni government was displeased with the media coverage of the attack. This strike was conducted after considerable cooperation between U.S. and Yemeni officials, including mounting a joint U.S.-Yemen intelligence team.[6] But some Yemeni leaders maintained that the public acknowledgment of the strike by the United States violated a secrecy agreement between the two nations, and could provoke domestic unrest in Yemen and reprisals by al Qaeda sympathizers.

Similarly, although Pakistan is a very critical U.S. ally in the war on terrorism because of its proximity to Afghanistan, domestic political concerns in Pakistan make close coordination with the U.S. military problematic. The Predator attacks in Pakistan brought tensions in the U.S.-Pakistani collaboration against terrorism to the surface. For example, the government responded to the January 2006 attack with a formal protest to the U.S. government, but the country's president also warned Pakistanis that they should not harbor foreign terrorists. U.S. officials insisted that Pakistan's government not only has shared intelligence with the United States about the terrorists' whereabouts, but also was informed about and agreed to the January attack.

Another issue is that the decision process and civil-military cooperation aspects of the Predator program are relatively untested and evolving. Will the program become more or less a CIA one, and, if it becomes predominantly one for the CIA, what legal vetting and limits will it face? Because there is always the danger of faulty intelligence and innocent deaths, the use of Predators should be handled with great caution.

Civil Affairs Operations

The military is also expanding its efforts to conduct civil affairs operations, to address the "hearts and minds" element of the war on terrorism. As noted earlier, special operations forces are increasingly combining military training operations with activities such as road building, medical aid, and other forms of humanitarian assistance as a way to gain the trust and support of the populations in the countries in which they are operating.

These activities are aimed at countries in which al Qaeda and other terrorist groups are known to have operated, or where the United States fears the influence of such groups may spread. For example, the United States deployed fifteen hundred troops in the Horn of Africa in 2007 to combat terrorism in the region. Along with more conventional missions such as intelligence operations and conducting military training with forces in the region, the troops built schools and medical clinics, dug wells, and provided medical and veterinary assistance to local populations. The Horn of Africa program is an experiment to determine whether such activities will help to create goodwill and reduce support for terrorists, but those involved recognize that it will take time to determine whether this policy is successful.

Although many of the functions undertaken in a mission like this one are not strictly military, they are currently being carried out by military troops, in part because the region is so dangerous and personnel from other U.S. government agencies are not necessarily able or willing to carry out such missions. For example, Foreign Service officers cannot be ordered to accept dangerous assignments, whereas military personnel can. The DoD also has more resources at its disposal than do the other branches of the government. But this situation raises an important question: should the "face" that the United States presents to the world be primarily military, or should civilians be more widely engaged in diplomacy and civil affairs operations intended to build goodwill?

That question comes into play in another form of civil affairs: the "provincial reconstruction team" (PRT) model. This model has its origins in Afghanistan, where the U.S.-led military coalition that overthrew the Taliban sought to secure and stabilize the countryside. Initially, the PRTs had several goals: to extend the influence of the Afghan national government, to enable the military to gather better information on what was happening in different regions, to aid in reconstruction, and to coordinate with UN assistance efforts in Afghanistan. PRTs now have two main goals in Afghanistan: to improve security and to facilitate the country's economic reconstruction and development.

PRTs are made up of a combination of military and civilian personnel, representatives of aid organizations working in the country, and often military contractors. Not only the U.S.-led coalition forces but also NATO has adopted this model, and it now has several PRTs working in Afghanistan. The PRT model is also being used in Iraq to promote reconstruction. According to the military, this model is particularly useful in Iraq because much of the countryside is too dangerous to enable the provision of aid and reconstruction without a significant security component, which the PRTs incorporate.

This model has not, however, been without criticism from within the military as well as from aid groups. The military acknowledges that PRTs have sometimes been problematic because their missions and roles are not always clear. In addition, the PRTs often suffer from insufficient resources to enable them to carry out their tasks. Nongovernmental organizations involved in aid and reconstruction have argued that the military does not have expertise in development and that the "quick impact" goal of many PRT projects limits their effectiveness. Simply building facilities such as schools or medical clinics ignores the need to undertake longer-term efforts to build community support and institutions to utilize these new facilities. Aid organizations and

NGOs have also expressed concern that the "militarization" of aid delivery will put them at risk. Most NGOs and aid organizations seek to maintain their neutrality to ensure they will be able to provide assistance to civilians in war zones. But if aid and reconstruction efforts are perceived to be linked to U.S. military efforts, then aid workers may become the targets of insurgents, and, in fact, they have become targets in parts of Afghanistan.

These are valid concerns, but the military faces the problem that in both Afghanistan and Iraq conditions on the ground are sufficiently dangerous that many aid groups have ceased operations there. Yet most observers agree that greater attention to economic development is critical to stabilizing these countries. There may be no alternative at present to the PRT model for the provision of reconstruction in these states.

Policy Dilemmas Posed by the Use of Force

The prospect of using military force to respond to terrorist attacks raises several dilemmas for policy makers. The first dilemma is the problem of attribution: it may be hard to determine precisely who is responsible for a terrorist attack. Because military responses are, by their nature, violent, international support for or condemnation of the use of military force will depend on clear proof of culpability.

Determining attribution is particularly difficult if attacks occur overseas. The host government may not wish to allow foreign investigators to examine the evidence or to question suspects. In addition, problems of proof are legion. After the Khobar Towers bombing in Saudi Arabia, for example, the Saudi government refused to allow U.S. personnel to question directly the suspected attackers. Such a situation can be vexing to investigators, because they hope to learn not only about the crime already committed, but also about attacks that may be planned in the future in order to prevent them.

Acting on its concern about future attacks, the Pentagon has adopted more aggressive guidelines for interrogating terrorist suspects and those designated as "enemy combatants." The Departments of Defense and Justice argue that harsh interrogation techniques are justified by the urgency of the threat. But some experts on interrogation argue that this policy is misguided, because the information obtained by using coercive interrogation techniques and torture is generally unreliable. Added to this problem, the widely publicized abuses by interrogators that occurred at Abu Ghraib prison in Iraq and elsewhere have damaged the reputation of the U.S. military and the United States, making it even more difficult to gain support for U.S. efforts to confront terrorism.

The second dilemma surrounding the use of military force is that, even if attribution is clear, is a military response appropriate? Retaliation for terrorist attacks requires not just knowing who is responsible, but being able to identify targets for attack that are clearly linked to the individuals or group that committed the terrorist act. This requirement is, however, complicated by several factors. One is state sovereignty. Any attack on terrorist bases or assets violates the sovereignty of the state that is subject to attack. If the state is a sponsor of the terrorist group, then there is no problem; indeed, the U.S. government has declared that state sponsors of terrorism should be held equally accountable for terrorist acts. But what should be done about states that are passive supporters—that is, those that merely tolerate the presence of a terrorist network inside sovereign borders? Or about states that are powerless to prevent terrorists from taking sanctuary in their territory—that is, the "failed" or "failing" states? Other factors are the difficulties encountered in conducting military attacks on targets in neutral or friendly states and the negative repercussions they may produce, as well as the problem of collateral damage. No matter how precise an air strike or cruise missile attack is, collateral damage may occur in the form of civilian casualties. Such damage may increase support for the terrorists by generating resentment against the attackers rather than weakening the terrorist group.

Military responses also confront the problem of proportionality. Although the UN Charter accepts that states have a right to self-defense, the international laws of war prohibit indiscriminate attacks that do not distinguish between military targets and civilians. Of course, terrorists that locate their assets in populated areas are themselves violating the laws of war by putting innocent populations at risk. This situation presents military planners with difficult dilemmas. If terrorists persist in using civilian areas as bases for launching attacks, the states targeted by the terrorists may have little choice but to target those areas, exercising caution to avoid civilian casualties to the extent possible.

The third and most far-reaching military response to terrorism, regime change, presents major dilemmas. Overthrowing a regime makes the victors responsible for securing the peace and the well-being of the population. Secretary of State Colin Powell nicely illustrated this point when he warned President Bush about the "Pottery Barn" rule of accountability with regard to Iraq: if "you break it, you own it." [7] Toppling Saddam Hussein would leave the United States in charge of the safety, security, and governance of Iraq. The military capabilities needed in the post-conflict period of occupation and reconstruction are quite different from those needed for invasion. Any state contemplating the use of force must take this factor into account.

Finally, a fourth dilemma to be considered in using military force is whether another response might be more appropriate. Indeed, as noted earlier, this consideration often prevented more forceful actions in response to some of the bloodier attacks against Americans. Not only must policy makers evaluate whether military force is the most effective response available, but they also must consider the negative repercussions that resort to force could have. In the 1983 U.S. Marine barracks bombing in Beirut, for example, no military retaliation was pursued because leaders feared that important political relations with states in the region would suffer if military force were used.

By its nature, the use of military force precludes prosecution and judicial means of punishment for terrorist acts; it may also inflame international public opinion against the state resorting to force for the reasons noted earlier. At the same time, states face the dilemma that if they do not respond with force to major terrorist attacks, they may be perceived as "weak," thereby provoking further attacks. Some critics maintain that the failure of the United States to respond to the Beirut attack, for example, emboldened Hezbollah and perhaps convinced the al Qaeda leadership that the United States would not "stand and fight" if attacked.

The contrasting examples of Afghanistan and Iraq illustrate many of these dilemmas. The United States overthrew the ruling regimes in these states to prevent further support for terrorism. Attribution of the September 11 attacks to al Qaeda was decisive, the Taliban's links to al Qaeda were clear, and U.S. actions in Afghanistan enjoyed widespread international support. In fact, today the international community continues to be engaged in Afghanistan, as evidenced by the ongoing roles played by both the UN and the NATO-led security force there. Even in Afghanistan, though, regime change has proved difficult, and Afghanistan's future looks tenuous.

In 2007 the deteriorating situation in Iraq appeared to be contributing to Afghanistan's problems. Bitter disagreements in the international community about whether the U.S. intervention was justified resulted in an invasion without UN sanction and one that was widely regarded as a unilateral U.S. action in spite of the Bush administration's insistence that it was a coalition effort. The disagreements about whether military force was legitimate to begin with have clouded efforts to gain international support for Iraq's reconstruction. A litany of military problems and political blunders, including the lack of preparation for stabilization and occupation, the de-Baathification of the Iraqi civil service, the firing of the Iraqi army, the abuses at Abu Ghraib prison, and the ongoing failure to ensure the safety and well-being of the Iraqi population, contributed to the emergence of an insurgency against the U.S. occupation that has grown steadily since mid-2003. Moreover, the same terrorist techniques—particularly the use of IEDs and suicide bombing—being adapted in Iraq appeared to be spreading to other places such as Afghanistan, and terrorist attacks linked to the Iraq conflict were being carried out in neighboring states such as Jordan, Egypt, Saudi Arabia, Iran, and Pakistan. It is fair to ask, then, whether the use of military force in Iraq has engendered more terrorism rather than helped to combat it.

Finally, successful military attacks raise the prospect that, in the long run, the use of military force may not effectively end terrorism. Rather, it may simply push terrorists into cities and other populated areas where they can hide and where it is harder to track them or to take actions against them. Indeed, the urban insurgency that has taken place in Iraq provides evidence of this phenomenon.

Conclusion

Military force is clearly an important component of the available policy options for responding to terrorist attacks. For the most part, however, military force is a tool that has been—and must be—used sparingly, and with caution. After September 11, 2001, military force was inevitable and surely appropriate, even if part of its rationale was the gut feeling shared by so many that Americans just had to "do something." The difficulties that have ensued in Afghanistan and Iraq raise serious questions about the utility of direct military operations against countries supporting terrorists, or suspected of supporting them. Military means may not succeed in defeating terrorist groups such as al Qaeda in Afghanistan, and the remnants of larger organizations can continue to pose serious problems. As for Iraq, assuming responsibility for running and rebuilding an entire country is immensely complicated, and, regardless of the motivations, it is likely to engender resentment against the occupiers.

Nor is it likely that the military responses to al Qaeda have deterred its terrorism. At least as likely is that the military response has begat more terrorism. Moreover, America's use of its overwhelming military power in such bold and expansive ways has generated considerable resentment against the United States. Further complicating the situation is that intelligence on terrorist attacks and on tracking terrorist movements has proved imperfect at best. Targeting mistakes have been made, further eroding support for the use of military responses to terrorism.

Special operations activities against terrorism have proved effective in the short run in Afghanistan, and special operations actions designed to strengthen cooperation with other states and militaries may be particularly useful, perhaps augmented by private contractors. The U.S. military is likely to expand its reliance on these forces and on the technological means available to confront terrorism such as the use of UAVs. But these tools, too, should be used carefully, because the covert use of military force can be just as problematic, as its overt use has proven. Finally, the utility of military force to confront terrorism is clearly enhanced when the United States works with other states to address shared problems rather than trying to go it alone.

FOR FURTHER READING

Avant, Deborah. *The Market for Force: The Consequences of Privatizing Security*. New York: Cambridge University Press, 2005.

Chandrasekaran, Rajiv. *Imperial Life in the Emerald City: Inside Iraq's Green Zone*. New York: Knopf, 2006.

Gordon, Michael, and Bernard E. Trainor. *Cobra II: The Inside Story of the Invasion and Occupation of Iraq*. New York: Pantheon, 2006.

Kagan, Frederick. *Finding the Target: The Transformation of American Military Policy*. New York: Encounter Books, 2006.

Ricks, Thomas E. *Fiasco: The American Military Adventure in Iraq.* New York: Penguin Press, 2006.

Woodward, Bob. *Bush at War.* New York: Simon and Schuster, 2002.
———. *Plan of Attack.* New York: Simon and Schuster, 2004.
———. *State of Denial.* New York: Simon and Schuster, 2006.

Notes

Chapter 1

1. Abouhalima, an Egyptian and former fighter in the Afghan resistance against the Soviet Union, was a follower of Sheikh Rahman. Ajaj arrived in New York City on the same flight from Pakistan as Ramzi Yousef. John V. Parachini, "The World Trade Center Bombers (1993)," in *Toxic Terror: Assessing Terrorist Use of Chemical and Biological Weapons,* ed. Jonathan B. Tucker (Cambridge: MIT Press, 2000), 185–206.
2. Yasser Arafat, "Address to the UN General Assembly" (November 13, 1974), in *The Israel-Arab Reader: A Documentary History of the Middle East Conflict,* ed. Walter Laqueur (New York: Bantam, 1976), 510.
3. For a description of al Qaeda's organizational structure, see Valdis E. Krebs, "Uncloaking Terrorist Networks," http://firstmonday.org/issues/issue7_4/krebs/index.html.
4. Brian Michael Jenkins, "International Terrorism: A New Mode of Conflict," in *International Terrorism and World Security,* ed. David Carlton and Carlo Schaerf (London: Croon Helm 1975), 15.

Chapter 2

1. Bruce Schneier, "Terror Profiles by Computers Are Ineffective," *Newsday,* October 21, 2003.
2. Nasra Hassan, "An Arsenal of Killers," *New Yorker,* August 2001.
3. Marc Sageman, *Understanding Terror Networks* (Philadelphia: University of Pennsylvania Press, 2004).
4. For further details on the Rajneeshi cult's use of a biological weapon, see W. Seth Carus, "The Rajneeshes (1884)," in *Toxic Terror: Assessing Terrorist Use of Chemical and Biological Weapons,* ed. Jonathan B. Tucker (Cambridge: MIT Press, 2000), chapter 8.
5. Louise Shelley and Robert Orttung, "Criminal Acts: How Organized Crime Is a Nuclear Smuggler's New Best Friend," *Bulletin of the Atomic Scientists* (September–October 2006): 22–23.
6. Ibid., 23.
7. See, for example, Graham Allison, *Nuclear Terrorism: The Ultimate Preventable Catastrophe* (New York: Henry Holt, 2004); Charles Ferguson, William C. Potter, and Amy Sands, *The Four Faces of Nuclear Terrorism* (Monterey, Calif.: Center for Non-Proliferation Studies, Monterey Institute of International Studies, 2004); or Brad Roberts, ed., *Hype or Reality: The "New Terrorism" and Mass Casualty Attacks* (Alexandria, Va.: Chemical and Biological Arms Control Institute, 2000).

Chapter 3

1. Marc Sageman and others have noted that none of the September 11 terrorists came from prototypically poor and underprivileged families. See Marc Sageman, *Understanding Terror Networks* (Philadelphia: University of Pennsylvania Press, 2004).
2. *Intifada* is an Arabic word that means "uprising." There have been two intifadas. The first began in 1987 and ended with the signing of the Oslo Peace Accords in 1993. The second intifada began in 2000 and has continued on and off until the present day.
3. The idea of creating a pan-Islamic state in Southeast Asia appears closely connected to the professed goal of Osama bin Laden and al Qaeda to reestablish an Islamic caliphate across much of Europe, the Middle East, and Asia.
4. It may well be argued that such perceptions of cultural threats are not unique to radical Islam and that, for example, the reaction among conservatives in Europe to the cultural practices of unassimilated immigrants from Asia and Africa is a manifestation of the same phenomenon.
5. Salafism is a puritanical fundamentalist movement whose adherents reject contemporary Islamic teachings in favor of a return to the Salaf, or Islam, as it was practiced during the first three generations after Muhammad founded Islam.
6. The caliphate is the theoretical government that would govern the Islamic world under Islamic law; a caliph would rule as head of state. From Muhammad's rule until the fall of the Ottoman Empire in 1923, various empires called themselves caliphates.
7. For example, Osama bin Laden has at times demanded the "return" of territory that is currently part of Spain.
8. The phrase "clash of civilizations" was coined by Harvard professor Samuel P. Huntington, and is fully described in his book *The Clash of Civilizations and the Remaking of the World Order* (New York: Simon and Schuster, 1996).
9. Huntington, *Clash of Civilizations,* 265–272.
10. The reference here is to the Christian crusaders who participated in a series of seven military campaigns in the Middle East between 1095 and 1291. Those campaigns sought to retake Jerusalem and to convert Muslims to Christianity.
11. There are no reliable statistics on the number of closed-circuit television surveillance units in Britain, but the estimates range up to four million.

Chapter 4

1. U.S. Department of Justice, Civil Rights Division, "Guidance Regarding the Use of Race by Federal Law Enforcement Agencies," Washington, D.C., June 2005.
2. Paul Sperry, "When the Profile Fits the Crime," *New York Times,* July 28, 2005, www.nytimes.com/2005/07/28/opinion/28sperry.htm.
3. Raymond Kelly, police commissioner, New York Police Department, quoted in Malcolm Gladwell, "Troublemakers: What Pit Bulls Can Teach Us about Profiling," *New Yorker,* February 6, 2006.
4. Ibid.
5. *U.S. Code* 18 (2004), §2339B(a)(2).

6. *U.S. Code* 8 (2004), §1182(a)(3)(B)(i)(IV&V).
7. *U.S. Code* 18 (2004), §2339B(a)(1).
8. *U.S. Code* 8 (2004), §1189(a)(1).
9. *United States v. United States District Court,* 407 U.S. 297 (1972) at 313.
10. National Commission on Terrorist Attacks upon the United States, *Final Report* (Washington, D.C.: Government Printing Office, 2004).
11. Ibid., 357.
12. Ibid., 399–400.

Chapter 5

1. *United States v. Rahman,* 189 F. 3d 88 (2d Cir. 1999).
2. Ibid.
3. *Humanitarian Law Project v. Reno,* 205 F. 3d 1130 (9th Cir. 2000).
4. See *United States v. Lindh,* 212 F. Supp. 2d 541 (E.D. Va. 2002).
5. Ibid.
6. "A Panicky Bill" (editorial), *Washington Post,* October 26, 2001, A34.
7. *The Paquette Habana,* 175 U.S. 677 (1900).
8. CNN, www.cnn.com/2003/LAW/01/31/reid.transcript.
9. *United States v. Yousef,* 327 F. 3d 56 (2d Cir. 2003).
10. *U.S. Code* 18 (2000), §2332(b).
11. *U.S. Code* 18 (2000 & Supp. IV 2004), §2339(a).
12. *U.S. Code* 18 (2000 & Supp. IV 2004), §2339(b).
13. *United States v. Goba,* 220 F. Supp. 2d 182, 190–191 (W.D.N.Y. 2002) (quoting the defendants in the case).
14. Senate Subcommittee on the Judiciary, *Hearing on DOJ Oversight: Preserving Our Freedom While Defending Against Terrorism,* 107th Cong., 1st sess., 2001.

Chapter 6

1. Federal Emergency Management Agency (FEMA), "U.S. Crisis Relocation Planning," Washington, D.C., 1981, 7.
2. Ibid.
3. Robert T. Stafford Disaster Relief and Emergency Assistance Act, *U.S. Code* 42 (West 2003 and Supp. 2006), §§5121–5206.
4. Office of Homeland Security, "The National Strategy for Homeland Security," www.whitehouse.gov/homeland/book.
5. Ibid.
6. Ibid.
7. Ibid.
8. White House, "Homeland Security Presidential Directive/HSPD-5," www.whitehouse.gov/news/releases/2003/02/20030228-9.html.
9. Federation of American Scientists, www.fas.org/irp/threat/212fin~1.html.
10. Richard A. Clarke, *Against All Enemies: Inside America's War on Terrorism* (New York: Free Press, 2004).
11. National Commission on Terrorist Attacks upon the United States, *Final Report* (Washington, D.C.: Government Printing Office, 2005), 262.

12. U.S. Commission on National Security/21st Century, http://govinfo.library.unt.edu/nssg/Reports/reports.htm.
13. James Jay Carafano and David Heyman, "DHS 2.0: Rethinking the Department of Homeland Security," at www.heritage.org/Research/HomelandSecurity/sr02.cfm.

Chapter 7

1. Amy E. Smithson and Leslie-Anne Levy, *Ataxia: The Chemical and Biological Terrorism Threat and U.S. Response* (Washington, D.C.: Henry L. Stimson Center, 2000), 269–270.

Chapter 8

1. "The Great Divide: How Westerners and Muslims View Each Other," Pew Global Attitudes Project, June 22, 2006, http://pewglobal.org/reports/display.php?ReportID=253; "A Rising Tide Lifts Mood in the Developing World," Pew Global Attitudes Project, July 24, 2007, http://pewglobal.org/reports/display.php?ReportID=257.
2. Richard Lugar, "The U.S.-Russian Front against Terrorism and Weapons Proliferation," July 18, 2002, http://usinfo.state.gov/journals/itps/0702/ijpe/lugar.htm.
3. "Secretary General Offers Global Strategy for Fighting Terrorism in Address to Madrid Summit," UN Press Release SG/SM/9757, March 10, 2005.
4. National Commission on Terrorist Attacks upon the United States, *Final Report* (Washington, D.C.: Government Printing Office, 2005), 381–383.
5. Financial Action Task Force, www.fatf-gafi.org.

Chapter 9

1. Jenkins quoted in "Terrorism Found Rising, Now Almost Accepted," *Washington Post,* December 3, 1985, A4; Thatcher quoted in David L. Paletz and Alex F. Schmid, eds., *Terrorism and the Media* (Thousand Oaks, Calif.: Sage Publications, 1992), 123.
2. Brigitte L. Nacos, *Mass-Mediated Terrorism: The Central Role of the Media in Terrorism and Counterterrroism* (Lanham, Md.: Rowan and Littlefield, 2002), 10.
3. Al-Zawahiri quoted by U.S. Secretary of Defense Donald H. Rumsfeld in a speech to the Council on Foreign Relations, New York, February 17, 2006.
4. Ronald Dick, assistant director, FBI, and head, U.S. National Infrastructure Protection Center, quoted in Gabriel Weimann, "How Modern Terrorism Uses the Internet," United States Institute of Peace, Washington, D.C., March 2004.
5. Ibid.
6. *Detroit Free Press v. Ashcroft,* 303 F. 3d 681, 683 (6th Cir. 2002).

Chapter 10

1. "U.S. Conducts a Second Airstrike Inside Somalia," *New York Times,* January 25, 2007.
2. Michael R. Gordon and Tim Weiner, "A Nation Challenged: The Strategy," *New York Times,* October 16, 2001, A1.
3. The separate military commands were long referred to as CINCs, or commanders in chief for the different theaters of operation, but in October 2002 Defense Secretary Rumsfeld changed these titles to combatant commanders. The goal was to reserve the title of commander in chief for the president.
4. Barton Gellman, "CIA Weighs 'Targeted Killing' Missions," *Washington Post,* October 28, 2001, A01.
5. Jason Burke and Imitiz Gul, "The Drone, the CIA, and a Botched Attempt to Kill bin Laden's Deputy," *Observer,* January 15, 2006.
6. This cooperation evolved after September 11; before then, U.S. officials had complained about the lack of cooperation in investigating the USS *Cole* bombing and other terrorist attacks in which suspects hiding in Yemen were potentially involved.
7. In Bob Woodward, *Plan of Attack* (New York: Simon and Schuster, 2004), 150.

Index

Notes: Boxes, figures, tables, and notes are indicated by b, f, t, and n following the page number. Surnames starting with "al-" are alphabetized by the following part of the name. Alphabetization is letter-by-letter (e.g., "Directorate of Intelligence" precedes "Director of central intelligence").